THE AMERICAN EXPRESS POCKET GUIDE TO LONDON

Michael Jackson

PRENTICE HALL PRESS
NEW YORK

The Author
Michael Jackson's previous books include *The English Pub*, *Michael Jackson's Pocket Cocktail and Bar Book* and *The World Guide to Beer*. He writes regularly for *Travel & Leisure*, *Food & Wine* and *Playboy*. He has also acted as a consultant on food and drink projects for the English Tourist Board.

This book is dedicated to the memory of Maggie O'Connor Jackson (1943-81), who loved London.

Contributors
John Roberts (Sights and places of interest, for earlier editions); Fiona Duncan and Leonie Glass (revised and updated text for this edition)

Acknowledgments
The author and publishers would like to thank the following for their help and advice: Stephen Clark, Valerie Cumming of the Museum of London, Pamela Fiori, Kidsline Projects, London Tourist Board.

Quotations
The author and publishers are grateful to Faber and Faber (UK) and Harcourt Brace Jovanovich (USA) for their kind permission to reprint the quotation from *The Waste Land* by T.S. Eliot on p58.

Few travel books are without errors, and no guide book can ever be completely up to date, for telephone numbers and opening hours change without warning, and hotels and restaurants come under new management, which can affect standards. While every effort has been made to ensure that all information is accurate at the time of going to press, the publishers will be glad to receive any corrections and suggestions for improvements, which can be incorporated in the next edition, but cannot accept any consequences arising from the use of the book, or from the information contained herein. Price information in this book is accurate at the time of going to press, but prices and currency exchange rates do fluctuate. Dollar amounts reflect exchange rates in effect in fall 1988.

Series Editor   David Townsend Jones
Editor (first edition 1983)   David Arnold
Editor (second edition 1986)   Leonie Hamilton
Editor (this edition)   Simon Ryder
Art Editor   Eric Drewery
Designer (this edition)   Christopher Howson
Illustrators   Jeremy Ford (David Lewis Artists), Illustra Design Ltd, Rodney Paull
Production (this edition)   Stewart Bowling

**Library of Congress Cataloging-in-
Publication Data**
Jackson, Michael, 1942-
  The American Express pocket
  guide to London.
  Includes index.
  1. London (England)—Description
  —1981-   —Guide-books.
  I. American Express
  Company.   II. Title.
DA679.J29   1989   914.21′04858
88-24641
ISBN 0-13-025255-7

Maps in 4-color by Clyde Surveys Ltd,
Maidenhead, England, based on
copyrighted material of John
Bartholomew & Son Limited. London
Transport Underground Map,
LRT Registered User No. 88/915.
Typeset by Bookworm Typesetting,
Manchester, England
Printed in Shekou, China

Contents

How to use this book

The American Express Pocket Guide to London is an encyclopedia of
travel information, organized in the sections listed on the previous
page. There is also a comprehensive **index** (pages 210-217), which
is accompanied by a **gazetteer** (pages 218-224) of the most
important streets that are shown in the full-color **maps** at the end
of the book.

For easy reference, all major sections (**Sights and places of
interest, Hotels, Restaurants**) and other sections as far as possible
are arranged alphabetically. For the organization of the books as a
whole, see *Contents*. For individual places with no separate entry
in *Sights and places of interest*, see the *Index*.

Abbreviations
As far as possible only standard abbreviations have been used.
These include days of the week and months, points of the compass
(N, S, E and W), street names (Ave., Pl., Rd., Sq., St.), Saint (St),
rooms (rms), C for century, and measurements.

Bold type
Bold type is used in running text primarily for emphasis, to draw
attention to something of special interest or importance. It is also
used in this way to pick out places — shops or minor museums, for
example — that do not have separate descriptions of their own. In
such cases it is usually followed in brackets by the address,
telephone number and details of opening times printed in italics.
In *Hotels* and *Restaurants*, look to see whether places mentioned
in bold in one entry also have a separate entry of their own.

Cross-references
A special type has been used for cross-references. Whenever a
place or section title is printed in *sans serif italics* (for example,
Tower of London or *Basic information*) in the text, this
indicates that you can turn to the appropriate heading in the book
for further information.

Cross-references always refer to sections of the book — *Basic
information, Planning and walks, Hotels* — or to entries in

How entries are organized

Tower Bridge
SE1 ☎403-3761. Map 13G&H17 🖼 ✱ ◀€ *Open Apr-Oct
Mon-Sat 10am-5.45pm; Nov-Mar Mon-Sat 10am-4pm. Tube
Tower Hill.*

With its towers and drawbridges, this landmark, adjacent to the
Tower of London, has become a symbol for London. Built in
1886-94, it is the most easterly bridge over the Thames, and
though designed so that large ships can pass beneath its easily
raised roadway, it is deceptively graceful when viewed from a
distance. Enter by the N tower to visit the glass-enclosed walkway
which has spendid views: Butler's Wharf downstream, *HMS
Belfast* to the W and *St Katharine's Dock* on the N bank. The
Tower Bridge Museum is located to the S of the bridge and
contains the original steam-driven machinery used to lift the
bridge. There are further exhibitions in the NW and S towers.
Recently Tower Bridge has been bedecked with lights, making a
superb night-time sight.

Sights and places of interest, such as *Tower of London*.

For easy reference, use the running heads printed at the top of the page (e.g., **The City**, p57 or **Hotels**, p140).

Floors

To conform with local usage, "first floor" is used throughout the book to refer to the floor above the ground floor, "second floor" to the floor above that, and so on.

Map references

Each of the full-color maps at the end of the book is divided into a grid of squares, identified vertically by letters (A, B, C, D, etc.) and horizontally by numbers (1, 2, 3, 4, etc.). A map reference identifies the page and square in which the street or place can be found — thus the **Tower of London** is located in Map **13G17**.

Price categories

Price categories are denoted by the symbols ☐ ◪ ◫ ▦ and ▥ which signify cheap, inexpensive, moderately priced, expensive and very expensive, respectively. In the cases of hotels and restaurants these correspond approximately with the following actual prices, which give a guideline at the time of printing. Although actual prices will inevitably increase, in most cases the relative price category — for example, expensive or cheap — is likely to remain more or less the same.

Price categories	Corresponding to approximate prices	
	for **hotels**	for **restaurants**
	double room with bath and breakfast; singles are somewhat cheaper	*meal for one with service, VAT and house wine*
☐ cheap	under $90	under $17
◪ inexpensive	$90-140	$17-25
◫ moderate	$140-190	$25-45
▦ expensive	$190-250	$45-60
▥ very expensive	over $250	over $60

_____ Bold blue type for entry headings.

_____ Blue italics for address, practical information and symbols.
For list of symbols see page 6 or back flap of jacket.

_____ Black text for description.
Sans serif italics used for cross-references to other entries or sections.

_____ Bold type used for emphasis.

Entries for hotels, restaurants, shops, etc., follow the same organization, and are usually printed across a half column.

In hotels, symbols indicating special facilities appear at the end of the entry, in black. ⎯⎯⎯

Kingsley ♣
☎242-5881 ☎ 211517. Map **10E11** ◫ 146 rms ▭ 146 ☰ AE CB ◈ ◉ VISA Tube Tottenham Court Road.
Location: Bloomsbury, near British Museum. Warm and inviting hotel, ideal for families, offering accommodations at good-value prices in a very convenient location. The Kingsley is a full-scale hotel, with a bar and carvery restaurant, owned by the Mount Charlotte Group.
‡ ☐ ⊿ 🎿 Y

Key to symbols

☎	Telephone	⊙	Diners Club
⊙	Telex	⊙	MasterCard/Access
★	Recommended sight	VISA	Visa/Barclaycard
☆	Worth a detour	⌷	Secure garage
❁	Good value (in its class)	⊟	Meal obligatory
i	Tourist information	⌂	Quiet hotel
⇌	Parking	⇕	Elevator
🏛	Building of architectural interest	౬	Facilities for disabled people
†	Church or cathedral	⬜	TV in each room
⊡	Free entrance	⬚	Telephone in each room
⊠	Entrance fee payable	✔	Dogs not allowed
⊠	Entrance expensive	✿	Garden
⌦	Photography forbidden	⊰	Outstanding views
K	Guided tour available	⇌	Swimming pool
⬛	Cafeteria	⬳	Tennis
✱	Special interest for children	✓	Golf
		⚓	Conference facilities
⌂	Hotel	⇌	Restaurant
⬛	Simple hotel	⬥	Simple restaurant
🏨	Luxury hotel	⌂	Luxury restaurant
⬜	Cheap	⌷	A la carte available
⬛	Inexpensive	⬛	Set (fixed-price) menu available
⬜	Moderately priced		
⬜	Expensive	⊑	Good wines
⬜	Very expensive	⬯	Open-air dining available
⬛	Rooms with private bathroom	⍾	Bar
		●	Disco dancing
⊞	Air conditioning	⬛	Nightclub
⌂	Residential terms available	✪	Casino/gambling
⸿	American Express	♫	Live music
⊡	Carte Blanche	⸜	Dancing
		⬛	Revue

6

An introduction to London

To see the pageantry of London, or the architecture, to visit the theater or the places of government and jurisdiction, is to be immersed for a moment in a city which was capital of half the world, and which enjoyed that position rather more recently than Athens, Rome or Constantinople. Nor has London cast aside the robes of her recent eminence. She may be wrinkled in some places, face-lifted in others, and over-painted here and there, but she has retained dignity in her middle age.

The attitude of Londoners to their own city can puzzle the newcomer. There is a defiant defensiveness in the proclamation, "I love New York"; Londoners are cooler and ostensibly more detached, but inclined nevertheless to be deeply and irremovably in love with their city. They will rightly evince anger at the handiwork perpetrated by planners and developers in the postwar period, but the irony is that such licensed vandalism prospered so long without restraint simply because the profusion of fine and historic architecture seemed inexhaustible.

To the newcomer, London is an overwhelming jumble of antiquity, a labyrinthine junk shop with 'finds' hidden all over the place, often apparently unnoticed and gathering dust. Sometimes it seems that every house was the birthplace of someone famous, or the scene of an invention, each corner the site of an important speech, a battle or an especially vile crime, each name one which has passed into the language.

The irrepressible curiosities of London manifest themselves from Greenwich in the east to Richmond in the west, two of the most interesting and pleasant little towns in England. Both maintain their identities while remaining parts of London, although they stand about 20 miles apart (London is at some points 35 miles from end to end), and each can be reached by pleasure boat from the heart of the capital.

London grew from the river; the Thames was its first thoroughfare, its lifeline and its mean of social irrigation. Because the first route to London was up the river, successive waves of immigrants, Italians, Jews, Huguenots and many others settled in what became known as the 'East End,' a series of waterside, working-class communities which has nurtured its own culture, patois and social mores. They settled in the east because, being foreigners, they had been barred in times past from entering the city.

Yet there were older immigrants in London from the beginning; Romans founded the settlement nearly 2,000 years ago, and many a Cockney today has a discernibly Roman nose.

This is how the city was born. Yet when Londoners talk about 'The City,' they mean specifically and exclusively that part which was originally walled and still vestigially is, and which covers no more than one square mile, located between Tower Bridge and Blackfriars Bridge.

The City is the financial district, the 'Wall Street' of Britain. The Lord Mayor of London represents only this square mile, and its streets are patrolled by the separate City Police. The City does not include the famous shopping streets, or theaterland, and does not care. It is an entity within itself, parochial yet worldly, with its own rituals and customs, and its preoccupation with bulls and bears and commodity prices.

London is governed not from The City but from the town halls of its more than 30 boroughs. Britain is governed not from The City but from Westminster, a mile upriver. Westminster, too, was once a small city, but it spread far from the river, and today takes in Covent Garden, Soho, theaterland and the main shopping streets of central London. Yet, because of its geographical relationship with the original walled city, today's center is known as the 'West End.'

While The City remained fiercely independent and introspective, Westminster was the royal seat, and London has good reason to be grateful. The royal residences of Westminster (St James's, Buckingham Palace and Clarence House) are joined to those of Kensington (Kensington Palace) by a long swathe of royal parks. Through St James's Park, Green Park, Hyde Park and Kensington Gardens, you can walk miles across the great metropolis amid the greenery. With Holland Park, Regent's Park, and the squares of Bloomsbury, Chelsea and Kensington, developed during the Georgian and Victorian periods, London has a remarkably green inner city.

Born from two separate cities on the river, modern London is, not surprisingly, a complex patchwork of villages. To anyone from outside, Chelsea is probably the most familiar district name in the capital. It is also a neighborhood which perfectly demonstrates London's enigmatic charm, contriving simultaneously to be grand and yet to be a pristine, dollhouse village. At one moment, it spreads itself elegantly on the riverside; in another it hugs itself in narrow streets, cozy as a cat. It has been smart, then bohemian, and is now both, and yet richer than ever. It has the most discreet streets in London, yet its main thoroughfare, King's Road, if no longer quite as *outré* as in the Sixties, remains bereft of caution. It is always unmistakably Chelsea, yet it has many moods. London is like that; a face which is unforgettably familiar, but which has an expression for every emotion.

London, that great sea, whose ebb and flow
At once is deaf and loud, and on the shore
Vomits its wrecks, and still howls on for more
> Shelley, *Letter to Maria Gisborne*, 1819

The changes of mood can be sudden. South Kensington has some of the wealthiest streets in Britain, North Kensington some of the poorest. Yet deprivation has not bred dullness, nor isolation; south of the river, Brixton, too, is less than a ghetto, despite its occasional tensions. In the delightful Brixton market, you can buy jellied eels, an old cockney delicacy, as well as yams and breadfruit.

The river may no longer influence population trends, but the subway ('tube') lines do. Parts of south London became places of cheap housing when they were ignored by the underground systems, but when the new Victoria line went south in 1969, these neighborhoods suddenly became attractive to a new generation of young, professional people who no longer wished to live out in the suburbs. The contemporary equivalent is the boom in London's Docklands. The same 'gentrification' has taken place in several districts which were built for the artisan; the social classes are as identifiable in London as they are anywhere else in Britain, but nowhere else do they quite so readily live together.

Strangers get lost in London. So do Londoners, unless they are cabdrivers. It is a city in which to lose oneself, an engrossing experience. People who are afraid of getting lost, who believe that every city should be built as a piece, at a single stroke, to a well-ordered plan, should not come. London was not built for efficiency. It is a city for explorers.

Before you go

Documents required

A valid national passport is often all that is needed to visit Britain, since citizens of the USA, Commonwealth and most European and South American countries do not need visas.

Health certificates are required only if you are a national of or are arriving from countries in Asia, South America or Africa, in which case you should carry certificates of vaccination against cholera, yellow fever and smallpox. A smallpox vaccination certificate will be required if within the previous 14 days you have been in a country with a designated smallpox-area.

Only your full valid national license is required to drive personal or rented cars. If you are bringing your own car make sure it is properly insured, and bring the vehicle registration certificate (logbook), and an insurance certificate or green card. A national identity sticker is also requried.

Travel and medical insurance

Make sure that you take out an insurance policy covering loss of deposits paid to airlines, hotels, tour operators, etc., and emergency costs, such as special tickets home and extra nights in a hotel.

Visitors from countries with no reciprocal health agreement are not covered for any medical help other than accidents or emergencies, and even then will be expected to pay if they have to stay the night in hospital. They should be properly insured. No charge is made for visitors from countries with a reciprocal arrangement, such as EEC member countries.

Money

There is no exchange control in Britain, so you can carry any amount of any currency through customs in or out of the country. The unit of currency is the pound sterling (£), divided into 100 pence (p). There are coins for 1p, 2p, 5p, 10p, 20p, 50p and £1, and notes for £5, £10, £20 and £50.

Travelers cheques issued by American Express, Thomas Cook, Barclays and Citibank are widely recognized; make sure you read the instructions included with your cheques. It is important to note separately the serial numbers of each cheque and the telephone number to call in case of loss. Specialist travelers cheque companies such as American Express provide extensive local refund facilities.

Major international credit cards, such as American Express, MasterCard (linked in Britain with the Access card), Visa (linked with Barclaycard) and Diners Club are widely accepted for most goods and services. Carte Blanche is less common.

Customs

If your are visiting the United Kingdom for less than six months, you are entitled to bring in, free of duty and tax, all personal effects which you intend to take with you when you leave, except tobacco goods, alcoholic drinks and perfume. Ensure you carry dated receipts for valuable items, such as cameras and watches, or you may be charged duty.

Duty-free allowances at the time of writing for import into Britain are given on p10. The figures shown in brackets are the increased allowances for goods obtained duty-free and tax-paid in EEC countries. Travelers under 17 are not entitled to the allowances on tobacco goods and alcoholic drinks.

Tobacco goods 200 (300) cigarettes *or* 100 (150) cigarillos *or* 50 (75) cigars *or* 250 (400)g tobacco. Or if you live outside Europe, 400 cigarettes *or* 200 cigarillos *or* 100 cigars *or* 500g tobacco.
Alcoholic drinks 1 (1.5) liters spirits or strong liquor (over 22% alcohol by volume) *or* 2 (3) liters of alcoholic drink under 22% alcohol, fortified wine or sparkling wine *plus* 2 (5) liters of still table wine.
Perfume 50g/60cc/2fl oz (75g/90cc/3fl oz)
Toilet water 250cc/9fl oz (375cc/13fl oz)
Other goods Goods to the value of £38 (£250)

Prohibited and restricted goods include narcotics, weapons, obscene publications and videos.

If you have anything in excess of the duty-free allowances, pass through the channel with red 'Goods to declare' notices, otherwise pass through the green 'Nothing to declare' channel.

For exemption from Value Added Tax (VAT) on goods bought in Britain for export see *Shopping*.

Getting there

London's Heathrow Airport is one of the busiest in the world, and there are regular flights from most countries on a wide range of international airlines. Gatwick, the city's second airport, is also heavily used, and both are within an hour of the city center (see *From the airport to the city*). Air fares vary enormously, so consult your travel agent.

Only Cunard now operates frequent transatlantic sailings, but it is possible to sail to English ports (usually Liverpool or Southampton) on other less regular routes. An efficient network of short-distance passenger, car and train ferries links Britain with France, Belgium, The Netherlands, West Germany, Ireland and Scandinavia. The main ferry ports are Dover, Folkestone, Harwich, Felixstowe, Portsmouth, Plymouth, Holyhead and Fishguard.

Climate

English weather is rarely given to extremes, but it is unpredictable and can change character several times a day. Indeed, it is a constant and characteristic topic of British conversation. Average daytime temperatures range from 6°C 43°F) in winter (Dec-Feb) to 21°C (70°F) in summer (June-Aug), only occasionally going below 0°C (32°F) or above 27°C (80°F). There is an annual rainfall of 24in (60cm), most of it in winter but likely at any time. There are, of course, considerable regional variations.

Clothes

In summertime light clothes are adequate, but remember to include some protection against showers and a sweater or jacket for cool evenings. During the rest of the year, bring warm clothes, and hope you won't need them all, although in winter overcoats, gloves, etc. will usually be necessary.

London has given the world some bizarre fashions, and is consequently relaxed about dress, but restraint is expected in some institutional buildings, the older hotels and restaurants, casinos and some clubs. If you are attending any formal or notably grand occasion, full evening dress, which the British refer to simply as 'black tie,' may be expected; check first.

Poste restante (general delivery)

Poste restante can be addressed to any post office. (See *Post offices* p17 for the two main locations.)

Getting around

From the airport to the city

Heathrow is the terminus of the underground's Piccadilly Line; trains link the airport with all parts of the city between 5am (6.45am Sun) and 11pm. The journey to the city center takes about 40min.

The M4 motorway is the other main link, the trip to the center taking 30min-1hr depending upon traffic. London Regional Transport operates a 24hr bus service (including the Airbus service) to points in central London, various bus companies run services to Victoria Bus Station, and some airlines run buses to meet arriving flights and connect with their various passenger terminals in central London. A more expensive alternative is to take a taxi, always readily available at the airport, but make sure you take a black metered cab and not one of the 'pirate' operators, who may overcharge.

Gatwick is farther out of the city and the easiest way into London is to take the Gatwick Express, the British Rail service from the airport station. This reaches Victoria Station in London in 30min and all parts of the city are easily reached from there. The airport is by the side of the M23 motorway, an hour or more from central London, and there are bus services around the clock. Because of the distance from London a cab is not a realistic proposition for most travelers, and could be expensive; ask the driver first how much the fare will be.

Arriving by other means

By rail: London's several major stations encircle the center, and all have underground interchanges, taxi stands and bus stops. (See *Railway services* p14.)

By road: The roads into London plough through the sprawling suburbs, after which signposting for 'West End' indicates the center. Try to avoid driving anywhere in the rush hours (8-9.30am and 5-7pm). The biggest bus terminus in London is at Victoria, and most cross-country buses (known as 'coaches' in Britain) arrive there.

Public transportation

London Regional Transport's network of buses and subway, or underground ('tube'), trains is extensive and efficient, although the usual warnings must be made about traveling in the rush hour. Free bus and tube maps and details of services are available at the Travel Information Centres located at the following tube stations: Heathrow Central, Euston, King's Cross, Piccadilly Circus, Oxford Circus, St James's Park and Victoria. There is also a telephone information service ☎222-1234: you may have to wait a while for an answer as the calls are stacked and dealt with in rotation.

Various special tickets are available, and it is wise to visit a Travel Information Centre and get details of them early in your visit. The tickets include flat-rate passes for bus or tube or both for various periods from three days to one month. See *London for children* for further information on children's fares. The Visitor Travel card, on sale outside the UK through travel agents, allows unlimited travel on buses and underground for 3, 4 or 7 day periods.

For public transportation remember to stand in line.

The underground ('tube')

The underground (see *Map 24*) is the easiest and fastest way to get around the city, if not the most interesting. The stations are easily recognized by the London Regional Transport symbol, a horizontal line through a circle. On maps, each line always has its own color (Circle line yellow, Central line red, etc.), so it is easy to plan your journey, noting where you have to change lines. The fare depends on how many zones you enter; see *Buses*. Buy your ticket before boarding, either from a ticket office or a machine in the station, where the fares will be on display. Show your ticket to a collector or, if it is a yellow one, put it in the automatic entry gate and walk through, picking it up as you go — you will need to present it at the end of your journey. Follow the signs to the platform for the line you want. Check with the indicators above the platform and on the front of the train that it is going to your station; some trains do not go to the end of the line, and some lines divide into two or more branches. Trains stop at every station, with only a few exceptions at weekends. The first tube trains run at about 5am, and they begin to close down after 11.30pm, when you might have trouble with connections. Smoking is forbidden in underground trains and in all stations that are underground.

Buses

(See table of central bus routes, *Map 22-23.*) London's red buses are usually slower than the tube, but are cheaper and more interesting, offering a good view from the upper deck. Do use them and don't be discouraged by the complex network of routes: people waiting in the line will usually help you, and the conductor will answer your questions and tell you when you have reached your destination if necessary. Each bus runs along part or all of a numbered route — find out which route you want from the map at the bus stop, and look at the indicator on the front of the bus to check that it is going far enough along the route for you. There are two types of bus stop; a normal stop, with the LRT symbol on a white background, where all buses stop; and a request stop, with a red sign bearing the word 'Request,' where the bus will stop only if you raise you hand or, if on the bus, ring the bell. Fares are tied to zones; a small flat-fare is payable for every zone you enter. Children under 16 pay less, and those under five travel free. Usually the conductor will come round and collect your far during the journey, but sometimes you will have to pay as you enter. Smoking is allowed only upstairs on double-decker buses. The buses run between about 5am and 11.30pm, although there are a few night buses on special routes, running once an hour or so. In central London, small 'hoppa' buses have been introduced on selected routes, specially designed to give speedier rides to people traveling just a few stops. Green Line Coaches run from central London into the country outside London Regional Transport's area. They stop only rarely in London, and are more expensive than red buses. Ask at a Travel Information Centre for details of routes.

Taxis

London's distinctive black taxis (other colors are now being introduced on the modern metrocabs) are driven by some of the best drivers in the world, who have to pass an exam to prove their detailed knowledge of the city before they get a license. They can be hailed as they cruise the streets (a cab which is free illuminates its yellow light), and you will also find them on ranks at stations and outside hotels and large stores, etc. Once they have stopped for you, taxis are obliged to take you anywhere you want to go within six miles of the pick-up point, provided it is within the metropolitan area. The fare, always shown on the meter, consists of a basic hiring charge and subsequent additions according to the length of your journey; there are additional charges for extra passengers, night or weekend journeys and for baggage. In all cases notices are displayed inside the taxi with details of all charges. Give the driver a 10-15% tip.

Private taxis (usually saloon cars and known as 'minicabs') cannot be hailed but must be ordered by phone. You will find the numbers by some public telephones and in the *Yellow Pages* under Mini Cabs. It is best, however to stick to the black taxis if possible; the strict regulations governing fares for black taxis do not apply to minicabs, so if you have to use a minicab try to fix the fare with the driver at the start of the journey to avoid problems when you reach your destination.

Getting around by car

Driving in London is not as aggressive as in most large cities, but the difficulty for foreign visitors is that everyone appears to be on the wrong side of the road, and that the city has a totally unplanned road system with an abundance of one-way routes. If you can face all of that, make sure that you are carrying your license, that your tires have at least 1mm of tread, and that all your lights are working.

You must drive on the left and you must pass only on the right. The speed limit in London and all built-up areas (i.e. streets with lampposts) is 30mph (48kph) unless otherwise indicated. Standard international road signs are generally used. A solid white line across the road means that you must stop, a broken one that you must give right of way; a solid white down the center of the road must not be crossed at all, but a broken line can be crossed if it is safe to do so. Pedestrian crossings are marked by black and white zones across the road and are sometimes controlled by traffic lights. In either case, pedestrians have the right of way and traffic must stop to let them cross, unless there is a green traffic light showing, in which case drivers have priority. Observe lane division rules, i.e. slower traffic on the inside (left), faster traffic on the outside, and be sure to get into the correct lane coming up to intersections, as different lanes may be controlled by different traffic signals. Horns must not be used from 11.30pm-7am except in emergencies, and the wearing of seat belts in both front seats is compulsory.

Parking is extremely difficult on streets in central London, usually possible only at meters for a maximum of 2hr. Two yellow lines by the roadside mean no parking at all, one yellow line no parking during the work day (8am-6.30pm, Mon-Sat). Always look for an explanatory sign in the restricted zones: there will be one giving details of the maximum stay allowed, or indicating that the space is for residents only. Parking is always prohibited near pedestrian crossings and intersections. If you violate parking regulations, you may be fined (but not on the spot). Or you may have your car immobilized by a wheel clamp; instruction on how to get it released will be displayed on the windshield, but you will have to pay a fine, on the spot, and wait until it is unlocked. In some instances the police may tow away your car. Go to the nearest police station to inquire if this has been the case.

Off the streets, there are various parking lots and garages, often indicated by a blue sign with a large **P**. Charges for these should be set out clearly somewhere near the entrance.

If you belong to an FIA-affiliated automobile club and are bringing your own car, the services of the two main British automobile clubs will be at your disposal:

Automobile Association   5 New Coventry St., WC2 ☎954-7373
Royal Automobile Club   49 Pall Mall, SW1 ☎839-7050

Basic information

Renting a car

Renting a car is probably not worthwhile if you do not intend to go outside London. To rent one, you must be over 21 and hold a full valid national license. You can opt for either a daily rate plus a mileage charge, or a weekly rate with unlimited mileage, often more economical. Insurance is usually included, but check before you leave. You may be asked to leave a cash deposit larger than your likely eventual overall charge, from which the difference will be refunded when you return the car.

Car rental can be arranged through travel agents or at desks in airports, major stations and large hotels. Or make a telephone reservation through one of the major companies: *Avis*, ☎848-8733; *Europcar*, ☎950-5050; *Hertz*, ☎679-1799.

All these companies can arrange for cars to be waiting if you arrive by air or train.

Getting around on foot

Although many Londoners ignore them, it is best to use zebra crossings, where pedestrians have priority, or underground passages.

A few outer areas are unsafe for pedestrians after nightfall: if outside the city center after dark, stick to the main streets.

Railway services

British Rail offers a fast Inter-City service between major towns throughout the UK, as well as Motorail and sleeper trains. First-class and, on some routes, Pullman tickets are available. Reduced-rate tickets are available for off-peak day or weekend trips, and the Britrail Pass, on sale only outside the UK through travel agents, offers unlimited travel on the whole network for weekly periods up to one month.

British Rail Travel Centres (visitors only)
4-12 Regent St., SW1. (*Map 10G10*)
407 Oxford St., W1. (*Map 9F8*)
Major British Rail stations in London
S and SE England (Information ☎928-5100)
Charing Cross, Strand, WC2. (*Map 10G11*)
Waterloo, Waterloo Rd., SE1. (*Map 11H13*)
Victoria, Buckingham Palace Rd., SW1. (*Map 17J9*)
East Anglia (Information ☎283-7171)
Liverpool Street, Liverpool St., EC3. (*Map 13E16*)
SW and W England, S Wales (Information ☎262-6767)
Paddington, Praed St., W2. (*Map 7F5*)
Midlands, NW England, N Wales, W Scotland (Information ☎387-7070)
Euston, Euston Rd., NW1. (*Map 4C10*)
St Pancras, Euston Rd., NW1. (*Map 4C11*)
NE England, E Scotland (Information ☎278-2477)
King's Cross, Euston Rd., NW1. (*Map 4B11*)

Domestic airlines

The principal airline operating from the capital to other major cities is British Airways. Other airlines include Air UK, British Midland Airways and Dan-Air. Unless you wish to go to one of the country's extremities, like Aberdeen in Scotland, it is often easier to go by car or train and arrive directly in the city center. London City Airport, situated in Docklands, catering mainly to businessmen, serves a few British and European destinations, including Paris, Amsterdam and Brussels. For information ☎474-5555.

Ferry services
Apart from the pleasure cruises on the Thames, the only ferry
service is the River Bus, which runs between London City
Airport and Charing Cross Pier, with stops at Swan Lane Pier
(near London Bridge) and Greenwich Pier (☎474-5555).

On-the-spot information

Public holidays
New Year's Day, Jan 1; Good Friday; Easter Monday; May Day
(first Mon in May); Spring Bank Holiday (last Mon in May);
August Bank Holiday (last Mon in Aug); Christmas Day, Dec 25;
Boxing Day, Dec 26. Most places are closed.

Time zones
London time is GMT in winter and changes to European Summer
Time (EST), 1hr ahead of GMT, from the end of Mar to late Oct.

Banks and currency exchange
All banks are open Mon-Fri 9.30am-3.30pm. On Sat a handful of
central London branches are open, e.g. Lloyds, 399 OxfordSt.,
W1, open 10am-3pm; or Barclays, 74 Kensington High St., W8,
open 9.30am-noon. Money can also be exchanged outside these
hours at *bureaux de change*, found as small separate shops and in
hotels, railway stations, travel agencies and airports, although the
exchange rate might not be as good as that offered by the banks.
Travelers cheques are widely accepted, the exchange rate being
roughly the same as for cash.

Shopping hours
Most shops are open Mon-Sat 9am-6pm, and some open Sat
9.30am-noon. Many large city-center shops stay open late on Wed
or Thurs (see *Shopping*). Office hours are Mon-Fri 9.30am-
5.30pm. A few shops, mainly grocers and newsagents, open on
Sun.
   Outside the city center, shops may close at lunchtime, usually
1-2pm, and for one afternoon during the week.

Rush hours
The rush hours are approximately 8-9.30am and 5-7pm on
Mon-Fri only. Unlike some cities, London does not become totally
choked, but getting around will take longer.

Post and telephone services
Post offices are usually open Mon-Fri 9am-5.30pm, Sat 9am-
12.30pm, with the notable exception of the post office in William
IV St., off Trafalgar Sq. (*Map 10G11*), open Mon-Sat 8am-8pm,
Sun 10am-5pm.
   Stamps are available at post offices and, occasionally, from
machines. There are two classes of inland mail, but as the second
class is only a little cheaper and sometimes a lot slower and more
unreliable, it is best avoided. You will also have to specify which
rate you want for international mail, as it will not automatically go
air mail. When sending a parcel out of the country you will have to
fill in a customs form declaring the contents. Besides the boxes in
post offices, mail can be posted in the red boxes placed at regular
intervals on main streets. There are various special services

available, such as express or recorded or guaranteed delivery. Ask for details.

Public telephones are found in kiosks and in booths on main streets and in post offices, hotels, pubs, stations, etc. They should all have London telephone directories; if you want a number outside London, dial 192 and Directory Enquiries will supply it. If you can't find a London number dial 142. There is always an area code, which may have up to six numbers. It is not necessary for local calls but must be used when telephoning from outside the area — London's is 01. Most international calls can be dialed direct (IDD) from public telephones; if the codes are included in the front of the A-D telephone directory. If you have any difficulty call 155 for the International Operator or 153 for International Directory Enquiries.

Some public telephones take coins, others take phonecards, which can be bought from post offices and shops displaying the phonecard sign. Follow the instructions displayed by the telephone; you will be refunded any unused coins. The ringing tone is a repeated double trill, and an intermittent shrill tone means that the line is engaged. See also *Telephone services*, p17.

Public rest rooms

The public rest rooms found in main streets (often in French-style, automated 'superloos'), parks and tube stations can often be dirty and vandalized, although there are some exceptions. Well-maintained rest rooms that can be used by anybody will be found in all larger public buildings, such as museums and art galleries, large department stores and railway stations. It is not acceptable to use the rest rooms in hotels, restaurants and pubs if you are not a customer. Public rest rooms are usually free of charge but you may need a small coin to unlock a rest room or to use a proper washroom.

Electric current

The electric current is 240V AC, and plugs have three square pins and take 3, 5 or 13 amp fuses. Foreign visitors will need adaptors for their own appliances, which should be bought before departure.

Customs and etiquette

The English are a tolerant people, and London is a cosmopolitan city, so foreign visitors are unlikely to offend by tripping up on some part of etiquette. The most important custom is that of 'queuing' — the British line up for everything and if you do not wait your turn they will not take it kindly.

Tipping

Tipping is customary in a few cases. A tip of 10-15% is usual in hotels and restaurants, unless a service charge is already incorporated into the check. Taxi drivers also expect about 10-15% of the fare. You need only give small tips to porters, hairdressers, rest room attendants and doormen.

Disabled visitors

Prior information is important. A useful publication is *Access in London*, published by Nicholson, and there is a Disabled Information Service run by *The Royal Association for Disability and Rehabilitation* (RADAR), 25 Mortimer St., W1 ☎637-5400.

Local and foreign publications

The weekly entertainments magazines, such as *Time Out, City*

Limits and *What's On & Where to Go*, are the most comprehensive guides to events and entertainments of all sorts. London's daily evening newspaper, the *Evening Standard*, also features a wide range of entertainments. Programs of special events (free concerts, ceremonies, etc.) are usually available from Tourist Information Centres and are listed in *The Times*.

Morning newspapers are produced for national circulation, and do not necessarily cover local London events.

Foreign newspapers are widely available from newsagents, the *International Herald Tribune* and many others on the day of publication, and most of the others a day or two later.

Useful addresses

Tourist information/tickets/hotel reservations
London Tourist Board and Convention Bureau information centers:
Harrods (4th floor), Knightsbridge, SW1
Heathrow Airport, Arrivals Concourse, Terminal 2
Heathrow Central Underground Station, Heathrow Airport
Selfridges (ground floor), Oxford St., W1
Victoria Station Forecourt, SW1
West Gate, Tower of London, EC3 (summer only)

Written inquiries and hotel reservation service (write six weeks in advance) Information Unit, London Tourist Board, 26 Grosvenor Gdns., SW1; LTB Tourist Information ☎730-3488. On-the-spot hotel reservation at Victoria Station and Heathrow.
British Travel Centre 12 Regent St., W1
American Express Travel Service 6 Haymarket, London SW1 ☎930-4411. A valuable source of information for any traveler in need of help, advice or emergency services.
City of London Information Centre St Paul's Churchyard, EC4 ☎606-3030
London Regional Transport Information Centre 55 Broadway, SW1. 24hr telephone service ☎222-1234
Travel Information Centres at the following stations:
Euston, Heathrow Central, King's Cross, Oxford Circus, Piccadilly Circus, St James's Park, Victoria.
British Tourist Authority and *English Tourist Board* Thames Tower, Black's Rd., W6 ☎846-9000
Kidsline ☎222-8070

Post offices
Poste restante (general delivery) can be addressed to any post office. The two main ones are:
Trafalgar Square post office 24 William IV St., WC2 ☎930-9580
City post office, King Edward Building, King Edward St., EC1 ☎601-9064 (general inquiries)

Telephone services
Time 123 (from London 01-numbers only)
Telegrams — Telemessages (UK and USA only) 190
International telegrams 193
Business news summary 246-8026
Weather forecast, London 246-8091

Embassies and consulates
Australia Australia House, Strand, WC2 ☎379-4334
Belgium 103 Eaton Sq., SW1 ☎235-5422

Basic information

Canada   1 Grosvenor St., W1 ☎629-9492
Denmark   55 Sloane St., SW1 ☎235-1255
Finland   38 Chesham Pl., SW1 ☎235-9531
France   24 Rutland Gate, SW7 ☎581-5292
Germany (West)   23 Belgrave Sq., SW1 ☎235-5033
Ireland   17 Grosvenor Pl., SW1 ☎235-2171
Italy   14 Three Kings Yd., W1 ☎629-8200
Japan   46 Grosvenor St., W1 ☎493-6030
Netherlands   38 Hyde Park Gate, SW7 ☎584-5040
New Zealand   80 Haymarket, SW1 ☎930-8422
Norway   25 Belgrave Sq., SW1 ☎235-7151
Spain   20 Draycott Pl., SW3 ☎581-5921
Sweden   11 Montagu Pl., W1 ☎724-2101
Switzerland   16 Montagu Pl., W1 ☎723-0701
USA   24 Grosvenor Sq., W1 ☎499-9000

Sightseeing tours
London Transport ☎227-3456. London sightseeing tour in open-top double-decker bus departs every half hour from Victoria St., Baker St., Marble Arch, Piccadilly Circus.
Cityrama ☎720-6663. Also departs every half hour from several points; eight language commentary.
Harrods ☎581-3603. Very luxurious; eight-language commentary.
Golden Tours ☎743-3300, *Frames Richards* ☎837-3111, and *Evan Evans* ☎730-2377, all offer various sightseeing tours by coach.
   All the above tours can be booked through the London Tourist Board Centres at Victoria, Harrods or Selfridges.

Major places of worship
Church of England churches cover the whole city, and Roman Catholic, Baptist and Methodist churches also abound.
American Church in London (Interdenominational)
79 Tottenham Court Rd., W1 ☎580-2791
Central Synagogue (Orthodox)   36 Hallam St., W1 ☎580-1355
London Central Mosque 146 Park Rd., NW8 ☎724-3363

Major libraries
Guildhall Library Aldermanbury, EC2 ☎606-3030.
Westminster Central Reference Library   St Martin's St., WC2 ☎828-8070. (International and local reference.)

Conversion tables

Emergency information

Emergency services (call free from any telephone)
Police   ☎999 (no coins needed).
Ambulance   } The operator will ask which
Fire   } service you require

Hospitals with casualty (emergency) departments
St Mary's Hospital   Praed St., W2 ☎755-6666
St Thomas's Hospital   Lambeth Palace Rd., SE1 ☎928-9292
St Bartholomew's (Barts)   West Smithfield, EC1 ☎601-888
St Stephen's   Fulham Rd., SW10 ☎352-8161
Other emergencies
If your complaint does not warrant an ambulance or
hospitalization you will have to ring up a doctor or dentist.
Consult the 'Yellow Pages' of the telephone directory under
'Doctors (Medical Practitioners)' and 'Dental Surgeons'.

Late-opening chemists/drugstores
Boots   Piccadilly Circus, W1 ☎734-6126, open Mon-Sat
9am-8pm
Bliss   50 Willesden Lane, NW6 ☎624-8000, open daily
9am-2am

Help lines
Capital Help Line ☎388-7575. Referral service.
Release ☎603-8654. Drug problems, legal and practical.
The Samaritans   46 Marshall St., W1 ☎439-2224 (24hr).
Personal callers 9am-9pm. Talk out problems.

Automobile accidents
— Do not admit liability or incriminate yourself.
— Ask any witnesses to stay and give a statement.
— Contact the police.
— Exchange names, addresses, car details and insurance
   companies' names and addresses with other driver(s).
— Give a statement to the police who will compile a report
   which insurance companies will accept as authoritative.

Car breakdowns
Call one of the following from the nearest telephone.
— The nearest garage/repair service.
— The police who will put you in touch with the above.
— The number you have been given if you rented the car.

Lost passport
Contact the police immediately and your consulate (see
pp17-18) for emergency travel documents.

Lost travelers cheques
Notify the local police at once, then follow the instructions
provided with your travelers cheques, or contact the nearest
office of the issuing company. Contact your consulate or
American Express if you are stranded with no money.

Lost property
Report your loss to the police immediately (many insurance
companies will not recognize claims without a police report).
There are some special lost property offices:
British Rail   At main stations. (See *Railway services* p14.)
Heathrow Airport Lost Property Office   ☎759-4321
London Regional Transport   200 Baker St., NW1.
Taxi Lost Property Office   15 Penton St., NW1.

Time chart

AD 43	The invading Romans under Claudius defeated the Celtic tribes of SE Britain and bridged the Thames close to the site of the later London Bridge. By AD 60, London was a thriving port and settlement at the center of the Roman road network.
60	Revolt by Iceni tribe from East Anglia, under Queen Boadicea, culminated in destruction of London.
200	England's capital, and a prosperous city of traders, London was fortified by the Romans. Walls from modern sites of Tower to Aldgate, along London Wall to Barbican and down to the river at Blackfriars.
200-400	Romans used Germanic mercenaries to help defend this outpost of their weakening empire.
410	Romans withdrew, and London reverted to a farming town under the Angles and Saxons, warrior kings.
700-820	England gradually reunited under kings of Wessex, from Winchester. London an important provincial market town. Christianity slowly reintroduced, and stimulated learning.
836	London sacked by Vikings. For almost two centuries it was a borderland pawn in their struggle with the western Saxon kingdoms, with divided loyalties usually determined by self-interest.
1014	London taken by storm for the last time; Olaf, an Anglo-Saxon, tied his boats to London Bridge and sailed downstream to destroy it. (Hence the song *London Bridge is Falling Down*.)
1052	Disgusted by London's switching of support to his enemies, King Edward the Confessor started to build a new abbey and palace named Westminster on Isle of Thorney. Tension between City and Crown was born.
1066	Norman invasion. William did not attack the well-fortified London, but forced it into submission by destroying surrounding farmlands.
1066-1100	London accepted and thrived under the civilized Norman rule. William I built Tower of London.
1140-90	As political stability was undermined by factionalism among the king and powerful barons, London exacted a price for its support. It won the power to raise taxes and elect its own governors. The powerful guilds, confederations of merchants, controlled trade.
1215	London accepted Charter of Incorporation from King John, confirming authority of the Lord Mayor, elected annually by 24 aldermen. Displeased by heavy taxes, it supported barons in drafting Magna Carta.
1217	First stone bridge over Thames, London Bridge.
1263	Trade guilds took control of city from aldermen during turbulence of baronial wars, and reinstituted government by citizens' assembly (Anglo-Saxon idea).
1269	Henry II began construction of new Westminster Abbey after boundary dispute with City.
1280	Old St Paul's Cathedral completed, half as tall again as current St Paul's. Precincts housed sports arena, markets and a brewery. 126 parish churches plus monasteries inside city displaced population.
1326	The new urban pressures of the city erupted in riots against the king. Foreigners and Jews attacked.
1338	Edward III made Westminster the regular meeting

	place of Parliament, previously irregular.
1348	Black Death. Half city's 60,000 population died.
1381	Peasants' Revolt. Seeking an end to feudalism, a working class 'army,' led by Wat Tyler from Kent, took over London for two days. Tyler killed by mayor.
1399	London supported Parliament in forcing deposition of the absolutist and heavily-taxing Richard II.
1411	Work began on Guildhall, the city's 'royal palace.' Professional soldiers and tradesmen formed new wealthy class threatening the old feudal aristocracy.
1461	London's support essential to Edward IV, victor of Wars of the Roses, in struggle to restore stability to country and its trade. King knighted many London citizens in return for support.
1500-1600	Population exploded from 50,000 to 200,000 during economic boom of relatively stable Tudor period. New slum areas arose outside London, all ungoverned suburbs, including red-light district of Southwark.
1533	Henry VIII's Reformation. New gentry class snapped up land vacated by dissolution of the monasteries. Henry founded downriver naval bases.
1553-58	Queen Mary reinstated Catholicism. Citizens martyred at Smithfield. London then supported the parsimonious Protestant Elizabeth I for 45yr.
1600-70	The new gentry, now aristocracy, began to develop their new land, moving westward, building on the edge of the countryside in Piccadilly and Leicester Sq.
1603-42	Puritanism flourished in the city as a reaction against the autocratic Stuart kings, James I and Charles I.
1642-49	London financed Parliament in Civil War. London and Westminster both embraced by new fortifications, and the citizens manned defense. London was the setting for Charles I's execution in 1649.
1649-60	The Commonwealth (republic). London traders gradually reacted against the religious radicals' egalitarianism, and supported the restoration of Charles II in 1660.
1665-66	The Great Plague. The last and worst outbreak. At least 100,000 died in just over a year.
1666	The Great Fire. Medieval London destroyed after fire, started in King's baker's in Pudding Lane.
1666- 1700	Reconstruction with stone buildings and wider streets. Wren's plan of grid of streets with piazzas infringed too many property rights; private ownership shaped new landscape. Instead Wren built 51 churches, culminating in St Paul's. By 1700, the 300,000 population was widely dispersed after the fire.
1700-50	Both the new urban poor and the fashionable elite pushed up the population to 675,000 by 1750. The villages of Knightsbridge and Marylebone were incorporated, and St James's and Mayfair were developed. To the E and S were slums, where gin consumption averaged two pints per person per week and only one child in four lived beyond age five.
1774	The City, still self-governing, elected the radical John Wilkes as Mayor after he was expelled from Parliament three times. It still distrusted the cultured West End and the almost omnipotent Parliament.
1780	The Gordon Riots. Anarchy in London for a week, but still no police force with day-to-day authority.

Culture, history and background

1780-1820	Middle and upper classes moved ever more to the suburbs in the w, as slums and urban pressures increased. Still no comprehensive local government.
1829	The Metropolitan Police or 'Peelers,' the first police force, founded. City founded its own force in 1835.
1820-38	Prince Regent, later George IV, and architect Nash developed Regent's Park and Regent St., Buckingham Palace and The Mall.
1835	Britain given local councils. London was exempted from this, and continued to be 'governed' by over 150 parishes, encompassing 300 administrative bodies. Slum clearance still partially executed by the Commissioner for Woods and Forests.
1839	New Palace of Westminster, the present one, was started after old one was burned down.
1844	Controlling monopoly in printing of money granted to the Bank of England.
1832-66	Cholera killed thousands: various Public Health Acts had no effect on London, until Metropolitan Board of Works founded in 1855. Destitution worsened by clearance of land for railways.
1851	The Great Exhibition in the Crystal Palace in Hyde Park celebrated British supremacy in trade, science and industry. Consolidated by Prince Albert's development of the museums and learned institutions of South Kensington.
1863	Railways available to working class for first time, and opening of first underground line. Increased mobility and belated public health and education measures.
1889	London County Council formed, giving London comprehensive local government for first time.
1897	Victoria's Diamond Jubilee. London described as "center of an empire on which the sun never sets."
1900-05	Opening of four new electric underground lines began rapid expansion into sprawling suburbs.
1914-18	Women took over many services in London during the War, and the suffragettes won the vote in 1918.
1920-30	'Homes for Heroes' program was part of growth of vast new estates quadrupling size of London.
1940	The Blitz. London bombed, mainly in The City and East End; St Paul's stood alone amid rubble.
1945-55	Private and local government redevelopment of the city resulted in fast modernization.
1951	Festival of Britain, one of the first world fairs.
1955-65	Boom years for property developers, who erected prestigious skyscrapers while London County Council concentrated on housing in suburbs. Population of central London lowest for centuries.
1956	Clean Air Act created smokeless zones and marked the end of central London as an industrial area.
1960-70	'Swinging London.' Economic boom, immigration and changing values and wealth patterns made London more cosmopolitan. In 1965, Greater London Council succeeded LCC.
1970-80	Local government gained strength, tempering modernization through such projects as Covent Garden.
1986	Labour GLC abolished by Conservative government. London Stock Exchange reformed — the 'Big Bang.'
1987	Margaret Thatcher's Conservative government re-elected for a third term of office. First black MPs elected.

Architecture

London was not the vision of an emperor or king. To their surprise, visitors who know by repute its showcase architectural masterpieces find not a city of grand avenues and broad boulevards, but a family of villages, offering delightfully distracting details more often than panoramic views. A uniquely pervasive grandeur derives from this blending of a rich heritage of fine buildings into the everyday life, past and present, of a bustling city.

A chronology of English architectural styles

Norman (1060-1200)   Sturdy buildings around massive piers; round arches; carved geometrical ornament; square towers and keeps.

Gothic (1180-1540)   Lighter, more dynamic buildings: flying buttresses, pointed arches and windows, spires. Main periods are: **Early English** (1180-1260), marked by simplicity and airiness; **Decorated** (1250-1370), extensive surface ornament and window tracery; and **Perpendicular** (1300-1540), with slender columns stressing vertical lines, fan vaulting and paneled windows.

Tudor (1540-1603)   The Renaissance influenced only decoration, with paperwork and carved gables. Brick buildings with symmetrical plan, often E or H; large mullioned windows.

Jacobean (1603-25)   Extravagant period and plaster decoration.

Classical (1615-66)   Inigo Jones introduced Palladian style. After Great Fire, Wren worked in styles from Classical simplicity to dignified but sophisticated Baroque.

But withal understand that in London many stately palaces, built by noblemen upon the river Thames, do make a very great show to them that pass by water; and that there be many more like palaces, also built towards land, but scattered and great part of them in back lanes and streets, which if they were joined to the first in good order, as other cities are built uniformly, they would make not only fair streets, but even a beautiful city, to which few might justly be preferred for the magnificence of the building.

Fynes Moryson, 1617

English Baroque (1690-1720)   Fluidity of Continental Baroque was tempered by Classical and medieval elements.

Palladianism (or Georgian) (1720-1820)   Italianate buildings with columns and porticoes, often relatively plain, combined with new art of landscape gardening.

Neo-Gothic (1740-80)   Brief vogue for Classical decoration gave way to Rococo-like frivolity and novelty.

Regency (1780-1830)   Simplistic Classicism with delicate interior ornament, often a stucco relief.

Victorian (1830-1900)   Extravagantly treated historicist themes, especially Neo-Gothic, contrast with functional public and industrial structures in iron and glass.

Domestic Revival (1870-1920)   Direct simplicity in domestic architecture, using brick, stone and wood.

International Modern (1930-60)   Functional airy buildings often worked into English Gardens.

Modernist (1945-present)   Imaginative use of space and new materials; concern for social basis of architecture.

London is still blessed with the stones and mortar of its Roman founders in the remnants of the 2ndC city wall, especially near the

Culture, history and background

Barbican. Defense was still the vital consideration when the Norman conquest of 1066 was followed by the construction in 1078 of the huge, square White Tower, one of the best existing examples of a Norman keep.

Westminster Abbey, begun in 1245, is London's finest remaining medieval building, the E arm epitomizing the elegant Early English style, with the later nave in the Perpendicular style. Timber roofing, one of the glories of the English Gothic, survives in the hammer-beam roof of Westminster Hall, in the Great Hall of Hampton Court (1536), and also in St James's Palace a superb red-brick example of the ornate Tudor adaptations of Gothic.

Inigo Jones, born in 1573 in Smithfield, brought the vigor and sophistication of Italian Renaissance styles to London, most notably the elegant symmetry of Andrea Palladio. Jones' particular contribution to the building of London was the development of Covent Garden, especially the Piazza (1631-39), and the first two Palladian buildings in London, the Banqueting House in Whitehall (1619-22) and the delightful Queen's House in Greenwich.

Sir Christopher Wren (1632-1723), an Oxford-educated

The **White Tower** (1078) in the Tower of London, the first of the square Norman keeps, is built of Caen stone.

The hammer-beam roof in **Westminster Hall** (1399), the only surviving part of the old Palace of Westminster.

The Anne Boleyn gatehouse of **Hampton Court Palace** (1540), built for Henry VIII in Tudor red brick.

The **Banqueting House, Whitehall** (1622), Inigo Jones' strictly Palladian masterpiece, incorporates Ionic columns.

scientist, and later Surveyor of the King's Works, was entrusted with the rebuilding of The City after the Great Fire. On the churches of The City he designed towers and steeples to lead the eye to the dome of St Paul's Cathedral. In his buildings, Wren used elements of the classical Renaissance style, but was obliged to adapt its geometrical grandeur and piazzas to the framework of the medieval city's alleys and courtyards.

Wren's secular buildings include the Royal Naval Hospital, Greenwich (1696-1702), and the Royal Hospital, Chelsea (1681-91). His assistant Nicholas Hawksmoor designed several churches that are increasingly appreciated; a fine example is St Mary Woolnoth (1716-24). Wren also influenced Sir James Gibbs, a leader of the English Baroque, and the combination of styles is exemplified by St Martin-in-the-Fields (1722-26).

In the Georgian period, fashion swung away from Baroque back to the rules and conventions of Classical architecture, a move typified by Palladian Chiswick House (1725-29), which also has a garden landscaped by William Kent. The same notions of refinement and good taste were evident in the Georgian terraces built at this time. The dominant designer was Robert Adam

St Paul's (1675-1710) has vast circular crossing, over which arches on piers support inner and outer domes.

St Mary-le-Strand (1714-17), by Gibbs, has an Italianate steeple on a Classical base.

Chiswick House (1725-29), by Burlington and Kent, is fronted by a Palladian columned portico.

Culture, history and background

(1728-92), one of a family of influential architects, whose terraced town houses were unified by an elegant facade.

In the later part of the Georgian period, the Regency architect John Nash (1752-1835) used these themes to give a sense of shape and elegance to the heart of modern London. Seen from Piccadilly Circus, the bold, sweeping curve of Regent St. echoes Nash's plan for a triumphal 'Royal Mile' from the Prince Regent's residence at Carlton House to Regent's Park. At either end of this mile are two pristine examples of Nash's work: Carlton House Terrace (1827-32) and Park Crescent (1812-22). These elegant terraces and crescents were mirrored in the development of Belgravia and Chelsea, largely by Thomas Cubitt, in the 1820s and 1830s.

The sterner values of the Victorian period were reflected in church-like buildings such as the Houses of Parliament (1840-50, Sir Charles Barry and Augustus Pugin). This Gothic Revival architecture had moments of fantasy, as the spires of St Pancras Station (1868-74, Sir Gilbert Scott) happily show. The railway era also brought some breathtaking examples of civil engineering, and the interior of Paddington Station (1850-4, Brunel) remains a good memorial to the best of these. Similarly inspired use of cast iron

20 St James's Square, a Georgian terraced town house, with a strictly Classical facade.

Cumberland Terrace (1825), Regent's Park, by Nash, has massive Classical pediments with stucco decoration.

The **Palace of Westminster** (1840-50) has a classically balanced plan decorated in Perpendicular Gothic style.

The enormous **conservatory** or **palm house** (1844-48) at Kew Gardens, a functional but elegant Victorian structure.

and sheet glass is seen in the magnificent conservatory at Kew Gardens (1844-48, Decimus Burton).

The 20thC has produced some of London's least attractive architecture, although the passing of time is leading to a greater appreciation of 1920s and 1930s industrial buildings like the Hoover factory on Western Avenue, and Battersea Power Station. Bauhaus refugees founded the design group Tecton, which designed Highgate's Highpoint Flats (1936), described by Le Corbusier as "a vertical garden city." Notable postwar buildings, both of which have provoked controversy, are Oxford Street's dominant Centrepoint (1965, Richard Seifert), which became a symbol of profligate speculation, and the National Theatre (1967-77, Denys Lasdun), in the cold, horizontal style of the South Bank complex.

The Prince of Wales' outspoken criticism of modern architecture in the capital has accelerated the trend away from the brutalism of the 1960s and 1970s. Curves have replaced hard lines, steel, glass and brick have replaced concrete, and architects are employing Classical motifs — pediments, porticoes, columns, moldings — within the context of modern architecture.

The **Hoover factory** (1932) shows the influence of Art Deco.

The revolutionary **Lloyd's** (1980-86), by Richard Rogers and Partners, has a vast central atrium.

Centrepoint (1962-66), whose honeycomb tower rises above a piazza.

The **National Theatre** (1967-77) has a superbly organized interior, with complex vertical and horizontal creation of functional spaces.

London and literature

The resonances of a city through its life are caught and retained in its literature, and few sidewalks echo these sounds as pervasively as those of London. The streets themselves are dotted with blue plaques to mark the birthplaces, homes and workplaces of writers, and the British Museum is heavy with the manuscripts of classics.

It was from London that English literature began its journey; from the Tabard Inn in Southwark, whence Geoffrey Chaucer (1340-1400), a court official and customs officer in London, dispatched his garrulous pilgrims with their *Canterbury Tales*. In so doing, he created a specifically English literature, graphically realistic and vernacular. The Tabard became the Talbot Inn, which survived until the 1870s, and Talbot Yard is still there, with six centuries of exits and entrances to remember. It is easy to perceive Chaucer's London in his descriptions of the walled city of Troy in *Troilus and Crisyde* — there is something familiar about a city surrounded by countryside but bursting inside with wonders like those detailed in the contemporary but anonymous *Piers Plowman*.

A tradition was established. Even for the great Renaissance writers, steeped in classical learning, London, noisy, fast and aggressive, dictated its own style, often drama. Shakespeare (1564-1616) worked in the circular galleried theaters of Southwark, which were thought too rowdy for The City proper, where art was brought for almost the first time to the working class, the 'groundlings' who stood in the 'pit' (see *Shakespeare Globe Museum*). He would also perform for more exclusive audiences — both *Twelfth Night* and *A Midsummer Night's Dream* are thought to have been first performed privately in the Inns of Court.

The plays of his contemporary Ben Jonson give perhaps the best idea of London, where the cunning and clever prosper, especially *The Alchemist*, *Bartholomew Fair* and *Every Good Man in his Humour*, which includes a scene in Paul's Walk, the central aisle of St Paul's. Jonson and others would often retire to The Mermaid Tavern, which stood where Bread St. meets Cheapside, but they sometimes wound up in Southwark's prisons, The Clink and Marshalsea, for writing plays which displeased the Crown. Others met a worse fate: much of Sir Walter Raleigh's finest writing was done during his 13yr in the Tower before his execution in 1618, and in 1593 Christopher Marlowe was stabbed to death in a tavern in Deptford.

John Donne (1573-1631), whose early lyrics have such sense of place, is claimed by some to symbolize London's temporary 'decline' into intellectualism by turning to religious poetry. In 1621 he became Dean of St Paul's. Admittedly, London only housed and did not inspire Milton and the great metaphysical poets. Yet from the ashes of the medieval city (burned down in 1666) and Puritanism rose arguably the greatest works about London, certainly two of the best diaries ever written, both social history and literature: those of Samuel Pepys and John Evelyn.

> The stones of St Paul's flew like grenades, and the lead melted down the streets in a stream. The very pavements glowed with fiery redness, and neither horse nor man was able to tread on them.

Evelyn's physical description is outstanding, but in both diaries

28

everyday life is also vividly pictured — that of Pepys so honestly that he always wrote in a secret shorthand not deciphered until 1820.

With the 18thC post-fire development of the West End came a new Augustan 'Age of Reason,' when London, a new Rome or Athens, inspired learned, urbane works. But its vigorous, down-to-earth character shone through. Satire became the new mode, irreverent modern classics about people, not gods, such as *The Dunciad* by Pope (1688-1744), often to be found at *Chiswick House* with his patron Lord Burlington; or *London* by Dr Johnson (1709-84), an archetypal English blend of common sense and classicism (see *Johnson's House*). Cliques need meeting places, and the most famous surviving one is the Cheshire Cheese on Fleet St.; Russell St., Covent Garden, housed the most renowned coffee houses.

But the age of reason was not all it thought itself. In 1679 Dryden was beaten up outside the Lamb and Flat pub in Rose St., WC2 (since nicknamed 'The Bucket of Blood'), having offended the Earl of Rochester, a fellow writer, in a satire. At Swift's suggestion, John Gay wrote *The Beggar's Opera* in 1728 as a 'Newgate pastoral,' depicting with a new moral stringency the slums of Covent Garden and the notorious Newgate prison. Henry Fielding, a pioneer of the new novel form with *Tom Jones*, was an innovative magistrate in Bow Street, trying to protect the same slum dwellers. Even writing had its seamy side — buried under the Barbican is the site of Grub Street, still the imagined habitat of ill-paid hack writers.

London is enchanting. I step out upon a tawny coloured magic carpet. . . . it takes up the private life and carries it on, without any effort. . . .

Virginia Woolf in her diary, 1926

Although Wordsworth was moved to write "Earth has not anything to show more fair" (*On Westminster Bridge*, 1802), and Keats (1795-1821) found peace enough in Hampstead to write *Ode to a Nightingale* (see *Keats' House*), it was urban squalor which moved Charles Dickens (1812-70), the most obsessive writer about London. Like that of his own Sam Weller, Dickens' "knowledge of London was extensive and peculiar." In his novels London is most often a brooding, malevolent presence, too powerful for the people in it, a city of slum tenements, an evil ruling class, prisons and 'London particulars' or 'pea-soupers,' poisonous mixes of fog and smog. To balance this, there is the comedy and vitality of his unforgettable cockneys, like Sam Weller, Mr. Micawber and Bill Sykes, with their own unique language. Yet underneath speaks the morally appalled social reformer. The references are endless (see *Dickens' House*), but some idea of his feelings can be gained from his treatment of the Thames, along which Abel Magwitch tries in vain to escape in *Great Expectations* and which is so often the recipient of corpses — as in the superb opening scene of *Our Mutual Friend*.

By the interwar years, things had changed. Virginia Woolf (1882-1941) wrote: "I ask nothing better than that all the reviewers. . . . should call me a highbrow. If they like to add Bloomsbury, WC1., that is the correct postal address." In Bloomsbury's leafy Georgian squares, where dark brick houses surround pleasant gardens, Lawrence, Yeats, Eliot and Forster found a calming peace, which is still there and can be felt in the modernist literature forged in the area.

Royal London

Like the pussycat in the nursery rhyme, people go "up to London to look at the Queen." For the visitor from other parts of the realm, the rituals, pageantry, and palaces of royal London are the tangible demonstration not only of a heritage but also of a unique record of stability. The monarchy has survived not because the kingdom is quiescent but because the Crown itself is a stabilizing influence. It has had its nadirs, of course: it was replaced by the Commonwealth from 1649-60; and more recently the abdication of Edward VIII in 1936, before his coronation, provoked something of a crisis of confidence in the institution. Today, most Britons regard it as the keystone of the state. That phenomenon is not unique, but it is rare.

> . . . . for within the hollow crown
> That rounds the mortal temples of a king
> Keeps Death his court, and there the antick sits,
> Scoffing his state and grinning at his pomp. . . .
> I live with bread like you, feel want,
> Taste grief, need friends: subjected thus,
> How can you say to me I am a king?
>
> William Shakespeare, *Richard II*, c.1593

The kingdom is not, of course, England, otherwise the Queen's husband and her son and heir would not be Duke of Edinburgh and Prince of Wales. The Queen is also head of state of many countries in the Commonwealth, but arguably the most important job of the monarchy is to represent the family of nations which together, and by consent, compose the United Kingdom. Because they have smaller populations, Scotland and Wales are numerically less represented in Parliament than England, but they are equal in the sight of the Crown. In countries of less age, national unity can be an objective in itself, but Britain is neither young nor one nation, and needs some means by which it can articulate its wholeness.

> There will soon be five kings left — the Kings of England, Diamonds, Hearts, Spades and Clubs.
>
> King Farouk of Egypt, 1951

At the time of the wedding of the Prince of Wales in 1981, Charles Douglas-Home, writing in *The Times*, conceded that the Queen has "almost no executive function to perform," but concluded that she has "a 'presence' in the highest reaches of the political process." Before a general election can take place the Queen must dissolve Parliament. After the contest, she appoints as Prime Minister the leader of whichever party has won the election and invites him or her to form a government. The monarchy, Douglas-Home pointed out, "is not yet constitutionally allowed to slip back into a world of sumptuous ceremonial."

Where to see the Royal Family

The daily Court Circular, which gives details of all the Royal Family's public engagements, is printed in *The Times*, *Daily Telegraph* and the *Independent*. Apart from this, the Queen presides at certain annual events, often accompanied by other members of her family.

   The State Opening of Parliament, at the beginning of each new session of Parliament, usually late Oct, is the most apparently political of the Queen's regular duties, in that she announces in her speech a program of proposed legislation. In fact, the measures outlined are put forward not at the discretion of the Queen but on behalf of her government.

Remembrance Sunday, on the Sun nearest Nov 11, sees the Queen placing wreaths on the Cenotaph in Whitehall to commemorate the dead of the two World Wars.

Trooping the Colour takes place on a Sat in mid-June to honor the Queen's official birthday. Each year a different Guards regiment presents itself for inspection; the 'colour' is its regimental flag. The Queen rides on horseback to Horse Guards' Parade, off Whitehall, receives the salute amid marching bands, and often makes an appearance on the balcony of Buckingham Palace on her return.

Royal residences

Buckingham Palace did not become the principal royal residence until the time of Queen Victoria (1836-1902), though it had been used by monarchs since George III bought it in 1762. However, the palace is in every sense the center, home and headquarters of the British monarchy.

Before Victoria, St James's Palace, built for Henry VIII (1509-47), was the sovereign's official residence. Its status is still honored in the accreditation of foreign diplomats to "the court of St James," and is the headquarters of the Gentlemen at Arms, who form a personal bodyguard for the Queen, and the home of the Yeomen of the Guard. These, rather than the Tower Yeomen, are the true 'Beefeaters,' a word probably derived from 'buffetier,' meaning an attendant at royal buffets. St James's Palace also includes Clarence House, home of Queen Elizabeth the Queen Mother, one of the most dearly loved members of the Royal Family in recent decades.

Kensington Palace was acquired as a home by William III, who wanted a place in the country around London. It was the home of the sovereign from 1689-1760, and is now the London home of the Prince and Princess of Wales, and the home also of Princess Margaret, the Queen's sister, and of other royals.

Windsor Castle (see *Excursions*) is still used extensively by the Royal Family. Originally the home of Edward the Confessor (1042-66), it is a country home much closer to London than Balmoral in Scotland, or Sandringham in Norfolk.

Who's who in the Royal Family

George V m. Mary of Teck

Edward VIII m. Mrs Simpson · George VI m. Elizabeth (Queen Mother) · Mary · Henry, Duke of Gloucester m. Princess Alice · George, Duke of Kent m. Marina · John

Queen Elizabeth II m. Prince Philip, Duke of Edinburgh · Princess Margaret m. Earl of Snowdon · Richard, Duke of Gloucester · Edward, Duke of Kent · Princess Alexandra · Prince Michael of Kent

Charles, Prince of Wales m. Lady Diana Spencer · Anne, Princess Royal m. Capt. Mark Phillips · Andrew, Duke of York m. Sarah Ferguson · Prince Edward · Viscount Linley · Lady Sarah Armstrong-Jones

William · Henry · Peter · Zara · Beatrice

Calendar of events

See also *Sports and activities* and *Public holidays* in *Basic information*.

January

1st week. Jan sales. Most stores offer good reductions; the most voracious shoppers camp out overnight in lines. Some now start late Dec

International Boat Show. Earls Court, SW5. Leisure boats

Last Sun, 11am. Charles I Commemoration. Whitehall, SW1. On the anniversary of his execution, the unofficial King's Army parades from St James's Palace to the Banqueting House

Jan/Feb. Chinese New Year. Chinatown, around Gerrard St., W1. Dragons, lanterns, flags, torches and the Lion Dance

Jan/Mar. Rugby Union Internationals. Twickenham. On two Sat afternoons England play

February

Cruft's Dog Show. Earls Court, SW5. The world's biggest, most prestigious show

First Sun, 4pm. Annual Clowns Service. Holy Trinity Church, Dalston, E8. The Clowns International Club attends its church in full costume to honor its founder, Joseph Grimaldi. All welcome to free clown show afterward

Shrove Tuesday, noon. Pancake races. Covent Garden. Followed by a band performance.

March

Mar 1. St David's Day. Windsor Castle. A member of the Royal Family presents the Welsh Guards with the national emblem, a leek

Ideal Home Exhibition. Olympia, W14. A huge exhibition of everything, but everything, found in and around the home

Camden Festival. The borough, from Bloomsbury to Hampstead, sponsors concerts, plays, etc.; always attracts big jazz names

2nd Tues, noon. Bridewell Service. St Bride's, Fleet St., EC4. The Lord Mayor and Sheriffs attend this thanksgiving service for the Bridewell children's home, now moved out of London

3rd or 4th Thurs. Oranges and Lemons Service. St. Clement Danes, Strand, WC2. As a reminder of the nursery rhyme, children are presented with the fruits during a service. The church bells ring out the rhyme daily at 9am, noon, 3pm, 6pm

Royal Film Performance. Royals and celebrities attend a gala premiere for charity

Mar 17. St Patrick's Day. Pirbright, Surrey. The Irish Guards are presented with shamrock by the Queen Mother

Mar/Apr. Country Music Festival. Wembley Arena. Festivities last a week.

Mar/Apr. Boat Race. Putney to Mortlake. Oxford and Cambridge University eights battle upstream with awesome power

Mar/Apr. Head of the River Race. Mortlake to Putney. Racing between teams from all over Europe

April

Maundy Thursday (Thurs before Easter). Maundy Monday. At a different church every year, the Queen presents specially minted coins to the elderly and to groups of children

Good Friday. Butterworth Charity. St Bartholomew the Great, Smithfield, EC1. After 11am service, hot cross buns and coins are laid out on tombstones for local children

Easter Sunday. Easter Parade. Battersea Park. Climax of the day-long fair is the huge colorful parade at 3pm. Also fairs on Hampstead Heath and Blackheath. Tower Church Parade. Tower of London, EC3. After 11am service, Yeoman Warders have official inspection

Easter Monday. Procession and Easter carols. Westminster Abbey, SW1. London Marathon. From Greenwich Park to Westminster Bridge. 30,000 competitors from the very fast to the very mad

Harness Horse Parade. Regents Park, NW1. A morning parade of heavy working horses in superb, gleaming brass harnesses and plumes

1st Thurs after Easter. Spital Sermon. St Lawrence Jewry, EC2. A service attended by all The City's pomp, Lord Mayor included, in full regalia

Apr 21. Queen's Birthday. 21-gun salutes in Hyde Park and on Tower Hill at noon. Troops in parade dress

May

FA Cup Final. Wembley Stadium. Showpiece soccer match

Rugby League Cup Final. Wembley Stadium. Showpiece rugby league match

Beating Retreat. Household Division. Horse Guards Parade, SW1. Military massed bands and marching

Summer Exhibition. Royal Academy, Piccadilly, W1. An extensive potpourri of much that is happening in British art. To Sept

2nd Sun. Punch and Judy Festival. Covent Garden. Procession at 10am, service at 11am, then Punch and Judy shows until 6pm at the site where Pepys watched England's first show in 1662

Ascension Day. Beating the Bounds. The boundary stones of parishes were traditionally 'whacked' with a stick in defiance. Today it happens around the Tower, and All-Hallows-by-the-Tower, EC3, one of the marks of which is in mid-river but is whacked notwithstanding

Private Fire Brigades Competition. Guildhall Yard, EC4. They spray targets with hoses. Again in Sept

Glyndebourne Opera Season. Sussex. Exclusive performances in a country house, with champagne picnics during intervals. To Aug

Chelsea Flower Show. Royal Hospital, SW3. A massive and superb 4-day horticultural display

May 29 or soon after. Founder's (Oak Apple) Day. Royal Hospital, Chelsea, SW3. The Chelsea Pensioners' annual parade

Late May. Samuel Pepys Memorial Service. St Olave, EC3. Lord Mayor and Co., 17thC band, all flock to Pepys' own church

June

1st Wed. The Derby. Epsom Downs. This great horse race is on common land, and so is attended by fairs, Gypsies, and huge crowds

Beating Retreat. Royal Marines. Horse Guards Parade, SW1. Military massed bands and marching

Test match. Lords, NW8. 5-day international cricket match

June 11 or nearest Sat. Trooping the Colour. Horse Guards Parade, SW1. The Queen, in uniform, leaves from Buckingham Palace in procession to receive the Colour from her Foot Guards amid full pageantry

3rd Week. Royal Ascot. The Berkshire racecourse sees some fine racing but more important for royalty on parade and 'society' out to impress each other and have fun

3rd Mon. Garter Ceremony. St George's Chapel, Windsor Castle. The 24 members of The Very Noble Order of the Garter attend a service, invest new members, and pay homage to the Queen

June 22 or near. Election of the Sheriffs of The City of London. Guildhall, EC2. Full pageantry and procession

June/July. Wimbledon Tennis Championships. The world's top players

Outdoor concerts. In all major parks, Kenwood Lakeside, Hampstead Heath, and Crystal Palace Bowl. Until Sept

July

1st week. Henley Royal Regatta. Henley, Oxfordshire. Another sporting event (rowing) which is also part of the 'season'

Royal Tournament. Earls Court, SW5. All the Armed Forces join in displays of gymnastics, motor-cycling and military skills. On the Sun before it begins, they all parade along a chosen route, sometimes in and sometimes outside London

Promenade Concerts. Royal Albert Hall, SW7. Until Sept. See *Concerts* in *Nightlife*

Royal International Horse Show. Wembley Arena. Showjumping

3rd week. Swan Upping. The Thames, from Sunbury to Whitchurch. The Dyers Company and Vintners Company, which share ownership of all swans with the Queen, take six boats upriver counting and marking the birds

2nd Wed. Vintners Roadsweeping. Wine porters sweep the road in front of a procession, from Vintners' Hall, Upper Thames St. to St James's Garlickhythe, EC4, at 11.58am, marking the inauguration of their new Master

Doggett's Coat and Badge Race. A race for single sculls rowing from London Bridge to Chelsea against the tide, founded in 1714

August

London Riding Horse Parade. Rotten Row, Hyde Park. Moss Bros cup goes to best turned-out horse and rider

Bank Holiday Weekend (last in Aug). Horse Show. Clapham Common. Bank Holiday Fair. Hampstead Heath. A traditional fairground. The Notting Hill Carnival. Ladbroke Grove, W11. West Indian street carnival

September

Test match. Kennington Oval, SE11. 5-day international cricket

Last Night of the Proms. Royal Albert Hall, SW7. See *Concerts* in *Nightlife*

Chelsea Antiques Fair. Chelsea Old Town Hall, King's Rd., SW3

Planning and walks

Sept 21. Christ's Hospital Boys March. Church of the Holy Sepulchre, Holborn Viaduct, EC1. The pupils and band of this ancient school march to Mansion House in 16thC 'bluecoats'

Private Fire Brigades Competition. EC4. See May

Sept 28. Admission of Sheriffs. See June; in another ceremony they are admitted to the Guildhall

Sept 29. Election of the Lord Mayor. Guildhall, EC2. Beforehand, the whole corporation proceeds in state from Mansion House

October

Oct 1 or 1st Mon. Judges Service. Westminster Abbey, SW1. At the start of the legal year, the judiciary process from Westminster Abbey to breakfast in the Palace of Westminster, and then parades in the afternoon at the Royal Courts of Justice in the Strand, WC2

1st Sun, 3pm. Pearly Harvest Festival. St Martin-in-the-Fields, WC2. The brightly caparisoned Pearly Kings and Queens, Cockney folk leaders, in full uniform

Horse of the Year Show. Wembley Arena. Show jumping, featuring top international competitors

2nd Sun. Harvest of the Sea Thanksgiving. St Mary-at-Hill, EC3, 11am. Billingsgate dealers fill the church with fish, and The City attends in state

Quit Rents Ceremony. Royal Courts of Justice, WC2. An official receives token rents on behalf of the Queen; ceremony includes counting of sticks and counting horseshoes

Oct 21, or nearest Sun. Trafalgar Day. National Service for Seafarers at St Paul's Cathedral, attended by Admiralty top brass; and a naval ceremony in Trafalgar Sq., WC2

National Brass Band Championships. Royal Albert Hall, SW7. A type of music at which the British excel

Oct/Nov. State Opening of Parliament. The processional route is Buckingham Palace, The Mall, Horse Guards Parade, Palace of Westminster. Usually the entire Royal Family attend; full regalia, ancient gilded coaches

November

1st Sun. London to Brighton Veteran Car Run. Hyde Park Corner, SW1. An early start (8am) for the aged cars

Nov 5. Guy Fawkes Night. To celebrate the 1605 Gunpowder Plot to blow up Parliament, fireworks and bonfires all over town, with effigies of the conspiracy's leader burned on top

Sun nearest Nov 11. Remembrance Sun. The Queen and State attend an 11am ceremony at the Cenotaph, Whitehall, SW1. The previous evening there is a moving Festival of Remembrance at the Royal Albert Hall, SW7

Fri nearest Nov 12. Admission of Lord Mayor Elect. Guildhall, EC2. The outgoing mayor hands over the insignia

Sat nearest Nov 12, Lord Mayor's Show. Guildhall to Law Courts, Strand, WC2. The state coaches follow the many colorful floats in this huge carnival

London Film Festival. National Film Theatre, South Bank. To Dec

Benson & Hedges Tennis Championships. Wembley Arena

Late Nov. Switching on of Christmas lights in Regent St. and Oxford St. Until Jan 6

December

Royal Smithfield Show. Earls Court, SW5. Agricultural show

Norwegian Christmas Tree. Trafalgar Sq. Carol-singing on most evenings beneath the tree

Dec 31. Watch Night. St Paul's Cathedral. Scots gather on steps for Hogmanay. Trafalgar Sq. is the other traditional spot for high-spirited revelers as well as Parliament Sq. for watching Big Ben strike at midnight

Weekly events

Mon. Bric-a-brac and antiques at Covent Garden market

Wed. Camden Passage antique market. Late-night shopping in Knightsbridge (see *Shopping*). Some theater matinees

Thurs. Late-night shopping in Oxford St. and Regent st. Some theater matinees

Fri. Bermondsey (New Caledonian) antique market (see *Shopping*)

Sat. Portobello Rd. antique market and Covent Garden crafts market (see *Shopping*). Theater matinees. Evening open-air concerts in June-July at Kenwood House, Hampstead Heath

Sun. Petticoat Lane, Camden Lock markets (see *Shopping*)

Daily events

11am (10am Sun). Changing the Guard. Horse Guards Parade

11.30am (only alternate days in winter). Changing the Guard, Buckingham Palace

9.50pm. Ceremony of the Keys. Tower of London. Ceremonial changing of guards. Write to Resident Governor for free ticket

When and where to go

Unlike the folks of some cities, Londoners do not all choose to take their vacations at the same time, so the capital never 'closes down.' It does, on the other hand, become very crowded at the height of summer. Consider side-stepping this stampede: the British climate may be unpredictable but it is rarely extreme, and London, being in one of the mildest parts of the country, can be very pleasant in the spring and fall. Moreover, a whole series of outdoor sporting (and social) events takes place from March (see *Calendar of events*).

Outdoor institutions, like the open-air theater in *Regent's Park*, begin to brave the elements in May, and in the same month Glyndebourne's opera season starts. The crowded months are July and Aug, but theater-lovers will want to avoid the summer in favor of fall and winter, often better times for new shows and certainly for accommodations.

Even in winter, London remains alive with activity, and several of the main exhibitions take place at this time of year. One famous winter institution which London has cast aside is the pea-soup fog, vanquished by clean-air legislation, and little else remains to stop Londoners going about their daily rounds.

The main airport being on the western side of the city, and the longer rail and road routes running into the w and N, those compass points have a powerful influence on activity in London. The greatest number of hotels is to be found in the w, whether in suburbs such as *Chiswick*, inner districts such as *Kensington*, *Chelsea* and Victoria, or in the West End, the area which most Londoners regard as the center by virtue of its shops, restaurants and theaters.

Farther E, *The City*, though it is jeweled with historical sights, is seen by the Londoner as being primarily a business district which empties in the evenings and at weekends. In much the way that The City is a buffer to the E, so is the river to the s. The implantation of the *Barbican* Centre in the City and the *South Bank Arts Centre* across the river were both conscious attempts to extend the geographical spread of nocturnal life. Beyond these outriders, however, central London fades in The City and only half-heartedly crosses the Thames. Central London does not formally define itself, but most inhabitants would probably accept the Circle line on the tube (subway) system as a fair boundary.

Few Londoners live within that circle, however, and their residential districts outside it are the source of much local rivalry. Not only does the topography of fashionable northern suburbs like *Hampstead* and *Highgate* provide their inhabitants with elevated notions, but it is also true than many Londoners feign disinclination to cross the river. Certainly many of the 'south-of-the-river' districts closer to London have little to recommend them to visitors, although among these are some residential enclaves that are gradually becoming fashionable. Nevertheless there is only one recommended tourist hotel at present s of the river; nor indeed are there many to the E of *Tower Bridge*. So for accommodations the visitor generally has to stick to the center, the N or the w.

Each of the compass points appears in the beginning of the postal codes and is also printed on street signs. Much of the West End is W1 (West One), addresses in The City usually carry EC (East Central), and so on. Nevertheless the system is not as logical as it might be and spoken directions will tend to be given in terms of the area's or the district's name. Many of the most interesting of these areas are described in the A-Z of *Sights and places of interest*.

Orientation map

Area planners

The City

Home not only of Mammon (in the Bank of England and the *Stock Exchange*) but also of God (in *St Paul's Cathedral* and the numerous churches) and the Godless (in *Fleet Street*). The *Royal Courts of Justice* and the *Old Bailey* are to be found in The City, and the whole square mile is guarded by the *Tower of London*.

The West End

Unlike The City, the West End has no precise borders, though it is divided by its main thoroughfares into clearly-defined neighborhoods. Simply by crossing the street it is possible to leave behind a neighborhood of one quite distinct character and enter what seems to be another world. See *Orientation map* on pages 36-37 for area limits.

Mayfair is the neighborhood of exclusive hotels, expense-account restaurants, embassies, haute couture houses and casinos, and its denizens usually ride in chauffeur-driven cars. Its 'village' shopping street is Bond St., with South Molton St. for the younger folks, and North and South Audley Sts. for the extra-extravagant. In hilly, elegant Brook, Mount and Curzon Sts. are smaller, old-established, conspicuously exclusive shops. The alleys of Shepherd Market offer sidewalk cafés for rest and refreshment on sunny days.

Soho is seductive not for its sex shops, which are no more inviting nor less sleazy than those in any other city, but for its delicatessens, patisseries, moderately priced restaurants, and a gossipy confluence of Italian waiters, Cockney movie editors, lengthy lunchers and other miscreants. Its trendiness has long attracted media folk. Over Shaftesbury Ave., its cosmopolitanism hardens into Chinatown.

Covent Garden has, despite the misgivings of purists, proved to be one of the most successful examples anywhere of a discarded facility (in this instance a wholesale fruit and vegetable market) being turned into an area for strolling, eating and shopping. The most fiercely community-conscious of all the inner city areas, it has come to stand for everything opposed to big business and development.

Bloomsbury has a bookish dignity which once hid all manner of intensity. It also has the *British Museum* and the nucleus of London University, whose visitors and students find perfect peace in its many green squares.

Belgravia is the most elegant part of the West End, with its early 19thC houses; Belgrave Sq., from which it takes its name, has beautiful gardens. Even the very rich who have always lived here are feeling the pinch and today the area is dominated by embassies. Belgravia's 'neighborhood shop' is Harrods; around the corner is Knightsbridge.

St James's is gentlemen's clubland, with Jermyn St. as its shopping thoroughfare. The name is broadly applied to the neighborhood around St James's St., and St James's Sq., on the hill running down from Piccadilly to *St James's Palace*, constituting an area which perhaps changed less than any other over the last 50yr.

Westminster is media shorthand for Parliament, in much the way that *Whitehall* is used to denote the Civil Service and *Downing Street* to suggest the Prime Minister. Apart from *Westminster Abbey*, all the dominant buildings in this area are concerned with government. There are no shops and very few residents —just a rich seam of pomp and circumstance.

Inner London
Beyond central London, several inner districts make their own
unique contributions to metropolitan life. The most obvious are
the two which give their name to the Royal Borough of Kensington
and Chelsea. *Kensington*, with its famous museums, also extends
to Notting Hill and Portobello Rd., eventually giving way to
Hammersmith, which has a couple of respected theaters. *Chelsea*,
elegant and fashionable, with its clothes shops and restaurants,
spills over into Fulham.

All these districts are in the w; in the N, Islington has emerged as
the outstanding example of the arty rejuvenation of London's old
working-class inner boroughs.

Outer London
Intellectual *Hampstead* and *Highgate* in the N, maritime
Greenwich in the E, villagey *Dulwich* in the the s, riverside
Richmond in the w. . . . All are to varying degrees outer districts,
though London stretches yet farther in an exhausting sprawl of
mainly 1930s suburbs.

Walks in London

Although London is vast in area, it is also a marvelous city for
taking a walk. Perhaps the chief reason for this lies in the close
proximity of the many separate and characterful neighborhoods
that it contains, and a number of these — *Chelsea*, *Holland Park*,
Little Venice, *Greenwich*, *Hampstead*, among others — make
walks in themselves (see A-Z of *Sights and places of interest*).

In a city that reached its prime before the days of motor
transportation, walking is also, naturally, the most effective way to
see and learn about London. For information about walks for this
purpose — routes, subjects of theme walks, starting times —
☎730-3488: London Visitor and Convention Bureau. Similar
information is also published on the back page of *The Times* in The
Times Information Service.

The walks described in detail on the following pages have a
different and special purpose: to give a taste of a Londoner's
London — its river, parks and pubs, and its cultural, especially
literary, heart.

There is no quick way of getting to know London. As an
introduction to this historic city, however, or to refresh the
memory after a long absence, the following stroll through its City
of Westminster, center of government and tradition and coner-
stone of the West End, links many of London's most famous
landmarks and serves as a convenient orientation tour as well.

Walk I/Introduction to London
Allow 2-3hr. Tube Westminster. See Map 9-10.
Begin by walking along Bridge St., past the statue of *Queen
Boadicea*, symbol of patriotism, on to Westminster Bridge itself,
from where the best view of the *Palace of Westminster* and **Big
Ben** can be gained. Look also to your right along the Victoria
Embankment to see the fine government buildings. Let your gaze
move around in full circle to cross the river with the Charing Cross
railway bridge; beyond it is the *South Bank Arts Centre* and, on
this side, County Hall, old headquarters of the now defunct

Greater London Council. The panorama continues past the huge stone lion at the E end of Westminster Bridge to the new St. Thomas' Hospital, and crosses the river again by Lambeth Bridge.

From the foot of Big Ben, walk back around the w side of the Palace of Westminster past Westminster Hall and then cross over the road to St Margaret's Church to arrive at *Westminster Abbey*.

Continue around Parliament Sq. almost to Bridge St. again, before turning left into Parliament St., which leads to *Whitehall*. The second street on the left, past the Cenotaph, is *Downing Street*, where the policeman at the door identifies 'Number 10'. Going N along Whitehall, the *Banqueting House* (1622) is on the right, nearly opposite the Whitehall entrance to *Horse Guards Parade*. At the N of Whitehall is *Trafalgar Square*, which is dominated by **Nelson's Column** and is a crowded area of constant activity.

As you cross the square toward the *National Gallery*, notice also James Gibbs' beautiful church of *St Martin-in-the-Fields* (1726). St Martin's Pl., in front and to the right of the church, has the central Post Office on its right; to the N, up St Martin's Lane, is the globe-topped spire of the **Coliseum**, home of the English National Opera (see *Nightlife*). Leading around to the left, however, past the entrance to the *National Portrait Gallery*, is Charing Cross Rd. Follow this road as far as Leicester Square tube station, then turn left along Cranbourn St. into **Leicester Sq.** itself.

The route continues along the N side of Leicester Sq. as far as the Swiss Centre, where a right turn up Wardour St. leads past Lisle St. and Gerrard St., the two main arteries of **Chinatown**, to Shaftesbury Ave., the heart of theaterland and the southern boundary of *Soho*. Turn left on Shaftesbury Ave. and walk down to **Piccadilly Circus**.

Arriving at Piccadilly Circus, pause a moment to orient yourself between Shaftesbury Ave., Regent St., curving majestically to the W and N and *Piccadilly* itself, leading W toward *Mayfair*, *Belgravia* and Knightsbridge. It is the fourth major street that you must follow: go down Lower Regent St. to the s, which borders *St James's* on the right, and crosses Pall Mall to the Duke of York Monument, at the top of the steps that run down past the elegant and imposing **Carlton House Terrace** to *The Mall*.

At the foot of the steps look left toward Admiralty Arch, and Trafalgar Square beyond it. Notice also the ivy-clad wartime extension to the Admiralty, the Citadel, beyond which can be seen the expanse of Horse Guards Parade. Then walk W along The Mall, with *St James's Park* on your left, toward the gilded **Victoria Memorial** and beyond it *Buckingham Palace*, passing *Marlborough House*, *St James's Palace*, Clarence House and *Lancaster House* on the way. Walk around the s side of Buckingham Palace to Buckingham Gate and Buckingham Palace Rd., to the entrances to the **Queen's Picture Gallery** and the **Royal Mews**.

To complete the walk, either continue along Buckingham Palace Rd. to Victoria Station, or retrace your steps to follow Birdcage Walk along the s side of St James's Park in front of the newly restored Wellington Barracks. The first street on the right, **Queen Anne's Gate**, leads to St James's Park tube station. To continue along Birdcage Walk into Great George St. takes you to **Parliament Square** and Westminster tube station, where the walk began.

Walk 2/London's cultural heart
*Allow 1-2hr. Tube Temple. Map **10-11**.*

The central areas of *Covent Garden* and *Bloomsbury* have always been nurseries of artistic endeavor and achievement.

Begin at the Aldwych, where **Bush House**, facing up Kingsway, is an appropriate symbol of British cultural prestige; from this building the BBC runs its foreign radio services. On the right, Houghton St. leads to Portugal St., and **The Old Curiosity Shop**. It is not certain that Dickens based his novel on this antique shop, but he knew it well.

Back on the Aldwych, turn up **Drury Lane**. The **Theatre Royal**, down Russell St. to the left and on the corner of Catherine St., was founded in 1663. Also in **Russell St**. were the famous coffeehouses of the 18thC; Dr Johnson and Boswell first met in a bookshop at no.8 in 1763. Drury Lane continues until it turns into Museum St. and pushes on into more elegant *Bloomsbury*, passing on the right in Bloomsbury Way the church of **St George**, used by Dickens as the setting for his Bloomsbury christening in *Sketches by Boz*.

Return to Museum St. and turn right, passing an occult and magic bookshop, the Rudolf Steiner Library, and a couple of famous publishing houses. At the far end is the **Museum Tavern**, at different times favored by Karl Marx and Dylan Thomas. Turn left here, past the *British Museum*, and then right into Bloomsbury St., passing the peaceful and unspoiled **Bedford Sq**., the home at times of many distinguished people and therefore of a crop of blue plaques. Continue down Gower St., pausing to see the statues of tragedy and comedy outside the **Royal Academy of Dramatic Art**.

A right turn into Torrington Pl. passes Dillon's University Bookshop and Woburn Sq. on the right, home of the *Courtauld Institute Galleries*. Gordon Sq., on the left, was a stamping ground of the Bloomsbury Group. Torrington Pl. leads on to Tavistock Sq.; the garden has as its focal point a statue of *Mahatma Gandhi*, and a tree planted by Pandit Nehru. Turn left along the far side of the square to Upper Woburn Pl. On the right, a blue plaque marks the site where Dickens lived from 1851-60, now the headquarters of the British Medical Association. Farther on the right, turn into **Woburn Walk**, with its bowfront shops and brass plaque in memory of the poet W.B. Yeats, who lived here at the turn of the century.

A left turn leads back to Euston Rd., for a bus or tube.

Walk 3/A riverside stroll
Allow 1-2hr. Tube Hammersmith. Map 20C4.

Upstream from central London, the Thames gradually abandons business for pleasure. As much of the route is unpaved you will need suitable footwear in wet weather.

From Hammersmith tube station, Queen Caroline St. leads straight to the river, with the option of a detour left into Crisp Rd. to visit **Riverside Studios** for a drink or snack, or a look at the art gallery or bookshop. Cross the river by Hammersmith Bridge and turn right for a surprisingly rustic walk along the overgrown bank to the **Bull's Head** pub at Barnes, or stay on the N side for historical and architectural interest.

Hammersmith Bridge is one of the most attractive on the river; a suspension bridge built in 1887. Just under the bridge are several balconied houses and boathouses, and there are a couple of pubs next door to each other on this stretch of the river; the most interesting is the **Blue Anchor**.

Just beyond the pubs, a small area of park opens out, and on the right is **Wescott Lodge** (1700), a former vicarage. Farther away to the right, across the main road, is the handsome 1930s facade of **Hammersmith Town Hall**.

On the river, an ugly iron jetty marks the spot, indicated by a plaque, where a creek and a small natural harbor gave birth to the village of Hammersmith. The path winds to the right, then an inlet to the left leads suddenly into a tiny Georgian street which once lay at the heart of Hammersmith, **Upper Mall**. On the left is the **Dove** pub, and on the right is **Kelmscott House**, once the home of William Morris. Over the coach-house door is a sign commemorating the Hammersmith socialists, and the building is still the headquarters of the William Morris Society. The same house can also boast of having witnessed the first demonstration of the electric telegraph.

The riverside walk continues past the crow's-nest lookout post of the Corinthian Sailing Club, through a modern cloisterlike construction under a block of apartments, past the balconied **Ship** pub, a pumping station and another pub called the **Black Lion**;

this pub has associations with the humorist and essayist A.P. Herbert.

Leaving behind a panoramic view of the river, the path then deserts the Thames for a moment to follow the fine Georgian terrace, **Hammersmith Terrace**. As the river comes back into view, from Chiswick Mall a ramp can be seen from which it is possible to walk at low tide to a small island, **Chiswick Eyot**. On the right is Fuller's brewery, then **St Nicholas** church, where Whistler and Hogarth are buried. Enter the churchyard from the river and the tomb of *Hogarth* is on the left, surrounded by a railing. Walk around the church into the graveyard, and the bronze tomb of *Whistler* is near the ivy-covered wall. The path leading out of the church, Powells Walk, leads to a main road, Burlington Lane, across which is *Chiswick House*. Back on the opposite side of the church, Church St. leads to **Chiswick Sq.**, on the left, said to be the scene of an episode in Thackeray's *Vanity Fair*. Around the corner is *Hogarth's House*.

Walk 4/The parks
*Allow 1-3hr. Use Maps **6-10** to enjoy the parks and wander off the skeleton route described. Tube Piccadilly Circus.*
A few minutes' walk from Piccadilly Circus tube station, London's royal parks begin, and they spread themselves airily to *Kensington*.

Stroll down Lower Regent St. to the very end, passing the Crimean War memorial and crossing *Pall Mall* into **Waterloo Pl**. Descend the steps to *The Mall*, with the **Institute of Contemporary Arts** on the left and the Admiralty building diagonally across the road. Cross the road, and enter *St James's Park*.

This small but pretty park is dominated by its lake, alive with waterfowl. Follow the lake to the opposite end offfff the park to leave by the gateway to the right, in front of *Buckingham Palace*. Renegotiate The Mall to enter **Green Park**, opposite. Walk diagonally across this hilly little park, and bear left to enter the pedestrian subway passage at Hyde Park Corner.

The tunnel emerges by the triumphal **Wellington Arch**, on an island of history surrounded by a tangled urban road system. It is best to leave this island, after a look at its imposing monuments, by another hole in the ground, this one signposted for Hyde Park Corner tube station. Bypassing the station itself, emerge by *Hyde Park*, backtracking to enter by the triple archway, then take one final tunnel to arrive in grassy safety. On this corner is *Apsley House*.

Inside the park, the thoroughfare to the left is **Rotten Row**, for horseback riders. Straight ahead is the path leading to the **Serpentine**, the descriptively named lake popular for boating, which also has two adequate restaurants. Follow the lake as far as the bridge carrying the main road, and cross to the other bank. A few steps beyond the bridge is the **Serpentine Gallery**, noted for its exhibition of contemporary artists. Behind the gallery are paths to the bandstand and Round Pond, with a striking view *en route* of the *Albert Memorial and Royal Albert Hall*. Return to the water's edge, on the Kensington side, to see the Art Nouveau statue of *Peter Pan*, whose whimsy pervades the gardens. At the head of the waters is a paved garden, and beyond them the Elfin Oak, a tree-stump carved with elves. Don't leave the gardens without visiting *Kensington Palace*. From this end of the park, it is not far to Bayswater or Kensington High St. tube station, to the N and S respectively.

Sights and places of interest

London's major sights are every bit as enjoyable as their worldwide reputation suggests, but remember that this is also a city of wonderful diversity, so try to take in some of the less well-known attractions too.

Opening hours are fairly regularly adhered to, although entry may not be allowed near closing time. Churches' hours may vary more than those of other buildings, especially in *The City*, and are always subject to closure for services. Rules on photography vary, but often only flash is prohibited.

Major sights classified by type

Ancient buildings
Aspley House
Banqueting House
Buckingham Palace
Chiswick House
Eltham Palace
Fenton House
Gray's Inn
Guildhall
Ham House
Hampton Court
Kensington Palace
Kenwood House
Lambeth Palace
Lancaster House
Leighton House
Lincoln's Inn
Mansion House
Marble Hill House
Marlborough House
Orleans House
Osterley Park
Royal Hospital, Chelsea
Royal Navy College, Greenwich
St James's Palace
Somerset House
Staple Inn
Strawberry Hill
Syon House
Temple
Tower of London
Westminster, Palace of

Churches
Brompton Oratory
St Bartholomew-the-Great
St George's, Bloomsbury
St James's, Piccadilly
St Martin-in-the-Fields
St Mary Abchurch
St Mary-le-Bow
St Mary-le-Strand
St Paul's, Covent Garden
St Paul's Cathedral
St Stephen Walbrook
Southwark Cathedral
Westminster Abbey
Westminster Cathedral

Districts
Belgravia
Bloomsbury
Chelsea
Chiswick
The City
Covent Garden

Docklands
Greenwich
Hampstead
Highgate
Kensington
Mayfair
Richmond
St James's
Soho
Westminster

Museums and galleries
Apsley House/Wellington Museum
HMS Belfast
Bethnal Green Museum
The British Museum
Commonwealth Institute
Courtauld Institute Galleries
Dickens' House
Dulwich College and Picture Gallery
Geffrye Museum
Geological Museum
Hogarth's House
Imperial War Museum
Dr. Johnson's House
Keats' House
Kenwood House/Iveagh Bequest
London, Museum of
London Transport Museum
Madame Tussaud's
Mankind, Musuem of
National Gallery
National Maritime Museum, Greenwich
National Portrait Gallery
Natural History Museum
Public Records Office Museum
Royal Academy of Arts
Royal Air Force Museum, Hendon
Royal Britain
Science Museum
Shakespeare Globe Museum
Sir John Soane's Museum
Tate Gallery
Theatre Museum
Victoria & Albert Museum
Wallace Collection
Whitechapel Art Gallery

Parks/gardens
Holland Park
Hyde Park
Kew Gardens
Regent's Park
Richmond Park
St James's Park
Zoo

44

Albert Memorial and Royal Albert Hall ⭑

Kensington Gore, SW7 ☎589-8212. Map 15I4. Tube Knightsbridge, South Kensington.

These fine examples of Victoriana are dedicated to Victoria's consort, who encouraged the institutionalization of arts and sciences which gives this corner of *Kensington* its character. The Albert Hall was erected in 1867-71, and today its huge amphitheater is used for everything from boxing to concerts, most notably the summer 'Prom' season (see *Nightlife*); visitors are allowed in when the hall is not in use.

Its bold, simple red outline is offset by a solemn ceramic frieze showing the triumph of the arts and sciences. Although the ornate spire of the *Albert Memorial* over the road sits uneasily on the huge Gothic canopy, and although the statue of Albert himself is utterly uninspired, there are endless details to admire in the inventive *mélange* of granite, marble, bronze and semi-precious stones. A multi-million pound restoration program is under way to prevent the memorial from falling down.

Apsley House, The Wellington Museum ⭑ ☆

149 Piccadilly, W1 ☎499-5676. Map 9H8 ▦ � Open Tues-Sun 11am-4.50pm. Tube Hyde Park Corner.

Once the first of a row of aristocratic houses a traveler from the w would encounter when approaching the city, and hence known as 'No.1, London,' Apsley House still puts on a brave show, despite being surrounded on three sides by London's busiest roads. Inside, the visitor is still assured of calm in the majestic rooms once occupied by the Duke of Wellington, Britain's greatest soldier.

Built by Robert Adam in 1771-78 for Baron Apsley, the brick-fronted mansion was bought in 1807 by Lord Wellesley, Wellington's elder brother who sold it to the duke in 1817. Wellington transformed the elegant house into a palace with the help of his architect Benjamin Wyatt, who clad the exterior with Bath stone and added the large portico in 1828; the house was clearly intended to impress at a time when the duke's political career was at its height (he was Prime Minister from 1828-30), and impress it did — during the Reform crisis of 1832, a mob stoned the house, and iron shutters replaced the windows.

Because of the transformation, two complementary styles are to be found in the interior. Adam's work has a fine elegance, whereas Wyatt's changes and additions are on a grander scale. This contrast is not too obvious on the ground floor, where some of the duke's personal mementos and his fine collection of porcelain and dinner services are displayed in rooms which retain some air of domesticity, but it strikes one forcibly on reaching the stairwell, where the graceful curve of Adam's design is offset by Wyatt's heavy and ornate banister. The stair now houses Antonio Canova's massive Neo-Classical statue of the nude *Napoleon as a Roman Emperor*.

The best example of Adam's interior work is the **Piccadilly Drawing Room** at the top of the stairs, with its vaulted ceiling, decorated with characteristically delicate Classical moldings, and curved apsidal E end. Wyatt's work is best seen in the splendid **Waterloo Gallery**, with an elaborate ceiling in his grand 'Versailles' manner. The eight large windows have shutters which slide out to reveal mirrors, turning the room into a glittering hall of light in the evenings. The **Dining Room**, also on the first floor, was adapted by Wyatt from 1816-29 to house the fantastic table service given to Wellington to commemorate his Portuguese victories by the Prince Regent of Portugal in 1816. The complete service

45

consisted of about 1,000 pieces, of which the most important is the centerpiece to be seen on the large oak table.

The fine paintings at Apsley House are largely those of the first duke, with a few additions and loans. Velázquez dominates the Spanish collections with *A Spanish Gentleman* and the profoundly serene *Water Carrier of Seville* (Waterloo Gallery). Murillo and Ribera are also represented, as are many Dutch and Flemish artists: look for Jan Vermeer of Haarlem's *Landscape with Bleaching Grounds* (Yellow Drawing Room) and Elsheimer's haunting *Judith and Holofernes* (Piccadilly Drawing Room). There are a great many portraits of Wellington's illustrious contemporaries, including several of Napoleon and a fine equestrian study of the duke himself painted by Goya (Waterloo Gallery).

A new gallery in the basement is devoted to prints of the duke, costumes and other memorabilia.

Banqueting House 🏛 ★

Whitehall, SW1 ☎930-4179. *Map* **10**H11 🚾 *Open Tues-Sat 10am-5pm, Sun 2-5pm. Tube Westminster, Charing Cross.*

The old prints in the entrance hall show this superb Palladian building as the focal point of the great royal palace of Whitehall; the single hall to survive a fire of 1688, it is today in a very different setting, across busy *Whitehall* from *Horse Guards Parade* and dominated by large government offices. Built by Inigo Jones in 1619-22, the Banqueting House has a flamboyance, but also a classical solemnity and clarity of design, that was entirely novel in its day, marking the final triumph of Italian Renaissance ideas in England.

On the ceiling are the giant canvases commissioned from Rubens by Charles I of the apotheosis of his predecessor and father, James I. Installed in 1635, their incredible scale and vigorous movement are entirely Baroque in feeling, contrasting strongly with Jones' Classicism. Rubens received a knighthood and a pension; Charles I, ironically, was led to his execution in 1649 from the window of this hall.

Barbican

☎628-8795. *Map* **12**E15. *Tube Barbican, Moorgate.*

The Barbican now rises as London's boldest piece of Utopian planning. It was a barren bomb site when, in 1956, it was chosen to reintroduce housing to the almost totally commercial City center. On a bad day, it can seem grim and forbidding, a monument to the failed dreams of modern architecture, but it does have a certain excitement, with angular towers soaring upward and walkways sweeping across. And sometimes the concrete comes to life: the Barbican Centre contains the London Symphony Orchestra's concert hall, the Royal Shakespeare Company's two theaters (see *Nightlife and the arts*), cinema, a gallery, conference halls, a roof garden and cafeterias and restaurants. Opened in 1982, its complex design and sumptuous interior constitute the largest social and arts center of its type in Europe. Also within the complex is the superbly designed new Museum of London (see *London, Museum of*).

Incongruous amid the concrete stand remains of bastions of the old City wall, and the church of **St Giles Cripplegate**, the gutted shell of which survived the fire-bombing. The 15thC tower is surmounted with a brick top story of 1683 and an attractive central turret and weather vane.

Battersea
Map 21D4. Train to Battersea from Waterloo, or bus no.19, 39, 45, 49.

Little remains of the old Thameside village of Battersea, part of which is now an industrial sprawl and part a gentrified residential area. Down by the river, **Battersea Park** is well laid out, with sculptures by Henry Moore and Barbara Hepworth, and is the site of the Easter Parade (see *Calendar of events* in *Planning*). Overlooking the river is an attractive **Japanese Peace Pagoda** completed in 1985. A dominant and increasingly admired landmark is the vast **power station**, brick-built in the modern, monumental style of the 1930s. It is currently being converted into Europe's biggest indoor theme park, **The Battersea**, due to open in May 1990.

HMS Belfast
Symons Wharf, Vine Lane, SE1 ☎407-6434. Map 13G17 ▨ Open daily Apr-Sept 11am-5.30pm, Oct-Mar 11am-4.30pm. Tube London Bridge.

This World War II warship, a Southampton-class cruiser, saw action in the Battle of North Cape in 1943, when the *Scharnhorst* was sunk, in the Normandy landings and even in the Korean War. Now she is a floating tribute to all that, and to wartime naval life in general. Conditions on board were cramped, and the visitor has to weave and duck through hatches and up ladders, but the imagination can run riot on the navigation bridge or next to the massive main guns.

Belgravia
Map 16&17H-K. Tube Hyde Park Corner, Knightsbridge, Sloane Square, Victoria.

London's most magnificent terraces, once the town houses of dukes, make up the great squares of Belgravia, the area around Belgrave Sq. developed by Thomas Cubitt in a frenzy of activity following the establishment of nearby *Buckingham Palace* as the royal residence in the 1820s.

Belgrave Square itself forms the centerpiece of the fairly regular plan, with its massive Classically decorated blocks by George Batesi and grand corner houses by other architects surrounding the private sunken gardens. Eaton Sq., to the s, is a long rectangle with the King's Rd. running through the middle of its massive stuccoed terraces. To the s again is Chester Sq., to some eyes the most appealing of the three.

In Motcomb St., Seth-Smith's Doric-fronted pantechnicon of 1830 looks back on Wilton Crescent, which was built by the same architect 3yr earlier. For refreshment, go to **The Grenadier** (see *Pubs*).

Bethnal Green Museum of Childhood ☆
Cambridge Heath Rd., E2 ☎980-2415. Map 21C5 ▢ ✱ Open Mon-Thurs, Sat 10am-5.50pm, Sun 2.30pm-5.50pm. Tube Bethnal Green.

In the heart of the authentic East End, off the usual tourist track, this museum was opened in 1872 as an extension of the *Victoria & Albert Museum*. There are numerous old toys to study, including board games, toy ships, trains and dolls from many periods. Among the dollhouses, the **Tate Baby House** stands out, a fully furnished Georgian mansion in miniature dating from about 1760.

The galleries upstairs include wonderful collections of children's clothes, books, educational toys and furniture.

Blackheath

Map 21D5. Train to Blackheath from Charing Cross.
This common near the royal residence of *Greenwich* and *Eltham Palace* used to be as grim a place as its name suggests. However, in the 18thC it became a fashionable country address, and now the refreshingly open, high clearing is surrounded by the fine, plain and elegantly unadorned Classical houses of that period. On the SE side, a semicircular arrangement, known as the **Paragon**, is quite stunning. Probably dating from the 1780s, it consists of a series of blocks linked by single-story colonnaded arcades.

To the NE of Blackheath is the superb red-brick **Charlton House** ☆ (☎856-3951 ✉ ✗ *open by appt. only, Mon-Fri*), the best Jacobean house in London. Built in 1607-12, it is entirely regular, with a central arched doorway, exuberant Mannerist carvings, and flanking towers.

Bloomsbury

Map 4C-E. Tube Euston, Russell Square, Holborn.
Bloomsbury, like so many other areas of London, is a 'village' with a reputation. The Bloomsbury Group was as well known for its mores as for its writings, but its patch of London remains the literary capital, housing a host of publishing companies and centered on London University and the *British Museum*. It is also enjoyed for its Georgian squares.

One of the most fashionable addresses in the 18thC, Bloomsbury was an inconspicuous residential area when Virginia and Leonard Woolf, Roger Fry, Lytton Strachey and Maynard Keynes made it their fortress from 1904-39. Before long, other voices were heard there: T.S. Eliot, Bertrand Russell and D.H. Lawrence were inevitably drawn to the center of the action, even if they did not agree with 'The Group.'

Bloomsbury Sq. is where it all began, when the Earl of Southampton built a palace for himself there in 1660. No original building survives, although the gardens are pleasant. **Bedford Square**, to the W past *St George's, Bloomsbury*, was built in 1775; it survives virtually intact as London's finest square. Its rows ('terraces') of plain houses are built of dark brick with stucco pedimented centers. The lush garden is exquisite, although private. The much larger Russell Sq., at the top of Bedford Pl. with its huge plane trees, has fared less well. South of the square, the enchanting streets around Museum St. are full of secondhand bookshops. To the N, Woburn, Gordon and Tavistock Squares all boast good gardens and some terraces surviving from the early 19thC. A short walk to the E brings you to the **Jewish Museum** (☎388-4525 ✉ *open Tues-Fri, Sun 10am-4pm, Nov-Mar Fri 10am-12.45pm*) and Cartwright Gdns., with a fine crescent-shaped terrace. A little farther on is Brunswick Sq., a major modern public housing development with brutal but interesting architecture, and the *Coram Foundation* (the foundling Hospital Art Museum).

The University has buildings throughout Bloomsbury, of which the best is the oldest, the original **University College** in Gower St. It is a splendid Classical building with dome and portico, dating from 1827-29. The Senate House in Malet St., by contrast, is an essay in 1930s Classicism. Also within this 'open campus' is the University Church of Christ the King in Gordon Sq., 1853 Gothic with an impressive cathedral-like interior. Nearby are two University art collections, the *Percival David Foundation of Chinese Art* and the *Courtauld Institute Galleries*, on either side of Torrington Pl.

Looming over Bloomsbury, the *Post Office Tower* in Cleveland St. is a familiar landmark: a 619ft (189m) cylinder topped by a jumble of transmitters and radio masts.

The British Museum 🏛 ★
Great Russell St., WC1 ☎636-1555. Map 10E11 ⊡ ◼ Open Mon-Sat 10am-5pm, Sun 2.30-6pm. Tube Russell Square, Tottenham Court Road.

Despite its age and venerable traditions, the British Museum is constantly changing, for this is one of the most adventurous of the world's great museums. It was founded in 1753 around the 80,000 items collected by Sir Hans Sloane, a successful physician. Sloane's will allowed the nation to purchase his collection for £20,000, well below its value, thus beginning a sequence of generous bequests. The nucleus consisted of Sloane's broad-ranging cabinet of curiosities: zoological and mineral specimens, antiquities, manuscripts, books and drawings. Natural history was best represented, but in time the museum became oriented more toward archeology.

In 1823 George III's huge library was given to the nation by his heir and the decision was taken to build a new and grand edifice to display the nation's collected treasures. With the young Robert Smirke as architect, the intention was to create a Neo-Classical structure around a quadrangle, which was completed by 1838. The quadrangle was later filled in with the famous Reading Room (see **British Library**).

The move of the natural history exhibits to the *Natural History Museum* in the 1880s and the ethnographic exhibits to the Museum of Mankind (see *Mankind, Museum of*) in 1970 has coped with much of the museum's space problem.

A comprehensive catalog would fill a bookcase. A selective visit should include the following.

Greece and Rome ★
The best place to start a visit; turn left in the entrance hall and for the moment pass through the Assyrian section. This leads to one of the best-laid-out sections, offering an excellent chronological survey and including some of the finest examples of Greek art in the world. It starts with simple idols of the 3rd and 2nd millennia BC (**Rm. 1**) found in the Cyclades. Bronze Age Greek art (**Rm. 2**) is followed by early ceramics (**Rm. 3**) that show a developing sophistication — as in the fine wine jar by Exekias (c.540 BC), decorated with mythological scenes in black on a red-earth background. The exit to this room is through a display of Greek vase decoration (**Rm. 4**). In **Rm. 5**, ceramics of about 500 BC, now with red figures on black, demonstrate that Greek artists had achieved a full understanding of the forms and movements of the human body.

The next room chronologically is the **Duveen Gallery** (**Rm. 8**), which contains some of the finest examples of Greek art: a sizeable group of the sculptures that once adorned the Parthenon in Athens, dating from c.440 BC when Pericles was beautifying Greece's greatest city. They have become world famous as the **Elgin Marbles ★** now the subject of controversy, with the Greek government making strenuous appeals for them to be returned to Athens. The Parthenon was ruined by an explosion in 1687; in 1803 Lord Elgin rescued the shattered fragments of the pediment sculptures, frieze and metopes and brought them to London. The **frieze**, displayed at eye level around the outside of the gallery, consists of marvelously natural figures and horses in a rhythmic procession to Mt. Olympus. The superb **pediment sculptures** recount the birth of Athena and the foundation of Athens.

Among the innumerable treasures of this collection is a **caryatid from the Erectheion** in Athens (c.410 BC) in **Rm. 9**. In **Rm. 7** are fragments of the great **Nereid Monument** (5thC BC) from a Greek colony at Lycia in Asia Minor, reconstructed into a facade. The Nereids themselves, wind spirits, are portrayed as dancing maidens with flowing garments clinging to their energetically moving bodies. In **Rm. 12** is a **frieze of the Battle of the Greeks and Amazons** from the Mausoleum of Halicarnassus, an extraordinary tomb of the late 4thC BC, built for Mausolus, which was one of the Seven Wonders of the Ancient World.

The smaller collection of Roman art (**Rms. 14 and 15**) begins with the famous **Portland Vase** (c.1stC BC), a cameo glass production, with the top white layer carved to reveal the blue underneath. There are also wall paintings from Pompeii, pleasant little architectural landscapes, and sculptures. Rooms above house smaller Greek and Roman antiquities, including fine figurines, busts, vases and household items. Particularly good are the Roman portraits in **Rm. 70**; the representations of Greek and Roman life in **Rm. 69**, with a small fountain actually in operation and a Roman waterwheel from Spain; the Cypriot antiquities dating from 4500 BC to AD 330 in **Rm. 72**; and artifacts from the Greek colonies in Southern Italy and Sicily (founded in the second half of the 8thC BC) in **Rm. 73**.

Ancient Mesopotamia ★

The collections from the ancient cities of Assyria rival those of Greece in importance — Britain's close relations with Turkey in the mid-19thC made extensive excavations possible. In contrast to the Greeks, the Assyrians seem to have been interested in a static, formal approach to representation, and the changes in style through the period are much less striking. The Nimrud Gallery (**Rm. 19**) has huge **reliefs from the palace of Ashurnasirpal II** (9thC BC), which show highly ritualized hunting and military scenes. From a century later are two huge winged bulls with human heads (**Rm. 16**), once forming an entrance to the palace at Khorsabad. The best observed and most enjoyable details to be found in the Assyrian sculptures are not shown in the king and his countless soldiers but in the animals, particularly the lions in the **relief series from Nineveh** (7thC BC), taken from Sennacherib's palace (**Rm. 17**).

Upstairs in **Rm. 54** can be found the smaller archeological finds from Sumeria and Babylon. From the Sumerian city of Ur in modern Iraq comes the extraordinary figure of a goat resting its legs in a tree (c.2500 BC), and a charming box inlaid with figures known as the **Standard of Ur**.

Ancient Egypt ☆

The nucleus of this collection of 70,000 objects fell into British hands after Napoleon's defeat at the Battle of the Nile in 1798. The large **Egyptian Sculpture Gallery** (**Rm. 25**) gives an impressive indication of the overpowering scale and stern quality of Egyptian art with its ranks of massive, shiny and hard-edged statues, often showing little sign of their great age. At the s end is the famous inscribed **Rosetta Stone**, discovered by the French in 1797, which, by giving its text in Greek as well as in Egyptian hieroglyphs, provided the key to a script that was previously unreadable. Among the huge **statues**, look out for a pair of 3rdC BC granite lions found at Gebel Barkal, a colossus of **Rameses II** (c.1250 BC) and a giant scarab beetle (c.200 BC), an image of the sun god. Upstairs, **Rms. 60-65** contain smaller Egyptian objects. The **mummies and mummy cases** have a macabre fascination — there

The British Museum

Upper floor

North entrance
Montague Pl.

Ground floor

Reading Room

Main entrance
Great Russell St.

are even mummies of animals. From the Roman period are mummy cases with unnervingly realistic portraits of the dead occupants.

Oriental art

From **Rm. 66** it is possible to descend to the Edward VII Gallery (**Rm. 34**), now given over to a superb collection of Oriental art, including the world's finest assembly of ancient **Chinese ceramics**. They are sophisticated and perfect — look out for a **large gray plate** of the Ming dynasty (1368-1644 AD), a flawless, smooth circle with the faintest pattern of a dragon just showing through the milky glaze. A more dramatic and expressive side of Chinese art is shown by the fine ceramic horses and camels, and even more fierce are bronze weapons and chariot fittings from 1500-1000 BC, and the impressive ritual vessels of the Shang period (1523-1027 BC).

Good Indian sculptures are also on display, some with the characteristic eroticism of Hindu art, together with Islamic and Japanese works.

Books and manuscripts ★

Leaving the Edward VII Gallery at the E end, pass through to the **British Library Galleries** (**Rms. 29-33**). These are devoted to regularly changed selections from the library's vast store of literary treasures around particular themes. The medieval manuscripts in particular are breathtaking, with their perfect miniature paintings and the unbelievably skillful calligraphy — on permanent display are the **Lindisfarne Gospels**, made in an isolated monastery on England's NE coast in about 698. The abstract mazes of its complex illustrations deserve scrutiny.

The collection of holographs and annotated typescripts of many literary classics is supplemented by other treasures: Leonardo da Vinci's sketchbook, and one of Dürer's; two of the four originals of the Magna Carta; the last dying scribblings of Lord Nelson and Captain Scott of the Antarctic; the two 5thC manuscripts which were important in the compilation of the gospels; and there are chronicles, Bibles and legal documents from the Dark Ages. Among the printed books are Caxton's pioneering production of *Canterbury Tales*, the famous Gütenberg Bible and the Authorized Version of 1603, and the First Folio edition of Shakespeare's plays (1623).

The **British Library** receives a copy of every book published in Britain. Thus, the collection is the world's greatest, and the library's **Reading Room ★** (*open to the public only by guided tours on the hour*), which is entered from the entrance hall, has attracted all the greatest scholars, most notably Karl Marx, who worked on *Das Kapital* in its hallowed calm. Opened in 1857, this spectacular room has a huge iron dome and massive windows, and a radial arrangement of reading tables around the circular bookcases containing the catalog. The dome is bigger than that of St Peter's in Rome.

Prehistory and early Britain

From the British Library Galleries one returns to the main entrance hall; upstairs to the E are the rooms devoted to prehistoric and Romano-British objects (**Rms. 36-40**). Stone Age products include carvings on mammoth and walrus tusks from France, and there is a rich collection of early metalwork. Lindow man, the 2,000yr old remains of a Celt discovered in 1984 at Lindow Moss in Cheshire, is on display in **Rm 37**. A hologram of the head affords a much closer examination of his red hair, mustache and features than was previously possible. Look out for the superbly twisted electrum **torque** of the 1stC BC, found in Norfolk, and the exquisite Roman silver of the **Mildenhall Treasure** (**Rm. 40**), including several superbly embossed platters.

Medieval and later

Rms. 41-7 are devoted to medieval (post-Roman) and later material and **Rm. 48** to European and American decorative arts (1840-1940). Some of these rooms are darkened, with the exhibits spotlighted, an effect which helps the visitor recognize the great quality of the items that may be easily overlooked. The technique works very well with the **Waddesdon Bequest**, for example, in **Rm. 45**, which consists of elaborately wrought metal, glass and ceramic work from the Renaissance and Mannerist periods.

In **Rm. 41** is the famous **Sutton Hoo Treasure ★** — a 7thC Angle burial ship unearthed in Suffolk in 1939. On display are finely wrought items of jewelry and weaponry, and a forbidding **helmet**, now reconstructed. Their craftsmanship speaks of a sophistication which belies the common image of the 'Dark Ages,' as they are usually called.

Famous objects in the medieval sections include the late Roman **Lycurgus Cup** and the **Franks Casket**, an Anglo-Saxon whalebone carving (both in **Rm. 41**). In **Rm. 42** is the Flemish parade shield of the 15thC showing a knight kneeling before a fairy-tale damsel; a skeleton looks over the knight's shoulder, and the inscription, representing the knight's words, can be translated as 'You or death.' Also in this room is the fabulous **14thC Royal Cup** of the kings of England and France, decorated with scenes from the life of St Agnes, in enamel.

The museum also possesses numerous important prints and drawings, including works by Michelangelo, Botticelli and other important masters. A periodically changed display can be found in **Rm. 67**, above the Edward VII Gallery. Sadly, only a fraction of the collection is shown at any one time.

The Brompton Oratory 🏛 †

Brompton Rd., SW3 ☎*589-4811. Open 7am-8pm. Map 16J6. Tube South Kensington.*

Converts are supposedly the most zealous adherents of any faith: certainly the Oxford Movement, a group of Victorian intellectuals turned Catholic, allowed no halfway measures when they created this church in 1884. All the drama of the Italian Baroque is here, in an interior dark with rich marbles, heavy with gilded detail. Some of the atmosphere is genuine — the huge marble *Apostles* (1680) by Mazzuoli come from Siena Cathedral.

Buckingham Palace 🏛 †

☎*930-4832. Map 17/9. Not open to the public. Tube Victoria, Hyde Park Corner.*

The royal standard flying signifies that the monarch is in residence, and many a hopeful eye scans the windows of the palace to catch a glimpse of a member of the Royal Family. On the whole, however, visitors are satisfied by the splendors of the palace, with the *Queen Victoria Memorial* and *The Mall* at their backs, and the solemn facade, guarded by soldiers in scarlet tunics and bearskins, behind railings to the front. (For the **Changing of the Guard**, see *Calendar of events* in *Planning*.)

Its familiarity and setting give it a certain grandeur, but in reality Buckingham Palace is an undistinguished example of early 20thC official architecture — it might be a rather large town hall. Behind, however, there is John Nash's older palace. In 1762, George III bought Buckingham House from the Duke of Buckingham, and Queen Charlotte moved in. In 1825 his son, the

Regent, commissioned Nash to rebuild on a larger scale. The *Marble Arch* was built as the entrance (later moved), but by 1850 the project was still incomplete, and Nash was sacked under some suspicion for having squandered huge amounts of money and having bought building materials from his own companies. The best parts of the palace are still his, however. To the right of the palace, there is a large arch leading to the gardens — the clearest part of Nash's work that can be seen from outside.

When Queen Victoria came to the throne in 1837, the palace became the official residence, and it has been so ever since. It was her need for additional accommodations that led to the large side wings and front being built, although it was more humble until the facade was added in 1913.

To the left of the palace is Buckingham Gate and the **Queen's Gallery** (📷 *open during exhibitions only Tues-Sat 10.30am-5pm, Sun 2-5pm*), where exhibitions of treasures from the fabulous royal art collections are mounted.

Farther along, the road becomes Buckingham Palace Rd., and here can be found the **Royal Mews** (📷 *open Wed-Thurs 2-4pm*), which can be visited when state processions are not taking place; on display are the Queen's beautiful carriages and harness. The state coaches are a great attraction; the star is the gilded and painted **Gold State Coach**, dating from 1762.

Cabinet War Rooms   See *Whitehall*.

Carlyle's House
24 Cheyne Row, SW3 ☎352-7087. Map 16L6 📷 Open Apr-Oct Wed-Sun 11am-4.30pm. Tube Sloane Square.
The houses in Cheyne Row were built in 1708, making them some of the oldest surviving residences in *Chelsea*, and when the Scottish writer Thomas Carlyle (1795-1881) was looking for a London home he was evidently impressed. He lived here from 1834 until his death, and the house can be seen today much as it was then, crammed with memorabilia and manuscripts of the famous, although now little-read, essayist and historian. It can also be enjoyed as a perfect example of a comfortable Victorian home. The **attic study**, with its doublewalls, was added in 1853 to provide a quiet working place.

Central Criminal Court   The imposing building is known
universally as the *Old Bailey* after the street in which it stands.

Charing Cross
Map 10G11. Tube Charing Cross.
At the s end of *Trafalgar Square*, a statue of *Charles I* looks down *Whitehall* to the place of his execution and occupies the site of the original Charing Cross, from where all distances to London are measured. This was the last of the Eleanor Crosses put up by Edward I in 1291 to make the resting places of his queen's funeral cortege on its way to Westminster Abbey; Charing is a corruption of *chère reine* (dear queen). The original cross was destroyed in the Civil War in 1647, but when E.M. Barry designed Charing Cross Station Hotel nearby in 1863-64, he added a Victorian Gothic Eleanor Cross to the forecourt, where it still stands.

Chelsea ★
Map 15&16K-L. Tube South Kensington, Sloane Square.
Chelsea is London's most fashionable address. On the one hand, the pretty, well-maintained houses in its quiet streets retain the

feel of an elegant backwater, almost a country village; by contrast, the King's Road is *outré*, noisy and Bohemian in a way nowhere else can imitate.

Only in the later 18thC did the quiet village nestling on the river's edge become a part of London. Charles II built the *Royal Hospital* from 1682 as a restful place of retirement for old soldiers. The military connection remains, with two large barracks and the *National Army Museum*.

In 1673 the Society of Apothecaries established **Chelsea Physic Garden** (*Swan Walk* ☎352-5646 ▨ *open mid-Apr to mid-Oct Wed and Sun 2-5pm, daily during Chelsea Flower Show*) to grow plants for the study of medicine. With its exotic trees and shrubs, aromatic herbs, rock garden and tranquil pond, and despite severe damage caused by the storm of Oct 1987, it is still a delightful place in which to stroll.

Apart from the Hospital and Physic Garden, little remains of old Chelsea. The area around *Cheyne Walk* includes the few old houses there are, such as **Lindsey House** of about 1674, and Cheyne Row of 1708, where *Carlyle's House* can be visited. Most of Chelsea's housing dates from the 19thC, some of it very grand (Cadogan Sq.), and some of it mere artisans' cottages, which are now so sought after.

In the late 1800s, Chelsea became known as an artists' colony. Pre-Raphaelites such as Rossetti, Burne-Jones and Morris lived here. Whistler painted his *Nocturnes* of the evening river here, and Oscar Wilde lived in Tite St. Americans, such as Henry James and Jack London, were attracted. The blue plaques marking the former abodes of the famous are everywhere.

After World War II the avant-garde again made this their home. The 'angry young men' grabbed attention at the **Royal Court Theatre** in 1956 (see *Theaters* in *Nightlife*), artists crowded into Finch's pub in the Fulham Rd., and, most significantly, Mary Quant began selling clothes in the King's Rd., which subsequently became and remained a major center for cult fashion (see *Shopping*).

Cheyne Walk ☆

*SW3. Map **15**M5-6. Tube Sloane Square.*

There were grand houses here before the famous and beautiful row was built in the late 17thC. **Lindsey House** (nos. 95-100), built about 1674, gives some idea of the detached stateliness of the even bigger Tudor mansions of *Chelsea*, built when this land sloped uninterrupted down to the waterline.

Once the red-brick Georgian terrace was built, Cheyne (pronounce the last 'e') Walk's rural charm went largely unnoticed until the 19thC, when it suddenly became a haven for artists. Turner lived at no.119 from 1846 until his death in 1851, under the name of Puggy Booth, and D.G. Rossetti moved into no.16 in 1862. In 1880 the novelist George Eliot died in no.4, a house dating from 1717. James McNeill Whistler lived at no.104 from 1863, and at no.96 from 1866-79, painting many of his most famous pictures here, including the series on the river itself, known as *Nocturnes*.

One of the most remarkable buildings, however, is earlier. **Crosby Hall** (☎352-9663 ▣ *open daily 10am-noon, 2.15-5pm, Sun 2.15-5pm*) was built between 1466 and 1475 by Sir John Crosby, a wool merchant, as the great hall residence in Bishopsgate in The City. It was moved to its present site in 1910 to save it from demolition. It has a superb **gilded wood ceiling** and a three-story **oriel window**, and displays a copy of Holbein's lost portrait of *Sir Thomas More and his Family*. Next to it, **Chelsea Old Church** contains a charming monument to *Thomas Hungerford* (1581) and Sir Thomas More's chapel (1528).

Between Crosby Hall and the church is Roper's Garden, next to an unusually ugly modern statue of *Sir Thomas More*, whose own gardens once occupied the site. There is a relief by Jacob Epstein in the garden. At the E end is Cheyne Row and *Carlyle's House*, and the gardens at the W end lead to **Albert Bridge** (1873), a decorative piece of Victorian suspension engineering.

Chiswick

Map 21C4. Tube Stamford Brook, Turnham Green.
Although on the main routes into the capital from the W, parts of the old riverside village of Chiswick survive, in a still and dreamy quarter to be found by turning sharp left into Church St. at the monster traffic circle where the Great West Rd. traffic is forced to pause. **St. Nicholas** church has a 15thC tower, although the rest is a Victorian reconstruction; buried in the churchyard are the painters James McNeill Whistler and William Hogarth. Back on the Great West Rd. is *Hogarth's House*, and just beyond it *Chiswick House* (see *Walk 3* in *Planning*).

Chiswick House 🏛 ★

Burlington Lane, W4 ☎995-0508. Map 21C4 ▦. Open mid-Mar to mid-Oct daily 9.30am-6.30pm; mid-Oct to mid-Mar daily 9.30am-4pm. Tube Turnham Green, Chiswick Park.
The Palladian architecture so favored by 18thC English gentlemen, with its forms reduced to simple geometrical shapes and all detail ruthlessly contained, reached near-perfection in this ravishingly beautiful mansion in *Chiswick*. Set in its own park, it retains the feel of a country house. The first Earl of Burlington bought the Jacobean mansion here in 1682, and little was changed until the third Earl of Burlington, an enthusiastic student of Classical art, decided to add a villa to one end of the house, built to his own designs in 1725-29, with an interior by William Kent.

The villa consists of an octagonal dome rising from a simple square block, with a portfolio and stairs forming the entrance. The link building and summer parlor survive at the E side, showing where the villa was joined to the main body of the old house. Through a low-challenged and severely Classical octagonal room one enters the three rooms that served as the earl's **library**. An interesting exhibition of engravings, plans and documents relating to the villa occupies the rooms on this floor. The upper rooms are reached by a spiral staircase, and immediately the style changes: these reception rooms, designed by Kent, are brighter in color, with richly patterned velvet wallpapers and heavily decorated cornices, architraves and fireplaces. At the rear is the three-chambered gallery and, to the sides, the dramatic **Red and Green Velvet Rooms**. In the center, the impressive **dome** has elaborate coffering. The **garden** has grown to the modern, wilder taste.

The City ★

Map 12&13E&F. Livery company halls do not have regular opening hours and will admit visitors only on open days. For information, contact i City of London Information Centre, St Paul's Churchyard, EC4 ☎260-1456/7.
For centuries it was just what its name suggests, and although London has now vastly outgrown it, The City retains its identity, its influence, and, to a degree which invariably surprises newcomers, its self-government.

Today, 'The City' is shorthand for money; this is where the great banking, insurance and commodity trading concerns are based. During the day, over 350,000 people work here, but at night and on weekends it can be a concrete and glass desert, with a resident population of less than 5,000. As a result, it may be best to visit The City on a weekend, when it is easier to find and enjoy the hidden, almost secret places that give the area its appeal. Be warned, however, for while the streets may be free of traffic, it may be hard to find a pub or restaurant that is open. Even the famous Wren churches are often closed on Sun — the best time to visit them is weekday lunchtimes.

The City does not easily yield up its past. First the Great Fire of 1666, then the bombs of 1940 and, most recently, the zeal of developers have swept away much that was old. In its place, there is an ostensibly haphazard collection of office buildings, for the most part demonstrating the poverty of modern architecture. As Sir Nikolaus Pevsner has pointed out, the skyline has none of the excitement of New York or Chicago, but has more in common with that of an unimportant Mid-West town. On the other hand, *St Paul's Cathedral* is too great a building to be dominated by its taller neighbors, Wren's churches too interesting not to be visited, and history proclaims itself too loudly even from the street names. And, of course, The City does have its own unique geography, described by a uniquely English phrase — nooks and crannies.

The key to exploring The City is not to content yourself with its obvious beauties. To an astonishing extent it retains elements of its medieval character. Within the area bounded by the old walls (the gates were at Ludgate, Newgate, Aldersgate, Cripplegate, Bishopsgate and Aldgate) one can easily work out what was where. Cheapside, for example, with the surrounding Milk St., Poultry and Bread St., marks the site of the main medieval market. The government of The City has not even changed on the surface. The Guildhall is still its parliament, Mansion House the palace of its head, the Lord Mayor. He is selected annually by a complex system based on ancient privileges rather than mere residence. City livery companies, descended from medieval trade guilds, have an important part to play in choosing and providing the aldermen and sheriffs from whom the Lord Mayor must come. The liveries still have their own halls, their own constitutions, and their own regalia, even though they are hardly ever connected with their original trades. The City still has its own police force (look at the badges on the helmets, different from those elsewhere in London), and on royal ceremonial occasions the monarch will not enter The City unless greeted on its borders by the Lord Mayor.

The square mile is a large area to visit on foot, with its many sites of interest widely scattered. To make it more manageable, it has here been divided into four parts, each of which can be seen separately.

The City: east

The City to the E of a line taken from London Bridge to Liverpool Street Station in the N includes many fine churches, but the predominant tone is set by the great maritime trading interests. Until the 19thC almost all the trade goods landed at London were brought ashore between London Bridge and the Tower of London. **Lloyd's** (☎ *623-7100*), the headquarters of a business largely founded on insuring ships and their cargo, is in a controversial new building in Lime St., designed by Richard Rogers and opened in 1986. Lloyd's grew, amazingly, from a coffee house; now its huge underwriting room, simply called 'the Room,' but housed in a massive glazed atrium (200ft/60m high), is a beehive of activity, centered around the 18thC Lutine Bell, traditionally struck once for news of disaster of a missing ship, and twice for a safe arrival. The atrium is the core of Rogers' striking glass, steel and concrete structure. From the Room on the ground floor, illuminated glass-sided escalators ascend to three galleries, the floors of the market. All the services are contained in six satellite towers, up and down which slide glass-sided observation elevators. The viewing gallery and exhibition on the history of Lloyd's (🔟) are open Mon-Fri 10am-2.30pm. Lloyd's Shipping Register, where the capacity and whereabouts of all the world's shipping is monitored, is in nearby **Fenchurch St**. In Mincing Lane is the Commodity Exchange of Plantation House.

In the SE corner of The City is the *Tower of London*. Just to the N is **Trinity Square** with, at its E side, a well-preserved portion of Roman wall. Opposite is **Trinity House**, headquarters of the charity operating Britain's lighthouses and lifeboats. To the W of Trinity Sq., in Byward St., is the church of **All-Hallows-by-the-Tower**; the attractive tower dates from 1658-59. The church is actually much older, dating back to the 7thC, and there is a Saxon arch at the tower base, revealed by bomb damage. Inside is a quite beautiful **font cover** of 1682 by Wren's great carver Grinling Gibbons.

Farther W along the riverfront toward *London Bridge* is the large **Customs House** of 1812-25, its Classical facade best seen from London Bridge. Opposite, up St Dunstan's Hill, is the ruined church of **St Dunstan-in-the-East**, converted into a delightful garden; Wren's extraordinary spire of 1698, supported on flying buttresses, still stands. Back on Lower Thames St. the next building along from the Custom House is **Billingsgate Market**, a typical 19thC covered market, closed in 1982, when the fish market which existed there since medieval times moved farther E into the dockland. A little farther along is the church of **St Magnus Martyr**, designed by Wren in 1671-76 although altered since. The tower is massive, with a spire of 1705.

O City city, I can sometimes hear
Beside a public bar in Lower Thames Street,
The pleasant whining of a mandoline
And a clatter and a chatter from within
Where fishermen lounge at noon: where the walls
Of Magnus Martyr hold
Inexplicable splendour of Ionian white and gold.

T.S. Eliot, *The Waste Land*, 1922

Over Lower Thames St. is Fish St. Hill and Wren's *The Monument*. At the top of Fish St. Hill is the major thoroughfare of Eastcheap, site of a medieval market. Some fanciful Victorian commercial buildings deserve study — nos 33-35, for example, all brick Gothic and gables. To the S is the splendid Wren church of **St Mary-at-Hill**, hidden in a maze of charming lanes, which forms a moving contrast to the great space and harmony of Wren's beautiful interior, built in 1670-76. The church is unique in that it still has box pews and is noteworthy for some wrought-iron sword-rests and a carved organ screen.

Back on Eastcheap, another Wren church will be discovered a little farther along on the left, **St Margaret Pattens**, named after a special type of shoe made here. This time the exterior, with a fine spire of 1687, has more to offer than the interior. A pretty early-19thC shop and house (now an American bank) next to the church completes an attractive corner. To the N is the Commodity

Exchange, with its facade in Fenchurch St., and behind the new Clothworkers' Hall up Mincing Lane on the left is the small 15thC tower of **All Hallows Staining**, incongruously surrounded by large buildings. Nearby in Hart St. is **St Olave**, an attractive 15thC church, damaged in the Blitz but well restored. It contains several good monuments, especially those to *Sir James Deane* (1608) and *Peter Cappone* (1582). Samuel Pepys the diarist used the church and there is a monument to his wife (1669). Hart St. leads into Crutched Friars, which passes under Fenchurch Street Station ('crutched' means 'crossed' — there was a priory here). No.42 is a fine early 18thC house.

North of Fenchurch St., **Leadenhall Market**, off Lime St., provides City workers with a welcome shopping area. Leadenhall St., a little farther N, contains the churches of **St Andrew Undershaft**, mostly early 16thC, and **St Katharine Cree**, a survivor from the early 17thC, but with a medieval tower.

This section of The City, straddling the course of the Roman and medieval wall along Camomile St. and Bevis Marks, contains three churches. **St Helen Bishopsgate** is an outstanding convent church dating back to the 13thC. Its many interesting features include an attractive W front topped by a little 17thC bell-tower, a poor box of about 1620 in the form of a one-armed beggar, and remarkable monuments. The other churches in Bishopsgate are **St Ethelburga**, with medieval fragments and a tower of 1775, and **St Botolph-without-Bishopsgate**, a pleasant 18thC building where Keats was baptized. The **Spanish and Portuguese Synagogue** in Bevis Marks deserves a visit; it dates back to 1700-1, and contains some lavishly decorated appointments of that period.

The City: south

This segment covers the central area between *St Paul's Cathedral* and London Bridge, s of Cheapside, Poultry and Cornhill.

The waterfront W of London Bridge, Upper Thames St., is now one of London's least attractive roads, bearing great quantities of traffic through a windy and noisy desert. The narrow alley of **Broken Wharf**, however, leads down to a good view of the river and the **Samuel Pepys pub** in an old warehouse. There is also a riverside walk to the W of this. But to the N, only the slender pinnacled tower of **St Mary Somerset** and the much-restored church of **St Nicholas Cole Abbey**, both by Wren, relieve the monotony.

Just beyond Queen St., the approach to Southwark Bridge, there are some smaller and older streets of Mansion House Station. Wren's **St James Garlickhythe** (1676-83) in Garlick Hill (where the herb was sold) has a fine tower, looking rather like a lighthouse with a stone lantern on top; it contains some fine ironwork. **Beaver Hall** in Great Trinity Lane is the center of the fur trade, the premises of which cluster in these narrow streets. Facing Upper Thames St. is the **Vintners' Hall**, one of the best of a number of livery company halls in this area. It was built in 1671, and although much restored has a fine paneled hall and a superb carved staircase. Queen St. itself contains two magnificent Georgian houses (nos 27 and 28).

Between Queen St. and Cannon Street Station there is another maze of little lanes, around the church of **St Michael Paternoster Royal**, built by Wren but much restored after war damage. Some good interior fittings have survived, including a carved pulpit and reredos. Three livery companies have their halls in Dowgate Hill, just w of St Michael: the Skinners (with a late 18thC facade), the Dyers, and the Tallow Chandlers (the last two are Victorian).

Between Cannon Street Station and King Williams St. (which

leads onto London Bridge) is yet another fascinating maze of small streets, with several historic pubs and wine bars. **Laurence Pountney Hill** to the E has two of the most beautiful 18thC houses in London, dated 1703, with elaborately decorated doorways and cornices. Other attractive buildings are to be found around the pleasant little churchyard left by the vanished church of St Laurence; the **Olde Wine Shades** bar in nearby Arthur St. offers good refreshments. Next to London Bridge is the **Fishmongers' Hall** of 1831-34, the best-sited and grandest livery company hall, with an imposing Classical facade overlooking the river.

Just N of Cannon St. are **St Clement Eastcheap**, containing some superb wood carving, and the extraordinary *St Mary Abchurch*, both by Wren. Farther N is Lombard St., an important banking street named after the Italian money-lenders who set up business here in the 14thC. It contains two fine churches: **St Mary Woolnoth** and **St Edmund the King**. The latter is again by Wren, with a harmonious exterior and well-preserved woodwork inside. St Mary Woolnoth was built by Nicholas Hawksmoor in 1716-27 and occupies its prominent corner site with a dramatic monumental facade. The interior, with massive Corinthian columns, is Baroque in feeling. North of Lombard St. are several attractive lanes: St Michael's Alley, Castle Court and Ball Court. Old hostelries tucked away in this enclave include **Simpson's**, which has been recently restored, the **George and Vulture**, and the **Jamaica Wine House**. There are two churches on the S side of Cornhill: **St Michael Cornhill** has a pretty churchyard, but is itself an unhappy mixture of styles by Wren and later architects; **St Peter-upon-Cornhill** by Wren is best seen from its little churchyard.

Moving W, large offices again dominate the area S of Cheapside and Poultry. The remains of the **Roman Temple of Mithras** (see the marvelous sculptures in the Museum of London, under *London, Museum of*) can be seen in Queen Victoria St. Nearby is the church of **St Mary Aldermary**, completed by Wren in 1692 in an extraordinary version of Gothic, with a tall tower, nave and aisles. The fan-vaulted roof uses a very free interpretation of the medieval style, with shallow domes between the fans, all richly covered with delicate tracery. On Cheapside is the major church of *St Mary-le-Bow*, with the grandest of Wren's steeples. Where Cheapside joins Poultry is the *Mansion House*, the Lord Mayor's official residence, with the important *St Stephen Walbrook* behind.

The City: north

The northern part of The City contains a number of important institutions and a great many lesser offices. As a result, it is less an area to stroll through than other parts of The City. In the N are Liverpool Street Station and the postwar developments of London Wall and the *Barbican*. To the S, forming really the center of The City, are the financial and administrative institutions, the *Guildhall*, the Bank of England, the Royal Exchange and the *Stock Exchange*.

In Foster Lane, N of Cheapside, is **St Vedast**, a Wren church built 1670-97 but reconstructed after war damage. Its finest feature is the elaborate and effectively sinuous spire. To the N is **Goldsmiths' Hall**, built with a massive Classical exterior by Philip Hardwick in 1829-35. Frequent exhibitions of the livery company's unmatched collection of historic and modern plate make it possible to see the palatial interior, with its tremendous dome-covered staircase of colored marble.

On nearby Gresham St. is the interesting Wren church of

St Anne and St Agnes, built of brick in 1680 on a square with a central dome supported on columns. In Wood St., to the E, there is a lonely Wren tower in the Gothic style, all that remains of the Church of **St Alban**. Next to the *Guildhall* in Gresham St. is **St Lawrence Jewry**, again by Wren (1671-87).

Lothbury, next to the Bank of England, contains Wren's **St Margaret Lothbury**. Good features include the 17thC screen brought from another Wren church, with its beautiful twisted columns. Look for no.7 Lothbury — Victorian architecture at its imaginative best. Lothbury leads into Throgmorton St., with the *Stock Exchange* on the right, which then becomes Old Broad St. This contains the tallest and one of the most exciting and dramatic of The City's new office buildings, the **National Westminster Bank tower**. Its thrillingly soaring height, emphasized by vertical ribbing, balances unnervingly on a narrowed base with a clear glass facade.

A new museum is due to open in the nation's controlling bank, the **Bank of England** (*Threadneedle St.* ☎601-3832 *for details*). Exhibits will include pieces of Roman pavement, medieval artifacts, coins, notes and reproduction gold bars. The displays will concentrate on the history of the bank from 1694 to the high technology of the present day.

The northern section of The City is dominated by the undistinguished Victorian pile of Liverpool Street Station with its large hotel. Nearby in Bishopsgate is **St Botolph-without-Bishopsgate**, rebuilt in 1727-29 and with a 19thC interior. **All Hallows London Wall** (1765-67) to the W has a fine simple and light interior, with an ornate plaster ceiling.

The City: west

Most of the western part of the modern City falls outside the old Roman walled town, including the whole section W of Ludgate Circus to the beginning of the *Strand* and Smithfield Market, the capital's wholesale meat market, housed in a fine Victorian building, to the N. Of prime interest are *Fleet Street*, the Inner and Middle *Temple* extending S to the river, and *St Paul's Cathedral*.

The stretch of riverside to the S of St Paul's is disfigured by the traffic of Upper Thames St., although **St Benet's** (1677-83) remains as one of the most delightful and best preserved of Wren's churches, small and simple in the Dutch style. Nearby in Queen Victoria St. is the 17thC *College of Arms*, together with the **British and Foreign Bible Society Library**. The church of **St Andrew-by-the-Wardrobe** stands on St Andrew's Hill to the W. Built by Wren in 1685-93, it is abutted by the offices of the men who maintained the state apparel.

To the S is the new **Mermaid Theatre** (see *Nightlife*), surrounded by the raging traffic of Puddle Dock. There is a fine Victorian pub in Queen Victoria St., called the **Black Friar** (see *Pubs*). In Blackfriars Lane next to the station is the **Apothecaries' Hall**, a fine livery company building with a facade of 1684 (altered in 1779). North again is Ludgate Hill, site of the medieval 'Lud Gate' until 1769-61; it offers the best view of the portico of St Paul's. **St Martin Ludgate**, a Wren church of 1677-87, has a most attractive lead-covered spire and some good carved woodwork inside. Just behind is the **Stationers' Hall**, a building of about 1667 with a stone facade of 1800.

Another of the old roads out of The City passed through Newgate, site of the notorious jail and now the *Old Bailey*. Newgate St. leads into Holborn Viaduct, built to span a little valley in 1863-69. Its heavy, ornate ironwork can be seen best from

Farringdon St. The church of **St Sepulchre** on the N side of
Holborn Viaduct is unusually large, with a great (although
restored) 15thC tower. **St Andrew Holborn** on the s side is a Wren
church with a 15thC tower restored in 1703.

North of Holborn Viaduct is Smithfield, long the site of the
famous medieval St Bartholomew's Fair, about which Ben Jonson
wrote his play in 1614, and the place where Wat Tyler and his
rebel peasants confronted Richard II in 1381; Lord Mayor
Walworth showed The City's customary independence by simply
drawing his sword and killing Tyler. Nearby are **Smithfield
Market** and *St-Bartholomew-the-Great*. St Bartholomew's
Hospital opposite dates back to the Middle Ages. Its church, **St
Bartholomew-the-Less**, has another 15thC tower. Behind Bart's,
as it is known, at the end of Little Britain, is **St Botolph
Aldersgate**, rebuilt in 1788-91 and with a well-preserved interior.
The **National Postal Museum** is in King Edward St.

Cleopatra's Needle
*Victoria Embankment, WC2. Map **11**G12. Tube
Embankment.*
Now appropriately sited by another symbol of timelessness, the
Thames, this pink granite obelisk was made in Heliopolis in Egypt
in 1500 BC, predating Cleopatra by centuries. Presented to Britain
by Egypt in 1819, it was finally towed by sea to its present site and
erected in 1878. New York has a similar obelisk in Central Park.

The College of Arms 🏛
*Queen Victoria St., EC4 ☎248-2762. Map **12**F15 ⊡ Hall only
open Mon-Fri 10am-4pm. Tube Mansion House.*
The official body controlling the heraldry of the United Kingdom
is housed in an interesting building constructed in 1671-88
following the Great Fire, which destroyed the older house given to
the college by Mary I in 1555. The wrought-iron gates and railings,
of uncertain date, are particularly splendid; the brick pilasters with
carved stone capitals preserve some of its grandeur. As a
professional body, the College of Arms will investigate queries
relating to genealogy and heraldry — nobody knows more about
argent chevrons, batons sinister or griffins rampant. Only the
entrance hall is open to the public.

Commonwealth Institute 🏛
*230 Kensington High St., W8 ☎602-3257. Map **14**I2 ⊡ ▣ ✳
Open Mon-Sat 10am-5.30pm, Sun 2-5pm. Tube Kensington
High Street.*
With its extraordinary green copper roof, all peaks and elliptical
curves, the Commonwealth Institute is an appropriately unusual
tribute to a unique association, the Commonwealth. It was opened
in 1962 as a study and display center, and houses a permanent
exhibition representing its peoples, customs and economics. There
is a fine library, together with a cinema and restaurant. The
exhibition area is open-plan, consisting of a large circle of galleries
on different levels around a central concourse. Each country has a
display, variously expressing the cultural traditions or economies
of the nations.

The Coram Foundation (*Foundling Hospital Art
Museum*) ☆
*40 Brunswick Sq. WC1 ☎278-2424. Map **5**D12 ▨ Open
Mon-Fri 10am-4pm (check first). Tube Russell Square.*
In the 18thC London was full of destitute children, and their

plight moved nobody more than Thomas Coram, a retired sea captain who set up a foundling hospital in 1739. The original buildings were shamefully demolished in 1926, but the magnificent **Court Room** can be seen in the Foundation's modern offices, along with a model of the original complex. After its foundation, artists led by Hogarth tried to raise funds. Consequently, it has fine collection of pictures, of which the highlight is Hogarth's **portrait** of the sanguine philanthropist *Coram* ☆ There are also works by Gainsborough and Reynolds, a study of Raphael, and a manuscript of Handel's *Messiah*.

Coram's Fields, a children's playground, is entered from Guildford St. through the hospital's original gateway.

Courtauld Institute Galleries ★

Woburn Sq., WC1 ☎*580-1015. Map 4D10* 🔲 🏧 *with flash. Open Mon-Sat 10am-5pm, Sun 2-5pm. Tube Euston, Russell Square.*

When the textile industrialist Samuel Courtauld helped found London University's main art history department, the Courtauld Institute, in 1931, he provided the nucleus of an important art collection. Swelled by several subsequent bequests, this has grown into an exceptional, broad-ranging group of pictures.

The first rooms contain the Princes Gate paintings. The outstanding feature is a group of no less than 32 paintings by Rubens (1577-1640), including a fine portrait of the *Family of Jan Brueghel the Elder*, a moving *Entombment* and the incomparable *Landscapes by Moonlight*, famous for its eerie beauty. Rubens' pupil Van Dyck is also well represented, and earlier Flemish art is superbly exemplified by the brilliant, jewel-like *Madonna* by Quentin Massys and two rare paintings by the Elder Brueghel — a perfect imaginary landscape and a deeply human grisaille rendering of *Christ and the Woman Taken in Adultery*. Italian paintings include a well-preserved triptych by Bernardo Daddi, a poetic and sensuous *Venus* by Palma Vecchio and 12 paintings by Tiepolo. The drawings are also excellent; there are six by Michelangelo.

Samuel Courtauld's collection amounts to one of the best publicly accessible groups of both Impressionist and Post-Impressionist paintings. Impressionist works include examples by Monet (*Autumn at Argenteuil*), Sisley, and Renoir, including the superbly colored *La Loge*. Manet is represented by a large oil sketch for the celebrated *Déjeuner sur l'Herbe* and by the sumptuous *A Bar at the Folies-Bergère*. Two large sketches by Degas show to perfection the artist's ability to fix an ordinary moment in time. The Post-Impressionists are represented by no fewer than nine Cézannes on one wall, a Van Gogh self-portrait (with bandaged ear) and two haunting studies of Tahitian women by Gauguin, including the dreamy *Te Rerioa*.

The Courtauld Institute Galleries are moving to the N wing of *Somerset House* in early summer 1989 and are due to open there in Oct.

Covent Garden ★

Map 10&11F-G. Tube Covent Garden.

Until 1974, London's fresh fruit and vegetable market was Covent Garden's chief fame, and the pubs stayed open all night for the thirsty workers, and others. When the market and its heavy traffic left to go to a new building s of the river at Nine Elms, a bitter struggle for the future of Covent Garden began. Conservationists and local residents were ranked against the developers, for whom this was a prime site for office buildings (dressed up, of course, with token community schemes). To the enormous relief of everyone but those who stood to profit, the attempt to turn the delightful and historic chaos of decaying buildings into a 'planned' desert was defeated. But it may have been a Pyrrhic victory — skirmishing continues, new buildings continue to eat away at the old, and the population of the area is falling. Even so, the best buildings remain, and although some pricey shops and bars have brought their smart set to invade the area, it retains an earthy feel of real old London, and there is some discerning and tasteful modern patronage. For visitors and Londoners alike, this is where the action is.

Until the 16thC, Covent Garden was an enclosed kitchen garden belonging to Westminster Abbey. The land was granted to Sir John Russell, later Earl of Bedford, in 1630, and a descendant of his obtained the right to develop it under the egis of the great Classical architect Inigo Jones in 1670. The plan was ambitious — a huge piazza on the Italian model surrounded by arcaded houses. All that survives today is the church of *St Paul's, Covent Garden*. The present **market buildings** appeared in 1828-32, with the fine iron and glass canopies added later. In its restored state, the marriage of its severe Classicism to the more ornate roof creates a stunning effect. Other later market buildings surround the piazza. The best, the **Floral Hall** (1858) is to the NE, a superb example of the iron and glass architecture that sprang up in emulation of the Crystal Palace that housed the 1851 Great Exhibition.

The **market** itself is now given over to trendy shops and restaurants, with market stalls in the middle; it is at its liveliest at lunchtime. On the S side of the piazza, the old Flower Market (1897) now houses the *London Transport* and *Theatre Museums*. Leave the piazza by Russell St. to the E, lined with fashionable wine bars thick with young advertising executives and publishers not so different from the *monde* who congregated in its famous coffeehouses in the 18thC. Russell St. crosses Bow St., so notorious for its street crime in the 18thC that it saw the foundation of the first police force, the Bow Street Runners. Its inspiration was the novelist Henry Fielding, a magistrate at the busy courts which are still there in a newer building. To the left is the splendid facade of the Floral Hall and next to it the **Royal Opera House** (see *Nightlife*); amazingly, both are by the same architect, the Victorian E.M. Barry. The present is the third theater on the site — built in 1857-58, its grand Corinthian portico has a frieze by J. Flaxman and statues from the previous building of 1809.

Fittingly for a quarter of such vitality, Covent Garden is traditionally London's theater area, and its church, *St Paul's*, is the actors' church. (For *Theaters*, see *Nightlife*.)

Continuing along Russell St. will take you to the other old royal theater, the **Theatre Royal, Drury Lane**, founded in 1663 by Charles II, whose Nell Gwynne was, of course, an orange-seller in Covent Garden. The present building dates from 1810-12, and is by general agreement London's most beautiful theater. Covent Garden is also bordered by two of London's main theatrical streets; to the S is the *Strand* and to the W, St Martin's Lane, where the largest theater is the imposing **Coliseum** of 1904, now home of the English National Opera. A good example of an ornate late Victorian pub, complete with cut glass and mirrors, is the **Salisbury**, a little farther up on the left (see *Pubs*). At the top of St. Martin's Lane, Garrick St. to the right includes the solemn and grimy building of the famous Garrick Club, a gentlemen's club with theatrical associations. Up tiny Rose St. on the left is the **Lamb & Flag**, the area's oldest and best pub (see *Pubs*).

The northern continuation of St. Martin's Lane is drab Monmouth St. which leads to Seven Dials, the scene of Hogarth's 'Gin Lane' of drink and vice in the 18thC and the cholera outbreaks of the 19thC. A little to the NW is **St Giles-in-the-Fields**, a fine Classical church of 1731-33, with a supremely calm interior. Near Seven Dials is **Neal's Yard** and Neal Street, with craft shops, vegetarian restaurants and health-food stores. Another craft market opened in 1987 in nearby Endell St. Housed in a glass-domed building, Endell Street Place has craft workshops, a shop and special exhibitions.

Dickens' House ☆

48 Doughty St., WC1 ☎405-2127. Map 5D12 ▨ Open Mon-Sat 10am-4.30pm. Closed for two weeks Dec-Jan. Tube Russell Square, Chancery Lane.

When Charles Dickens lived at Doughty St. between 1837 and 1839, he was experiencing his first taste of success. The *Pickwick Papers*, which brought him sudden prosperity, was still being published, and he also worked on his first novels while in the house: *Oliver Twist*, *Barnaby Rudge* and *Nicholas Nickleby*.

In Dickens' time, Doughty St. had gates at either end tended by liveried porters. It is still a handsome house but, unfortunately, the interior preserves almost nothing of its original appearance; instead, however, there is an extensive museum of Dickens memorabilia. There are pieces of furniture from later houses, numerous letters and manuscripts, portraits of the writer and his family, and contemporary illustrations of his famous characters.

Docklands

Map 21C5. Tube Tower Hill, then Docklands Light Railway.

With the demise of the British Empire, London's docks fell into decline, and by the late 1960s Docklands was derelict: an area of poverty, slums and high unemployment. In 1981 the London Docklands Development Corporation (LDDC) was formed to redevelop Wapping, the Isle of Dogs, the Royal Docks and Surrey Docks in the largest, most ambitious scheme of its kind in Europe. Office space in The City was at a premium, so Docklands attracted businesses as well as private investors, who were prepared to plunge millions of pounds into offices, houses and recreation facilities.

Covering a vast 450 acres (182 ha), Docklands is a 21stC river city in the making. Since it is an official enterprise zone, architectural restrictions have been suspended. As a result a variety of styles are in evidence, from office buildings clad in tinted glass, framed by bold primary colors, to mellow brick buildings, which recall the past with gothic windows or the hint of a pediment. Within the maze of modern architecture, it is still possible to stumble across a beautiful old church, such as Hawksmoor's **St George in the East**, a pretty terrace of Georgian or Victorian houses, or a listed building, such as the ancient and allegedly haunted *pissoire* in the Royal Docks.

The conversion of old warehouses in Wapping and Limehouse have made these fashionable residential areas, with **Tobacco Dock**, a vast complex of restaurants and leisure facilities, conveniently nearby. On the Isle of Dogs, **Canary Wharf**, with its toy-town buildings, is the financial heart of Docklands. A two billion pound development, covering 70 acres (28 ha), it was designed to be an eastern extension of The City and has realized this aim. The country's largest and best-equipped sports complex, **Dockland Arena**, is due to open nearby in an old banana shed.

Farther E are the Royal Docks, where a waterside arena and the **Museum of the Docklands** are planned at Royal Victoria Dock, and King George V and Royal Albert Docks are intended to be centers for water sports. Here too, **London City Airport** provides businessmen with fast access to other UK cities and the continent.

On the S side of the river at Surrey Docks, the Victorian warehouses of **Butler's Wharf** have been refurbished by Sir Terence Conran to provide offices, workshops, houses, shops and restaurants, and will contain the new **Conran Foundation Design Museum** (previously the Boilerhouse Collection at the *Victoria and Albert Museum*).

The best way to see Docklands is from the **Docklands Light Railway** (☎*538-0311*), which was opened in Sept 1987. Suspended 20ft (6m) above the ground for much of its route, it affords panoramic views of the area. The red, white and blue computer-driven trains, looking even more like toys than the buildings below, run daily from 5.30am to midnight.

The LDDC (☎*515-3000*) arranges guided tours by bus, riverbus, helicopter and even by horse-drawn coach, and **Citisights** (☎*241-1323*) offers guided walks.

Downing Street
SW1. Map 10H11. Tube Westminster. Charing Cross.
There must be something significant about the way Downing Street, the Prime Minister's residence, is so overwhelmingly dominated by the massive government buildings of *Whitehall*. In fact, the interior of 'no 10' is more elegant and spacious than the unassuming facade might suggest, and from its Cabinet Room the country has been run since Sir Robert Walpole accepted the house ex officio from George II in 1735. No.11, home of the Chancellor of the Exchequer, is the only other survivor of Sir George Downing's original terrace of 1683-86. Steps at the end of the street lead to *St James's Park*.

Dulwich
Map 21D5. Train to West Dulwich from Victoria.
The charming village of Dulwich, with wooden signposts, broad open spaces and historic buildings, is a jewel preserved in the rock face in a way typical of London. The presence of *Dulwich College* is strong here: in **College Road** there are several 18thC houses and considerable style, nos.103-107 dating from around 1700, and nos.57 and 97, as well as substantial Georgian homes. College Rd. heads S across the refreshing Dulwich Common through a toll gate. In Lordship Lane is the **Horniman Museum** (☎*699-2339* 🖾 💷 *open Mon-Sat 10.30am-6pm, Sun 2-6pm*), in an Art Nouveau building of 1902. It houses a bizarre variety of objects: dolls, tribal art, even stuffed animals, and a fine collection of musical instruments.

Dulwich College and Picture Gallery 🏛 ☆
College Rd., SE21 ☎693-5254. Map 21D5 🖾 ✿ with flash. Open Tues-Sat 10am-1pm, 2-5pm, Sun 2-5pm.
In 1619, Edward Alleyn, a successful actor and colleague of Shakespeare, founded the 'College of God's Gift' at Dulwich, and the large almshouses that were part of the original bequest have been added to, making Dulwich College today one of London's greatest schools.

Of particular interest is the remarkable **Picture Gallery**, in a severe Neo-Classical building designed by Sir John Soane in 1811-14, which incorporates a mausoleum for the college's benefactors. The Dutch school of the 17thC is especially well represented: there are six Cuyps, for example, including some fine landscapes. Look out for the majestic *Landscape with Sportsmen* by Pynacker and important works by Poussin; also represented are Watteau, Claude and Canaletto. There are Rubens sketches, and English portraiture, including works by Gainsborough, and Reynolds' amusing portrait of his era's great actress, *Mrs Siddons as the Tragic Muse*. But pride of place goes to the awe-inspiring **Rembrandts**, including *Titus*, a moving portrait of his sick son.

Eltham Palace 🏛 ☆
Eltham ☎859-2112. *Map 21D5* 🅿 *Open Nov-Mar Thurs, Sun 11am-4.30pm; Apr-Oct Thurs, Sun 11am-6.30pm. Train to Eltham from Charing Cross.*

History has played some teasing games with this medieval palace near *Blackheath* and *Greenwich*. A favorite royal hunting retreat until the time of Henry VIII, it must have witnessed some huge banquets, such as when Henry IV received the Byzantine Emperor here in 1409. By the 1600s, it fell into ruins; only the Great Hall survived the Civil War, because it made a good barn. In the 1930s it was rescued by the Royal Army Educational Corps, which now occupies the site. You pass a lovely group of half-timbered houses in the outer court, known as the **Lord Chancellor's Lodgings** after Cardinal Wolsey, and cross a 15thC bridge over a moat with swans and geese. At the heart stands the **Great Hall** on the mound of the palace, with its superb **hammerbeam roof** and the two great **oriel windows** at either side of the dais.

Fenton House 🏛 ☆
Hampstead Grove, NW3 ☎435-3471. *Map 21C4.* 🅿 *Open Mar Sat, Sun 2-5pm; Apr-Oct Mon-Wed, Sat, Sun 11am-5pm. Tube Hampstead.*

Although *Hampstead* is rich in fine houses, this is its jewel. Dating from 1693, Fenton House is a brick mansion of disarmingly simple design, hardly changed except for the benign addition of the Classical portico on the E front soon after 1800. The luxurious Regency decor of the interior reflects the alterations carried out by James Fenton in about 1810. Among older items of furniture, look out for the charming little 'grandmother' clock of about 1695 on the stair landing. Meissen and Nymphenburg ware as well as English pieces are among a fine **porcelain collection**. Also kept in the house, and perhaps its crowning glory, is the **Benton-Fletcher Collection of Musical Instruments**, which comprises mainly early keyboard instruments.

Concerts are performed in the house in summer and a Shakespeare play is staged in the delightful walled garden every July.

Fleet Street
EC4. Map 11F13-14. Tube Aldwych, Temple, Blackfriars, St Paul's.

Leading from the *Strand* in *The City*, Fleet Street, named after the small river which now flows unseen beneath its sidewalks, is famous as the home of British journalism, although only one major newspaper and some press agencies now have offices in the 'street of shame' itself. Fleet Street begins at Temple Bar, the western limit of The City. Walking eastward, the gateways to the *Temple* on the right date from the 17thC. On the left, **St Dunstan's in the West** is a fine example of an early Victorian church in the Gothic style; it incorporates an extraordinary clock with giants striking bells (1671) and a statue of *Elizabeth* (1586). **El Vino's** wine bar on the right (see *Nightlife*) is famous for providing newspapermen with liquid inspiration. Farther along on the left (in Wine Office Court) is the **Cheshire Cheese**, an ancient pub frequented by Dr. Johnson and Boswell. Soon after comes the unusually ugly building (1928) built for and occupied by the *Daily Telegraph* until the paper moved to Wapping in 1987, followed by the *Daily Express* building of 1931, aggressively modern with its entirely plain, shiny black facade. Toward the end of Fleet Street, the wonderful wedding-cake spire of **St Brides** is visible over power buildings on the right. Built to Wren's design in 1701-3, it is the tallest and one of the most elaborate of his spires.

Geffrye Museum 🏛

Kingsland Rd., E2 ☎*739-8398. Map 21C5* ☐ ▣ *Open Tues-Sat, bank hol. Mon 10am-5pm, Sun 2-5pm. Tube Old Street.*

Shoreditch, in the East End, was traditionally the home of the furniture industry, and this museum was opened in 1914 not only to pay tribute to that past, but also to provide models for local craftsmen of the 20thC. The buildings are interesting enough, with a fine set of almshouses built in 1715 at the bequest of Sir Robert Geffrye, a former Lord Mayor whose statue stands over the door of the central block containing the coverted chapel. The collection is imaginatively arranged as a series of rooms representing different periods, and household items and pictures give a lived-in feeling. Look out for the fine chimneypiece in the Elizabethan room and the splendidly fussy Victorian parlor.

Geological Museum

Exhibition Rd., SW7 ☎*589-3444. Map 15J5* ▣ *Open Mon-Sat 10am-6pm, Sun 1-6pm. Tube South Kensington.*

Founded in 1837, the Geological Museum opened in its present building in 1935, appropriately sited between the *Natural History Museum* and *Science Museum*. The traditional displays upstairs on the regional geology of Britain and world economic mineralogy are of limited interest compared with the stunning exhibitions on the ground floor. Here, the collection of **gemstones** includes some beautiful specimens, both crude and cut. There are also two adventurous exhibitions entitled 'The Story of the Earth' and 'Treasures of the Earth,' and two smaller exhibitions, 'Britain before Man' and 'British Fossils.' On the first floor, displayed on a structure resembling a real offshore platform, 'Britain's Offshore Oil and Gas' tells the hydrocarbon story from both geological and operational viewpoints.

Grand Union Canal ☆

Maps 2-7.

At the end of the 18thC, London was triumphantly linked to the industrial Midlands by canal, then the most efficient form of travel. The canal is still there, ignoring and largely hidden by the roads that have superseded it.

Its walks offer particularly interesting views of London not normally seen by visitors: the backs of houses, gardens rich and poor, crumbling industrial buildings of the 19thC, and the many details of the working canals themselves, such as brightly painted canal barges ('narrowboats'), locks, bridges and tunnels. Camden

Lock is a good place to start — you can take a boat trip (see *Useful addresses* in *Basic information*) or walk either to the w (*Regent's Park* and Little Venice) or to the E (*St Pancras Station* and Islington).

Gray's Inn
High Holborn, WC1 ☎ *405-8164. Map 11E12. Tube Chancery Lane.*

This ancient society of lawyers, one of the four *Inns of Court*, has occupied this site since the 14thC. South Sq., the first quadrangle encountered, has one old set of chambers (no.1), dating from 1685. Opposite is the hall, badly burned but accurately restored. The fine carved late 16thC screen perhaps formed a backdrop to the first performance of Shakespeare's *Comedy of Errors* here in 1594. In the center of South Sq. is a modern statue of *Francis Bacon* (1561-1626), the great Elizabethan statesman and scholar, one of the Inn's most distinguished former members. Beyond the hall is Gray's Inn Sq., full of the calm grandeur of legal London; at the s end is the frequently restored and curiously characterless chapel. More appealing is Field Court, with no.2, a most attractive house of about 1780, and the dignified wrought-iron gates of 1723 that lead to the gardens. Designed in formal style by Francis Bacon himself, the gardens are the best of the Inns of Court, with a grand central walkway flanked by huge planes trees.

Greenwich ★
Map 21C5. Best approached by river boat — see Useful addresses in Basic information; alternatively train to Greenwich from Charing Cross.

It is no longer regarded as the center of the world, despite the continuing primacy of the Greenwich Meridian (0° longitude) and Greenwich Mean Time (GMT), and yet the sheer self-confidence of this most easterly of the Thames-side royal residences suggests otherwise. Bold and grand in every way, the metropolis' most spectacular architectural ensemble sweeps down to the riverside through fine parkland, unifying its blend of splendid buildings in an elegant Classicism.

It owes it prominence to its position as the capital port of a great seafaring nation, and its maritime character strikes the disembarking visitor in the tall form of the masts of a great British Ship. The *Cutty Sark* (☒ *open Oct-Easter Mon-Sat 10am-4.30pm, Sun noon-4.30pm; Easter-Sept Mon-Sat 10am-5.30pm, Sun noon-5.30pm*), built in 1869, was one of the greatest of the graceful tea clippers which raced to bring back tea from the Orient. Inside the hold is a display on the ship's history and a collection of old ship's figureheads. Nearby is the diminutive *Gypsy Moth IV* (☒ *open Easter-Sept Mon-Sat 10am-5.30pm, Sun noon-5.30pm*) in which Sir Francis Chichester sailed around the world in 1966.

Dominating the river is the magnificent Baroque creation of the **Royal Naval College**. It was begun in 1664 as a replacement for the old royal palace, was designated a royal hospital for navy seamen in 1694, and not completed until well into the 18thC. The original plans were by Wren, but other leading architects, including Vanbrugh and Hawksmoor, made substantial contributions. Of the interior, the amazing **Painted Hall** and the **chapel** can be visited (☒ *open Mon-Wed, Fri-Sun 2.30-4.45pm, closed Thurs*). Sir James Thornhill's **hall** of 1708-27 is a Baroque tour de force. The enormous painting on the ceiling represents the glory of the Protestant monarchy, the effect increased by the rich gray columns and pilasters, with illusionistic painted flutings. The

chapel opposite is in a much lighter Neo-Classical style; it was redecorated in 1779-89 after a fire.

Farther back from the river are the main buildings of the **National Maritime Museum** centered on the **Queen's House** (☒ *open late Mar to late Oct Mon-Sat 10am-6pm, Sun 2-6pm, late Oct to late Mar Mon-Sat 10am-5pm, Sun 2-5pm*). Henry VIII was born here, as were his two daughter queens, Mary and Elizabeth. James I gave the palace to his queen, Anne of Denmark, in 1613, and it was completely rebuilt to the designs of Inigo Jones between 1616 and 1635. The Queen's House is a building of extreme Classical simplicity, in the Palladian style quite revolutionary in its day. The most interesting rooms are the entrance hall, a perfect cube, and the graceful circular stairwell. To the sides are two wings added from 1807-16.

The National Maritime Museum housed here is the greatest seafaring museum in the world. Its extensive collections range from the finds of marine archeology to an entire paddle tug. The main entrance is in the East Wing, where new galleries house temporary exhibitions. The Queen's House, which is currently closed for restoration, but will reopen in the spring of 1990 to house, among other exhibits, a 17thC silver display. The West Wing is dominated by the New Neptune Hall, with the 1907 paddle tug, *Reliant*. Exciting displays here include the decorated royal riverboats: Queen Mary's shallop of 1689 and Prince Frederick's barge of 1732. On the top floor of the West Wing, a new gallery entitled 'Discovery and Seapower 1450-1700' charts England's transition from economic obscurity to its position, by the end of the 17thC, as one of the great naval and commercial powers in Europe. The exhibition traces the voyages of discovery, the origins of the Royal Navy and the exploits of Elizabethan seamen such as Drake and Hawkins, and includes artifacts from the *Mary Rose*.

After the Queen's House, you pass into **Greenwich Park**, crowned with several hills and sloping down steeply toward the river. One hill is topped by a Henry Moore statue, others by the buildings of the Royal Observatory.

The **Royal Observatory** (☒ *hours as Maritime Museum*) was established in 1675-76, when Wren was commissioned by Charles II to build a house for the first Astronomer Royal, John Flamsteed. A well-proportioned red-brick building with a fine octagonal room on the top floor, it commands extensive views down over Greenwich and the river. On top of one of Flamsteed House's towers can be seen a large red ball mechanism erected in 1833. Each day the ball falls at exactly 1pm to enable ships in the river to set their clocks accurately. At the rear of the house is a 19thC extension topped by a huge bulbous dome of 1894 (open only on sunny days) which houses a 28in (71cm) refracting telescope, one of the largest in the world. The astronomers have moved to Sussex and more modern equipment, and Flamsteed House is now a museum, with exhibits that include clocks and telescopes used by Halley, Herschel and other royal astronomers.

Next to Flamsteed is the mid-18thC **Meridian Building**, where there is also a display on the theme of time, for this is the site of the meridian on which all the world's clock time is based through Greenwich Mean Time; visitors can have a foot in each hemisphere.

At the top end of the park is **Ranger's House** (☒ *open Mar-Oct daily 10am-5pm, Nov-Feb daily 10am-4pm*), its front fringing *Blackheath* on Chesterfield Walk. Built of red brick, the stone center framing the main doorway dates from the early 18thC; the bowfront wings were added by the Earl of Chesterfield in about 1754. The best room, in the s wing, contains pictures of the Suffolk Collection, including a number attributed to William Larkin of members of the Jacobean aristocracy.

Chesterfield Walk leads into Croom's Hill, which proceeds back down to Greenwich town. This old road has several detached houses and terraces of the 17th-18thC along its steep slope. Near Ranger's house are **Macartney House** and the **Manor House**, both of the early 1700s. Greenwich has an attractive town center a little inland from the *Cutty Sark*, with wine bars and antique shops. Its massive and monumental parish church of **St Alfege** was built in 1711-30.

Downstream is **Woolwich**, with a large naval dockyard. It is also the traditional home of the Royal Artillery. The **Royal Arsenal**, **Military Academy** and **Artillery Barracks** of the 18th-early 19thC are extraordinarily large and imposing buildings. Nearby is the **Rotunda** (⚏ *open Apr-Oct Mon-Fri noon-5pm, Sat, Sun 1-5pm, Nov-Mar Mon-Fri noon-4pm, Sat, Sun 1-4pm*), a strange tent-shaped building of 1814 moved here from St James's Park in 1820, which now houses a collection of artillery pieces from 17thC to the present day. The river is straddled by the **Thames Barrier**, an extraordinary engineering achievement opened in 1984, which will protect London from flooding. A free exhibition demonstrates how it works.

Guildhall ⋔ ☆

Aldermanbury, EC2 ☎606-3030; ask for Keeper's Office. Map 12E15 ⚏ Open Mon-Fri 10am-5pm, Sat 10am-4pm (check first). Tube Bank, St Paul's Moorgate.

Despite being hidden away in its own yard in *The City*, the Guildhall has been parliament and palace for the Corporation of The City of London for almost 1,000yr. The present facade is not the one which would have greeted the powerful medieval Lord Mayors such as Dick Whittington; it was constructed in 1788-89 to the design of George Dance, an attractive but bizarre melange of 18thC Gothic ideas. The entrance porch, however, dates from the 15thC building, as do parts of the **Great Hall**. The most entertaining of the statues inside are the giants Gog and Magog, new versions of old mythical figures. Below is the large 15thC crypt, notable for its Purbeck marble columns supporting a vaulted roof.

The **Guildhall Library**, in an unremarkable new building on the w side, houses a sumptuous collection of books, leaflets and manuscripts giving an absorbing and unparalleled view of London. This building also houses the oldest **Clock Museum** in the world: the Collection of the Worshipful Company of Clockmakers. On show are many of the Company's 500 magnificent watches, 50 clocks and 30 marine chronometers, including the work of Tompion, Graham, Harrison, Arnold and Breguet. A 'scull' watch allegedly once owned by Mary Queen of Scots, an astronomical clock said to have belonged to Sir Isaac Newton and a deck watch which accompanied Capt. George Vancouver aboard *Discovery* are also displayed.

Ham House ⋔ ☆

Ham St., Richmond ☎940-1950. Map 20D3 ⚏ Open Tues-Sun 11am-4.30pm. Tube (or train from Waterloo) to Richmond.

One of several great mansions that border the Thames to the w of London near *Hampton Court*, Ham House is unique in that it preserves virtually intact a grand Baroque interior of the 17thC. The house was built in 1610 in conventional Jacobean style, but in the main its present appearance comes from the occupancy of Elizabeth Dysart, wife of the Duke of Lauderdale, one of Charles II's ministers. She remodeled the house in the 1670s in the grandest style of the period.

Behind the high-ceilinged entrance hall is the **Marble Dining Room**, perfectly proportioned and facing centrally down the formal garden. Even so, the ground floor rooms were only for normal domestic use; upstairs were the grand reception rooms and state bedrooms, reached by a massive staircase, carved in the 1630s with pierced reliefs of trophies. One bedroom was originally decorated for Charles II's queen. You can also see the library, several closets (or private rooms) and the fine **North Drawing Room**, with marble fireplace, rich wall hangings and gilded chairs. Most spectacular is the **Long Gallery**, with rich dark and gilded paneling and superb furniture. There is a good collection of miniatures on display in one room, including works by the masters of the genre: Hilliard, Oliver and Cooper. Rabbits, strung up ready for the pot, and crusty pies can be glimpsed through a door in the recently restored period **kitchen**.

Hampstead

Map 21C4. Tube Hampstead.

Hampstead Heath's high and hilly grassland, scattered ponds and dense woodland seem much farther than just 4 miles (6km) from a great city center. Hampstead 'village' itself still follows the street patterns of an earlier time: around the hills wind convoluted lanes lined with attractive houses of the 19thC and earlier, now favored by successful academics, artists and media folk, who give Hampstead its arty reputation.

In the 17thC, a few large out-of-town residences were established in the rural village of Hampstead; of these, *Fenton House* is a notable survivor. The craze for health-giving waters in the 18thC boosted the village into a fashionable spa which began to spread down the sides of the hill, becoming in the process a favorite haunt for artists: George Romney lived in Holly Bush Hill and John Constable at Lower Terrace, Downshire Hill and Well Walk.

The best-preserved part of old Hampstead Village is to be found around the parish church of **St John** to the w of the High St. The massive cedar trees of its calm churchyard shade Constable's grave. **Church Row**, which leads down toward the modern center, has superb row houses of 1720, reflecting the period of expansion following the discovery of the spa. To the N of Church Row are a number of charming little streets, most notably **Holly Walk** with its early 19thC cottages. A later fashionable period is represented to the s, with the Victorian and Edwardian mansions of Frognal and Fitzjohn's Ave. Look out for **Kate Greenaway's Cottage** in Frognal, in a fairy-tale style appropriately similar in feeling to her illustrations. Farther s toward Swiss Cottage, at 20 Maresfield Gdns., is the **Freud Museum** (☎435-2002 🖃 ✕ *open Wed-Sun noon-5pm*), where, among the fascinating memorabilia, is his famous psychoanalyst's couch. Freud escaped here from Nazi Austria in 1938, with his extensive library, his furniture, rugs and collection of Greek, Roman, Egyptian and Oriental antiquities. After his death in 1939, his daughter Anna preserved the house exactly as it was in his lifetime.

The winding, hilly streets of Church Row lead to **West Heath**, the wildest and most densely wooded part of Hampstead Heath.

To the E, on North End Way, is the famous **Jack Straw's Castle**, an old weatherboard inn rebuilt in the 1960s, named after the peasant leader who supposedly gathered his rebels here in 1381. Farther N on the same road is the equally famous **Bull and Bush** of the music hall song (see *Pubs*).

Back into the village, Hampstead's shopping is concentrated in Heath St. and High St. From the station, Flask Walk, where the **Flask** (see *Pubs*) is a good lunch spot, and Well Walk, where **Burgh House** (☎431-0144 ⊡ *Wed-Sun noon-5pm* ▣) mounts local exhibitions, lead past attractive cottages toward East Heath, and the strange enclave of the Vale of Health, a wooded valley crammed with 19thC houses. Down the heath to the S and on the right are Downshire Hill, with an interesting church, and Keats Grove, both with cottages and houses of around 1820, including *Keats' House*.

The Heath itself stretches across to *Highgate*; parts are wild and open, other enclosed and wooded. Across to the N is the **Spaniards**, an 18thC inn in Spaniards Rd. with a toll house, and the Georgian splendor of *Kenwood House*, a good focus for a walk. To the S is Parliament Hill, festooned with kites on weekends and offering a fine view over the dense housing of Kentish Town to The City beyond.

Hampton Court ▥ ★

Hampton, Middlesex ☎977-8441. *Map 20D3* ▨ *ƙ summer Mon-Fri only* ▣ *Open late Mar to late Oct daily 9.30am-5.30pm; late Oct to late Mar Mon-Sat 9.30am-4pm, Sun 2-4pm. Train to Hampton Court from Waterloo.*

This riverside palace, to the W of London, is not only the apotheosis of the great English Tudor style of architecture, but incorporates a grand Baroque palace designed by Wren. This dual character reflects its two periods of building, with only three patrons playing a significant part: Henry VIII's powerful Chancellor Cardinal Wolsey, the man who personified the zenith of Church and State power; Henry himself; and, over a century later, the joint monarchs William and Mary. Queen Victoria, who much preferred Windsor Castle as a Thames-side home, opened it to the public in 1839. A tragic fire in 1986 devastated eight private apartments, the lobby and cartoon gallery, which are now closed to the public while restoration work is under way.

The main entrance to the palace is through the mid-18thC Trophy Gates and along a walk which runs parallel to the river toward the West Front. The balancing projecting wings of Wolsey's magnificent gatehouse offer a regular and impressive aspect. Inset into the walls are roundels with relief busts of Roman emperors, bought as a set by Wolsey in 1521 from the Italian artist Giovanni da Maiano. Henry VIII enriched the gatehouse with a superb oriel window with his coat of arms over the door, and also built the moat and bridge. The latter now has fine stone **heraldic beasts** along its parapet brought from the garden. Through the gate is **Base Court**, the first of Wolsey's quadrangles, a peaceful space surrounded by domestic buildings of mellow red brick decorated with diamond patterning. At the far end is **Anne Boleyn's Gateway**, built by Wolsey but later named after Henry's queen whose introduction at the expense of Catherine of Aragon Wolsey had to arrange with Rome. Her emblem, a falcon, is on the tracery decorating the vaulted roof beneath the arch, together with the monograms H and A. The arch leads through to **Clock Court**, with, above the belfried gate, a fabulously complex **astronomical clock** of 1540, by Nicholas Oursian. To the S side is a Classical colonnade, added by Wren as the entrance to the State Apartments he constructed beyond this court to replace those of the Tudor period.

To enter the **State Apartments** is to move on to a different age — the walls and ceilings of the King's Staircase are decorated with exuberant frescoes, with gods and heroes of the ancient world swirling illusionistically through Corinthian columns. They were painted after 1700 by an Italian artist, Antonio Verrio. Next comes a huge **Guard Chamber**, its walls decorated with 3,000 pistols, muskets and swords. A door from here leads into some of the rooms of Wolsey's palace, with the 16thC linen-fold paneling, but this brief diversion ends with the formal sequence of rooms designed by Wren. **William III's bedroom** has a ceiling by Verrio, a soaring Baroque bed and gilded furniture originally designed for the room. Rich and heavy tapestries still hang on some of the walls: in the Cartoon Gallery are tapestries made to Raphael's famous designs (for which the room was planned; the designs now hang in the *Victoria and Albert Museum*). In the **Communication Gallery** are a number of paintings by Lely, the so-called *Windsor Beauties* court portraits.

The Cumberland Suite shows a different taste, that of the 18thC, with regal pomp giving way to elegant comfort. An important collection of paintings hangs throughout these rooms, largely from the Italian High Renaissance. Titian, Tintoretto, Correggio, Raphael and Duccio are all represented; perhaps the most striking are Mantegna's series *The Triumph of Julius Caesar*, but look out also for the chilly gloss of Parmigianino's *Minerva*. Other schools of painting are also to be seen: Brueghel's *Massacre of the Innocents* and Cranach's lovely *Judgment of Paris* stands out. There are also works by Holbein, an artist associated closely with the Tudors. There are splendid views over the park and on to **Fountain Court**, a first glimpse of Wren's superb architecture in pink brick and white stone.

Before emerging, three rooms of special interest are encountered, all dating from the Tudor period. The small **Wolsey's Closet**, probably the cardinal's study, has panelled walls, a finely wrought ceiling of timber and plaster and recently discovered paintings from the 16thC. The **chapel**, also built by Wolsey, is then seen from the Royal Pew; it has an elaborate ceiling added by Henry VIII, with pendants carved in the form of angels. The reredos was designed by Wren and its marvelously carved plant forms are the work of Grinling Gibbons. Finally, as a suitable climax, there is Henry VIII's **Great Hall** of 1531-36, hung with contemporary Flemish tapestries and with a **hammerbeam roof**. Small rooms which help make the place come alive are the authentically equipped **kitchen** and Henry VIII's **wine cellar**.

Emerging into Clock Court, an arch at the opposite end leads through to Fountain Court past the **Queen's Staircase**. Here Wren's bold but harmonious use of the contrast between stone and brick can be seen to dramatic effect from the cloister along the little courtyard. Another arch leads through to the center of the **East Front** and the lake, **Long Water**.

All round the buildings are spectacular gardens in the various styles of different periods, some sunken and enclosed, other broad and open, some in the Tudor 'knot' pattern, others with great avenues of trees. Note the 200yr-old vine in its special greenhouse (its stem is 78in (2m) thick) which produces 600 bunches of grapes yearly, and the maze, dating in its present form from 1714. The Chestnut Avenue stretches for over 1 mile (1.5km), and flowers spectacularly in May.

Highgate ☆
Map 21B4. Tube Highgate, Archway.

This twin village of *Hampstead*, looking down on London from the N, takes its name from a tollgate that used to bear its center and its dizzying height, best appreciated by approaching steep Highgate Hill or Highgate West Hill. Highgate Hill has a few fine mansions, most notably **Cromwell House**, a red-brick house in Dutch style of about 1637-40. Here also is **Whittington Stone** where, according to legend, Dick Whittington rested on his way home in c.1390, gazed down at The City and heard the bells chiming, 'Turn again Whittington, thrice Mayor of London.'

The High Street has good 18thC row houses, and South Grove on the left leads past the attractive Waterlow Park and Pond Sq. to the intersection with West Hill and **The Grove**, with an attractive terrace built around 1700. A plaque commemorates Coleridge who lived in one of the houses; his tomb is in the aisle of the nearby church of St Michael, an imposing 19thC Gothic (1832) edifice with Highgate Cemetery (see below) behind it. In complete contrast with these charms are two large and influential blocks of apartments to the N on North Hill, the **Highpoint Flats**, constructed in 1936 and 1939 by the Tecton group.

Highgate Cemetery is one of the most extraordinary relics of Victorian London gone to seed, a romantic wilderness that pays tribute to nature's power to reclaim its own. A tour of the w side (✗ *compulsory, on the hr every hr summer 10am-4pm, winter 10am-3pm*) takes you to Christina Rossetti's grave, a weird Gothic Chapel and the Egyptian catacombs. The most famous grave on the newer E side is the **grave of Karl Marx**, now surmounted by an ugly monument erected in the 1950s. Many other well-known people are buried here, including George Eliot.

Hogarth's House
Hogarth Lane, W4 ☎944-6757. Map 21C4 ◙ Open Apr-Aug, last 2 weeks Sept, Mon, Wed-Sat 11am-6pm, Sun 2-6pm; Oct to early Dec, Jan-Mar Mon, Wed-Sat 11am-4pm, Sun 2-4pm. Closed first 2 weeks Sept, last 3 weeks Dec. Tube Chiswick Park, Turnham Green.

The painter William Hogarth (1697-1764) was an urban artist, and only lived in the delightful riverside village of *Chiswick* in the summer. The house which he occupied from 1749-64 is now stranded between industrial buildings on the noisy Great West Rd. Inside the pretty old buildings, however, a quieter atmosphere prevails as an ironic background to the good selection of Hogarth's bustling, sarcastic and sometimes scurrilous engravings. The house also contains some contemporary furniture, and the artist himself is buried in the nearby village churchyard.

Holland House and Park
Map 6H1. Tube Holland Park.

Although Holland House has hardly survived, its park retains the elegance of its prime. Narrow paths wind among mature woods, peacocks and other ornamental birds roam in a large enclosure, a formal flower garden, with a traditional pattern of box hedges, is decorated with statues, and music drifts from the Orangery in summer.

The bombs of 1941 destroyed most of the house and now only the E wing stands complete, with its attractive Dutch gabled roof line. There is also a marvelous arched loggia, with strangely checkered carvings and fleur-de-lys crenelations. The Classical gateways (1629) was designed by Inigo Jones.

Horse Guards Parade 🏛

Map 10H11. Tube Westminster.

The Horse Guards of Whitehall is a curiously jumbled Classical building of the mid-18thC, all arches, pediments and separate wings. Troopers of the Household Cavalry will be seen mounting guard in resplendent uniforms astride their equally well-groomed horses. The large parade ground beyond the central arch sees the great **Trooping of the Colour** ceremony in June (see *Calendar of events* in *Planning*); past the Guards' Memorial, it leads into *St James's Park*. State buildings surrounded the other three sides. Looking back from the park, the Old Admiralty is on the left, an ugly brick and stone extravaganza of 1894-95; to the right of the Horse Guards is the more dignified Scottish Office, actually a fine mid-18thC house; and farther right are the Treasury and the rear of no.10 *Downing Street*.

Hyde Park

Map 7G-H. Tube Marble Arch, Hyde Park Corner, Lancaster Gate.

You can stand in the middle of the largest open space in London, formed by Hyde Park and Kensington Gardens, and see nothing but wooded, rolling grassland, punctuated only by the lake know as the *Serpentine*, made in 1730.

Rotten Row, along the southern edge, was *the* place to parade in the 18th-19thC, and is still used by horseback riders, although sadly it has lost its trees to Dutch Elm disease. In the SE, at Hyde Park Corner, is *Apsley House* and a graceful screen that once formed an entrance to the park's carriageway. A little to the N there is an absurd statue of *Achilles*, made in 1822 from captured French cannons. A much better statue is *Rima* by Jacob Epstein (1922) near the Hudson Bird Sanctuary in the center of the park. On the NE side is *Speakers' Corner*.

Imperial War Museum 🏛

Lambeth Rd., SE11 ☎735-8922. Map 19J13 🖼 🅿 ✳ Open Mon-Sat 10am-5.50pm, Sun 2-5.50pm. Tube Lambeth North.

'Lest we forget,' the Imperial War Museum was established soon after the end of World War I to preserve the relics and memory of that terrible conflict. Since then, its terms of reference have been expanded to include all wars involving Britain or the Commonwealth since 1914. We should not forget, either, that war means more than fighting; there are exhibits about life on the home front, an unparaleled display of newspapers, photographs and films, and even an important collection of modern art — pictures by artists such as Henry Moore, Paul Nash, Stanley Spencer and Augustus John, who were commissioned to record their impressions of wars in progress.

The museum's Lambeth building used to be the central range of the Bethlem Royal Hospital, built in 1812-15, appropriately perhaps an asylum for the insane, successor to the notorious 'Bedlam' in The City. The present building's portico and large dome were added in 1835-40.

The most appealing exhibits range from models of warships and battles to full scale displays built up with mannequins in authentic uniforms around genuine tanks and guns. Great attention is paid to realism, with foliage, camouflage and props carefully inserted. The museum displays a number of famous aircraft, including a Sopwith Camel from the 1914-18 war and a Spitfire from the Battle of Britain. The upper floors are devoted to temporary exhibitions, a room of documents, including the German surrender signed in 1945, and art galleries.

The museum's galleries closed in Nov 1988 so that new displays could be installed as part of a major redevelopment program. The museum will reopen in late Mar 1989 with four floors of exhibition space, including a new extension (due to open in June 1989) as well as a restaurant and shop. Displays will feature 'experiences' to bring alive the story of war in the 20thC.

Inns of Court

All barristers must belong to one of these four institutions, and many work from their dignified ancient buildings. They are: *Gray's Inn*, *Lincoln's Inn*, and the Middle and Inner *Temple*.

Dr. Johnson's House

17 Gough Sq., EC4 ☎ 353-3745. Map 11F13 ▨ Open Mon-Sat May-Sept 11am-5.30pm, Oct-April 11am-5pm. Tube Blackfriars, St Paul's.

In this substantial row house, dating from about 1700, Dr. Samuel Johnson lived from 1748-59; this man of letters *par excellence* was the center of a whole literary world which flocked to see him here and in the nearby **Cheshire Cheese** (see *Pubs*) in *Fleet Street*. In the large gabled attic, he and his six assistants worked on the celebrated *Dictionary*.

Unfortunately, little can be seen of the house's original contents — a few chairs and tables, however, do give some idea of its historic atmosphere. Pictures and memorabilia give a picture of literary life in 18thC London. Look out for a first edition copy of the *Dictionary* and Johnson's will.

Keats' House

Keats Grove, NW3 ☎ 435-2062. Map 21C4 ▣ K by appt. Open Mon-Fri 2-6pm, Sat 10am-5pm, Sun 2-5pm. Tube Hampstead, Belsize Park.

The Romantic poet John Keats (1795-1821) was already in the grip of tuberculosis when, in 1820, he left the house in *Hampstead* where he had spent his two most productive years to journey to Italy, where he died ten months later. Nevertheless, the house is a monument to his happiness and the rural seclusion that inspired *Ode to a Nightingale* and other poems. At the time is was split into two cottage homes sharing a garden; in the other half lived Fanny Brawne, with whom Keats fell famously and poetically in love. The engagement ring she wore until her own death is part of the memorial collection, as are Keats' manuscripts and annotated books, and letters to and from friends such as Shelley.

Kensington ☆

Map 14&15. Tube South Kensington, High Street Kensington.

Modern Kensington is pleasant and prosperous, with a few enclaves of ostentatious wealth, but the predominant pattern is of good 19thC terraces and villas, large late-Victorian and Edwardian apartment blocks, major shopping streets that include the better department stores, and little roads of classy boutiques and antique shops — good taste abounds.

In the 17thC, two great houses emerged from the manors scattered among the fields: *Holland House and Park*, and Nottingham House, which became *Kensington Palace* in 1690 when William and Mary moved there and gave the impetus to a new crop of aristocratic houses. **Kensington Square** was one such development, of about 1700, and a few attractive houses are preserved, such as no.29. The part just s of Kensington Palace is a lovely enclave, **Canning Place** in particular. **Kensington Palace Road**, running w of the palace, is known as 'Millionaires' Row'; it was begun in 1843 and consists of grand detached mansions, now largely occupied by embassies or their staff, and is a private road. The public road running N from **Kensington High Street**, a busy shopping area, to Notting Hill Gate is **Kensington Church Street**, with its many good antique shops and clothes boutiques (see *Shopping*). Nearby are *Leighton House*, the *Commonwealth Institute* and **Linley Sambourne House** at 18 Stafford Terr. W8 (✉ *open Mar-Oct Wed 10am-4pm, Sun 2-5pm; run by the Victorian Society, 1 Priory Gdns., W4* ☎*994-1019*), where an engraving on the brass letterbox reads: 'Mr Linley Sambourne Not At Home.' The home of the well-known *Punch* cartoonist, great-grandfather of the Earl of Snowdon, has changed little in three generations. It is crammed with Victoriana — photographs, chiming clocks, china and glass — the walls are covered in William Morris wallpaper, the windows hung with heavy Victorian drapes. Inside it feels a very long way from the late 20thC.

The central part of Kensington, thought of as **South Kensington** since that is the name of the tube station serving it, is dominated by a complex of museums and colleges set up on land bought with the proceeds from the Great Exhibition held in Hyde Park in 1851. Albert, Prince Consort to Queen Victoria, was the leading sponsor of the scheme and much of the character of this monument to Victorian optimism comes from his vision. He is commemorated by the *Albert Memorial* and *Royal Albert Hall*.

Next to the Albert Hall is the **Royal College of Art**, a supposedly 'brutal' but in fact dull building of 1960-61. A little to the E of the Albert Hall is the **Royal Geographical Society**, an attractively informal house in Dutch style designed by Norman Shaw in 1874. Statues show *David Livingstone* and *Scott of the Antarctic*, both fellows of the RGS.

To the s is Prince Consort Rd. Here, at the center of the large 20thC buildings of **Imperial College** (London University's leading science department), is the **Royal College of Music**, a red-brick pseudo-medieval building of 1883-84. The 280ft (85m) **Queen's Tower** (☎*589-5111* ✉ *open July-Sept daily 10am-5.30pm, no* ✿), is a survivor of the 1887-93 Imperial Institute buildings, and affords a spectacular, uninterrupted view of London.

South of Imperial College are the great museums that, together with the colleges, represent the fulfillment of Albert's dream: the *Science Museum*, the *Geological Museum*, the *Natural History Museum*, one of London's finest buildings, and the *Victoria & Albert Museum*.

The eastern part of Kensington is predominantly residential. Beyond the Victoria & Albert Museum is the *Brompton Oratory*, with the shopping center of the Brompton Rd. beyond, and the incomparable **Harrods** department store. Behind the main road, attractive housing of the 19thC stretches up to Knightsbridge and s into Brompton. An interesting building, well worth a detour, is **Michelin House**, an Art Nouveau gem of 1910, on Fulham Rd, now the Conran Shop (see *Shopping*). Its ceramic decorations include panels with charming scenes of early auto races.

Kensington Palace 🏛

Kensington Gdns., W8 ☎*937-9561. Map 6H3* ✉ ✿ *Open Mon-Sat 9am-4pm, Sun 1-4pm. Tube High Street Kensington, Queensway.*

Kensington Palace was first made a royal residence when it was bought by William and Mary in 1689. The house had large grounds, now **Kensington Gardens** (see *Walk 4* in *Planning*), and was next to the expanse of *Hyde Park*. Sir Christopher Wren was instructed to enlarge the palace and, apart from further work in the 1720s, most of what is seen was built under his supervision. It is a simple building, around three courts, and surprisingly unpretentious for a royal palace. Perhaps the most striking building is the **Orangery** of 1704, a little to the NE, probably designed by Nicholas Hawksmoor.

The interior is mostly private but the State Apartments can be visited. Some of the rooms are largely as Wren left them, others were made grander by William Kent in the 1720s. Kent's own Baroque paintings adorn several walls and ceilings, most notably in the **King's Staircase**, the **King's Gallery** and **King's Drawing Room**. One of the most attractive rooms is the **Queen's Bedroom**, sumptuously but intimately decorated, with fine 17thC furniture including the bed made for James II's queen. Look out for the fine carving by Grinling Gibbons, Wren's carver, over the fireplace in the Presence Chamber, enhanced by Kent's 'Etruscan' ceiling, and also the wind vane above the fire in the King's Gallery. There is an interesting display of paintings of and exhibits from the Great Exhibition of 1851 in the **Council Chamber**. Several good paintings are on display in addition to the fine furniture: most notable is Van Dyck's seductive *Cupid and Psyche* ☆ but look for Artemisia Gentileschi's powerful *Self-portrait*, an important work by a woman artist.

On the ground floor, the **Court Dress Collection** was opened in 1984. A unique display of court dress and army uniforms from 1750 to the 1950s, it also includes Princess Diana's wedding dress.

The royal tradition is kept up by the Prince and Princess of Wales, who have their London home here.

Kenwood House *(The Iveagh Bequest)* ⬛ ★
Hampstead Lane, NW3 ☎ *348-1286. Map 21C4* ▣ ▣ *Open daily Feb-Dec 10am-5pm; Jan 10am-4pm. Tube Highgate.*
After a short walk through old and well-established woods, on *Hampstead* Heath, the exquisite 18thC mansion comes into view, with Robert Adam's superb Classical facade flanked harmoniously by wings containing the orangery and library. Adam was commissioned to adapt an old Stuart house in 1766 by the first Earl of Mansfield. The result was some of the Scottish architect's finest work, including the South Front, with its decorated pilasters and the stucco portico that forms the main entrance. Several Adam details survive; the **library** is outstanding. The room was intended for 'receiving company' as well as housing books, and this explains its splendor.

Kenwood was saved from the hands of speculative builders in 1925 when the first Earl of Iveagh (Edward Cecil Guinness, of brewing fame) bought the house. He died only 2yr later, leaving the house, a sizeable bequest and a collection of pictures to the people of London. Apart from the library, the house is now laid out as an art gallery.

English 18thC painting is best represented, with excellent examples of Gainsborough and Reynolds in particular; Gainsborough's sumptuous *Mary, Countess Howe* is a masterpiece of the artist's elegant later style. Kenwood's real stars, however, are Dutch paintings, with fine examples by Cuyp and Van de Velde. Linger over Vermeer's *Guitar Player* and, supreme, Rembrandt's **Self-portrait** of c.1663. Other notable artists represented include Van Dyck, Guardi, Boucher and Turner.

In summer, concerts are given by the lake (see *Nightlife*). Dr. Johnson's summerhouse was moved here in 1968.

Kew

Map 20D3. Tube Kew Gardens, or train to Kew Bridge from Waterloo.

Close to the ideal of an English country village, Kew Green is not as rustic as it first seems. It is actually flanked by 18th-19thC detached and row houses which lend an air of substantial prosperity, and its unusual parish church, **St Anne's**, was built under royal patronage in 1710-14 (and extended in 1770). An interesting feature is the Royal Gallery above the w door, donated by George III in 1805.

At the narrow end of the green is the **Herbarium** (open only to professional botanists), the library and collection of some five million dried plant specimens which presages the area's great attraction, **Kew Gardens**, by whose gate it sits.

Providing a contrast to the natural splendors of the Gardens, **Kew Bridge Steam Museum** (*Kew Bridge Rd., Brentford* ☎*568-4757* ▨ *open daily 11am-5pm*) boasts some fine 19thC steam engines used to supply London's water. They can only be seen working on Sat and Sun.

Royal Botanic Gardens ★

☎*940-1171* ▨ ✿ *Open daily, gardens Jan, late Oct-Dec 9.30am-4pm; Feb 9.30am-5pm; Mar, late Sept to late Oct 9.30am-6pm; Apr to late Sept Mon-Sat 9.30am-6.30pm, Sun 9.30am-8pm; glasshouses from 10am; galleries, museums from 9.30am; closing times vary considerably, but as a general rule, summer Mon-Fri 4.30pm, Sat, Sun 5.30pm; winter 3.30pm.*

The full name of Kew Gardens comes as a salutary reminder to those who know it well, for they are apt to be seduced by its supreme beauty and forget that it is a scientific institution. As such, it is unmatched, studying, classifying and cultivating a vast number of plants from all around the world. Despite the devastation suffered in the storm that struck southern England in Oct 1987, Kew still boasts superb walks and dreamlike views, in spring it is sublime.

Kew Gardens was formed from the grounds of two royal residences: Richmond Lodge and Kew Palace. George III united the two estates and from 1722-1819 Sir Joseph Banks, who had accompanied Captain Cook to the South Seas, established a true botanic garden in the large park, sending young botanists all over the world in search of specimens. It was with the help of Kew Gardens that breadfruit was introduced to the West Indies and rubber to the Malay Peninsula. In 1841, the gardens were handed over to the State and the first director was formally appointed. Further grants of land by the Crown in 1897 and 1904 took the total to over 300 acres (121.5ha). Expansion continues; a new exhibition area, designed to be partly glass concourse and partly underground, is due to open in 1989.

Begin at the main gates by Kew Green, and turn sharp left for the vast new **Princess of Wales Conservatory**. It contains ten different habitats from Namib Desert and mangrove swamp to cloud forest and tropical pools. Proceed up the Broad Walk, which turns left at the Orangery, leading to the pond and Palm House, returning by smaller paths through flower-filled woodland, rock, iris and other gardens.

A more extensive tour will take in the many extra attractions. On the right of the Broad Walk is the **Aroid House**, a Nash-designed glasshouse in Classical style brought here from

Buckingham Palace in 1836; inside is re-created a dense and lush
tropical rain forest. Farther along on the right is the **Dutch House**,
all that remains of the buildings of **Kew Palace**, the rest of which
were demolished in 1802. The Dutch House actually predated the
main palace buildings, being built in red brick with steep Dutch
gables by a wealthy merchant in 1631. To the rear is the **Queen's
Garden**, an accurate reconstruction of the type of garden the house
might have had in the 17thC, with tightly-clipped hedges and
aromatic herbs. Back at the Broad Walk, the **Orangery** (1761)
contains temporary exhibitions.

Instead of continuing along the Broad Walk, bear to the right.
The long Riverside Ave. here passes through cedar, plane and
oak-planted woods. A detour to the left will take in the
rhododendron dell (if you are visiting in spring, it is almost a
crime to miss this), the bamboo garden and azalea garden, with the
beautiful lake to the s. Walk around the riverside to obtain a fine
view across the Thames to *Syon House*. Farther along to the sw
are the grounds of **Queen Charlotte's Cottage**, thatched in rustic
style and built in the 1770s as a focal point for elaborate garden
parties. It is now surrounded by an area left wild as natural habitat
for native British plants and wildlife. Walking to the E leads to the
Japanese Gateway, a fine replica erected in 1910 on a little hill,
and surrounded by pines and flowering azaleas. Farther E again is
the **Pagoda**, built in a more fanciful Oriental style in 1761-62, at
163ft (50m), pushing up through the surrounding woods.

From here, Pagoda Vista returns toward the entrance. On the
way, take in the **Temperate House**, a large 19thC complex of
greenhouses containing fine camellias, with the **Marianne North
Gallery** to the E, home of an extraordinary collection of botanical,
paintings. A little farther N, mock temples and ruins survive from
the 18thC garden layout. The **Palm House** (*closed until early 1990
for major repair work*) then comes into view — a magnificent and
graceful iron and glass construction of 1844-48 by Decimus
Burton. It contains a fabulous collection of tropical plants, many of
which have grown to great size. Between the Palm House and the
main entrance to the N are numerous little gardens and complexes
of greenhouses devoted to particular types of plants; particularly
impressive are the fine **water lilies**.

Lambeth Palace ▥

*SE1 ☎928-8282. Map **19**J12. Open only to organized groups
reserving in advance; apply in writing to the Bursar
✗ usually Wed or Thurs 2.15-3.30pm. Tube Lambeth North.*

In the possession of the Archbishops of Canterbury since 1197,
Lambeth Palace grew into prominence as the Primate's residence
in the later Middle Ages. In 1547, Thomas Cranmer wrote the
English Prayer Book here, but caused great controversy by eating
meat during Lent in the Great Hall. The superb red-brick
gatehouse dates from 1495, and next to it stands the 15thC tower
of the now closed church of St Mary Lambeth. Beyond the walls
can be seen the Classical stonework decorating the **hall**, rebuilt
after the Civil War.

Lancaster House ▥

*Stable Yard, The Mall, SW1 ☎839-3488. Map **9**H9. Currently
closed to the public. Tube Green Park.*

Previously known as York House and Stafford House, according
to the aristocrat in residence, Lancaster House (begun in 1820) is
the most westerly of the palaces of *The Mall*, with its facades
overlooking Green Park to the w and *St James's Park* to the s.

Benjamin Wyatt designed the exterior in cool Bath stone with massive and severe Classical porticos similar to his *Apsley House*, together with the imposing stairwell. Charles Barry, who took over in 1838, completed the interior in a much more grandiose and highly decorated Baroque style. Paintings by Veronese and Guercino, brought to the house to decorate ceilings of the antechamber and gallery, conform to this taste for richness.

Law Courts   The popular name for the fine Victorian Gothic *Royal Courts of Justice* on the *Strand*.

Leighton House 🏛
12 Holland Park Rd., W14. Map 21C4 ☎602-3316 ⊡ Open Mon-Sat 11am-5pm; during special exhibitions Mon-Fri 11am-6pm. Tube High Street Kensington.
Looking like one of several plain red-brick houses in a street once favored by successful artists, Leighton House contains a remarkable surprise. Lord Leighton was the most famous of Victorian artists and, in building his house from 1865, he gave vent to his taste for the exotic, creating a rich interior in Moorish style. It is fantasy, a harem in London. The highlight is the **Arab Hall**, with its two stories culminating in a dome, and its walls covered with rich 13th-17thC Islamic tiles. Interesting Victorian paintings on show include works by Leighton himself and Edward Burne-Jones.

Lincoln's Inn 🏛 ★
☎405-1393. Map 11E12 ⊡ ✗ Open Mon-Fri 9am-6pm; Great Hall and Old Hall open Mon-Fri 9am-12pm, 2.30-6pm when not in use (check first); apply at porter's lodge. Tube Holborn, Chancery Lane.
Reminiscent of one of the grander Oxford or Cambridge colleges, this most unspoiled of the *Inns of Court* was founded in the 14thC. The best way in is from Chancery Lane, through a gatehouse (with the original gates) of 1518 and the Tudor red-brick **Old Buildings** (before 1520). Opposite the gate is the **Old Hall** (1490-92) which contains an uncharacteristically serious painting by Hogarth and a fine wooden roof. On the N side of the court is the **chapel**, dating from about 1619-23, standing on an open undercroft of Gothic vaulting with rich ribbing. Its high-backed boxed pews, and its stained-glass windows of numerous coats of arms of treasurers dating back to the 17thC, contribute to a deep serenity. To the SW is **New Square**, not originally built as part of the Inn but a large and remarkably well-preserved square of about 1685-97; its dignified brick houses, with decoration restricted to the open pediments above the doors, enclose a splendid lawn. To the S is a gateway of 1697 leading into Carey St. The northern part of the Inn includes the great bulk of Stone Buildings of 1774-80, with a severe Classical facade on the W side; the large sundial on this wall is dated 1794. Opposite are the Inn's attractive private gardens, together with the impressive Victorian brick-Gothic library and New Hall. Beyond these lie the open spaces of Lincoln's Inn Fields, one of London's largest public squares.

London Bridge
Map 13G16. Tube Monument, London Bridge.
London's *raison d'être*, one might call it — the Romans discovered that this was the farthest downstream they could easily cross the river, and built their town accordingly. In fact, their wooden bridge was almost certainly a little to the E of the present structure,

but survived with periodic reconstructions until the medieval stone bridge appeared in 1176-1209. This stood for over 500yr, encrusted with houses, shops, even chapels, and the famous iron spikes where traitors' heads were displayed. Eventually, all its buildings were removed and the bridge modernized in about 1749, at the same time as London's second bridge was built at Westminster. A new bridge, now moved to an amusement park in Arizona, was built in 1825-31. The present structure of three arches dates from 1967-73.

In the shadow of London Bridge, St Mary Overie Dock is home to the last surviving topsail schooner, the 85yr-old **Kathleen and May**.

London Dungeon

34 Tooley St., SE1 ☎*403-0606. Map 13G16* 🔲 ⬛ *Open daily Apr-Sept 10am-5.30pm; Oct-Mar 10am-4.30pm. Tube London Bridge.*

Enjoying the London Dungeon requires a special sense of humor — and a strong stomach. Its location in a series of dark, damp vaults under railway arches has been carefully chosen to foster discomfort, and is ideally suited to its exhibits on the 'darker side of British history.' The vaults echo to the recorded sounds of screams and moans, and even the rumble of the occasional passing train. The ancient British heroine Boadicea, for example, is shown thrusting a blood-smeared spear into the throat of a gurgling victim, and in a new attraction, The Fire of London, ingenious special effects create the illusion of being in Pudding Lane engulfed by flames. Not for the faint-hearted.

London, Museum of ★

150 London Wall, EC2 ☎*600-3699. Map 12E15* 🔲 ⬛ ✱ *Open Tues-Sat 10am-6pm, Sun 2-6pm. Tube Barbican, Moorgate, St Paul's.*

Recently reorganized, and moved to a new building on the corner of the *Barbican*, this museum traces the social history of London from prehistory to the present day in 'social' manner.

The museum possesses a substantial part of the stock of important archeological finds made in London, and is chronologically arranged so visitors follow a single winding course, with the two floors joined by a glass walkway.

Archeological finds from the **Stone, Bronze and Iron Ages**, most originating from sites in the Thames Valley to the w of London, are grouped in settings that show the purposes to which they were put by ancient people. Ax heads, for example, have been fitted with handles to demonstrate how they would have been used. Models and drawings reconstruct the appearance of prehistoric settlements and explain early hunting methods and agriculture.

Roman London is well represented in the museum and, as an added surprise, a carefully placed window looks down on one of the best-preserved parts of the Roman wall outside, with its medieval bastions. Inside, the display ranges from leather sandals to board games to the superb sculptures found buried in the floor of the Temple of Mithras discovered in 1954 during the construction of an office block in Queen Victoria St. The **head of Serapis** is particularly exquisite. A famous **mosaic floor** found in 1869 can be seen in a reconstructed room setting, with reproduction furniture showing the luxurious Roman way of life.

The displays of **Anglo-Saxon and medieval London** begin with the strange gravestone in the Viking Ringerike style, inscribed with runes dating from the 11thC. An excellent model of the original Tower of London shows it as a single stone tower surrounded by a wooden palisade. A model of old *St Paul's Cathedral* is even more impressive, and shows how the great Gothic cathedral must have been before its destruction in the Great Fire of 1666.

A Ming porcelain cup mounted on a silver-gilt stand and an exquisitely embroidered glove show the sophisticated tastes and superb workmanship of the **Tudor and Stuart** periods. Also noteworthy are a copper plate of c.1558, engraved with a contemporary map of London, and the Cheapside Hoard, a collection of 16thC jewelry. Politics now feature more prominently: the Civil War, Great Plague and Fire of London all receive ample attention. A darkened room with a large model graphically shows the progress of the fire; old London actually appears to disintegrate as you watch, with a commentary from Pepys' diary. The exhibits from the **18th-20thC** are even more varied, if more familiar, and the **Georgian** gallery has recently been completely renovated. **Shop fronts and interiors** are reconstructed, including a superb 18thC barber's, a 19thC pub, and an early broadcasting studio. There are some extraordinary barred doors from the notorious Newgate Gaol, an 1862 fire engine, and even an Art Deco elevator from Selfridges department store. On a smaller scale, look out for some charming Victorian Christmas and Valentine cards and toys. However, grandeur steals the show: the **Lord Mayor's Ceremonial Coach ★** (1757), removed once a year for the Lord Mayor's Show, stands resplendent with its elaborate painted and gilt decoration.

London Toy and Model Museum
23 Craven Hill, W2 ☎*262-7905. Map 7F4* 🔲 💻 ✳ *Open Tues-Sat 10am-5.30pm, Sun 11am-5.30pm. Tube Queensway, Lancaster Gate.*

This remarkable museum appeals as much to adults as to the children for whom the exhibits were originally intended. Several of the toys on display can be activated by the touch of a button. Dolls, nursery toys, mechanical toys and a collection of model railroad locomotives fill a warren of rooms. There is also a miniature railroad, which children can ride on, in the small garden, and a 'hands-on' video and activity area in the basement.

London Transport Museum
39 Wellington St., WC2 ☎*379-6344. Map 10F11* 🔲 ✳ *Open daily 10am-6pm. Tube Covent Garden.*

As part of the renovation of *Covent Garden*, the Flower Market (1871-72) now houses a large number of historic public transportation vehicles in its spacious galleries. This 'hands-on' museum chronicles the history of the capital's transportation, with illustrations, photographs, audio visual displays, relics such as tickets and posters, and fine models of everything from the 'wherries' that plied the river to electric streetcars. Children can press a button to operate an Underground elevator, drive a streetcar and a bus, and work the deadman's handle in a Tube train. The vehicles include a replica of the first omnibus of 1829, a development London copied from Paris, two late 19thC, horse-drawn buses, with open-top decks, and early motor buses and streetcars, also with open-tops and painted in the familiar fire-engine red of today. The tube (subway) engines and carriages go back to the 19thC, and there is a simulation of the Circle Line from the driver's eye.

Madame Tussaud's ☆

Marylebone Rd., NW1 ☎935-6861. Map 2D7 🖼 💻 ⚕ *Open Mon-Fri 10am-5.30pm, Sat, Sun 9.30am-5.30pm. Tube Baker Street.*

The redoubtable Madame Tussaud lived to be 89. Having begun her wax modeling in France with the aristocracy and royalty of the *ancien régime*, and having continued to work through the Revolution (the severed heads of king and queen as modeled by Madame can be seen in the museum's Chamber of Horrors), she came to England in 1802 and settled her waxwork museum in London in 1835.

It is now linked to the *Planetarium*. The modern display combines the old and the new: a famous tableau called 'the Sleeping Beauty' has a central figure cast from one of Madame Tussaud's oldest molds, thought to have been made of Madame du Barry, Louis XV's mistress, with a mechanism which simulates breathing. More recent celebrities include Ian Botham, Bob Geldof, Michael Jackson and Mikhail Gorbachov, and there is a new figure of Margaret Thatcher.

Nowhere are the visitors quieter than in the greatest draw of all, the **Chamber of Horrors**, which has among other terrors a reconstruction of the dark streets of Whitechapel where Jack the Ripper stalked.

The Mall ☆

Map 10H10. Tube Charing Cross, Green Park.

Whenever pomp and circumstance are on hand, the Mall is where the crowds gather. Originally laid out by Charles II in 1660-62 as a formal avenue through *St James's Park*, it is now a triumphal processional way leading from *Trafalgar Square* to *Buckingham Palace*. As such, it is largely the work of one man, Sir Aston Webb, between 1900-11.

Majestically lined with plane trees, it slopes gently but impressively down along the side of the park to the Victoria Memorial and Buckingham Palace facade, both also designed by Webb. Looking from Admiralty Arch, the first building on the right is **Carlton House Terrace**, built by John Nash in 1827-29 on the site of his earlier Carlton House, the great palace built for the Regent. Its two massive stucco facades are separated by the Duke of York Steps. The view is best from St James's Park — the balancing ranges, with their Corinthian colonnades, broad terraces at raised ground-floor level, and supporting dumpy Doric columns, are one of London's most exciting architectural views. On the s side of The Mall is the **Admiralty** of 1722-26 with the aggressively concrete Citadel next to it, a bold bombproof structure from World War II.

The rest of The Mall is surrounded by the park, but with the palaces that are scattered along its N side visible on the right. *Marlborough House*, of stone-dressed red brick, is followed by the complex making up *St James's Palace* and then the white stucco of **Clarence House**, built by Nash in 1825-27 for the Duke of Clarence, later William IV, and now the home of the Queen Mother.

Lancaster House follows, in more solemn yellow Bath stone. The **Victoria Memorial** occupies a circus at the end of the avenue, a huge structure covered with elaborate sculpture of high quality in the florid Edwardian style. Queen Victoria's likeness faces up The Mall toward Admiralty Arch, topped by a gilded statue of *Victory*. The circus was laid out in 1900-1901 and the memorial built in 1911.

Mankind, Museum of

6 Burlington Gdns., W1 ☎*437-2224. Map **9**G9* ⊡ *Open Mon-Sat 10am-5pm, Sun 2.30-6pm. Tube Piccadilly Circus, Green Park.*

The museum is the result of the recent upsurge of interest in non-European cultures. Since 1972 the British Museum's ethnographic collections have been based in this elaborate Victorian building, decorated with statues of British philosophers, built in 1866-67 as a part of London University. The sandstone and Portland stone facade looks good since its cleaning. At present, the museum is organized as a series of temporary exhibitions on particular cultures or themes, but they achieve considerable depth of coverage.

The British Museum's ethnographic collection is outstanding in African textiles, pottery, and sculpture, American art from Plains Indians and those of the Northwest Coast, and Pre-Columbian Central and South America. From the Pacific Ocean, the collection is strengthened by objects brought back in the 18thC by Captain Cook. From Indonesia there is the important collection of puppets, masks and other items built up by Sir Stamford Raffles in Java in the 19thC. The entire collection can never be on display at one time, but a permanent exhibition of the museum's greatest treasures is kept in **Rm. 7**, including a life-size skull carved from a solid piece of crystal from Mexico, a hauntingly beautiful object. **Rm. 5** provides an introduction to the collection, and stunning Aztec turquoise mosaics in the forms of a skull-mask and double-headed serpent are displayed in **Rm.1**.

Mansion House

Walbrook, EC4 ☎*626-2500. Map **13**F16* ⊡ ⚑ *Open only to organized groups reserving in advance (minimum age 12); apply in writing to the Assistant Private Secretary* ✗ *Tues-Thurs 11am, 2pm. Tube Bank.*

As if in reference to the ancient city-states, the residence of the Lord Mayor of London, symbol of the independence of *The City*, is Classical in character. It owes its Palladian simplicity to George Dance the Younger who designed it in 1739-53. Its six giant columns support the only decoration, a pediment with sculptures representing the dignity and opulence of The City. The interior, by contrast, is extremely ornate, with a series of state rooms leading back from the portico to the grand climax of the **Egyptian Hall** — Roman in style, despite its name. The annual **Lord Mayor's Show** which arrives here in Nov (see *Calendar of events* in *Planning*) is the climax of a still largely medieval system of government, and during the year you can see here the liverymen, aldermen and sheriffs who choose the Lord Mayor, parading at various antiquated ceremonies. But their power is real — this is the only private residence in the kingdom with its own court and prison cells.

Marble Arch

*Map **8**F7. Tube Marble Arch.*

Now in the center of a major traffic island, the Marble Arch retains only part of the grandeur intended when John Nash built it in 1828 as the entrance to Buckingham Palace. Modeled on the Arch of Constantine in Rome, it was moved to its present site in 1851 when the palace was enlarged by Queen Victoria. Its traffic island was also the site of Tyburn Tree, London's traditional place of execution from the Middle Ages until 1783. A plaque marks the site of the permanent large triangular gallows where regular

hangings, drawings and quarterings attracted large crowds.
Speakers' Corner is close by on the corner of *Hyde Park*.

Marble Hill House 血

Richmond Rd., Twickenham ☎892-5115. Map 20D3 ⊡
Open Mon-Thurs, Sat, Sun 10am-5pm; Nov-Jan 10am-4pm.
Tube Richmond, train to St Margarets from Waterloo.
A house of elegant Palladian regularity, this fine riverside mansion
w of London began life with some 'irregular' occupants: it was
built for George II's mistress, the Countess of Suffolk, in 1723-29,
and then Mrs Fitzherbert, George IV's secret wife, lived here in
the 1790s. Its stuccoed, pristinely white exterior has little
decorative detail — the rear, garden side is particularly impressive
— and it stands in a fine open park.

The interior of the house is quite beautiful, with a series of
lovely rooms culminating in the splendid **Countess of Suffolk's
Bedroom**, with Corinthian columns framing the alcove intended
for the bed. Some attractive furniture has been put back into the
house, together with a number of interesting paintings, including
good copies of Van Dyck portraits. The new **Lazenby Collection**,
displayed on the second floor, includes Chinese paintings on
mirrors, furniture and pottery. Flanking one side of the park is the
exquisite **Montpelier Row**, a perfect terrace of 1720.

Marlborough House 血

*Pall Mall, SW1 ☎839-3411. Map 10H10. Currently closed for
restoration. Tube Green Park, St James's.*
This red-brick house with bold stone dressings, the finest of the
palaces bordering *St James's Park*, was built by Sir Christopher
Wren for the Duke and Duchess of Marlborough in 1709-11,
following the duke's series of victories over the French in the War
of Spanish Succession which also won him Blenheim Palace near
Oxford (see *Excursions*). Various additions were made in the
18th-19thC, notably the attic stories, but Wren's powerful
conception can still be appreciated when viewed from the park.
The entrance on the *Pall Mall* side, however, is curiously
unimpressive. Most of the present decoration dates from the
19thC, but a series of original murals depicts Marlborough's
battles, and the ceiling of the Blenheim Saloon is decorated with
Gentilleschi's series painted for the Queen's House at *Greenwich*
in 1636. The house now serves as the Commonwealth Centre.

Marylebone

Maps 8&9D-F. Tube Baker Street, Great Portland Street.
During the 18thC, the fashionable West End expanded N to
surround the village of St Marylebone (St Mary-le-bourne meaning
St Mary-by-the-brook). The streets form a near-perfect grid, with
the major ones running N-S from *Regent's Park* toward Oxford St.
It now consists largely of smart houses and apartment blocks, with
some busy shopping streets. Although it has several squares and
some good buildings, it is a curiously anonymous area. The first
part to be laid out was Cavendish Sq. in 1714. St Peter's Chapel
nearby in Vere St. was designed in 1721-24 by James Gibbs, and
prefigures *St Martin-in-the-Fields*. The finest houses are **no.20
Portman Square**, designed by Robert Adam in 1775-76, and
Hertford House in Manchester Sq. (the *Wallace Collection*).
Other famous addresses are **Harley Street**, home of top doctors
and clinics, **Baker Street**, of Sherlock Holmes fame, and **Wimpole
Street**, where Robert Browning wooed Elizabeth Barrett. On
Marylebone Rd. are *Madame Tussaud's* and the *Planetarium*.

Mayfair ☆
Map 8&9F-H. Tube Bond Street, Green Park.
The very name is synonymous with wealth and elegance —
nowhere in London will you see more Rolls Royces or more fur
coats. It was not always so. The annual fair which lent its name to
the area was suppressed by George III in 1800, so riotous had it
become. Mayfair today is a roughly square-shaped section of the
West End, bordered by the shopping streets of Oxford St, Regent
St. and Piccadilly, and Park Lane, lined by large 20thC hotels and
the backs of grand 19thC mansions. Inside this area are expensive
shops, luxurious hotels, casinos, and homes of the rich.

The development of this area began in about 1700, and by 1800
it was largely filled with squares and terraces. **Grosvenor Square**
is the largest, without its original houses and with the large United
States Embassy of 1961 at its western end. Of the squares,
Hanover Square is the oldest (about 1715); original houses survive
in **St George's Street** to the s. **Berkeley Square** is best known,
thanks to its mythical nightingale; it has huge plane trees (almost
200yr old) in its fine gardens and attractive 18thC houses surviving
in the sw corner. Only one really grand mansion survives among
the houses: **Crewe House** in Curzon St., begun in 1730. Two
churches date back to the early development of the area: **St
George's, Hanover Square**, in St George's St. (1721-24); notice
the grand portico and bronze hunting dogs standing guard); and
Grosvenor Chapel in South Audley St., a more modest edifice
from about 1730. The Jesuit **Church of the Immaculate
Conception** (1844-49), in the same street, is worth a visit, with a
high altar designed by Pugin.

The shopping streets scattered through Mayfair best preserve its
reputation for high living. Around Bond St. (New and Old) are
found the best art and antique dealers. Savile Row has the world's
finest gentleman's tailors (see *Shopping*). **Shepherd Market** is a
19thC enclave of alleyways lined with smart shops and cafés.

The Monument 🏛 ☆
*Monument St, EC3 ☎626-2717. Map 13G16 ☒ Open
Apr-Sept Mon-Fri 9am-5.40pm, Sat, Sun 2-5.40pm; Oct-Mar
Mon-Sat 9am-3.40pm. Tube Monument.*
Deprived of its commanding appearance by the many modern
buildings that surround it. The Monument, on its little hill close to
the river, nevertheless retains the Baroque drama of its conception.
Designed by Wren and built in 1671, it commemorates the Great
Fire of London which began on Sept 2, 1666 in the bakery in
nearby Pudding Lane. A relief on the base plinth shows Charles II
in Roman dress protecting the citizens of London; the original
inscription unjustly blamed the disaster on a Catholic plot. A giant
Doric column, 202ft (62m) high, contains 311 steps up to a
balcony and a gilded urn. It is a stiff climb but still worth it for the
view.

National Army Museum
*Royal Hospital Rd., SW3 ☎730-0717. Map 16L7 ☒ X for
groups only, by appt through Education Dept ☎ Open
Mon-Sat 10am-5.30pm, Sun 2-5.30pm. Tube Sloane
Square.*
Opened in 1971 in a new building close to the *Royal Hospital,
Chelsea*, the National Army Museum brings together objects
from several older collections. The **Weapons Gallery** is a
self-contained exhibition displaying a comprehensive collection of
small arms used by the British Army from the 17thC to the present

day; the use of both edged weapons and handguns, from muskets to self-loading rifles, is expertly explained. '**The Story of the Army**' is divided into two galleries: the first takes the visitor through army history up to the outbreak of World War I, with maps and models of campaigns, uniforms, weapons and other mementos. The second tells the story from 1914 to the Falklands War, using life-size displays, audiovisuals and dioramas. There is also an impressive **uniform gallery**, a picture gallery and a reading room.

National Gallery ★

Trafalgar Sq., WC2 ☎839-3321. *Map* **10**G11 ▣ ☜ *K* ▬
Open Mon-Sat 10am-6pm, Sun 2-6pm; July-Sept Wed 10am-8pm. Tube Charing Cross.

Enlarged with its northern extension in 1975 and now possessing over 2,000 pictures, the National Gallery is one of the world's finest collections of art. Few rivals can boast such a comprehensive account of Western art, and the way the paintings are shown provides a model for other great national collections: they are clean, clearly labeled, well-lighted and given adequate space.

This freshness of approach accords with the National Gallery's relative youth. When most European capital cities already had public collections, in 1823, the threat of the sale of John Julius Angerstein's great collection to William of Orange forced a tight-fisted parliament to produce the money to found a national collection. Angerstein's pictures were bought for £57,000 and housed with other bequests in Angerstein's house in Pall Mall. By 1832, with the collection growing, a larger building was needed. It was designed by William Wilkins and completed in 1838, stretching the full length of the N side of *Trafalgar Square*, but was never the imposing building intended, and has frequently been expanded since. The northern extension is superbly functional, with excellent hanging space making it possible to put on temporary exhibitions and, after much controversy over the choice of architect, the foundation stone for Robert Venturi's Sainsbury wing, an extension to the w of the gallery, was laid in Mar 1988 and is due to open in 1991. The extention will provide new galleries to house the Early Renaissance collection and for temporary exhibitions, as well as a lecture theater, movie theater and numerous other facilities.

The collection of pictures has expanded steadily, with its character changing in accordance with the taste of the different periods of acquisition. After some exploratory Italian forays in the 1840s, the pioneering director, Sir Charles Eastlake, purchased many early Italian works from 1855-65, a time when these pictures were little known. As a result the gallery has a collection of Italian art unequaled outside Italy. In 1861, Queen Victoria gave 20 German and Flemish pictures in memory of her husband Albert; this inspired a new round of acquisitions, resulting in a magnificent group of Dutch and Flemish works. In the 20thC attempts have been made to strengthen the French collection.

British art is the specialty of the *Tate Gallery*, as is modern art, but the National Gallery does have some fine 18thC British masterpieces. There are also outstanding Spanish works.

Since 1946, the National Gallery has had a conservation department and it has been in the forefront in applying science to the care and restoration of paintings. As a result, a high proportion of National Gallery paintings can be seen in the most beautiful condition, cleaned of dirt or past overpainting. Temporary exhibitions, usually in the **Sunley Rm.**, bring in pictures on loan to

National Gallery   Entrance   Trafalgar Square

develop particular themes. Paintings usually on display in **Rms. 1-5** and **11-13**, but moved temporaily to Gallery A on the Lower Floor, should be returned by mid-1989.

The turning to the left from the main entrance leads into the early Italian section. In **Rm. 1** is the *Wilton Diptych* ✩ which is actually not Italian but was put here because of its early date (c. 1395). Probably French, it shows the English monarch Richard II being presented to the Virgin and Child, with saints and angels in attendance. The other glowing medieval icons are further testimony to faith as well as artistic genius; Duccio's **Maestà altar-piece panels** ★ from Sienna Cathedral are outstanding. **Rms. 2-6** show the transition to a more realistic style. In **Rms. 2-6**, Lorenzo Monaco's *Coronation of the Virgin* is in the graceful International Gothic style, while Masaccio's innovative *Virgin and Child* ★ (**Rm. 4**) has the spiritual gravity and solid forms of the Renaissance, thrown into relief by Paolo Uccello's *Battle of San Romano* (**Rm. 2**), with its unsuccessful attempt at realistic perspective. The Renaissance can also be seen emerging in Botticelli's early *Adoration of the Magi* and his *Venus and Mars* ✩ (both **Rm. 5**), admired for the purity of its line, and in Piero della Francesca's *Baptism of Christ* (**Rm. 4**). In **Rm. 7**, Leonardo's famous and beautiful black-chalk *Cartoon* ★ has been restored after it was damaged by gunfire in 1987.

In **Rms. 8-14**, the superb collection of Italian Renaissance art unfolds. Among too many highlights to list are: Michelangelo's unfinished *Entombment*, a rare easel picture; Raphael's *Pope Julius* ★ which was only recently discovered to be the original among several versions around the world; Correggio's charming *Mercury instructing Cupid before Venus* ✩ ; Leonardo's mysterious *Virgin of the Rocks* ★ and Bronzino's *Allegory*, with its chilly eroticism and obscure subject. One of the original pictures bought from the Angerstein collection is Sebastiano del Piombo's huge *Raising of Lazarus*, for which the artist received guidance from Michelangelo. Of the Venetian works in **Rm. 9**, Titian's breathtaking *Bacchus and Ariadne* ★ is ablaze with color and movement. Other important Venetian works include Tintoretto's dramatic *Origin of the Milky Way* and Veronese's *Family of Darius* *before Alexander.* All the greatest masters of the period are here.

The Renaissance was not such an Italian monopoly as is sometimes supposed. The carefully observed naturalism of Northern painters greatly influenced their Italian counterparts; the Dutch and Flemish collection in **Rms. 15-28** illustrates this better than anywhere else in the world. The most famous work here is Jan Van Eyck's *Arnolfini Marriage* ★ (**Rm. 24**), full of realistic but symbolic detail. In the same room is a beautiful jewel-like altarpiece by Memlinc showing the *Virgin and Child with Saints and Donors* and a recent acquisition, *The Virgin and Child in an Interior,* a tiny but fine panel painting by Robert Campin. As a reminder of the range of the northern painters, look out for a wonderfully grotesque *Adoration of the Kings* by Bruegel, and a weird rocky *Landscape with St Jerome* by Patenier (both **Rm. 25**). The German and Early Netherlandish pictures are less numerous, but include some important masterpieces in **Rm. 23** such as Dürer's **portrait of his father**, the exquisite little Altdorfer *Landscape with a Footbridge* and Cranach's *Charity,* a charming early nude. In **Rm. 25** is Holbein's *Ambassadors* ☆ which was probably the most important picture painted in England in the Tudor period; as a reminder of frailty the oblique shape in the bottom left corner shows itself to be a skull when viewed for the right angle.

The Dutch 17thC, the golden age of painting in the Netherlands, is strongly represented: there are several Rembrandts, including the extraordinary *Self-portrait* ★ of 1640, with its sad dignity, and the quietly powerful *Woman Bathing* (both **Rm. 26**). There are two Vermeers, of which the *Woman Standing at a Virginal* ☆ (**Rm. 28**) best demonstrates the sense of intimate silence that the artist generates. There are many fine landscapes, of which the most famous is the *Avenue at Middelharnis* ☆ (**Rm. 27**) by Hobbema, and also scenes of everyday life, with the restrained, precise style of the Dutch school.

The art of the 17thC in Flanders (**Rms. 20-22**) was altogether grander, dominated by Rubens and Van Dyck. Major works by both can be seen, including Van Dyck's *Equestrian Portrait of Charles I* (**Rm. 21**); in **Rm. 20** Rubens' joyous, colorful *Judgment of Paris* contrasts with the dignity of his landscape *Château de Steen* ☆ (**Rm. 22**).

Rms. 29 and 34 are occupied by 17th-18thC Italian works. Caravaggio's *Supper at Emmaus* ★ (**Rm. 29**) shows the artist's revolutionary use of naturalism in religious art: the disciples are seen as real working people with coarse clothes; look at the drama even in the hands. A popular acquisition, found on the ceiling of a London house, is Tiepolo's *Allegory with Venus and Time* (**Rm. 34**), full of light and air.

French painting of the 17th-18thC (**Rms. 32 and 33**) is shown with emphasis on Poussin and Claude, both of whom have been assiduously collected in Britain. Poussin's *Bacchanalian Revel* demonstrates his influential cool Classicism. Claude's mysterious and peaceful landscapes are altogether more approachable; the *Enchanted Castle* ☆ has an astonishing, dreamlike quality, achieved largely by superb mastery of light. The French 18thC is poorly represented by National Gallery standards; even so it offers Watteau's *La Gamme d'Amour,* Chardin's acute *Young Schoolmistress* ☆ and Boucher's *Landscape with a Watermill.*

The gallery's strongest English period is the 18th-19thC (**Rms. 35-39**). Outstanding works include Hogarth's satirical *Marriage à la Mode* paintings, the basis for the more famous series of engravings, and magnificent examples of that period's two best

National Portrait Gallery

genres, Gainsborough's portrait of *Mr and Mrs Andrews* ★ and
Constable's landscape *The Hay Wain* ★ Turner opens new vistas
with this magical *Rain, Steam and Speed* ★ and *The Fighting
Téméraire*.

In **Rms. 41 and 42** are a small number of Spanish pictures of
extraordinary quality. El Greco's *Christ driving the Traders from the
Temple* (about 1600) is the finest of several paintings by this
remarkable artist. From the later 17thC there is Velázquez's
sensual tour-de-force, *The Rokeby Venus* ★ and a portrait of
Philip IV, together with Zurbarán's *St Francis*, showing the dark
religious passion so characteristic of Spanish art. There are also
several good Goyas, including the famous portrait of the *Duke of
Wellington*.

Rms. 40 and 43-46 now house the gallery's acquisitions charting
the emergence of modern art. An impressive collection of
Impressionist works include Renoir's *Les Parapluies* ★
(periodically moved to Dublin) and Monet's stunning
Water-lilies ☆ as well as Degas' *Beach Scene*. Van Gogh's intense,
dynamic *Sunflowers* introduces a Post-Impressionist collection
which also includes Seurat's *Bathers, Asnières* ★ , works by
Gauguin and Klimt's *Hermina Gallia*.

National Portrait Gallery ☆

*2 St Martin's Pl., WC2 ☎930-1552. Map **10G11** 📷 🚻 with
flash. Open Mon-Fri 10am-5pm, Sat 10am-6pm, Sun 2-6pm.
Tube Charing Cross.*

Opened in 1859 as a kind of 'national pantheon,' the emphasis was
placed from the start on the subjects of the pictures rather than on
artists or on art for art's sake. Nevertheless, the effort to obtain the
best portraits has meant that the collection has acquired many fine
paintings and drawings. Since 1968, photographs have been
systematically included and caricatures are now also accepted. In
fact, the emphasis on history gives great coherence to the
exhibition, which is arranged chronologically with relevant
background material, such as a pictorial essay on the Industrial
Revolution. The excellent **temporary exhibitions** (🖼) also
expand on themes or figures from the starting point of the
portraits.

The present buildings were constructed next to the *National
Gallery* in 1896 and extended in the 1930s. The collection begins
at the top (several flights of stairs have to be climbed), with a room
devoted to medieval portraits. Portraits in a modern sense were not
produced in the Middle Ages, so the images are few in number; a
copy of the fine representation of *Richard II* in Westminster Abbey
dominates. Portraits became common from the Tudor period and
perhaps the most interesting examples in the whole collection
come from this early section. There is an excellent version of *Henry
VII* by Michel Sittow of 1505, painted for the Holy Roman
Emperor when Henry was seeking his daughter's hand in
marriage. Perhaps the finest work of all is Holbein's magnificent
cartoon for a lost fresco at Whitehall Palace showing *Henry VIII
with his father Henry VII* ☆ There is an exquisite full-length image
of *Lady Jane Grey*, who was executed in 1554 after she had become
queen at the age of 17. Several portraits of Elizabeth I are in the
incredibly detailed style of the period, with the queen decked out
in rich clothes and incrusted with jewelry. A portrait of *William
Shakespeare*, dated about 1610, is the only one with any real claim
to authenticity.

The gallery continues through the Jacobean and Stuart periods,
with the increasing formality of the court painters, giving way to

the more lively images of the 18thC. Figures from the arts and sciences increase gradually in proportion to the political and military leaders. This was another golden age of English portraiture; look for Hogarth's *Self-portrait*, several works by Gainsborough and Reynolds, and pictures of *Dr. Johnson and Charles James Fox*. A fine unfinished portrait of *Nelson* by Sir William Beechey and a romantic one of *Byron* in Greek costume show the greater concentration on the individual that becomes apparent in much of the 19thC work. Royalty, however, is still shown in highly idealized fashion: *Victoria and Albert* sculpted in the costume of ancient Saxons is the most amusing example.

The portraits from the last years of the 19thC and later are varied in style. There are superb studies of *Edith Sitwell* by Wyndham Lewis, and some fine bronze busts by Epstein. Royalty, however, is still idealized with deference.

National Theatre 🏛

Upper Ground, South Bank, SE1 ☎*633-0880. Map 11G12* ⊡
Ɩ up to 5 times a day 🎭 *Tube Waterloo.*

It is a blessing that the institutionalization of the theater in London has not led to a stultifying subservience to the establishment. The drama remains as true to its nature of subversiveness as when it was banished to the South Bank in the Middle Ages, and this latest addition to the *South Bank Arts Centre* created its own furore. The building itself, designed by Sir Denys Lasdun in 1970-75, is a prime example of the Brutal style, a lumpy abstract sculpture in concrete. The interior, however, is much more universally admired, with a superb intersection of horizontal and vertical planes creating a honeycomb of useful and interesting space.

See *Theaters* in *Nightlife*.

Natural History Museum 🏛 ★

Cromwell Rd., SW7 ☎*938-9123. Map 15J5* ⊡ 🎭 ✳ *Open Mon-Sat 10am-6pm, Sun 1-6pm. Tube South Kensington.*

When the *British Museum* was formed from Sir Hans Sloane's collections in 1753, a high proportion of material consisted of plant, animal and geological specimens. Appropriately, these categories grew at enormous speed (they still do, at the rate of 300,000 items each year), and in 1860 it was decided to split off the natural history collections. Between 1873-80 the present building was erected in South Kensington with Alfred Waterhouse as architect. His creation is a cathedral to nature, a vast Romanesque construction with a central porch opening onto a great iron-roofed nave. Unlike a cathedral, however, it has two immensely long side wings creating an impressive facade along the Cromwell Rd. Once criticized as austere and heavy, cleaning has revealed the bright colors of the cream and blue terra-cotta tiling, and the countless relief details that cover the exterior — a fitting showcase for the treasures housed within.

In the 1970s, a new policy was adopted by which the museum shows a series of self-contained exhibitions, rather than attempting to show all of its millions of specimens in old-fashioned cabinets. At the main entrance, however, parts of an older, dramatic display have survived: the giant Central Hall, with huge dinosaur skeletons towering over the visitor. There they stand, absurd and terrifying, the center of an exhibition about their evolution and disappearance. The left side of the hall is given over to an exhibition explaining the theory of evolution. Also on the ground floor is an exhibition of British birds arranged by habitat, and an exceptionally lively presentation on every aspect of human biology.

Look for the display on British insects, and the **Whale Hall**. This is one of the museum's most effective sections, although unmodernized, containing the vast skeletons and jawbones of the great mammals and a life-size model of a blue whale.

A monumental staircase leads from the Central Hall to the upper floor, where an exhibition traces a controversial subject: the evolution of man. Another, on the origin of the species, covers Darwin's work with admirable thoroughness. The traditional hall, devoted to minerals, rocks and gems, serves as an effective contrast to the newer exhibition techniques, and is notable for the incredible diversity and beauty of its specimens.

Old Bailey *(Central Criminal Court)*
Old Bailey, EC4 ☎248-3277. Map 12F14 ⊡ ✗ ▣ Open Mon-Fri 10.30am-1pm, 2-4pm. Tube St Paul's.

The Old Bailey's famous gilt figure of *Justice*, complete with scales and sword, looks down on a site with a grim history. The Central Criminal Court replaced Newgate Gaol, dating from the Middle Ages, for many years a place of execution and eventually the 19thC reformers' ultimate symbol of penal squalor. The current Portland stone building dates from 1900-07. Inside its heavy Baroque frame justice can be seen to be done from the public galleries, but you will have to line up early when a major criminal case is being heard — the crowds of the Newgate gallows have their modern counterparts.

Orleans House Gallery ▥
Orleans Rd., Twickenham ☎892-0221. Map 20D3 ▧ ✗ Open Apr-Sept Tues-Sat 1pm-5.30pm; Sun 2-5.30pm; Oct-Mar Tues-Sat 1-4.30pm, Sun 2-4.30pm; Bank Hol Mon 2-5.30pm. Tube Richmond, train to St Margaret's from Waterloo.

Although it takes its name from the Duc d'Orléans, later King Louis Philippe of France, who lived here in the early 19thC, this house in Twickenham, near *Strawberry Hill*, dates from 1710. Regrettably, much of it was demolished in the 1920s, but the superb **Octagon** survives amid attractive woodland. It was designed by James Gibbs in 1720. The interior is richly decorated with Baroque stucco work: heads of George II and Queen Caroline can be seen on medallions. The Octagon is now a gallery, and a few fine early English landscape paintings are on show, although the building is generally used for temporary exhibitions. Nearby is *Marble Hill House*, and the grander *Ham House*, which can be reached by ferry.

Osterley Park ▥ ☆
Isleworth, Middlesex ☎560-3918. Map 20C3 ▨ ▣ in summer. Open Tues-Sun 11am-5pm. Tube Osterley.

Already one of the finest country houses in the London area, Osterley gained even more prestige after being completely refurbished between 1761-82 by the great Scottish architect Robert Adam for the banker Francis Child, who was trying to emulate the other country houses nearby, such as *Syon House*. It still contains much of the furniture he designed for it, and is set in a large area of parkland, with lakes and woods, and an attractive brick stable block to one side, which probably contains the buildings of the medieval manor house which originally stood on the site.

Adam's building is a large hollow square, with corner turrets and a great portico that opens to the central courtyard. This unusual scheme for the 18thC was dictated by the existing house, built on a magnificent scale by Sir Thomas Gresham (the wealthy merchant who founded the Royal Exchange) in the 1570s. By Adam's time it had fallen into decay, and he completed the covering of the exterior with an entirely new skin of brick, and built the portico.

At the end of the courtyard the main door leads into the hall, the centerpiece to the whole design, beautifully decorated in Adam's Classical style, with white stucco reliefs on a gray background. At either end, copies of ancient Roman statues inhabit niches within apses. Note how the ceiling decoration is echoed in the marble floor pattern. Beyond the hall is the great **gallery**, a plainer room probably designed a few years earlier by Sir William Chambers. The remaining rooms open to the public are by Adam, who even designed the door handles and friezes. The **Drawing Room** has a ceiling of extraordinary richness and contains fine original commodes. The **Tapestry Room** is hung with works from the French royal Gobelins workshop, in extravagant pink with Rococo designs from paintings by Boucher. The **State Bedchamber** has an absurdly elaborate four-poster bed. Plainer, but just as effective, is the **Etruscan Dressing Room**, with delicately painted walls.

Pall Mall
Map 10H10. Tube Charing Cross, Green Park.
When *St James's Palace* became the main royal residence in the 17thC, this avenue quickly became established as its main route into London and the site for the favorite Stuart game of palle-maille, resembling modern croquet. The street is now the most important in *St James's*, famous for the traditional gentlemen's clubs that line its s side, a sequence of stern Classical buildings reflecting the importance of tradition in this most conservative of areas.

From the *Trafalgar Square* end, Pall Mall becomes interesting beyond the soaring glass slab of **New Zealand House** (1957-63). This is at the bottom end of John Nash's great city planning scheme of the early 19thC that stretched up Regent St. and incorporated *Regent's Park*. Just past New Zealand House will be found the delightful little **Opera House Arcade**, built by Nash in 1816-18 and the first in London; note the splendid wrought-iron lamps. At Waterloo Pl. the **Duke of York's Column**, built by Benjamin Wyatt in 1831-34, can be seen in front of the steps of **Carlton House Terrace**.

Back on Pall Mall, the gentlemen's clubs begin. These uniquely English and very exclusive institutions, designed to provide the gentleman with a 'country house' haven to which he can retire in the city, thrive unchanged, still offering, in various mixes, snoozing, business talk and witty conversation, and hallowed peace. The corners with Waterloo Pl. are occupied by the impressive **United Services Club**, designed in 1827 by Nash (now the Institute of Directors), and the **Athenaeum** of 1828-30, traditionally the clergy and academics' club. Farther along in a dignified terrace come the **Travellers' Club** (1829-32), a Victorian version of Italian Renaissance for those who have been more than 1,000 miles from London; the **Reform Club** (1837-41), a Liberal political grouping formed after the 1832 Reform Act; and then more modern buildings, including the **Royal Automobile Club** of 1908-11. Beyond comes **Schomberg House**, built in 1698, a tall brick structure with projecting wings. Other clubs are the **Army and Navy** on the N side, jokingly known as 'The Rag' after the toughness of its meat; the **Oxford and Cambridge** on the s; and the **Junior Carlton**, a stepping-stone for the famous singer Tory

(Conservative) club. Pall Mall ends with the lower, brick buildings of *St James's Palace*, past the entrance to *Marlborough House*.

Parliament, Houses of   See *Westminster, Palace of*.

The Percival David Foundation of Chinese Art
53 Gordon Sq., WC1 ☎*387-3909. Map 4D10* 🔲 📷 *with flash. Open Mon-Fri 10.30am-5pm. Tube Euston.*

Gathered with scholarly precision by Sir Percival David and given by him to the University in 1951, this remarkably rich collection of Chinese ceramics of the 10th-19thC is aptly sited in *Bloomsbury*, surrounded by intellectual and artistic endeavor. Unfortunately, the presentation of the collection is rather too scholarly, and the great numbers of bowls, jars, vases and figurines grouped in display cabinets by classification tend to cancel each other out by their profusion. But the individual items are of great beauty, glazed in rich and subtle colors.

Piccadilly
Map 9G-H. Tube Piccadilly Circus, Green Park.

As the famous 'hub of Empire', **Piccadilly Circus** has of late put on a pretty poor show, with a motley collection of buildings covered in illuminated signs. But recently the **Trocadero** center, with its shops, restaurants and exhibitions, has brought a new sense of life, helped by the Criterion brasserie (Victorian mosaics and tiles, next to the charming Criterion theater), and the London Pavilion, a shopping complex which includes a rock and pop outpost of Madame Tussaud's. The focus of the Circus is the *Shaftesbury Monument*, a statue and fountain of *Eros* (1893) around which international youth likes to gather while temporarily dropping out. Recently restored, it is now the center of a pedestrian mall, no longer marooned on its central island. Piccadilly itself, stretching w to Hyde Park Corner, is lined with imposing commercial buildings. Some of the stores are justifiably famous: **Hatchard's** for books, **Simpson's** for clothes and **Fortnum and Mason** for anything expensive (see *Shopping*). In addition, there are arcades of smart little shops, with the Piccadilly Arcade of 1909-10 to the s and the most attractive Burlington Arcade of 1815-19 to the N. Wren's *St James's*, the **Ritz** (see *Hotels*) and Green Park are of greatest interest on the s side; Burlington House (the *Royal Academy*) on the N. By Hyde Park Corner is *Apsley House*.

Planetarium
Marylebone Rd., NW1 ☎*486-1121. Map 2D7* 🎫 𝑋 📷 *'Starshows' every 40min 11am-4.30pm. Tube Baker Street.*

Attached to *Madame Tussaud's*, the Planetarium's greater green copper dome is a striking landmark, providing convincing displays and 'starshows' on astronomy. The auditorium inside the great dome is at the top of a long ramp through the Astronomers' Gallery, past imaginative displays on the great astronomers. But the highlight for all visitors is the moment they tip back their seats and gaze at the heavens projected on the dome above them.

Post Office Tower ⅢⅢ
Cleveland St., W1. Map 9E9. Not open to the public. Tube Great Portland Street.

Renamed **British Telecom Tower**, but still faithfully known as the Post Office Tower, this 619ft (189m) landmark has a purpose beyond display, having been erected in 1964 to achieve effective

TV and radio telephone broadcasting above surrounding buildings. The architecture is pleasantly familiar to Londoners, neither inspired nor pretentious, with a jumble of transmitters and radio masts above an elongated cylinder.

Public Records Office Museum 🏛

Chancery Lane, WC2 ☎876-3444. Open Mon-Fri 10am-5pm. Map 11F13. Tube Chancery Lane.

Most of the public records are now kept at Kew, but in this successful example of Victorian Gothic official architecture one room and a corridor are given over to a museum, unimaginative in its presentation but boasting some remarkable treasures. Outstanding are the two volumes of the **Domesday Book**, the great survey of England carried out for William the Conqueror in 1086. Among later documents are a copy of the Magna Carta, Guy Fawkes' confession to participation in the Gunpowder Plot, and William Shakespeare's will. There is an extensive display of royal seals, with their elaborate designs showing the image of the king, a knight in armor or suchlike. Several monuments from the Rolls Chapel, which once stood here, include an example of early Renaissance sculpture by Pietro Torrigiano, with the recumbent figure of *John Young*, a Master of the Rolls (d. 1519), in a Classical architectural surround. There are also fine medieval and later strong-boxes.

Regent's Park ☆

Maps 2&3A-D. Tube Regent's Park, Baker Street.

Regency London was certainly sophisticated; and the legacy is one of the most impressive examples of town planning in the country. Marylebone Fields, a hunting preserve of Henry VIII's, reverted to the crown in 1809, and the Prince Regent's friend, John Nash, was put in charge of an ambitious scheme that would link it with Carlton House to the s via the new Regent St. Carlton House has gone but the park retains much of the original plan. It is approached from Portland Pl., leading into the elegant terraces of **Park Crescent** and **Park Square**, built from 1812-23. To E and w around the flanks of the park stretch magnificent Classical terraces, mostly built in the 1820s. To the w the amazing length of **York Terrace** and, best of all, the imaginative, almost Oriental-looking **Sussex Place** with its octagonal domes. The dome motif is repeated in copper on the brand new **Mosque** nearby. On the E side of the park, **Chester Terrace** and **Cumberland Terrace** are ostentatiously grand, with vast decorated porticos.

The park itself is attractively landscaped, with a massive straight **Broad Walk** continuing the line of Portland Pl. through the center. Two circular roads (the Inner and Outer Circles) carry road traffic; on the Inner Circle, **St John's Lodge** incorporates parts of a villa of about 1818. Here too is the marvelous **open-air theater** where superb productions of Shakespeare's plays can be enjoyed in summer months (see *Nightlife*). There is a small lake in **Queen Mary's Gardens** within the Inner Circle, and a larger one with islands to the w. Across the N side is a branch of the *Grand Union Canal*, picturesquely incorporated as part of Nash's plan, and the *Zoo*.

Registry of Births, Deaths and Marriages

St Catherine's House, 10 Kingsway, WC2 ☎242-0262. Map 11F12 ⓘ 🖈 Open Mon-Fri 8.30am-4.30pm. Tube Aldwych, Temple.

With perseverance and a little money, it is possible to trace ancestry in England or Wales back to 1837, the date centralized registration of births, deaths and marriages began. To go further back, local records have to be consulted. The system is not difficult but it is time-consuming, a factor which seems to discourage few people, for the offices are always busy. Simply look up the reference for yourself or an ancestor born in England or Wales (listed alphabetically by year) and order the birth certificates, which takes about two days. This will usually give the names, addresses and occupations of the parents. By searching for their marriage certificate or birth certificates it is possible to repeat the process back into history.

Richmond ☆
Map 20D3. Tube Richmond.

The Palace of Sheen was first occupied by Henry I in 1125, beginning an important royal connection which gave impetus to the growth of this still beautiful Thames-side town. The name came later; after a fire in 1499, Sheen was rebuilt as Richmond Palace by Henry VII, the title coming from his former title as Earl of Richmond (in Yorkshire). Henry died in the palace, as did Elizabeth I in 1603. Charles I was the last king to live there, moving his court during a 1634 plague; in due course it then fell into decay.

Of the great Tudor palace, the most magnificent before the building of Wolsey's nearby *Hampton Court*, very little remains. What there is can be seen on the western side of **Richmond Green**. A Tudor gatehouse marks the position, but within are private houses of later date which, in some cases, incorporate portions of the old brickwork — the fine early 18thC pedimented facade of **Trumpeters' House** predominates. Richmond Green itself boasts exceptional 18th-19thC houses on all four sides — most notable is **Maids of Honour Row** of about 1724, built for the companions of Caroline, wife of the future George II, who then lived at Richmond Lodge in Old Deer Park in *Kew* to the N. Richmond Theatre, built in 1899, lies across the green to the W. Old Palace Lane leads down to the river, where the attractive ocher **Asgill House**, a mansion of the 1760s, can be seen on the left.

Richmond's busy and crowded shopping center, with its infuriating traffic tangle, contains some 17thC almshouses in The Vineyard near an interesting church with a 16thC tower, St Matthias, and, up Hill Rise, the fine Queen Anne houses of Ormond Rd. To the S of the noble 18thC bridge rises **Richmond Hill**, offering one of London's most remarkable views. The preservation of this unspoiled vista over *Marble Hill House* and *Ham House* across the wooded expanse of the Thames Valley is a rare and triumphant planning success. It has been painted by several of Britain's greatest artists, such as Reynolds, Turner and Constable. Some good 18thC houses can be seen at the top of the hill, including **Wick House**, built for Reynolds by Sir William Chambers in 1772.

A gate into **Richmond Park** of 1700 is thought to have been erected by Capability Brown. The park is the most telling reminder of Richmond's royal connection; with over 2,000 acres (814ha) first enclosed by Charles I and still a royal park, it is the most natural stretch of green land in London. Its rough heath and woodland contain a great variety of native plants, birds and animals, even protected herds of red and fallow deer. The highest points offer excellent views NE across London. The several private houses in the park include **White Lodge**, built for George II in 1727-29, now the Royal Ballet School, and **Pembroke Lodge** of about 1800, now a restaurant.

Royal Academy of Arts 🏛

Burlington House, Piccadilly, W1 ☎*439-7438. Map 9G9* ■■
🎨 ▣ *Open daily 10am-6pm. Tube Piccadilly Circus, Green
Park.*

First built as a mansion for the first Earl of Burlington in the newly
developed Piccadilly area in about 1665, Burlington House was
remodeled in 1717-20 in the elegant Palladian style. The third earl
made this as celebrated a forum for the artists whose patron he
became as his *Chiswick House*; Pope, Arbuthnot, Gay, all often
attended. Unfortunately, between 1868-74 the profile of the
Georgian house was obliterated by the rebuilding that marked its
adoption by the Royal Academy of Arts. This new building is in
the Victorian Renaissance style, with a screen along *Piccadilly*
opening on to a forecourt with a statue of *Sir Joshua Reynolds* in
the center. Other learned societies occupy the buildings to the
right and left.

The Royal Academy was founded in 1768 with Reynolds as its
first and greatest president to foster the arts of Britain. Except for a
few decades after its foundation, however, the most interesting
developments in British art have consistently taken place outside
of, and even in opposition to, the dictates of the Royal Academy.
This is still true: the Academy's free-for-all **Summer Exhibition**
(see *Calendar of events* in *Planning*) may be popular and enjoyable,
but no one would claim that it does much to influence
developments in art. The modern academy consists of 40
academicians and 30 associates, the country's most successful
establishment artists. Today a most important function is as a
home for major temporary exhibitions.

The academy has an important collection of works of art,
including much by past academicians: Reynolds, Gainsborough,
Constable and others (not on public display except during
exhibitions in the private rooms, otherwise by appointment). The
decorative schemes of its grand interior include paintings by artists
such as Benjamin West and Angelica Kauffmann (the entrance
hall), and Marco Ricci. The academy's outstanding treasure is
Michelangelo's beautiful relief tondo depicting the **Madonna and
Child ★**

Royal Air Force Museum, Hendon

Grahame Park Way, NW9 ☎*205-2266. Map 21B4* ▣ ▣ *Open
Mon-Sat 10am-6pm, Sun 2pm-6pm. Tube Colindale.*
The northern suburb of Hendon itself lays claim to the interest of
aircraft enthusiasts: there was a pioneering flying school here
before World War I, and it became one of the first aerodromes,
staging regular air displays and becoming famous as the starting
point for the first nonstop London-to-Paris flight in 1911. The
museum was opened in 1972 in an excellent modern building
which incorporates two historic World War I wooden hangars.
Interesting displays trace the history of flight and show the
development of the Royal Air Force, with its vital role in two
world wars.

However, it is the aircraft themselves that take pride of place.
They range from the Blériot XI, similar to that in which Louis
Blériot made the first cross-channel flight in 1909, to the English
Electrical Lightning which travels at twice the speed of sound.

Famous World War I aircraft include a Sopwith Camel from
Britain, a Caudron G3 of French design and a Hanriot HD1,
which was used extensively by the Belgian Aviation Militaire and
was presented to the Museum by Mr Marvin K. Hand of San
Francisco.

From World War II there is the oldest surviving Spitfire Mk1 which fought in the Battle of Britain, a Beaufighter and the only known Typhoon left in the world. More modern jet aircraft include the early Vampire and Gloster Meteor and the remarkable Canberra.

The splendid **Battle of Britain Museum** 🖼 nearby contains a unique collection of British, German and Italian aircraft which were engaged in the great air battle of 1940. Also in the same complex is the vast new **Bomber Command Museum** 🖼 which contains a striking display of famous bomber aircraft including the Lancaster, Wellington, Mosquito and Vulcan.

Royal Britain
Aldersgate St., EC2 ☎*588-0588. Map 12E15* 🖼 💷 ✶ *Open daily 9am-5.30pm. Tube Barbican.*
Covering 35,000sq.ft (3,250sq.m) and 1,000 years of history, Royal Britain opened in Aug 1988 and is designed to make visitors feel as though they are seeing, hearing and experiencing history first-hand. The exhibition boasts 23 'feature environments,' which combine visual displays, special and sound effects to bring historical events to life. You can listen to the noise of battle as Boadicea makes her heroic stand against the Romans; witness Edgar's coronation as the first King of England in 973AD; eavesdrop on Richard the Lion Heart as he prays in his tent during the Crusades; and take Mary Queen of Scot's final tragic walk down a corridor in Fotheringay Castle to her execution. Then, stepping into the present, you can experience the life led by members of the Royal Family today, shaking hands and receiving posies, amid the bevy of flash photographers.

Royal Courts of Justice 🏛
Strand, WC2 ☎*936-6000. Map 11F13* 🖼 ✿ 💷 *Open Mon-Fri 10am-4.30pm; entry depends upon use of courts. Tube Temple, Chancery Lane.*
Better known as the Law Courts, this extravagant complex in the *Strand*, built by G.E. Street in 1874-82, houses the courts where important civil, as opposed to criminal, law cases are heard. The buildings are now admired by many, after having long been despised as an example of Victorian plagiarism — for they are in Early English Gothic style. Cleaning has helped, for the rich colors and intricate patterns in the stone can be appreciated. In addition, the Courts show a dignity suited to their purpose, and their complex irregularity and inventive detail feast the eye. Inside, the sheer scale of the **great hall** is quite as impressive as the exterior.

Royal Hospital, Chelsea 🏛 ☆
Royal Hospital Rd., SW3 ☎*730-0161. Map 16L7* 🖼 *indoors. Grounds open 10am-8pm, Sun 2-8pm; chapel and dining hall Mon-Sat 10am-12pm, 2-4pm, Sun 2-4pm. Tube Sloane Square.*
Amply surrounded by parkland and retaining all the dignity of its riverside setting, Wren's stately Royal Hospital from 1682-92 is still a majestic sanctuary of calm, although now surrounded by *Chelsea*. It was founded by Charles II in 1682 as a refuge for aged and disabled soldiers on the model of Louis XIV's Les Invalides in Paris. It now houses some 400 pensioners, including a dwindling number of World War I veterans, who can be seen around and about Chelsea in their old-fashioned uniforms, red in summer and blue in winter; and in May it stages the **Chelsea Flower Show** (see *Calendar of events* in *Planning*).

The best view is from the s, where an open courtyard looks down the extensive gardens towards the river. At the center of the courtyard is a statue of *Charles II* as a Roman emperor by Grinling Gibbons, Wren's master carver. The hospital is entirely symmetrical and quite plain, its red-brick facades embellished with minimal stonework. At the center of each block a tall white portico of four columns or pilasters, and the central block is capped by a graceful, spire-like lantern.

The severely domed **vestibule**, lighted by the lantern above, is entered through the portico in the courtyard. To the right is the **chapel**, little altered since Wren's time. It has a fine carved reredos in dark wood, matching the organ gallery at the entrance end and, in the apse, a painting (about 1710-15) by Sebastiano Ricci, *Christ in Majesty*, a colorful burst of Baroque splendor. The **Great Hall** occupies the corresponding space to the chapel on the other side of the vestibule. It is more solemn, with paneled walls and military standards hanging from the ceiling. At the far end, there is a dark and ponderous painting by Verrio showing *Charles II* with mythological companions in front of the hospital buildings. A small museum in one of the eastern wings covers the hospital's history.

St Bartholomew-the-Great 🏛 † ★
Little Britain, EC1. Map 12E14. Tube Barbican.

The churchyard through the 15thC gateway with the charming Tudor house on top used to be the nave of this, one of the oldest churches in London. Now only the chancel and transepts remain with their 19thC refacing of flint and Portland stone. The church belonged to a wealthy priory, founded in 1123 by a courtier of Henry I, Thomas Rahere, who had a vision of St Bartholomew during a bout of malaria in Rome. The priory was sacked in 1529, one of the first to suffer in the Dissolution. Inside, many original features have survived. Rahere's church must have been impressive, for the high, massive **nave** of the present building was only the choir of the original. Huge columns support a Romanesque triforium, surmounted by a clerestory built in 1405 in Perpendicular Gothic style to replace the original; the cool gray stone in three regular tiers has a peaceful solidity typical of Norman architecture. A lighter touch is give by the late Gothic **oriel window** built into the triforium on the s side of the choir. It dates from 1517 and was built by Prior Bolton, whose rebus is carved upon it — a crossbow bolt piercing a wine tun.

Beyond the altar is the **Lady Chapel**, dating to 1335. This has been much rebuilt after the depredations of the intervening centuries, during which it was not part of the church at all but used as a workshop; in 1725 Benjamin Franklin worked here.

At the w entrance, the massive crossing which once supported a huge stone tower can be seen. The present tower in brick is above the s aisle and dates from 1628, by which time surviving parts of the old priory were being used as a parish church. Five medieval bells are housed in the tower, making this one of the oldest peals in the country. On either side of the crossing are the much restored transepts. The best preserved is to the s, and from this stretches one side of an elegant cloister, almost entirely 19thC restoration work, imitating the style of the few original stones that survived long use as a stable and forge. A plain but beautiful font stands in the s transept, dating from the early 15thC.

There are a number of fine monuments, including the medieval tomb of the founder, *Rahere*, which has a delicate canopy of 15thC Gothic tracery. Outstanding examples of later tombs include a

Renaissance monument of 1589 in Italian marble to *Sir Walter Mildmay*, founder of Emmanuel College, Cambridge, and one from 1615 to *Sir Robert Chamberlayne*, whose effigy kneels in ceremonial armor beneath a carved canopy. The monument to *Edward Cooke*, who died in 1652, actually weeps in damp weather as a result of condensation — a phenomenon referred to in the inscription.

St George's Bloomsbury 𝕞 †
Bloomsbury Way, WC1 Map 10E11. Tube Holborn.
This splendid church compares well with the near contemporary but much more famous *St Martin-in-the-Fields*. Built by Nicholas Hawksmoor in 1720-31, it is in some ways an even more dramatic design than Gibbs', with a huge portico of Corinthian columns and a layer-cake spire, topped with a statue of *George I as St George*, a typical piece of Baroque overstatement. The interior repeats the boldness of the exterior — simple shapes, plenty of light and more giant columns. Notice the fine patterned inlay of the wooden reredos.

St James's
Map 10G-H. Tube Piccadilly Circus, Green Park.
Despite being unprotected by conservationists, there are still in the world examples of that strange breed, the English gentleman. Come to St James's, and you would never know that they are rare, for this is *their* district, still existing to provide the quiet, comfortable life long enjoyed by the upper-class.

Occupying the area between *St James's Park* and *Piccadilly*, the land was granted to the Earl of St Albans in 1665 in recognition of his loyalty while the king was in exile. The earl began building straightaway, and the proximity of the palace ensured that his square and streets soon became fashionable. The centerpiece was **St James's Square**, with a large central garden. No 17thC houses survived, but there are several fine examples from the 18thC: **Lichfield House**, no.15, with its Classical facade, is the best. At the center of the gardens is an equestrian statue of *William III* from 1807. To the n up Duke of York St. is the area's church, *St James's Piccadilly*.

To the s, running parallel to the park, is *Pall Mall*, a splendid road lined with gentlemen's clubs. *St James's Palace* is at the western end, with **St James's Street** stretching n to Piccadilly. Here are many more of the gentlemen's clubs built in the 19thC: **White's** for hard-drinking Conservatives; **Boodles**, a famous gambling club in the days of Beau Brummell, the Regency dandy; **Brooks'**, the Whig club founded in 1788; and the **Carlton**, the Conservatives' club.

Those mausoleums of inactive masculinity are places for men who prefer armchairs to women.

V.S. Pritchett on London clubs

St James's Place leads off to the w toward Green Park, a quiet street lined with 18thC houses and with the magnificent **Spencer House** (1756-66) overlooking the park at the end. Opposite is one of the two most interesting modern office developments in St James's — aggressively modern, in fact, and built in 1959-60. The other is the **Economist** complex, built around a central plaza just to the w of St James's St.

Another feature of St James's is the shops, with the most traditional approach to service and quality in London (see

Shopping). For refreshment, try the Victorian **Red Lion** pub in Duke of York St. (see *Pubs*).

St James's Palace 🏛 ★
*Pall Mall, SW1. Map **9**H9. Not open to the public. Tube Green Park.*

Despite its much greater antiquity, London has an architectural threshold formed by the plague and fire of 1665-66. This royal palace is unique in surviving intact, unadorned, and preserving a glimpse of Tudor London. There it sits, sandwiched by its larger offspring of *St James's* and *The Mall*, and yet dwarfing them, for all their grandeur and boldness, by its very antiquity and history. The official residence from 1698, when Whitehall Palace burned down, until *Buckingham Palace* took over in 1837, its seniority is still recognized; the Queen's court is 'the Court of St James's' and new monarchs are still proclaimed from this palace. Today it consists of 'Grace and Favour' quarters for yeomen-at-arms, lords and ladies-in-waiting, and the Lord Chamberlain.

Henry VIII took over the site from a leper hospital in 1532, and had his palace built entirely in brick, with battlements and diapering (diagonal patterning in the brickwork). Even the State Rooms added by Wren in the 17thC, also with battlements, maintain the low, informal approach, echoing the domesticity of Tudor architecture. The best original feature, visible to the public from *Pall Mall*, is the tall **gatehouse**, with its octagonal corner towers.

The interior is closed to the public but includes some fine features: the Throne Room has an overmantle by Grinling Gibbons; both the Armoury and Tapestry Room were decorated by William Morris in 1866-67; and the Chapel Royal, home of the Queen's liveried choir and scene of many royal weddings — George IV and V and Victoria — has a ceiling by Holbein. The **Queen's Chapel**, across Marlborough Rd. but originally within the palace, is in style entirely different from the rest of the buildings. Designed by Inigo Jones, it was built from 1623-27 in the Classical manner, with rendered white walls and Portland stone dressings. The beautiful interior boasts some more ornate Baroque work from the 1660s, including fine carving by Gibbons. To the w, attached to the palace, is **Clarence House**, built in 1825-27 by Nash and now the Queen Mother's home; when she is in residence, a piper (bagpipes) plays in the garden at 9am. The palace is flanked by two grand mansions from later periods: *Marlborough House* to the E and *Lancaster House* to the w with *St James's Park* to the s.

St James's Park ☆
*Map **10**H-1. Tube St James's Park.*

London's first royal park was always nearer to art than nature. In 1536 Henry VIII drained a marsh to make a park between *St James's* and Whitehall Palaces, filled with deer (for ornament rather than hunting). In 1662, Charles II made it a public garden, laid out in the formal style of the period with avenues of trees, *The Mall* as a carriageway, and a long straight canal. In 1828, it was remodeled on the present pattern by John Nash, who created the lovely complex of trees, flower beds and views across the natural-looking lake that we see today. The waterfowl, some of which breed on Duck Island at the E end, have always continued the contrivance — there are even pelicans. The view from the bridge over the lake back toward *Whitehall* is one of the most beautiful in London.

St James's Piccadilly 🏛 †
Piccadilly, W1 ☎734-5244. Map 10G10. Tube Piccadilly Circus, Green Park.

When *St James's* was developed as a residential area after 1662, Sir Christopher Wren was commissioned to build the new church, completing it in 1674. It is basically one great room with plain galleries, with a vaulted ceiling decorated with plaster moldings. Although damaged by bombs in 1940, the church has been well restored and preserves some fine fittings. The organ is 17thC, moved here from the old Whitehall Palace, and topped by gilded figures carved by Grinling Gibbons, who also produced the marvelous marble **font**, with its virtuoso relief of Adam and Eve, and the rich floral arrangements carved on the wooden **reredos**.

St Katharine's Dock ☆
Map 13G18. Tube Tower Hill.

While confusion hung over the future of the vast area of *Docklands* downstream, St Katharine's Dock, next to the *Tower of London*, was the first to be given an entirely new role. Originally built in 1827-28 by the great engineer Thomas Telford, this was for many years one of the leading docks in the Pool of London, with the advantage of being closest to The City. Today, St Katharine's again profits from its proximity to The City — as a residential and tourist center and a yacht marina. The large modern World Trade Centre looks down on the brick-brown sails of the Thames sailing barges and gleaming hulls of luxury yachts moored in the docks. Telford's **Ivory House** (later modified) shows off 19thC industrial apartments, shops and an exhibition area. A timber-built warehouse is now the Dickens Tavern, and several blocks of fashionable apartments sit between the docks and the river.

The dock's collection of old ships has now dispersed, with the exception of the Thames estuary lightship, *Nore*, and the steam tug *Challenge*, moored near the smart yachts and barges.

St Martin-in-the-Fields 🏛 †
Trafalgar Sq., WC2. Map 10G11. Tube Charing Cross.

The first buildings in a new architectural style often seem oddities, and this church has maintained its nonconformity. Today it is the venue for concerts on Mon and Tues lunchtimes, and a shelter for vagrants and drug addicts, as well as a church. The broad views allowed by *Trafalgar Square's* open spaces make enjoyment of this magnificent church's proportions possible, and it is now recognized for the seminal building it was. Designed in 1722-26 by James Gibbs (the foundation goes back to 1222) in a solemnly Classical style, it is very close to a Roman temple, except for the novel placing of a tower and spire above the Corinthian portico. The interior is similar to Wren's churches of a few decades earlier — spacious and light, with galleries to the sides and a splendidly molded ceiling. The crypt contains several interesting relics, including a whipping post dating back to the 18thC. It also houses the **London Brass Rubbing Centre** (☎437-6023 🖾 *open Mon-Sat 10am-6pm, Sun noon-6pm*) where rubbings can be made from replicas of medieval monumental brasses.

St Mary Abchurch †
Abchurch Lane, EC4. Map 13F16. Tube Cannon Street.

After its small cobbled churchyard, simple brick exterior and lead spire, the glories of St Mary Abchurch's interior are unexpected. Built by Sir Christopher Wren in 1681-86, it consists of little more than one huge dome on top of a square room, creating a sense of space with architectural detail kept to a minimum. The dome was painted in Baroque style by William Snow between 1708-14, and shows the name of God in Hebrew surrounded by figures representing the virtues. Although damaged in World War II, the church has been expertly restored; the **reredos** carved by Grinling Gibbons, for example, was rebuilt from fragments. Note the richly carved pulpit, the paneling and some original pews.

St Mary-le-Bow ⌂ †
Bow Lane, Cheapside, EC2. Map 12G15. Tube Bank, St Paul's.

When Wren rebuilt London's churches after the Great Fire of 1666 he put particular emphasis on their steeples, and this is the most magnificent. A great tower capped by an intricately designed stone spire, it is still prominent among the larger modern buildings around. The church was built in 1670-80, with the tower separated from the body of the church by a vestibule. The design and execution of the two doors to the tower which serve as the porch are particularly fine. The interior is large and simple, much restored after gutting during the war, and the crypt retains elements from the original Norman church. St Mary's bells are of sentimental importance to Londoners — being born within range of their sound is the qualification for being a Cockney. The bells were destroyed in the Great Fire of 1666 and again in the Blitz, although the current ones include recasts from remnants salvaged in 1941.

St Mary-le-Strand ⌂ † ☆
Stand, WC2. Map 11F12. Tube Aldwych, Temple.

It is hard to imagine a more ironic fate for a jewel of the Baroque: the island in the middle of the *Strand* is so small that the continuous traffic passes within inches of its walls, which, as a result, have needed drastic renovation. James Gibbs built this in 1714-18 fresh from the joys of Rome. The facade especially is a delight: from the portico, with its ornate capitals, the eye sweeps up to the triangular pediment and the bold layered spire. The interior has a richly coffered ceiling with two tiers of columns and a pediment dramatically framing the apse. Notice the fine carving of the pulpit, which was originally on a taller base with a scallop-shell sounding board behind, all part of the grand theatrical effect.

St Pancras Station ⌂ ☆
Euston Rd. NW1. Map 4C11. Tube King's Cross, St Pancras.

That a railway station could be made into a Gothic fortress speaks much for the Victorians' confidence. St Pancras Station, with its accompanying hotel building (now used as offices), was the glory of Victorian London. It was designed by Sir George Gilbert Scott in 1868-74, freely using the northern Italian and French Gothic styles. Notice the harmony of its red bricks with the pink and gray stone, and the way the detail combines with complex shapes and angles to feast the eye. It was also a tremendous feat of engineering, with the great train shed covered by a single span of iron and glass.

St Paul's, Covent Garden ⌂ †
The Piazza, WC2. Map 10F11. Tube Covent Garden.

As the Duke of Bedford neared completion of his *Covent Garden* development, money became tight, and so he instructed Inigo Jones to build an economical church, suggesting as a model

St Paul's Cathedral

something like a barn. Jones definitely declared that he would
build "the handsomest barn in Europe," and today it stands as the
sole surviving elements of the piazza. In fact it cost a small fortune,
but the barn analogy is not entirely inappropriate to the extreme
simplicity of what was London's first entirely Classical parish
church, completed in 1638. The main features are the overhanging
eaves and the superb Tuscan portico, ironically never used as an
entrance because the alter was moved in 1636 and a smaller door
made at the rear in Bedford St. Today it is the 'actors' church, and
every so often a grand theaterland funeral adds another monument
to the collection.

St Paul's Cathedral 🏛 † ★
*Map 12F14. Entrance and movement restricted during
services. Tube St Paul's.*
There are a very few great churches in the world which strike all
visitors, whatever their religious convictions, as a sublime witness
to man's ability to reach toward the infinite. St Paul's was built as
both a religious and secular statement of London's faith and
self-confidence after the devastating Great Fire of 1666, and almost
300yr later it was to soar alone amid the total destruction of the
surrounding buildings in the Blitz, preserved miraculously to
breath fresh hope into the beleaguered Londoners.

No building so clearly demonstrates Sir Christopher Wren's
prodigious skill and energetic inventiveness: detail is used with
characteristic Baroque exuberance but always subordinated to the
highly controlled overall scheme which makes the cathedral so
harmonious. The dominant dome still defies the encroaching
modern buildings.

The current cathedral is the third to stand on this site, and not
the largest. The first was founded in 604 and periodically enlarged
until destruction by fire in 1087. A medieval cathedral was
constructed in the 11th-12thC; in the 13thC it was enlarged, and in
1315 a huge spire was completed. It was one of the great churches
of medieval Europe, with a spire that reached 489ft (149m) from
the ground, taller and longer than the present St Paul's. (For a fine
model, see *London, Museum of.*)

Decline set in as the Middle Ages waned, however. The spire
burned down in 1561 and was not replaced. The building in
general fell into disrepair and became used more as a market-place
than as a place of worship. The central aisle, 'Paul's Walk,' was a
famous social forum. In 1634, Inigo Jones carried out substantial
repairs, but the medieval structure continued to deteriorate, and in
1666 Christopher Wren came up with his first scheme for drastic
renovations. In the same year, the Great Fire destroyed most of
London, raging in St Paul's for several days and reducing it to
ruins.

Given the task of reconstructing the cathedral, Wren proposed
sweeping away what remained of the medieval building and
starting afresh. He began with daringly modern designs which
were rejected by the ecclesiastical authorities. In the end, he was
forced to return to the basic plan for a Gothic cathedral, even if not
in appearance, and his design of 1675 was just that—with a nave,
aisles, a crossing, transepts and a chancel, all forming a Latin
cross. But the crossing was to be covered by a dome rather than a
tower or spire, the first in England, following the example of the
great Renaissance churches of Italy. Wren also fought for, and
won, the freedom to alter the 'ornamentation' of the cathedral,
which in effect left him able to design the building's appearance as
he went along.

St Paul's Cathedral

Wren's **exterior** actually owes much to Inigo Jones'
Banqueting House. There are two stories, with pilasters
decorating rusticated walls and a balustrade at the top — a first
stroke of ingenuity, for the aisles behind the exterior side walls are
only one story high, as in a Gothic cathedral. The upper is thus a
false wall (hence the blank niches instead of windows) connected to
and supporting the walls of the nave by means of flying buttresses
inside — all entirely Gothic device, but out of sight.

In Paul's Walk, at one time . . . shall you see walking the Knight,
the Gull, the Gallant, the Upstart, the Gentleman, the Clown, the
Captain, the Applesquire, the Lawyer, the Usurer, the Citizen, the
Cheater, the Puritan, the Cut-throat, the High-men, the Low-
men, the True-men and the Thief — of all trades and professions
some, of all countries some.
                    Thomas Dekker, *Seven Deadly Vices of London*, 1604

The E end of the cathedral, containing the chancel, was built
first. It has a rounded end, thus forming an apse as in a medieval
church, but with a curved roofline giving a Baroque flourish. This
effect is echoed in the curved porches to the N and S transept
facades, but these have more solidly Classical pediments at the
roofline. The W end, the ceremonial entrance, was built later
(1706-8), with massive towers at either side — the ornate tops to
these are the most complex elements in the whole building,
architecture handled as sculpture. The central portico is on two
stories with pairs of Corinthian columns, another emphatically
Baroque motif. All this serves to balance the solemnity of the
dome, suitably weighty and dignified as the dominant element of
the composition. It is arguably the most beautiful dome in the
world, 365ft (111m) high to the tip of the lantern and 100ft (30m)
across inside.

The quality of the carving of such elements as the garlands just
below the frieze, or the capitals to the columns and pilasters, is
superb. The sculptures, too, are well executed. The reliefs in the
transept pediments are by G.B. Cibber and Grinling Gibbons, the
statues by Francis Bird, who also carved the relief in the W
pediment showing the *Conversion of St Paul*.

The area around St Paul's has been effectively spoiled by
modern developments. Views of the cathedral are cut off by
uninspired or ugly modern buildings, and traffic whistles around
alarmingly close to the walls. There remain, however, the fine

railings that surround the churchyard, made in 1714 and an early example of the use of cast iron. In front of the portico stands a statue of *Queen Anne*, made in 1866 to replace the original of 1709-11 by Bird (but did the original look so like Queen Victoria?). In the churchyard gardens to the NE is **St Paul's Cross**, a bronze structure of 1910. Two of the old cathedral buildings survive, both designed by Wren: to the s is the little **Deanery** of 1670, and to the N the larger red-brick **Chapter House** of 1712-14. To the E, still inside the road, is the tower and elongated onion spire of the ruined church of St Augustine, designed by Wren in 1680-83, now attached to the new buildings of the celebrated St Paul's Choir School.

The **interior** gives an impression of the great bulk of the structure, but this is offset by the height of the nave and by the vast open space at the very center beneath the dome. The roofs are supported on a series of shallow cupolas, and the decorative elements are richly and finely carved, but limited in extent to the capitals of the pilasters, with garlands between, and geometrically patterned bands around the cupolas. The emphasis is on the sweeping drama of the Baroque. The eye is led along the nave or aisles, or across the transepts, and there seems to be a calculated attempt to create vistas with a sense of distance, focusing on the open space beneath the dome but leading ultimately toward the long chancel beyond the crossing. A great deal of light enters the cathedral from the clerestory windows of the nave, windows that are invisible from the outside because of the false upper story of the external wall.

Walk to the left from the main w entrance. The small **All Soul's Chapel** contains **Lord Kitchener's monument** of 1925, one of the more effective of the cluster of memorials to national heroes introduced since about 1790, with an effigy of the soldier in deathly white marble. The **St Dunstan's Chapel** follows behind a superbly carved wooden screen of 1698. Outstanding monuments are to *Lord Leighton*, the leading Victorian painter, and to *General Gordon* of the Sudan. In one of the arches farther along this N aisle is the great **monument to the Duke of Wellington**, erected in the mid 19thC and the most elaborate in St Paul's, with an equestrian statue of the duke on top of the canopy. The N transept is reserved for private prayer; it contains a number of monuments to the fallen heroes of the Napoleonic Wars, and the marble font, carved in 1727 by Francis Bird.

At this point the **crossing** can be admired, the focal point of the entire design. It is a huge space, with the circle of the **dome** supported on eight massive arches. The mosaics in the spandrels are Victorian, in the style of Michelangelo's Sistine Chapel frescoes, and there are Victorian statues in the niches above the Whispering Gallery. The breathtaking dome itself actually consists of three layers: an outer skin, a cone supporting the masonry of the lantern and a shallow frescoes ceiling. This is painted with illusionistic architectural frescoes in monochrome depicting scenes from the life of St Paul, by Sir James Thornhill, dating from 1716-19. Monuments in the crossing include those to *Dr. Johnson* (in an unlikely toga) and *Sir Joshua Reynolds*, first president of the *Royal Academy*. The lectern was made in 1720 but the pulpit is modern.

The **chancel**, stretching off toward the high altar, makes a sumptuous display, although it is not at all as Wren left it: the gaudy and fussy mosaics that decorate the ceiling date from the 1890s and are really not in keeping. The modern baldachino, attempting to follow Wren's original scheme for a high altar canopy as a focal point, is only partly successful, in an unhappy marriage with the ceiling decorations. However, the **choir stalls and organ case**, which originally closed the chancel off from the crossing, are quite magnificent, with exquisite carving by Grinling Gibbons, made in the 1690s. The chancel aisles can be visited, giving a fine close-up view of the rear of the stalls and of Jean Tijou's extraordinarily fine **wrought-iron gates**, again of the 1690s but moved to their present site in 1890. Behind the altar is the Jesus Chapel, now a memorial to the American dead of World War II.

Returning along the s chancel aisle **John Donne's monument** shows the poet, who was Dean of St Paul's from 1620-31, wrapped in his shroud, just as he posed during the (soon justified) bouts of melancholy before his death in 1631. It is the only monument to survive from the medieval cathedral.

Returning back toward the crossing, the s transept includes several military monuments, of which *Sir John Moore's* (1851) is the most moving, although *Lord Nelson's* include a fine portrait. In the s aisle is a striking example of high Victorian religiosity, a late version of Holman Hunt's painting *Light of the World*, and a fine wooden screen of 1706 in front of the **Chapel of St Michael and St George**.

Crypt

Entrance from s transept 🚇 *Open Mon-Fri 10am-4.15pm, Sat 11am-4.15pm.*

The piers and columns support a crypt the size of the whole cathedral, a quiet and dignified place crammed with monuments to national figures. A few battered remains to be seen of monuments surviving from before the 1666 Great Fire, but the majority are from the 19th-20thC. By far the most impressive are the **tombs of Wellington**, a massive porphyry block on a granite slab, and **Nelson**, an elegant black sarcophagus originally made for Cardinal Wolsey in 1524-29 but denied him after his fall from royal favor. Other monuments include numerous generals and admirals, and in 'Painter's Corner,' the tombs of *Turner* and *Reynolds* and monuments to *Van Dyck, Constable* and *William Blake*. Wren himself is buried nearby.

The **Treasury of the Diocese of London** also has an exhibition in the crypt, containing elaborate vestments, illuminated medieval manuscripts from the cathedral library, and some fine plate from London churches of the 16th-20thC.

Whispering Gallery and Dome

Stairs in s transept 🚇 *Hours as crypt.*

The stiff climb to the gallery inside the dome is repaid with stupendous views of the concourse below and the painted inner dome. The acoustics which give it its name enable the slightest sounds to be heard across the span; the traditional trick, much loved by children, is to whisper against the wall and wait for the sound to travel around to the next auditor.

The next section of the ascent is not for the fainthearted, with steps winding up throughout the struts supporting the outer dome. The stunning views from the **Golden Gallery** at the base of the lantern make the 542-step climb worthwhile.

St Stephen Walbrook 🏛 † ☆

Walbrook, EC4. Map 13F16. Tube Bank.

Although a parish church, its position behind the *Mansion House* means that St Stephen Walbrook is also the Lord Mayor's church. It is appropriately grand for this ceremonial function, with a simple exterior giving way to a magnificent structure inside, with

Corinthian columns, and eight richly molded arches supporting a coffered dome. Wren built the church in 1672-79 and it is thought that he was trying out some ideas for *St Paul's Cathedral*. The contrast with his *St Mary Abchurch* is illuminating, for here the dome is not used to create a simple, large space but to contribute to the series of constantly changing views as the visitor moves through the columns. The tower is slightly later, 1717, and the crypt survives from the 15thC.

Science Museum ★

Exhibition Rd., SW ☎938-8000. Map 15J5 ◎ ■ ✳ Open Mon-Sat 10am-6pm, Sun 2.30pm-6pm. Tube South Kensington.

The Science Museum originated in 1857 within the great South Kensington museum complex conceived by Prince Albert. It was separated from the *Victoria & Albert Museum*, housing the products of art rather than science, in 1909. Its present building, solemn and functional, was constructed in 1913, with the *Geological Museum* and *Natural History Museum* nearby.

On entering the ground floor, children make an immediate break for the **Launch Pad**, a marvellous new 'hands-on' exhibition where everyone can get down to working the machines themselves. The development of motive power is then covered in the East Hall, a large room with galleries above on three levels and a glass roof. Industrial machinery, vast and now seemingly crude in its construction, shows the development of steam power in the 18thC. By contrast, a huge mill engine of 1903, with a great gleaming fly wheel, shows the continuing use of steam into the 20thC. A gallery to the rear covers electric power rather more modestly. A new dramatically staged exhibition then introduces exploration, with full-scale models of the most modern space and underwater craft. The following section on transport is a great favorite, with famous steam locomotives such as Stephenson's *Rocket* of 1892 and the magnificent *Caerphilly Castle* of 1923 outstanding; the fascination with the visible working parts explains why something as messy and noisy as a steam train should have such a romantic appeal — there is something of the scientist in all of us. There are also horse-drawn carriages, automobiles and free engines. Below the rear part of the museum the **Children's Gallery** has many practical displays, although it pales in comparison with the Launch Pad. Domestic appliances are also found on this floor.

The displays on the upper floors (the galleries around the central East Hall and a few separate rooms) cover a great many aspects of science in turn. On the first floor, industrial processes such as iron, steel and glass manufacture and also agriculture are prominent.

On the second floor, subjects range from chemistry to nuclear physics to computers; there are some superb **models of ships**. Fascinating new exhibitions on the third floor cover photography, cinematography and optics, as well as more theoretical areas such as heat and temperature. Stairs lead up to the excellent **Wellcome Medical Museum**, where the history of medicine and its most up-to-date manifestations are shown in spirited dioramas. Here too is the **National Aeronautical Gallery**: see a Spitfire, Amy Johnson's 'Jason' in which she flew to Australia, and the first ever jet engine.

Shakespeare Globe Museum

1 Bear Gdns, Bankside, SE1 ☎928-6342. Map 12G15 ▩ Open Tues-Sat 10am-6pm, Sun 2-6pm; times vary, check. Tube London Bridge.

Until the 18thC, Southwark acted as London's pleasure center, an area of taverns, brothels and theaters. The Museum houses an exhibition on the circular theaters of the area where Shakespeare worked. The famous Globe theater burned down in 1613 during a performance of *Henry VIII*. At present the international Shakespeare Globe Centre (*due to open in 1991 ☎261-1353 for information*) is building a Tudor-style circular theater close to the Globe's original site, and next to the museum.

Sir John Soane's Museum

*13 Lincoln's Inn Fields, WC2 ☎405-2107. Map **11E1** 🔟*
✗ Sat 2.30pm or by arrangement. Open Tues-Sat 10am-5pm.
Tube Holborn.
Nothing could be further from modern ideas of museum display than Soane's Museum, for the great architect left his house as a museum on his death in 1837 on the condition that nothing be changed. His enormous collection of pictures, architectural fragments, books, sculptures and miscellaneous antiquities is crammed into every available space, giving some idea of his eccentricity as well as his tastes.

Born in 1753, Soane lived at no.12 Lincoln's Inn Fields from 1792, in a plain Geogian house he designed himself. In 1812-14 he added the much more elaborate no.13 with its grand facade, rebuilding no.14 to complete a balanced design in 1824. The interior, joined between the three houses, is the most ingeniously complex layout, offering numerous vistas through the houses, both laterally and vertically, as several of the rooms and yards extend through two or more stories. Mirrors are carefully placed to create additional illusory space. Most exciting are the paired **Dining Room** and **Library**, and the lovely domed **Breakfast Room**.

The fascination of the great number of objects on display from fossils to furniture is only increased by the capricious, even humorous, way in which they are jumbled together. Among them are several important works of art, as well as Soane's own architectural models. In the **Picture Room** are Hogarth's original paintings for two series, *The Rake's Progress* and *The Election*, 12 paintings in all, and elsewhere a Canaletto and a Turner. In a first-floor Drawing Room is Watteau's *Les Noces*. Outstanding is the beautiful alabaster **sarcophagus**, covered with hieroglyphics, of Seti I, a pharaoh who died in 1290 BC, for which Soane paid the then princely sum of £2,000.

Soho ☆

*Map **10**F-G. Tube Piccadilly Circus, Tottenham Court Road, Leicester Square.*
Every city has its low-life area, of course, but in few are the red light woven into a texture of such richness and variety as in London's Soho. These densely packed little streets in the heart of the West End, bounded by Oxford St., Regent St., Shaftesbury Ave. and Charing Cross Rd., are famous for their nightlife, their restaurants, the best delicatessens in London, their seedy but famous pubs, and, above all, for the gloriously cosmopolitan mix of their people and trades.

Much has been heard in recent years about the decline of Soho, for its thriving sex industry has threatened to engulf the area's other amenities. Even a pub where Dylan Thomas used to drink himself into oblivion has become a sex movie theater. However, the destruction has now largely been halted and there are clear signs that respectable businesses are returning, with fashionable restaurants and shops prospering. And Soho wouldn't be Soho without a scattering of sex parlors.

Within Soho there are two squares reminding us of its *early* development in the 17thC: **Golden Square** in the *w was* founded in 1673, and some 18thC houses survive around *its* undistinguished gardens with a 1720s statue of *Charles II*, but more impressive is **Soho Square**, laid out in 1681, *with* the few survivals of early buildings largely disgui*sed by* later additions, but offering a pleasant garden *with* a half-timbered summer house and a 17thC statue of *Charles II*. On its s side, in Greek St., is Soho's finest hou*se*, **The House of St Barnabas** (⊡ *open Wed 2.30pm-4.15pm, Thurs 11am-12.30pm*), a luxurious 1746 town house with a plain exterior but a magnificently decorated Rococo interior, with rich plasterwork on walls and ceiling. Soho's other public open space is **St Anne's churchyard**, a little park in Wardour St. overlooked by a splendid tower of 1801-3 surviving from the bombed church.

The southern part of Soho crosses Shaftesbury Ave., a busy street of many theaters, to London's **Chinatown**, centered on Gerrard St. — small, authentic and packed with excellent restaurants. But Soho's heart, with marvelous French and Italian delicatessens, together with fine butchers, fishmongers and wine merchants, is found farther N on **Brewer St., Old Compton St.** and **Berwick St.**; the latter is also an excellent open-air fresh food market, becoming more expensive and exotic at its continuation in Rupert St., s through sexy Walker Court. To the N of Old Compton St., Dean St., Frith St. and Greek St. have fine little restaurants, pubs and clubs, such as **Ronnie Scott's** for jazz (see *Nightlife*). In Wardour St., the respectable British movie industry has its center. Throughout, blue plaques mark apparently run-down buildings with famous associations: Blake was born in Marshall St., Chopin gave recitals in Meard St., and in Frith St., Marx worked, Baird first demonstrated television, and Hazlitt died. . . .

The northwestern part of Soho has less character: Carnaby St. was the Mecca of the Swinging Sixties, but most of its current visitors wonder why everyone else is a tourist.

Somerset House 🏛

Strand, WC2 ☎*438-6622. Map **11**G12. Fine rooms open only during temporary exhibitions. Tube Aldwych, Temple.*
The boldly Classical style of this riverside frontage was created by Sir William Chambers in 1776-78, and strongly carved details stand out from the Portland stone facing. The entrance is from the *Strand*, through a triple arch into a courtyard. In its time it has housed learned societies like the Royal Academy and, until recently, the *Registry of Births, Deaths and Marriages*. It is shortly to become the new home of the *Courtauld Institute Galleries*.

South Bank Arts Centre

*Map **11**G12. Tube Waterloo.*
The plans for a national arts center were formulated in the years after World War II, and crystallized when this derelict South Bank site was developed for the Festival of Britain in 1951, with the first stages of the Festival Hall and National Film Theatre ready for the event.

The **Festival Hall** is one of Britain's outstanding postwar buildings. Not finally completed until 1956, its impressive glassfacade makes full use of its panoramic riverside location. Like later South Bank buildings, however, the exterior is more massive and monumental than appealing, and it is the interior which is most successful. This has a complex arrangement of spaces, exceptional skill and is now the church of the Royal Air Force. Behind is a statue to *Samuel Johnson* erected in 1910, and to the front is a more pompous monument to *Gladstone* (1905).

The **Aldwych** follows on the N side of the street, an ambitious planning scheme begun in 1900. Its crescent shape is made up of massive, somber buildings in heavy Edwardian style, including Australia House and the BBC's Bush House. The exquisite church of *St Mary-le-Strand* occupies another island in the middle of the road at this point, with the 1971 concrete facade of King's College almost opposite. *Somerset House* comes next on the S side, just a little farther along from the Aldwych. Two large hotels are farther W: the Art Deco-ish **Strand Palace** (**Simpson's** ultra-traditional restaurant opposite) and the famous **Savoy** (see *Hotels*). Several theaters are to be found along the N side of the Strand from here, in a section largely given over to bustling shoppers. The W end, opening onto *Trafalgar Square*, is marked by *Charing Cross*, with the remarkable **Coutts' Bank building** opposite.

Strawberry Hill 🏛

Strawberry Vale, Twickenham ☎*892-0051. Map 20D3* 📷 𝗫
Open Jan-June, Oct-Dec Wed, Sat afternoons; prior appointment necessary. Train to Strawberry Hill from Waterloo.
At a time when country houses were being built in cool Classical style, Horace Walpole's Strawberry Hill, built in Twickenham, SW of London, in 1749-76, was revolutionary. Although influential in the 19thC, its curious 'Gothick' is entirely 18thC—a Rococo plaything, a complex melange of turrets and battlements. Walpole's attempt to revive the Gothic spirit was a total failure. What he produced instead was a quaint pastiche, a style now named after this house. The interior of the house is most effective, carved, molded and painted in complex detail. The entrance and staircase are particularly splendid. Now St Mary's Training College for teachers, it could not present a greater contrast with the nearby *Ham House* and *Hampton Court*.

Syon House 🏛

Brentford, Middlesex ☎*560-0881. Map 20C3* 🏞 ⚔ 𝗫 🅿
Open Apr-Sept Sun-Thurs 12-4.15pm; gardens daily 10am-6pm, sunset if earlier. Tube Gunnersbury.
Syon House was originally a convent, founded by Henry V in 1415 and exceptionally rich until suppressed by Henry VIII in 1534. In 1547, it was taken over by the Lord Protector, the Duke of Somerset, who transformed it into a large mansion on the pattern of a hollow square. Somerset went to the scaffold in 1552 as did his successor to Syon, John Dudley, and also Lady Jane Grey, who set out from the house to be Queen of England for eight days in 1553. Since 1594, the Percy family, Dukes of Northumberland, have held the house.

In 1762, Robert Adam was brought in to 'modernize' the Tudor house, thus creating the extraordinary contrast between the plain square exterior with battlements and corner towers, and the incomparable interior. As at *Osterley Park* nearby, the centerpiece of Adam's planning is the **Great Hall**, a cool and elegant room with restrained Classical decoration in stucco, including Doric columns, giving the house a dramatic entrance. To complete the scholarly effect, there are genuine Roman statues and some copies of famous antique models, including a fine bronze version of the *Dying Gaul*. Adam's intention was to create a sequence of pleasurable contrasts: the next room, **The Ante**

Room, is altogether more lavish, with rich gilding, dark green marble columns and a brightly patterned floor in colored artificial stone. The suite of state rooms continues the contrast, with **Dining Room, Red Drawing Room** and **Long Gallery** all in different, variously elaborate styles; some furniture is gilded, some is in beautifully inlaid wood. In the Red Drawing Room there is a fine carpet designed by Adam, and in the Long Gallery, landscape panels by Zuccarelli. Paintings in the house include works by Van Dyck, Lely and Gainsborough.

The gardens, remodeled in the late 18thC by the great Capability Brown, take in many rare botanical specimens, as well as many carefully planned vistas. The **Great Conservatory** was added in 1830, with its large, almost Oriental, glass dome, and now contains an aviary and aquarium. In the park there is also an experimental butterfly house, where British and tropical specimens can be seen all year round under glass.

Tate Gallery ★
Millbank, SW1 ☎821-1313, recorded info ☎821-7128. Map 18K11 ▣ 𝕏 ▤ Open Mon-Sat 10am-5.50pm, Sun 2-5.50pm. Tube Pimlico.

Appropriately for a gallery famous for modern art, the Tate was founded by the modern type of patron, a businessman, when in 1892 the sugar millionaire Sir Henry Tate gave his collection of British paintings to the nation, together with funds to build a special gallery. In fact, only later, in 1916, was the decision taken to add modern foreign art, largely because at the time the Tate was seen as an adjunct to the *National Gallery*. Several extensions have increased the available space many times over, recently in the large galleries opened in 1979, and with the new Clore Gallery extension opened in 1987. The two collections, British and modern art, are now exhibited adequately and distinctly, although the British collection is more complete. Works are shown in rotation, to allow as much of the collections to be displayed as possible.

The British collection
Mostly to the left of the entrance. The first rooms cover the 16th-17thC, when foreign artists working in England ruled the roost. A few works, such as the superb portraits by William Dobson, show what a benign influence Europeans could be.

In the 18thC, a truly national school appeared, particularly with William Hogarth, whose eye for contemporary life was unrivaled. His *Study of the Heads of Six Servants* shows a great and original understanding of the ordinary people making up his household, whereas *Calais Gate* reveals his biting satire. In the 18thC, with Reynolds and Gainsborough, two contradictory approaches to portraiture emerged, although in the end both artists concentrated on pleasing their sitters. Reynolds favored a grand, Classicizing manner (as in *Three Ladies Adorning a Term of Hymen*), while Gainsborough concentrated on charm and prettiness with his extraordinarily fluent technique. The Tate has good examples of the development of landscape painting in the 18thC: Richard Wilson's *Cader Idris* demonstrates an emerging naturalism. Two other important artists of the 18thC should not be missed: George Stubbs (sporting and animal scenes, including the finest horses ever painted), and Joseph Wright of Derby (highly individual night scenes closely bound up with advances in science and industrialization).

The **Clore Gallery for the Turner Collection** (James Stirling, architect— beautifully proportioned and lit) houses Turner's bequest of his works to the nation, a dazzling display of light and color, revealing an unmatched understanding of nature in all its moods and prefiguring the Impressionists' innovations by several decades. The late works, such as the studies of *Norham Castle*, are outstanding. Constable, too, in studies and finished works such as *Flatford Mill*, showed an appreciation of the real appearance of the countryside which was revolutionary in his time.

By contrast, the eccentric mysticism of William Blake and his followers is shown most effectively in a darkened room. The Pre-Raphaelites are well represented at the Tate, and Millais' *Ophelia* and Rossetti's *Beata Beatrix* are among the most famous examples. Victorian painting is now admired and the Tate has an admirable selection ranging from John Martin's apocalyptic *The Great Day of His Wrath* to Frith's *Derby Day*, with its unbelievably complex storytelling detail. From the later 19thC, Whistler stands out. This American painter working in England placed great emphasis on abstract pictorial qualities such as color harmony.

The 20thC collection

The Tate's modern collection, shown mostly to the right of the main entrance, gives an effective survey of the main movements in 20thC art.

The collection starts with the Impressionists and Post-Impressionists with all the major figures represented with works of varying quality. Degas' bronze *Little Dancer* and Gaugin's *Faa Iheihe* are notable. Two important masterpieces by pioneering artists of the Fauve group are Derain's *Port of London* and Matisse's late collage *The Snail*. The Bloomsbury Group of British artists, perhaps more noted for their writings than their derivative paintings, are also represented. Cubism, short-lived but vitally important, is demonstrated with a few works of high quality of Picasso and Braque, together with Futurism. The move to complete abstraction is shown by Delaunay, Kandinsky and Mondrian. The gallery has some excellent Expressionist works, including Munch's *Sick Child* and Grosz's *Suicide*, and important works by Picasso, the giant of modern art, including the famous *Tree Dancers* in his unique version of the Surrealist style. The Surrealists themselves, Miró, Ernst, Magritte and Dalí, are well represented, as are the American Abstract Expressionists. The two most important contemporary British artists, Bacon and Hockney, are usually on view, as is Naum Gabo (the Tate has a leading collection of his work). Arguably the high point of the modern collection comes with one room entirely devoted to a group of powerful abstract canvases by Mark Rothko in somber black and purple; they serve as a potent reminder of the achievements of modern art.

The remaining rooms of the 1979 extension are given over to fine **temporary exhibitions** (■■ *hours may be extended*), generally of both contemporary artists and historical subjects.

Temple 🏛 ☆
Map 11F13. Tube Temple.

It can be easy to miss the gateway to the Inner and Middle Temples amid the bustle of *Fleet Street*, yet behind them lies a large and relatively peaceful enclave of historic buildings and gardens down toward the Thames. The Temple is named after the Knights Templar, a religious order founded in the Middle Ages to further the Crusades, who came to this site — then outside The City walls — in about 1160. They were disbanded in 1308, but not before they had constructed a great complex of monastic buildings, of which the chapel survives. Some time in the 14thC, the buildings were taken over by lawyers, and there they have remained, today organized into two of the four *Inns of Court*.

The red-brick **Middle Temple Gateway** was built in 1684 to a design using Classical motifs, and leads through to Middle Temple Lane, lined with chambers and courtyards. Much was destroyed by wartime bombing, although some buildings date back to the 17thC and beyond. Outstanding is the **Middle Temple Hall** of 1562-70 (■ *open Mon-Sat 10.30am-noon, 3pm-4pm*), expertly restored and retaining a superb **hammerbeam roof** and **oak screen** from the Elizabethan period, with Doric columns and arches, and finely carved figures. It is likely that Shakespeare himself appeared in the performance of *Twelfth Night* given here in 1602.

To the E, narrow alleys lead through to the **Inner Temple**. Here, the most important building is the **Templar church**, one of London's most interesting medieval structures. It is one of five circular churches in England, based on the Church of the Holy Sepulchre in Jerusalem. The round nave was begun in about 1160 and completed by 1185, one of the earliest Gothic structures in England. The chancel is from about 1220-40, in a more unreservedly airy Gothic style. On the floor of the nave are nine 13thC effigies of knights in Purbeck marble.

The **Inner Temple Gateway**, leading back to *Fleet St.*, is an attractive half-timbered house of 1610-11, restored in 1906. On an upper floor is Prince Henry's Room, with an elaborately decorated plaster ceiling. The Prince of Wales Feathers and the initials 'PH' suggest the connection with James I's son.

Theatre Museum

1E Tavistock St., WC2 ☎*836-7891. Map* **10F11** ■ *K* ■ *Open Tues-Sun 11am-7pm. Tube Covent Garden.*

Opened in 1987, this is an outpost of the *Victoria and Albert Museum* appropriately sited in *Covent Garden*, close to theatreland and the Royal Opera House. It is rich in theatrical history and memorabilia. In the lobby, a giant gilt angel, rescued from the Gaiety Theatre, Aldwych, beckons. Entry tickets are sold from a box office from the Duke of York's. All aspects of the performing arts are included; there are models, costumes, playbills, posters, puppets, props and much more besides. Here you will find Noël Coward's monogrammed dressing gown and slippers, original models for the opera by master designer Oliver Messel, Elton John's platform boots and Mick Jagger's jumpsuit. There is also a box office for all London shows and concerts, and a theatrical reference library.

Tower Bridge

SE1 ☎*403-3761. Map* **13G&H17** ■ ✳ ◄€ *Open Apr-Oct Mon-Sat 10am-5.45pm; Nov-Mar Mon-Sat 10am-4pm. Tube Tower Hill.*

With its towers and drawbridges, this landmark, adjacent to the *Tower of London*, has become a symbol for London. Built in 1886-94, it is the most easterly bridge over the Thames, and though designed so that large ships can pass beneath its easily raised roadway, it is deceptively graceful when viewed from a distance. Enter by the N tower to visit the glass-enclosed walkway which has spendid views: Butler's Wharf downstream, *HMS Belfast* to the w and *St Katharine's Dock* on the N bank. The **Tower Bridge Museum** is located to the s of the bridge and contains the original steam-driven machinery used to lift the bridge. There are further exhibitions in the NW and s towers. Recently Tower Bridge has been bedecked with lights, making a superb night-time sight.

Tower of London 🏛 ★

EC3 ☎ *709-0765. Map* **13G17** ▨ *summer* ▨ *winter* ✗ *Open Mar-Oct Mon-Sat 9.30am-5pm, Sun 2-5pm; Nov-Feb Mon-Sat 9.30am-4pm. Tube Tower Hill.*

The Tower's great keep rises from its complex accretion of massively fortified walls, moats, towers and bastions, and today its forbidding but thrilling appearance is often used as a symbol for London. The best views are from Tower Hill to the N and w, by All Hallows church, from *Tower Bridge*, or perhaps from the river itself, on a boat trip from Tower Pier (see *Useful addresses* in *Basic information*). The Tower is London's most substantial medieval monument, steeped in a bloody past and containing a superb collection of arms and armor together with the priceless Crown Jewels. As a result, it is a prime tourist attraction and is often crowded; a visit near opening time is recommended.

It was founded by William the Conqueror just inside the Roman wall at the E end of London following his arrival in 1066, to encourage the loyalty of the townspeople as much as to defend them. William's castle was initially a wooden structure, but from about 1077 the great stone White Tower began to rise, to be completed by 1097 in the reign of the Conqueror's son, William Rufus. At this time, the White Tower stood alone, joined to the river by an enclosed bailey, but Richard the Lionhearted began to build a curtain wall in the late 12thC, a process continued in the reign of Henry III. Edward I (1272-1307) completed the transformation of the Norman stronghold into a full-fledged medieval castle; the White Tower was now surrounded by a continuous curtain wall with 12 towers. The moat surrounding the whole was up to 12ft (38m) wide, with a barbican on the far side guarding the drawbridges. This is substantially as the Tower is today.

Until the reign of James I (1603-25) the Tower was a leading royal residence. It strength meant that is was also used as a principal armory and house for royal treasure. These functions have continued, and the Tower still holds the Crown Jewels and weaponry amassed over the ages. The Tower's security also commended it as a prison, and kings and queens have kept many of their most notable enemies within its walls: Anne Boleyn, Sir Thomas More, Elizabeth I (while a princess), Sir Walter Raleigh and, most recently Rudolf Hess during World War II.

The continuous traditions of the Tower have cloaked it in rich ceremony. It is guarded by the Yeomen Warders, or 'Beefeaters,' a company founded by Henry VII in 1485, who still wear Tudor costume, with blue tunics carrying the sovereign's monogram on the chest, and broad, flat caps. On ceremonial occasions, a more elaborate scarlet version of the same dress is worn. Together with guardsmen from the Regular Army, Yeomen Warders participate in the **Ceremony of the Keys** at 10pm each day, formally locking up the Tower for the night (see *Calendar of events* in *Planning*). Another tradition hangs around the six ravens that live inside the Tower's walls these are kept jealously, with a meat allowance, because of a legend that the Tower will fall when the ravens depart.

The outer fortifications

The main entrance to the Tower is, as in the Middle Ages, to the w, near the river. Evidence can be seen of the medieval causeway that led up to the vanished Lion Tower, so called because it housed the royal menagerie — lions and leopards included — until 1834. The whole entrance defense work, or barbican, was originally surrounded by water and reached by drawbridge. Another drawbridge led to the **Middle Tower**, the present outer gateway, an 18thC reconstruction. From here, a causeway leads across the broad moat (once with another drawbridge) to the gate in **Byward Tower**, built by Edward I. The moat was drained in 1843 and is now grassed over. Byward Tower leads into the corridor between the curtain walls, with the angled **Bell Tower** on the left, probably built soon after 1200 by King John, one of the oldest surviving parts of the curtain defense. Farther along on the right is the notorious **Traitors' Gate**, through which royal barges and boats bearing prisoners (or provisions) could enter the castle.

The inner buildings

The inner precincts of the Tower can be entered through the gate in the **Bloody Tower** opposite, overlooked by the heavily fortified round structure of **Wakefield Tower** to the side. The Bloody Tower is by tradition the site of the murder of the young princes by their uncle, Richard III, in 1485, hoping to secure his succession to the throne, although modern historians are less certain about the event than was Shakespeare. Inside the tower, a winch used to raise the portcullis can be seen and two rooms are furnished as they might have been when Sir Walter Raleigh was imprisoned here. Other notable prisoners included Thomas Cranmer, Archbishop Laud, and the notorious Judge Jeffreys, who died here in a fit in 1689.

The great open space enclosed by the fortification of the curtain walls can now be appreciated. On the right is a portion of 12thC wall, surviving from the Norman bailey, only exposed in 1940 when a bomb destroyed a 19thC building. When the top of the steps ahead is reached, the **Queen's House** (not open to the public), a pretty half-timbered structure begun in about 1540, is on the left. In its rooms, Guy Fawkes was tortured following the 1605 Gunpowder Plot. To the N is the entrance to **Beauchamp Tower**, used again and again as a prison. The interior is covered with carved graffiti, giving witness to the suffering of prisoners. Nearby is the **Chapel of St Peter ad Vincula**, built in the early 16thC on a 12thC foundation, in Perpendicular Gothic style. It retains some late medieval monuments. Beyond the chapel, **Bowyer Tower** contains a display of torture instruments.

The Crown Jewels ★

Nearby begin the long lines for the Crown Jewels, the Tower's greatest single attraction. The lines move quickly so you cannot expect more than a brief look.

Kept below the 19thC Waterloo Barracks, the jewels are reached through a suitably dramatic pair of polished steel doors, and are the Tower's best-guarded prisoners ever. The fire and brilliance of the stones are even more spectacular than their reputation or their worth. Almost all the royal regalia was melted down or sold off by Cromwell, so most of what is left dates from after the 1660 Restoration. The display begins with a selection of plate, massive and ornate pieces in silver-gilt; loot out for the fabulous **wine cooler** of 1829, gilded state maces and bejeweled swords. The rich vestments of the knightly orders are on display, but overshadowed by the coronation robes of the sovereign, elaborately covered in gold embroidery. The Crown Jewels themselves are in the next room. Two items of coronation regalia survive from the Middle Ages: an exquisite **spoon**, probably made for King John's coronation in 1199; and a much restored early 15thC **ampulla** in the form of an eagle (for which the anointing oil is poured). The **Royal Sceptre** contains the largest diamond ever cut (530 carats), one of the 'Stars of Africa' from the Cullinan diamond found in 1905. Another piece was added to the **Imperial State Crown**, originally made in 1838, which also incorporates an immense and beautiful ruby, probably the one given to the Black Prince by Pedro the Cruel after the Battle of Najara in 1367 and worn by Henry V at the Battle of Agincourt. The oldest crown is 'King Edward's,' made for Charles II's coronation in 1660. It weighs 5lb (2.3 kilos) and is worn by the sovereign at coronations. The **Queen Mother's Crown**, made for her coronation in 1937, contains the ancient Kohinoor diamond, which was bought by the British Crown in 1849 and was recut in 1852 to its present size of 109 carats.

The White Tower and armories

The dominant White Tower is the oldest and largest of the Tower's buildings; its massive walls are up to 15ft (4.6m) thick, supported by external buttresses and carrying square or curved turrets at the corners. The large semicircular protruberance at the SE contains the apse of the chapel; the round turret on the NE corner contains a spiral staircase. The medieval facade was even starker — since then the decorative cones have been added, and Wren enlarged the windows.

Inside are displays from the Tower's superb collections of arms and armor. On the first floor, the **Sporting and Tournament Galleries** contains crossbows, muskets, lances, swords and the specialized armor made for jousting, already in the late Middle Ages a leisurely exercise in archaism.

The **Chapel of St John** on the second floor is the finest example of early Norman architecture in England, almost totally without ornament, massive and severe. More armor is displayed in the other two rooms; notice the awesome bulk of a suit made for a giant almost 7ft (2.13m) tall.

The third-floor rooms contain outstanding examples of Tudor and later armor, with several suits that belonged to Henry VIII, growing progressively larger as their owner grew older and fatter. The ceremonial armor of the 17thC is decorated to a high degree — a suit belonging to Charles I from 1630 is chased and gilded over its entire surface. Stairs descend to ground level where a fine selection of handguns, uniforms and cannons from various periods can be seen. The Oriental armor, including fine examples from India, China, Japan, even Africa, is housed in the **Waterloo Barracks**, worth visiting in particular for the elaborate elephant armor captured at the Battle of Plassey in 1757. Of many interesting cannons and other artillery pieces scattered throughout the Tower's enclosures, note a Turkish bronze cannon of 1530-31.

Trafalgar Square

Map 10G11. Tube Charing Cross.

Trafalgar Square is known as a rallying point for political demonstrations and New Year's Eve revelries, and even as a sanctuary for pigeons. When Nash began its redevelopments in the 1820s, it already had the fine equestrian statue of *Charles I* on the site of *Charing Cross*, and the superb church of *St Martin-in-the-Fields*. Since then, the surrounding architecture has let down Nash's vision: the *National Gallery*, added on the high N side in 1832-38, is too small in scale to make the triumphant statement its site demands, and Admiralty Arch (1911), a monument to Queen Victoria which saves its best face for *The Mall*, is equally uninspired. Still, it does allow Nelson, newly cleaned, to steal the show, as Nash intended; he was placed atop the 170ft (52m) granite column in 1842. The base is decorated by spirited reliefs made from the guns of ships captured at Trafalgar, and the justifiably famous lions added by Landseer in 1858-67.

Trocadero

*Piccadilly Circus, W1. Map **10**G10. Open daily 10am-10pm.
Tube Piccadilly Circus.*

No less than three exhibitions, plus a **Brass Rubbing Centre**, now
jostle for attention in this shop-and-restaurant complex on the
corner of Shaftesbury Ave. Built as a dance hall at the turn of the
century, it became a popular Lyons restaurant between the wars.
Today it is worth a visit for the **Guinness World of Records** alone,
which is the Guinness Book of Records brought to life by means of
models, movies, tapes and push-button machines (☎439-7331 ▓).
Light Fantastic is an impressive holography display and
showroom for its technology and practical application (☎734-4516
▓). The **London Experience** is an audiovisual canter through
London's history to the present (☎439-4938 ▓).

Victoria & Albert Museum ★

*Cromwell Rd., SW7 ☎938-8500. Map **15**J5 ▣ ▣ ♣ Open
Mon-Sat 10am-5.30pm, Sun 2.30pm-5.30pm. Tube South
Kensington.*

Probably the world's greatest museum of the decorative arts, it is a
vast storehouse of extraordinarily varied treasures. While fine art is
emphatically included, the reverence of the art gallery is absent.
The 'V & A' is thus a lively, informal place, and one of London's
most popular museums. The range of the exhibits is
overwhelming, including everything from entire furnished rooms
brought from the great houses of Britain and the Continent to
spoons, shoes and locks.

The museum is, however, a labyrinth of galleries and passages in
which it is easy to become lost, and around which it is almost
impossible to plan a coherent or comprehensive tour. But, to an
extent, this drawback, contributes to the museum's appeal, for
even regular visitors know that no matter how often they came,
there are still new treasures to be discovered.

The initial impetus and financing for the Victoria & Albert came
from the Great Exhibition of 1851, the profits of which were used
to purchase the large site in South Kensington on which it stands.
Under the enthusiastic direction of Prince Albert's friend Sir
Henry Cole, it first opened as the Museum of Ornamental Art in
1852, temporarily at *Marlborough House*, dedicated to fostering
the 'application of fine art to objects of utility,' but in 1857 the
museum moved to its iron and glass construction at South
Kensington.

Almost from the first, Cole's ideals became diluted by the desire
to fill the museum with great works of art. In 1865 Raphael's
tapestry cartoons arrived from the Royal Collection. In 1888, the
Constable Collection was bequeathed by a member of the great
painter's family, adding another fine-art element of the greatest
importance but having little to do with the museum's intention.
Before long, the museum felt free to acquire any item of esthetic or
historical interest.

Similar uncertainties have dogged the museum's building
programs, contributing to the sense of confusion. After 1863, the
red-brick buildings were constructed around the gardens in a
northern Italian Romanesque style with terra-cotta and mosaic
ornament. The leading artist, Lord Leighton, and the firm of
William Morris contributed to the decoration of the interior, but
shortage of funds prevented the scheme's completion. The library,
especially attractive and now the **National Art Library**, was
completed by 1882. But all this was haphazard and without any
underlying plan. The final phase came in 1899-1909 with Sir Aston

Webb as architect. The museum was re-named the Victoria and Albert in 1899. From this time date the great facades along Cromwell Rd.

It is not possible to suggest a complete route through the V&A — the result would be both difficult to follow and exhausting. Instead, two particularly well-displayed but contrasting departments are proposed as the starting and ending points — the Jones Collection and Constable Collection — and suggestions are made for sections to be visited in between. Visitors should stay alert on their travels for the countless minor surprises that the museum has to offer. Good large plans for the galleries are available at the main entrance. Note that the collection is supposedly arranged into 'art and design' collections, cutting across the arts of a given culture or period, and 'study collections,' grouped by material and techniques.

Begin from the main entrance by turning left and following the signs from the **Jones Collection**, a dazzling display of French interior decoration, painting, furniture, ceramics and other decorative arts. Elaborate furniture, some of which belonged to Marie-Antoinette, is inlaid with brass or with finely-grained woods, or covered with enameled panels. The rich, aristocratic mood is complemented by paintings such as Boucher's *Portrait of Madame de Pompadour*. German, Dutch and Italian decorative arts on display echo the French Rococo of the 18thC. The 17thC follows, just as elaborate but more solemn in mood. Several Dutch cabinets, inlaid with complex floral designs, are outstanding, as are German metalwork and Venetian glass.

At the end of these splendidly laid-out galleries steps lead up to the section devoted to the Renaissance, a series of rooms grouped around the court containing the gardens. In a less organized collection, some superb works stand out. There is a statue, for example, by Giovanni Bologna of *Samson and a Philistine*, a full-size marble composition of Mannerist complexity. From the High Renaissance, there is the famous elegantly glided **Antico miniature bronze** of Meleanger (c.1500), and from the 15thC several important **reliefs by Donatello**, the greatest sculptor of the early Renaissance, including an exquisite and moving *Dead Christ tended by Angels*. Rooms on the side of the gallery opposite the garden have been restored to their original decoration; one was carried out by William Morris's workshops. Another has tiles by Minton and stained glass designed by James Gamble.

The northern Renaissance is also well covered. Particularly beautiful are two late Gothic carved limewood angels made as candlesticks by Tilman Reimenschneider in the early 16thC. At the end of the gallery of Gothic art is a vast and gruesome Spanish altar piece of the early 15thC, showing scenes from the life of St George, which, according to this account, consisted almost entirely of hideous torture. Be sure to study the **Syon Cope** closely — this early 14thC example of *opus anglicanum* needlework is one of the finest pieces of embroidery ever executed.

Also on the ground floor is the large and stunning **costume court** ☆ with one of the world's great clothing collections of everyday garments and high fashion. It is a subject visitors relate to instantly, of course, but note that even some outfits of a decade or two ago seem as strange as an 18thC ball gown or Jacobean court dress. Above this is the collection of **musical instruments**, especially strong in the 16thC keyboards such as virginals and the first harpsichords, many with exquisite carving and inlaid work.

A huge gallery nearby exhibits the seven **Raphael cartoons** ★ on permanent loan from the Royal Collection. These vastly influential designs of the *Acts of the Apostles* were carried out in 1516-19 as designs for tapestries for the Sistine Chapel in the Vatican. Next to this room, is the main museum shop, housed in a gallery containing part of the **woodwork collection**.

Oriental arts are also represented on the ground floor, although even the large galleries allow room for only a small part of the V & A's great holdings. From India, there are several beautiful temple sculptures to see. More unusual is **Tipoo's Tiger**, a large wooden model of a tiger mauling a European, identified as British by his red coat; made in about 1790 for an anti-British sultan, it has organ pipes which simulate the grams of the victim. Outstanding is the exquisite **jade wine cup** made for Shah Jahan in 1657, with a lotus-flower base and a graceful antelope head as the handle. The **Islamic gallery** is dominated by the vast **Ardabil Carpet** of 1540, from a Persian mosque and some superb lacquered pottery. Outstanding in the **Chinese Collection** is an incredibly elaborate carved lacquer throne of the mid-18thC, ceramic and jade horses of more than 1,000yr earlier, and finely embroidered court costumes, all testifying to the unchanging sophistication of Chinese art. The new **Toshiba Gallery** of Japanese art, opened in 1986, contains exquisite collections of *netsuke*, kimonos, armor and ceramics.

The important **British Collection** stretches through sizable galleries on two upper floors to the left (or w) of the main entrance. First encountered is the furniture, especially beautiful, but generally simpler than the Continental equivalents, often relying more on shape and the quality of the wood than on elaborate decoration. Several complete rooms transplanted into the museum include the massively Baroque gold and white **Music Room for Norfolk House** (mid-18thC) and Robert Adam's much more delicate **Glass Drawing Room from Northumberland House** (1773-74). Two beds dominate the furniture: the huge Elizabethan **Great Bed of Ware**, which became instantly legendary for its size and was mentioned by Shakespeare; and a chinoiserie fantasy by Chippendale of 1750-55. Quite outstanding are several **miniatures**, a form of painting which reached its peak in 16th-17thC England, including Nicholas Hilliard's famous *Young Man Amongst Roses*. The same artist is thought to have produced the miniature on the **Armada Jewel**, produced for Elizabeth I in 1589 to celebrate the destruction of the Spanish Armada, and the highlight of a fine jewelry collection. British decorative arts are brought right up to 1960, and there are several important examples of the work of William Morris and the Arts and Crafts Movement which had so much influence on modern British design.

Before leaving, make sure that you visit the **Henry Cole Wing**, opened in 1984 at the rear of the museum to the w. Here you will find the **Ionides Bequest**, largely but not entirely of 19thC paintings, and with several important works: a Degas ballet scene, Millet's *Wood Sawyers*, Burne-Jones' *Day Dream*, Gainsborough's portrait of his two young daughters, and works by Turner are outstanding. Here is also the **Constable Collection** which presents the best coverage anywhere of the work of the most English of painters, providing a refreshing, open-air view for even the most jaded visitor. The fleeting effects of the changing weather of the English countryside are here shown more convincingly than ever before or since. Clouds rush over Hampstead Heath, rainbows hover over Salisbury Cathedral, and the trees of Suffolk rustle in gentle breezes. Besides finished paintings by the master there are some superb small oil and watercolor 'sketches.'

Next to the Henry Cole Wing, in the main body of the museum, is the **20thC exhibitions gallery**. It houses temporary exhibitions, often imaginative, on leading figures and aspects of 20thC design production.

Wallace Collection ★

Hertford House, Manchester Sq., W1 ☎*935-0687. Map* **9E8**
☒ ⌨ *Open Mon-Sat 10am-5pm. Sun 2-5pm. Tube Bond Street.*

Flying in the face of the renowned English insularity, this magnificent monument to Francophilia is, in fact, arguably the finest selection of French art to be found outside France, together with many other paintings and objects d'art of exceptional quality. It is a great private art collection of the 19thC 'frozen' in the grand house equipped by its wealthy owner to contain it.

Hertford House in Manchester Sq. was built for the Duke of Manchester in 1776-88 and acquired by the Second Marquess of Hertford in 1797. After some years as the French Embassy, it was used to store pictures by the Fourth Marquess who did most to build up the fabulous collection while living in Paris, adding to that of his father. He bequeathed both house and works of art to his natural son, Sir Richard Wallace, who returned to London and transformed Hertford House in the 1870s into a showcase for the collection. In 1897, his widow left it to the nation and it was opened as a public gallery in 1900. It thus reflects the tastes of three generations of Victorians.

The finest objects are on the first floor, which should be seen first. Large paintings by Boucher are on the walls of the top landing, full of the frivolous eroticism of the Rococo court style. Turning to the left, **Rm. XII** contains several scenes of Venice by Guardi and Canaletto. **Rms. XIII-XV** are devoted to Flemish and Dutch art, including fine studies by Rubens. Look out for Potter's animal scenes—even the cows have personality. Caspar Netscher's *Lace-Maker*, quietly realistic, is serenely hauting; the landscapes include marvelous works by Hobbema, and Rembrandt's eerie *Landscape with a Coach*. **Rm. XVI** is a large picture gallery built by Sir Richard Wallace, containing many oustanding works: Titian's *Perseus and Andromeda*, Rubens' deeply human portrait *Isabella Brant*, and Velázquez's cool *Lady with a Fan* are the most important. Works by Rembrandt, as always, stand out, including a buoyant *Self-portrait* and a deeply sympathetic *Portrait of Titus*, his son; also Reynolds' famous portrait of the beautiful courtesan *Nelly O'Brien* and Frans Hals' *Laughing Cavalier*.

Among the superb examples of the richly ornate Rococo furniture is a rolltop desk made by J.J. Riesener for the King of Poland in the 1760s, and a chest of drawers made for Versailles by Charles Cressent. **Rm. XVII** contains an impressive collection of gold boxes, mostly elaborate French 18thC. Some of the best French Rococo pictures are in **Rms. XVII-XIX**, leading in an unparalleled procession through Watteau, Lancret, Pater, Boucher and Fragonard and complemented by richly decorated furniture in the same style, much of which came from French royal palaces. Watteau's *Lady at her Toilet* and Fragonard's *Swing* sum up the leisured mood and Boucher's *Portrait of Madame Pompadour* shows unexpected candor. **Rm. XX** contains the best public collection of works by R.P. Bonington, an English artist working in France in the early 19thC — the clear light of his seascapes is exquisite. **Rm. XXI-XXII** contain more French works, the furniture deserving most attention.

The ground floor is more an Aladdin's cave of miscellaneous treasures, many grouped into specialist collections of great merit — of armor, miniatures or pottery, for example. There is a splendid collection of terra-cotta statuettes, mostly from the Italian Renaissance, and a unique cabinet of wax portraits. Furniture including works attributed to the great A. C. Boulle, and Sèvres porcelain, continue the French bias of the collection. Italian majolica pottery, and Limoges enamels of the Renaissance are as well represented here as anywhere in the world. Painting include works by Murillo, Canaletto, Guardi and Andrea del Sarto. From all this rich diversity, the **arms and armor** stand out. It is a remarkable collection of elaborately wrought and decorated items — look out for the northern Italian body armor and helmet of about 1620-35.

Westminster

Map 18H-J. Tube Westminster.

Even the visitor who has never heard of Westminster can instantly appreciate the significance of this most stately of London's districts, for, like its longtime rival *The City*, it has remained almost free from residential invasion and is devoted to business, in this case government. Its activity is dominated by the mother of parliaments at the Palace of Westminster (see *Westminster, Palace of*) attended by the officialdom of *Whitehall*. Next to the Houses of Parliament is the great church of *Westminster Abbey*.

Parliament Square, an open space created at the time of the building of the Palace of Westminster, is appropriately studded with statues of great statesmen: *Disraeli, Palmerston, Abraham Lincoln, Winston Churchill*. Surrounding the square, apart from Westminster Abbey and the Palace of Westminster, there is the Middlesex Guildhall (Neo-Gothic of 1906-13) and the Home Office. In front of the abbey is the smaller church of **St Margaret**, founded as the parish church of Westminster possibly as early as the 11thC and now the parish church of the Houses of Parliament, and always a fashionable place for weddings (Pepys, John Milton and Churchill were all married here). The present building dates from the early 16thC although it was restored almost out of recognition in the 18thC. Among its interesting monuments is the tomb of *Sir Walter Raleigh*; the E window is Flemish 16thC.

Earth has not anything to show more fair. . . .
The City now doth, like a garment, wear
The beauty of the morning; silent, bare,
Ships, towers, domes, theatres, and temples lie
Open unto the fields, and to the sky;
All bright and glittering in the smokeless air. . . .
Never saw I, never felt, a calm so deep!
The river glideth at his own sweet will:
Dear God! The very houses seem asleep;
And all that mighty heart is lying still!

Wordsworth, *On Westminster Bridge*, 1802

To the E of Parliament Sq., just E of Birdcage Walk and *St James's Park*, is **Queen Anne's Gate**, with some of the best early 18thC houses in London, and a statue of *Queen Anne* dated 1708. In Victoria St., two important landmarks are *Westminster Cathedral* and **New Scotland Yard**, the Metropolitan Police's modern headquarters. There is an attractive enclave to the S of Westminster Abbey with Georgian houses in Cowley St. and Lord North St. The latter opens into Smith Sq., which includes some 18thC survivors on its E side, and in the center of the square is one of the most magnificent Baroque churches in London, **St John's**, built in 1714-28, a massive and monumental structure. It was burned down in World War II but has been restored and often hosts concerts.

Back in Birdcage Walk lies Wellington Barracks. Here a new museum, the **Guards Museum** (*open Mon-Sat 10am-3.30pm* 💶) traces the history of three-and-a-half centuries of the five Regiments of Foot Guards (Grenadier, Coldstream, Scots, Irish and Welsh); both their fighting record and their famous ceremonial role is covered.

Westminster Abbey 🏛 † ★

Broad Sanctuary, SW1 🕾*222-5152. Map 18I11* 💶 *Royal chapels* 🗺 *✗ Mon-Fri 9am-4pm, Sat 9am-2pm, 3.45-5pm. Tube Westminster.*

Since William the Conqueror chose the new, incomplete Westminster Abbey for his coronation as king of his new subjects on Christmas Day, 1066, it has been the scene of the coronation, marriage and burial of British monarchs, a place of tribute to Britain's heroes, and in every way Britain's mother church. While *St Paul's Cathedral* belongs to London, Westminster Abbey belongs to the nation. It is also, of course, one of Britain's finest Gothic buildings, a soaring and graceful offering to God, with a strikingly unified interior.

The date of Westminster Abbey's foundation is uncertain. Legend takes it back to the 7thC; in any case, there was certainly a religious foundation here by the 9thC. In 1050 Edward the Confessor began work on a large new abbey church, in the Norman style, and it bacame a Benedictine monastery attached to the new Palace of Westminster.

Work continued on the Norman buildings well into the 12thC, and remains can be seen in the ruined infirmary chapel of St Catherine to the s of the present abbey church. In 1245, Henry III began a vast new building program in the latest French Gothic style of the cathedrals of Amiens and Reims. Work proceeded quickly and the chancel, transepts and part of the nave were complete by 1259, together with the chapter house. The great speed of the construction gave the building a remarkable unity of style and, when work was resumed more than a century later in 1375, it was decided that the existing parts should be imitated in the rest of the nave.

The mid-16thC was a time of religious upheaval, which first threatened and then confirmed the abbey's role. The royal connection preserved it from destruction at the dissolution of the monasteries and, in 1540, Henry VIII made it a cathedral, with its own bishop. Queen Mary, briefly restoring Catholicism, turned it back into a monastery in 1556. The permanent establishment of the protestant Church of England came under Elizabeth I, who in 1560 gave the abbey the status of a collegiate church independent of both the Bishop of London and the Archbishop of Canterbury. It thus became a Royal Peculiar, a great church serving Crown and State.

The building of Westminster Abbey did not end with the Middle Ages, although what has come since has tended to detract from its beauty. In 1698, Sir Christopher Wren began the designs for the w towers and facade. These were continued by Nicholas Hawksmoor and completed in 1745 — in pseudo-Gothic style but sitting uneasily all the same with the existing structure. In the 19thC, restoration work was carried out on a substantial scale — much of it destroying the medieval detail. Thankfully, the restoration work currently under way concentrates on conservation rather than improvement.

Westminster Abbey

The exterior

A huge program of restoration lasting from the mid-'70s until the early 1990s is under way. Cleaning has revealed the beauty of the abbey's soft Reigate stone (although where replacement is necessary Portland stone is being used, which will better stand the test of time). The w facade, with the main entrance, is perhaps the most dramatic approach, although Hawksmoor's towers are insubstantial — just too narrow and too high to suit the medieval facade — and their provenance can be detected in the Baroque stonework above the clock face and matching round windows in the opposite tower.

The abbey looks best from the N; the N transept forms a tremendous centerpiece, with its great triple porch and huge rose window, framed by a superb series of flying buttresses. Unfortunately, all the stonework is a product of 19thC restoration and only indicates in a general way the detail that was there before.

To the E lies the far more elaborate exterior of Henry VII's chapel, entirely covered with dense late Gothic tracery. The outer walls have turrets capped by 'pepperpots' and connected to the chapel's nave by delicately pierced flying buttresses. The nave is topped by a pierced balustrade and narrow pinnacles, all creating a wonderfully decorative effect. To the s of the chapel can be seen the earlier, much plainer chapter house. The pointed roof is 19thC.

The area around Westminster Abbey once formed a part of it and was densely covered with buildings. The open space to the NW was the Sanctuary, where anyone could seek the Church's protection in medieval times; as a result it became packed with timber buildings inhabited by felons on the run. The s of the abbey was made up of the monastic buildings, and the cloister remains, but this is best visited from within the abbey, as is the Chapel of St Faith. Other monastic buildings to the s are now incorporated in Westminster School, the leading public school that has evolved from the monastery's teaching function. To the N is Dean's Yard, now an open space, which can be entered through a 19thC arch to the w of the abbey. Until the 18thC it was covered over by monastic buildings.

The interior

The abbey is entered from the w, immediately presenting the visitor with a stunning view along the nave. Sweeping exaltedly upwards, it is very like a French Gothic cathedral, much higher and narrower than other English churches, supported on piers of dark Purbeck marble. Above the main arches is the triforium containing a gallery (unlike the French style); then the clerestory containing the windows, beneath the gracefully vaulted ceiling, completing the majesty. The western end of the nave was built last to match the style of the 13thC work to the E; the huge, plain window above the w door is late 15thC.

Set in the floor ahead of the entrance is a memorial to *Winston Churchill* with the **Tomb of the Unknown Warrior** beyond; the brass lettering is made from cartridges brought back with the body from the World War I trenches. On the first pier of the nave to the right hangs a famous and rare medieval **portrait of Richard II**, probably painted in 1398. Both the aisles are filled with monuments, jumbles of marble statuary, both good and bad. In the s aisle, that to *Colonel Townshend*, killed at the Battle of Ticonderoga in the American War of Independence, is of particular merit. It was designed by Robert Adam and made soon after 1759. The N aisle is even more crowded with monuments. Most notable is that to *Charles James Fox* of 1823. Look out also from the small kneeling wall effigy of *Mrs Jane Hill* of 1631, with

Westminster Abbey

Death in a Shroud and the *Tree of Life* above. Buried in the nave are David Livingstone, the explorer, and the engineers Thomas Telford and Robert Stephenson, among many national figures. The E end of the nave is closed by a brightly colored Neo-Gothic choir screen of 1848. On the left in one of its arches is the monument to *Isaac Newton* of 1731, one of the finest sculptures in the abbey, designed by William Kent and carved by J.M. Rysbrack.

The rest of the abbey is reached through a gate in the N side. Memorials to scientists cluster near Newton's tomb: Lister, Darwin, Faraday, Rutherford; musicians including Elgar, Vaughan-Williams and Benjamin Britten are commemorated by plaques in the floor near Purcell's monument. In the N transept the monuments come thick and heavy, and include those to 19thC statesmen. The architecture is of Henry III's time (1216-72), except that the great rose window was heavily restored in the 19thC. In the E of the transept, among several older monuments, is one of the most impressively carved and imaginatively conceived of all — that to *Mrs J.G. Nightingale*, made by Roubiliac in 1761. It shows a grim figure of Death pointing a lance at the unfortunate lady, who died after being struck by lightning. The fine monument to *Sir Francis Vere* from 1609 is also remarkable.

At this point notice the **crossing**, with its temporary ceiling where a tower should rise. The wooden pulpit is early 17thC. To the W, the choir stalls are overdone Victorian Gothic, and to the E is the sanctuary, with an elaborately gilded reredos of 1867. To its right are rare and important early 14thC wall paintings, together with an early Renaissance Italian altarpiece. The medieval monuments either side of the sanctuary are best seen from the ambulatory. Particularly fine is that to the *Earl of Lancaster* of 1296.

Before approaching the centerpiece of the whole abbey — the chapel and shrine to Edward the Confessor — visit the superb **Henry VII's chapel** at the E end of the abbey. Begun in 1503 and completed in 1512 by Henry VIII, it is in the much more richly elaborate Gothic style of the late Middle Ages, a mature, sophisticated farewell flourish. The whole surface is adorned with carvings — there are more than 100 statues, and the ceiling is a marvel of delicate tracery. The choir stalls are equally finely carved in wood — be sure to inspect the misericords, carvings that are visible when the seats are folded up. Henry VII's tomb in the chapel was started in 1506 in the same rich Gothic style, with a bronze screen. For the momument within, however, the Italian Pietro Torrigiano produced the first Renaissance sculpture in England in 1512-18; the heads of the corner angels are specially beautiful.

Henry VII's chapel has its own subsidiary chapels and aisles. In the N aisle is the joint tomb of *Elizabeth I*, completed in 1606 with a suitably stern effigy, and her hated rival *Mary Queen of Scots*. Beyond are two monuments to daughters of James I. The S aisle contains several Tudor monuments rather grander than that to Queen Elizabeth herself. The easternmost chapel is dedicated to the Royal Air Force.

From Henry VII's chapel, **Edward the Confessor's shrine**, which is located just behind the main altar of the abbey, is reached by a bridge, and entered past the wooden effigy and chantry chapel of Henry V, a Gothic structure of the early 15thC. Only the base remains from the magnificent tomb built by Henry III to contain the remains of the Confessor, but there is enough of the gold mosaic to indicate how splendid it must have been. It was made by an Italian artist in about 1270, as was the fine mosaic floor and Henry III's own similar tomb. Also in the chapel is the **coronation throne** of 1300-01, where almost every monarch since William I has been crowned. It contains, under the seat, the **Stone of Scone**, the mystical coronation stone of the Scottish kings, captured by Edward I in 1297. Legends identify it with Jacob's pillow when he dreamed at Bethel, and also as a holy stone in Ireland. It was certainly in use as a coronation stone for Macbeth and other Scottish kings from the 9thC. Its symbolic value persists: in 1950 it was stolen by Scottish nationalists but was recovered a year later. Beside the throne are the state sword and shield of Edward III, and all around are the tombs of the medieval monarchs, some of the finest sculpture surviving from this period in England.

After this holy of holies, the chapels of the S ambulatory are an anticlimax. In the ambulatory itself are the remains of a 13thC painted retable, with a well-preserved figure of *St Peter* on the extreme left. St Edmund's Chapel contains a fine effigy of *William of Valence*, Henry III's half-brother, from 1296. Look for the lovely miniature alabaster effigies of a knight and his lady.

The S transept has two beautiful carved angels from the mid-13thC in the spandrels of the main arch, but is more famous as **Poet's Corner**. Here are buried, or commemorated, many of the greatest writers in the English language. The best monument, *Geoffrey Chaucer*, was placed here in 1555, but probably includes older elements. More recent poets commemorated include Ben Jonson, Milton, Blake, Longfellow and Shakespeare — a very undistinguished statue. Browning, Byron, Tennyson and Henry James have plaques in the floor. On the S wall are two fine late 13thC wall paintings, discovered in 1936.

In the S choir aisle a doorway leads through to the cloister, as dignified as a monastic cloister should be. The earliest part is to the E and N, dating from the 13thC and among the oldest parts of Henry III's work on the abbey; the cloister was finished in the 14thC, and much restored in the 19thC. It now contains a brass-rubbing center, where copies can be made from replicas of medieval brass monuments. On the E side, a passageway leads through to the **chapter house** ⅢⅢ ☆ (*open daily Oct-Feb 9.30am-3.30pm, Mar-Sept 9.30am-6pm*), an exquisitely symmetrical octagon, with its vaulted roof supported on a slender Purbeck marble pier. It was built c.1250 and has been well restored to its medieval state, with beautiful red and gold tiles decorating the floor, and wall paintings. The chapter house was used throughout the Middle Ages for the occasional meetings of Parliament. To the N of the entrance is the small chapel of St Faith, with a high vaulted roof and, behind the altar, a well-preserved painting, probably late 13thC.

Beyond the chapter house is the **Norman Undercroft**, where the **Abbey Museum** (▨ *open daily 10.30am-4.30pm*) houses a display of the abbey's history. Apart from examples of carving, there are a number of royal funeral effigies. Those of the Middle Ages are wood, later ones are wax, clothed in contemporary costume. Armor from Henry V's funeral is particularly interesting.

Westminster Cathedral 🏛 ✝ ☆

Ashley Pl., SW1 ☎834-7452. *Map 17J9* ▨ *Campanile, open Easter-Oct 10am-5pm. Tube Westminster, Victoria.*
When designs were being considered in the late 19thC for the Roman Catholic Cathedral of Westminster, intended to be London's most important Catholic church, a Neo-Gothic structure at first seemed the inevitable choice. In the end, however, an early Christian approach was courageously adopted, against all the prevalent dictates of the era. The result of this farsighted decision is a building of great originality, a strange Byzantine basilica unique in London and cleverly avoiding a false comparison with nearby *Westminster Abbey*.

The cathedral was built under the direction of J.F. Bentley between 1895-1903, using as a model Santa Sophia in Istanbul, together with some Italian Renaissance ideas, the most striking of which is the huge campanile, similar to that of Siena Cathedral but in red brick with lighter stone striping. The top of the tower, 273ft (83m) high, can be visited (by elevator) in summer, and affords marvelous views.

The interior is deeply impressive, with a massive open space created by the great nave, supporting a roof of four shallow domes, purely Byzantine in inspiration. The decoration is still incomplete, with rough brick exposed above the lower levels contributing to the solemn effect. The piers of the nave are giant columns of dark green marble, supposedly from the same quarry as those in Santa Sophia. Other marbles, dramatically patterned in gray and black, cover the walls, and over the altar is a great baldachin of even more brightly colored marble, but again to a restrained design. It is expected that eventually the whole interior be covered with mosaics; unfortunately, those parts completed do not reflect the grandeur of the overall conception and tend toward fussiness. The outstanding works of art in the cathedral are the **Stations of the Cross**, reliefs carried out by Eric Gill in 1913-18.

Westminster, Palace of 🏛 ★

Parliament Sq., SW1 ☎219-4272 *(House of Commons), 219-3107 (House of Lords). Map 18J11* ▣ ⚑ Ⅹ *Visiting arrangements subject to repeated change, check first. During parliamentary sittings admittance to public galleries from St Stephen's entrance. Tube Westminster.*
The effect is stunning: sheer size combines with immense variety and inventive detail to create an architectural triumph so instantly recognizable that it has come to symbolize the very system of government, representative democracy, housed within. In fact, this riverside complex of buildings is only the new home of the mother of parliaments, a high Victorian exercise in medievalism. The buildings are often known simply as the Houses of Parliament.

A royal palace was probably moved from Winchester to Westminster in about 1000, being established on the Island of Thorney in the marshes next to an existing monastery, and Edward the Confessor began an ambitious building programme in 1050-65, the monastery becoming *Westminster Abbey*. The Norman kings followed his lead and William Rufus, the

Conqueror's son, built Westminster Hall in 1097-99, at the time almost certainly the largest hall in Europe. When in residence, medieval kings would call their councils of noblemen to meet at Westminster, a forerunner of the House of Lords. In 1265, a powerful baron called Simon de Montfort began the practice of calling additional councils of knights and burghers to represent the shires and towns. Meeting together from 1332, these subsequently became the House of Commons. A medieval king was not obliged to call a parliament, and only did so when he needed the cooperation of his lords and knights. In theory, they came to advise him, but, in practice, he needed their assistance in the raising of taxes. From this grew the fact, unpalatable to medieval monarchs, that the country could not be governed without the consent of lords and commons.

In the 16thC, when Henry VIII moved his residence to the nearby Whitehall Palace, the Palace of Westminster became the permanent and more exclusive base of Parliament, the Commons using from 1550 the abandoned royal chapel of St Stephen. Westminster Hall was not used for Parliament, however, but retained for the royal courts.

The 17thC saw the long struggle which would eventually lead to the constitutional preeminence of Parliament. In 1642 Charles I attempted to assert the royal power and crush the Commons, losing both crown and head in the process. Since his last desperate entry in 1648 to arrest parliamentary opponents, no monarch has entered the Commons. In 1660 Charles II was recalled to the throne and the struggle between King and Parliament was renewed. During the 18thC, the monarchy lost ground steadily and parliamentary government became a reality, with a prime minister appointed by the monarch according to the electoral wishes of the country.

In constitutional terms, Parliament consists of Monarch, Lords and Commons, all of whom have to assent to the laws by which the country is governed. But, by a process of recurring struggle, members of the Commons have come to have the dominant role — the Lords can now only delay legislation by one year and royal assent is never refused. The Lords is still the highest Court of Appeal in the land. A much criticized survival is that the Lords is still largely composed of hereditary peers, although an increasing number of peers are now created for life only. The system has developed slowly, through reforms and bitter struggles, with a unique combination of traditional ritual and democratic reality. The palace is still a web of ancient regulations: in the Commons, the hatless must take opera hats provided for them in boxes.

Tightened security limits access to the interior of the palace. The medieval royal palace, with its 17th-18thC additions, was largely destroyed by fire in 1834. In 1840, rebuilding began, with only the old cloister, Westminster Hall and the crypt of St Stephen's Chapel being preserved. The architect was Sir Charles Barry, with the younger A.W.N. Pugin as his assistant. Barry was essentially a Classicist, forced by the brief to work in the Gothic idiom. Pugin, on the other hand, was a passionate medievalist — indeed, it was his meticulous drawings that won the commission. The House of Lords chamber was complete by 1847, the Commons by 1850. Both men died in 1852, and the work was not completed overall until 1860.

The most splendid views of the palace are from Westminster Bridge or across the river, taking in the great regular facade Barry constructed along the riverside, with large asymmetrical towers at either end: the huge square **Victoria Tower** to the s and the more slender and original **Clock Tower** to the N, the superb clock of which is Britain's most authoritative. Although this tower is often known as **Big Ben**, that name actually applies to the huge bell inside the clock itself, named after Benjamin Hall, Commissioner of Works at the time.

From the landward side, the visitor sees several different facades and views of the towers, spreading to N and S behind the central bulk of medieval Westminster Hall. Golden-brown Yorkshire limestone was chosen, but it was badly quarried and has needed constant repairs. Recently it has been cleaned to remove the blackened grime and reveal its original mellow color. Every part of the exterior is covered with tracery, statues and pinnacles, with a dominant pattern that echoes Herry VII's chapel across the road.

Of the few remaining medieval elements of the palace, **Westminster Hall ★** is outstanding. The lower walls are the oldest part, dating from the late 11thC. In 1394-99, Richard II replaced the upper walls and roof with the remarkable structure seen today. It is one of the world's greatest timber constructions, and the apogee of English Gothic, a huge and beautiful oak **hammerbeam roof**, with wonderfully carved tracery and angels on the ends of the beams. Statues of early kings, also dating from Richard II's reign, can be seen in niches. The only other survivor from the medieval palace is the **Jewel Tower**, across Abingdon St. and actually closer to the abbey. Strongly fortified and moated, it was built in 1365 as a royal treasure house, and was later used to store records.

There are two public entrances to the Victorian parts of the palace. For those wishing to 'lobby' their members of parliament (a practice whereby constituents can ask their representative to come to the lobby to discuss a particular issue), there is St Stephen's Porch beside the hall. This entrance leads above the medieval crypt, now the Parliament chapel, and to the great lobby beneath an elaborate, spiral lantern which can be seen from outside. This entrance also gives access to the public galleries of the two debating chambers.

For the tour of the palace, which is sometimes allowed, entrance is made by the Norman Porch next to the Victoria Tower. The gate beneath the tower itself is used by the Queen only, for official ceremonies such as the **State Opening of Parliament** (see *Calendar of events* in *Planning*). The porch leads through to the **Robing Room**, a spectacular paneled chamber which amply demonstrates Pugin's effective use of Gothic and Tudor motifs; note especially the ornate fireplace. The **Royal Gallery** beyond, more spectacular yet, has a colorful ceramic floor and gift statues of monarchs.

Through the Prince's Chamber is the **House of Lords**, an absolutely stunning chamber surrounded by sumptuous red leather benches. The leather and wood, the rich colors, and the deep calm make it feel like a monumental clubland lounge, an analogy not altogether inappropriate for the more detached, learned deliberations of the upper house. The Lord Chancellor, who chairs the debates, sits on a red-covered woolsack, and behind him is the royal throne the Lords still maintain (the State Opening takes place in this chamber) beneath an extraordinarily fine gilded canopy, Pugin's masterpiece.

Beyond the Peers' Lobby, Central Lobby and Commons' Lobby is the **House of Commons** itself. It was burned during an air raid in 1941 and the entrance arch has been rebuilt, using some of the damaged stones, between statues of *Winston Churchill* and *Lloyd George*. The chamber itself was built in 1945-50 in a plainer style — neither Pugin-elaborated nor obviously modern. The governing party occupies the benches on one side, the opposition the other. Neither side is supposed to cross the red lines in the carpet, traditionally the distance apart of two drawn swords.

The rest of the Houses of Parliament, consisting of over 1,000 rooms and two miles of corridor, is not open to the public. It is a place of work: committees struggling over the details of legislation and MP's taking care of their constituency business. Restaurants and terraces for the MPs look out over the river, as does Pugin's magnificent **House of Lords Library**.

Whitechapel Art Gallery 🏛

80 Whitechapel High St., E1 ☎*377-0107. Map* **13**F18 ⟦☉⟧ ⊠
▣ *Open Tues-Sun 11am-5pm, 8pm on Wed. Tube Aldgate East.*

A scruffy row of shops in the East End is an unlikely place to find one of England's most celebrated Art Nouveau buildings, but there it is, with a large arched doorway in a plain facade topped by a delightful foliage relief. It was built in 1897-99 by C. Harrison Townsend, a follower of the influential Arts and Crafts Movement, who also designed the Horniman Museum in *Dulwich*. The gallery currently enjoys a high reputation for staging important temporary exhibitions of contemporary art.

Whitehall

Map **10**G-H. *Tube Charing Cross, Westminster.*
The word Whitehall is so firmly embedded in English that it is applied to people, institutions and buildings quite irrespective of whether they belong to the street of that name. Nevertheless, Whitehall has not changed — it is still lined by large government offices, and is still Britain's administrative center. Running s from *Trafalgar Square* toward *Westminster*, it began to take on this character in the late 17thC, as government departments began building around the Royal Palace of Whitehall.

Before 1514, Whitehall Palace was York Place, a house belonging to the Archbishop of York. Henry VIII took it over from Cardinal Wolsey in 1530 and turned it into a huge rambling palace, and in 1619-25 Inigo Jones' magnificent *Banqueting House* was added, the only building that survives.

The northern end of Whitehall resembles any other commercial street in central London until the **Admiralty** is encountered on the w side, a brick building (1722-26) with a large Ionic portico. In front is a handsome screen designed by Robert Adam in 1759-61 with winged sea horses surmounting the gates. Government buildings from about 1900 are followed by the Banqueting House, with the attractive Welsh Office, occupying a private residence from 1772, soon after. On the w side, opposite, is the *Horse Guards Parade* built in 1750-60 to William Kent's designs. Next to it is Dover House (the Scottish Office) with an elegant facade of 1787. Unfortunately, Whitehall at this point is dominated by the great bulk of the Ministry of Defence building, a Portland stone monster finished as late as 1959. Somewhere beneath it are Henry VIII's wine cellars, surviving from the old palace. The diminutive-looking modern statues in front depict *Sir Walter Raleigh* and *Field-Marshal Montgomery*. Opposite is *Downing Street.*

From here, Whitehall becomes Parliament St., with massive 19thC government buildings in Italian Renaissance style. The Cenotaph of 1919, the national monument to Britain's war dead, is in the center of Parliament St.

Beneath the offices, with a public entrance is King Charles St., are the fascinating **Cabinet War Rooms** (⊠ *open Tues-Sun*

10am-5.50pm). This fortified bunker, deep in the bowels of the earth, housed Churchill's emergency center of operations during the war. It can now be seen as it was, with maps, telephones and even the great man's cigars on display.

Wimbledon

Map 20D4. Tube Southfields, Wimbledon, Wimbledon Park.
The modern tennis duels, which have made this sw suburb world famous, had an earlier counterpart, on **Wimbledon Common**, a large expanse of heath once notorious for settling disputes of honor. The **All-England Tennis Courts** themselves are in Church Rd., and the two-week championships in June-July transform the area, attracting both tennis fans and those who come for the copious strawberries and cream and champagne. Inside the splendid ivy-clad main building is a **Lawn Tennis Museum** (▨ *open Mon-Sat 11am-5pm, Sun 2-5pm*).

The Zoo 血 ☆

Regent's Park, NW1 ☎ *722-3333. Map 2B7* ◼ *X* ▣ ✻ *Open daily 10am-6pm, dusk in winter. Tube Regent's Park, Mornington Crescent, Camden Town.*
More properly named the gardens of the Zoological Society of London, the zoo occupies an attractive portion of *Regent'sPark* bisected by the *Grand Union Canal*. Founded in 1826, it is the oldest such institution in the world, and one of the most important. Together with Whipsnade Park in Bedfordshire, where the animals are kept in large open paddocks in the countryside, London Zoo has no less than 5,000 species and, as well as showing animals to the public, it enjoys worldwide repute in the fields of conservation and animal medicine.

Innovation has changed the ways of showing animals, and bold architectural experiments have displaced the old iron cage approach. In many cases the animals are in larger compounds, designed to reflect their natural habitats and separated from the public by moats rather than bars. The most spectacular example, the **Mappin Terraces**, were opened as early as 1914. Here, an artificial mountain is divided into layers, devoted to different animals on succeeding levels. There are at present closed for redevelopment. Similarly, the big cats can be seen at close range in their dens through glass or watched as they roam their paddocks stocked with suitable vegetation. These animals do not have that bored, lethargic appearance that can make zoos so depressing. Precisely because they are so active, the monkeys and apes in the **Michael Sobell Pavilion** (opened in 1972) are perhaps the most enjoyable of the zoo's creatures. More morbidity alluring is one of the world's most extensive collections of reptiles and insects, poisonous snakes and giant spiders.

Two special features are **The Moonlight World**, where nocturnal animals can be seen behaving as if in the dead of night, and the **children's zoo and farm**, with tame animals which will give children rides or can be handled.

London Zoo also has some important examples of modern architecture. The **Penguin Pool** of the 1930s used pre-stressed concrete in a pioneering way, and still looks modern. The **Snowdon Aviary**, opened in 1965, contains a variety of birds in a large open space — superbly functional even if criticized for looking rather like a collapsed radio mast.

The zoo has recently won a much needed 'one-off' government grant and extensive refurbishment of existing exhibits, and the addition of many new ones, is commencing.

Where to stay

London's hotels were described, in one well-bruited year, as the most expensive in the world, then 12 months later found themselves easing to a less-publicized 22nd position in the same *Financial Times* league table. It must be said, of course, that such calculations are greatly influenced by the value of the pound sterling against the visitors' currency, given to considerable fluctuation over recent years, though it is an inescapable fact that prices have recently taken another enormous leap.

The same differing viewpoints attend the hotels' reputations, while the most reflective judges argue that, at both ends of the price spectrum, standards are much the same as those elsewhere in Europe. Though London has not escaped the international trend toward the provision of fewer services, it might be contended that overall standards have improved in recent years.

Categories of hotel

At the most expensive end of the spectrum, what might be described as the grand old hotels of London bear witness to the Englishman's notion of style as an attribute not to be worn on the sleeve. They know that a gentleman does not have to prove anything, and neither do they. They assume that quality, though hideously expensive these days, is timeless, and so can seem old-fashioned to some. They were built for people with ancient country estates who needed a home-from-home in town. The traveler with the resources to understand this will enjoy them. Others may prefer something less English.

Most of the international chains have at least one establishment in London, offering the style of accommodations and service to which their regular patrons are accustomed, though at rather cosmopolitan prices. As most of them offer conference facilities, and are popular with the international executive, advance reservation is essential.

Of the British chains, Trust House Forte is the largest, with the **Grosvenor House** as its flagship. Inter-Continental retains a stronghold in London with several top hotels including the **Inter-Continental, Britannia** and **May Fair** under its egis. The deluxe Savoy group includes the **Savoy, Berkeley, Connaught** and **Claridge's**. Thistle is a good chain of mainly business hotels, concentrated in and around London, as are Ladbroke's hotels.

In the middle price range 'house hotels' are becoming increasingly popular. They usually only have a few rooms and are often converted from attractive row houses. They range from the designer-decorated, such as **Dorset Square** and **L'Hôtel**, to the quaint, such as **Ebury Court**.

The cheaper type of British hotel is often known as a boarding house, or a 'bed-and-breakfast' (or simply 'B & B'). At their best, they are clean, comfortable and friendly, but currently, good 'B & B's' in London are in very short supply; they are rarely to be trusted unless you have a recommendation. **The British Tourist Authority** is promoting a pleasant alternative—staying with a British family. Send for the booklet *Stay with a British Family*, British Tourist Authority, Thames Tower, Blacks Rd., London W6 9EL, or from the many BTA offices throughout the world.

Reservation

If you want to choose the particular hotel you stay in, advance reservation is essential, preferably at least a month ahead. Depending on the time of year, you might be lucky with short-notice reservations, but you might have to be flexible.

Advance reservation of an inexpensive to medium-priced hotel can be arranged by writing to the **London Tourist Board** (Accomodation Services), 26 Grosvenor Gardens, SW1W ODU. Write at least six weeks in advance, suggesting a price bracket and any general preference for location, and the organization will then make a provisional reservation before writing to you to confirm it.

Given some flexibility, it is possible to make an instant reservation at **London Tourist Board and Convention Bureau Information Centres** at Heathrow Airport or Victoria Station (see *Useful addresses* in *Basic information*).

Price

See *How to use this book* for the price guidelines corresponding to the symbols used in all hotel entries. London hotels usually charge by the person, rather than by the room, and sometimes include breakfast in the price, although it is increasingly only a 'Continental breakfast' of toast or croissants and coffee, with a supplement for the fried 'English breakfast.' Check whether VAT (Value Added Tax) is included.

Service is usually included. If you are very pleased with the service, give a small tip to the chambermaid or receptionist.

Meals

The dining facilities range from some of the best restaurants in London to those which do not expect to attract most of their guests. What they nearly all offer, at extra cost, is the great British breakfast of bacon and eggs or kippers. Residential terms, with an evening meal included in the price, are rare.

Hotels classified by area

Bayswater/Paddington
Great Western Royal ▮□
Royal Lancaster ▮▮▮▮
Belgravia/Knightsbridge
Basil Street ▮□ ✿
Berkeley Hotel ▮▮▮▮ ▭
Capital ▮▮▮▮ ▭
Claverly ▮□
Eleven Cadogan Gardens ▮▮▮▮
L'Hôtel ▮□
Hyatt Carlton Tower ▮▮▮▮ ▭
Sheraton Park Tower ▮▮▮▮ ▭
Blackheath
Bardon Lodge □ ▬ ✿
Bloomsbury
Imperial ▮□ ✿
Kingsley ▮□ ✿
City
Great Eastern ▮□
Howard ▮▮▮▮
Covent Garden/Strand
Hazlitt's ▮□ ✿
Savoy ▮▮▮▮ ▭
Strand Palace ▮□ ✿
Waldorf ▮▮▮▮
Hampstead
Sandringham □ ▬ ✿
Kensington
Alexander ▮▮□
Blakes ▮▮▮▮
Gore ▮□ ✿
Halcyon ▮▮▮▮
Kensington Close ▮□ to ▮▮□

Kensington Palace ▮▮▮▮
Pembridge Court ▮□ to ▮▮□
Portobello ▮▮□ to ▮▮▮▮
Marylebone/West End
Berners ▮▮▮▮
Churchill ▮▮▮▮ ▭
Dorset Square ▮▮□ to ▮▮▮▮ ✿
Durrants ▮▮□
Montcalm ▮▮▮▮
White House ▮▮□ ✿
Mayfair
Britannia ▮▮▮▮
Brown's ▮▮▮▮
Claridge's ▮▮▮▮ ▭
Connaught ▮▮▮▮ ▭
Dorchester ▮▮▮▮ ▭
Grosvenor House ▮▮▮▮ ▭
Hilton ▮▮▮▮
Inn on the Park ▮▮▮▮ ▭
Inter-Continental ▮▮▮▮ ▭
May Fair ▮▮▮▮
Westbury ▮▮▮▮
Piccadilly
Athenaeum ▮▮▮▮ ▭
Meridien Piccadilly ▮▮▮▮ ▭
Park Lane ▮▮▮▮
Ritz ▮▮▮▮ ▭
St James's
Dukes ▮▮▮▮
Stafford ▮▮▮▮
Victoria
Collin House □ ▭
Ebury Court ▮□ to ▬
Goring ▮▮▮▮

Alexander
9 Sumner Pl., SW7 ☎*581-1591/5*
☎ *917033. Map* **15K5** ▥ *37 rms*
▣ *37* ⬛ AE ⓓ ⓒⓓ VISA *Tube
South Kensington.*
Location: South Kensington. S.J.
Perelman once issued the entreaty
"Please don't give me nothing to
remember you by," but they haven't
forgotten his stays at The Alexander;
they named a room after him. If he
observed the strangeness of a hotel in
a street so attractive that it is not
allowed to hang a sign, he didn't say
so. The Alexander is announced only
by a brass plate outside, and
maintains a similar note of restful
discretion inside. It is a Victorian
house, in which all bedrooms have
been impeccably modernized, with a
lovely, high-walled garden for the
use of guests. Those visitors who
have a bar at home will feel
comfortable in the self-service
lounge, operating on an honesty
system.
🛏 ⚓ 🔲 🖼 🛥 ⛾

Athenaeum ▦
116 Piccadilly, W1 ☎*499-3464*
☎ *261589. Map* **9H8** ▥ *112 rms*
▣ *112* ▦▦ ⬛ AE CB ⓓ ⓒⓓ
VISA *Tube Green Park.*
*Location: West End, between Mayfair
and Green Park.* Although it is
especially well known for its
unrivaled selection of malt whiskies,
this smallish, pristine 1940s hotel is
full of good ideas. Aptly-named
Lady Athenaeum Club makes sure
lone female travelers are welcomed
and pampered. Guests who want to
jog in the park are loaned tracksuits.
Attention to detail is the keynote. If
you have an afternoon nap, your
sheets will be changed again before
bedtime. Unlike so many present-
day hotels, the Athenaeum doesn't
stint on towels — there are mounds
of them, and luxury bathrooms too.
⚓ ⚕ 🔲 🖼 ⛾

Bardon Lodge ♣
Stratheden Rd., Blackheath, SE3
☎*853-4051* 🔲 *37 rms* ▣ *1* ⬛
ⓒⓓ VISA
*Location: South London, between
Greenwich and Blackheath.* Good
inexpensive hotels are hard to come
by in London at present, and it may
be necessary to look farther afield for
a fair deal. Blackheath is on the edge
of the city, an impressive place with
its vast common and fine Georgian
houses; close by is Greenwich.
Bardon Lodge, owned and run with
some pride by Barbara and Donald
Nott — hence the name — is a
beautifully kept hotel with spacious
rooms (one with a private bathroom,
the rest with a shower cubicle) and a
pleasant dining room.
🔲 🖼 🛥 ⛾

Basil Street Hotel ♣
8 Basil St., SW3 ☎*581-3311*
☎ *28379. Map* **16I7.** ▥▥ *102 rms*
▣ *102* ⬛ ⓒⓓ VISA *Tube
Kensington.*
*Location: Knightsbridge, behind
Harrods.* Much loved not only for the
high standard of service it provides,
but also for its depth of personality.
A woman's hotel in the days when
ladies came from the country to do
their shopping in Knightsbridge, it
still runs the female counterpart to a
gentlemen's club. In the hotel,
however, guests of both sexes are
offered what the Basil describes with
some accuracy as "an island of
hospitality in our brusque, modern
world." Decorated with British and
Oriental antiques, in an Edwardian
building part of which was once the
reservation hall of a station, the Basil
has a coziness that belies its size; it
remains small enough to offer the
personal touch, but sufficiently large
to provide the services of a first-class
hotel.
⚕ 🔲 🖼 🛥

Berkeley Hotel ▦
Wilton Pl., SW1 ☎*235-6000*
☎ *919252. Map* **16I7** ▥▥ *159 rms*
▣ *159* ▦▦ ⬛ ⬛ AE ⓓ ⓒⓓ VISA
Tube Knightsbridge.
*Location: Knightsbridge, opposite
Hyde Park.* Noël Coward's old
Berkeley is gone, yet much of its
character has re-emerged in the new
one, built by the same management
in 1972. "The last really deluxe hotel
to be built in Europe," they claim.
Deluxe rather than grand because,
by today's standards, it is small for a
hotel of this style. The hotel is
known for its service, organized
separately on every floor, has a
rooftop swimming pool, a
gymnasium, sauna, movie theater,
beauty salon, one of London's better
French restaurants, the **Le
Perroquet** bar, and the **Buttery**.
⚕ ⚓ 🔲 🖼 🛥 🛥 ⛾

Berners
Berners St., W1 ☎*636-1629*
☎ *25759. Map* **10E10** ▥▥ *237 rms*
▣ *237* ⬛ AE CB ⓓ ⓒⓓ VISA *Tube
Tottenham Court Road.*
Location: Off Oxford St. A
magnificent job of refurbishment has
been carried out in this grand old
hotel, the splendid interior of which
seems at odds with its never having
been famous or fashionable. The

location is wrong for that, yet right for shopping, and near to theaterland. Bedrooms round the central well are very quiet. A dozen rooms are specially designed for the benefit of handicapped people. There is a carvery-type restaurant.

♨ ᕴ ▢ ⬚ ⚆ ⛳ ♟ ⛾

Blakes
33-35 Roland Gdns., SW7 ☎*370-6701* ☎ *8813500. Map 15K4* ▥ *50 rms* ▭ *50* ⚊ AE ⊕ ◉ VISA *Tube South Kensington.*
Location: South Kensington, off Old Brompton Rd. Mandatory for media folk, who are suitably at home in an hotel owned by a designer. It shows, too, with that beautiful birdcage, the black and white dining room and a sunken bed in one suite. And which other small London hotel serves pastrami on rye? Also one of the best hotel restaurants in town, and what the management describes as "all the best services to be expected from a first-class hotel," all in a prim Victorian street.

⌂ ▢ ⬚ ⚆

Britannia
Grosvenor Sq. (entrance Adam's Row), W1 ☎*629-9400* ☎ *23941. Map 9G8* ▥ *354 rms* ▭ *354* ▤ ▦ ⚊ AE CB ⊕ ◉ VISA *Tube Bond Street.*
Location: Mayfair, near Oxford St. and Hyde Park. This very large Georgian square, lined with embassies, has largely been rebuilt and restored, and there is little to suggest that behind its facades lies a large hotel. Even more surprisingly, the Britannia was built only in 1970, and its interior is a well-achieved blend of original and reproduction Georgiana. Nonetheless, its built-in 'pub' can claim to stand on the site where a Cabinet meeting learned from a horse-borne messenger that Wellington had beaten Napoleon at Waterloo. The hotel has undergone extensive refurbishment of late, with the creation of fewer but more spacious bedrooms. It now sports an Anglo-American café, and two restaurants, one Japanese.

♨ ▢ ⬚ ⚆ ⚘ ♟ ⛾

Brown's
22-24 Dover St., W1 ☎*493-6020* ☎ *28686. Map 9G9* ▥ *133 rms* ▭ *133* ⚊ AE CB ⊕ VISA *Tube Green Park.*
Location: Mayfair, near Bond St. and Piccadilly. The original Mr Brown was butler to Lord Byron, and the hotel he founded became the most renowned among those intended to

be a London home-away-from-home for the gentry. It still retains this character in the charm, individuality and style of its rooms, though many are, by modern standards, rather small and gloomy. Theodore Roosevelt was married from Brown's, and FDR and Eleanor honeymooned there; the Dutch Government in exile declared war on Japan and Queen Wilhelmina and Princess Juliana stayed here. Brown's still takes pride in maintaining the privacy of its guests, but life is inevitably less serene in the late 20thC. It is now owned by the Trust House Forte chain.

⌂ ♨ ▢ ⬚ ♟

Capital ▦
Basil St., SW3 ☎ *589-5171* ☎ *919042. Map 16/7* ▥ *52 rms* ▭ *52* ▤ ▦ ⚊ AE CB ⊕ ◉ VISA *Tube Knightsbridge.*
Location: Knightsbridge, behind Harrods. So friendly and informal that the designation 'luxury hotel' seems unfairly intimidating. Yet this sophisticated little modern hotel is the sort of place that provides each guest with a toothbrush and bathrobe, leaves a rose for every lady, and has a *concierge* who attends to every need. Public rooms and reception areas decorated by Nina Campbell highlight the feeling of intimate luxury. Upper floors have recently been redecorated in Ralph Lauren fabrics by the owner's wife Margaret Levin, who was also responsible for their bed and breakfast establishment next door, **L'Hôtel**. The Capital has a good French restaurant (see *Restaurants*).

♨ ᕴ ▢ ⬚ ⛾

Churchill ▦
30 Portman Sq., W1 ☎*486-5800* ☎ *264831. Map 8F7* ▥ *489 rms* ▭ *489* ▤ ▦ ⚊ AE CB ⊕ ◉ VISA *Tube Marble Arch.*
Location: Off Oxford St. The glittering, marbled lobby is a suitably impressive introduction to this modern luxury hotel, recently purchased from the Loews group for an impressive sum by Mr Charles Chan, which sits in a busy elegant square behind Selfridges store. The public rooms and the thickly-carpeted bedrooms are in a more relaxed, but equally sumptuous, Regency style. The Churchill has an international restaurant, the Arboury, and a 24hr lounge for drinks and snacks. Service is efficient, unobtrusive and faultless.

♨ ᕴ ▢ ⬚ ⚆ ♟

Hotels

Claridge's ▨
Brook St., W1 ☎ 629-8860
☎ 21872. *Map* **9F8**. ▥ 204 rms
and 54 suites ▣ 258 ▧ ≈ AE
⊙ ⊙ VISA *Tube Bond Street.*
Location: Mayfair, near Oxford St.
Visiting royals and statesmen are
inclined to choose Claridge's which,
despite its fame, is imperturbably
discreet. No bar, because such
trappings don't fit a country house,
even if it is in the middle of London.
Drink in the sitting room (not
'lounge' — it isn't an airport), where
a small orchestra plays at lunchtime
and in the evening. Nor would it be
very dignified to publish a tariff, so
they don't. Lots of Art Deco, but the
tone is better set by log fires in the
suites. A guest who has been
shopping returns with a brace of
pheasants; without batting an eyelid,
the porter carries them for her as if
they were Gucci suitcases.
‡ ▢ ⬀ ⚄ ♟

Claverly
14 Beaufort Gdns, SW3 ☎ 589-
8541 *Map* **16I6** ▥ 36 rms ▣ 2 VISA
Tube Knightsbridge.
Location: Close to Harrods. Beaufort
Gardens, a quiet enclave off busy
Brompton Rd., has attracted two
new upscale bed and breakfast
hotels, this one and, at No. 33, the
Beaufort (☎ 584-5252 ▥ *to* ▥),
which is more expensive with a good
support system for businessmen.
The Claverly has won a British
Tourist Award owing to its general
friendliness, cleanliness and comfort.
▢ ⬀ ⚄

Collin House ▨
104 Ebury St., SW1 ☎ 730-8031
Map **17J8** ▢ 13 rms ☺ *Tube
Victoria.*
*Location: Belgravia, close to Victoria
Station.* One of the very few reliable,
relatively inexpensive bed and
breakfast hotels in central London,
run with care by Welshman Mr D.L.
Thomas for the past six or so years.
Ebury St. is an excellent location
which has spawned many small
hotels such as Collin House, many of
them not to be recommended,
although see **Ebury Court**.
▢ ⬀ ⚄

Connaught ▨
16 Carlos Pl., W1 ☎ 499-7070.
Map **9G8** ▥ 90 rms ▣ 90 ▧ ◨
⊙ VISA *Tube Bond Street.*
*Location: Mayfair, near Hyde Park
and Oxford St.* The finest of
London's grand old hotels, according
to its devoted following, and
certainly the best gastronomically

(see *Restaurants*). The Connaught
is smaller than other hotels in its peer
group, and accordingly offers a little
less in the way of facilities and
services, but that kind of
expansiveness isn't its style; the
luxury is more personal. Likewise,
the cozy public rooms make a virtue
of their intimacy. The clubby
atmosphere fits this part of
Mayfair. The hotel does have its
detractors: for the faithful nothing
could ever be wrong, but newcomers
have dared to whisper that it may be
resting on its laurels just a tiny bit.
‡ ▢ ⬀ ⚄ ▾

Dorchester ▨
Park Lane, W1 ☎ 629-8888
☎ 887704.
Location: Overlooking Hyde Park.
With its stately terraces, the
Dorchester looks like an ocean liner
that has somehow been moored on
Park Lane. Bought in 1985 by the
worlds richest man, the Sultan of
Brunei, the hotel closed at the end of
1988 for a £70 million refit lasting
more than a year.

Dorset Square ♣
39 Dorset Sq., NW1 ☎ 723-7874
☎ 263964. *Map* **8D7** ▥ *to* ▥ 37
rms and 12 suites ▣ 49 ▧ ◨ AE
⊙ VISA *Tube Marylebone.*
Location: Close to Marylebone Station,
s *Regent's Park.* Situated in a
lovely Regency square (guests have
the use of the central garden), this is
one of London's best and more
stylish 'house hotels.' One is
immediately impressed by the
carefully contrived decoration,
almost alarming in its perfection, but
nevertheless a charming evocation of
the country house style. All the
bedrooms are impressive, with
marble bathrooms: the suites,
housed a few doors along the street,
are sumptuous, with huge bowls of
fresh flowers and crowded drinks
trays, one even with a grand piano.
Service is intelligent and efficient.
‡ ▴ ⚄ ▾ ⊙ ▱ ⬀

Dukes Hotel
34-36 St. James's Pl., SW1 ☎ 491-
4840 ☎ 28283. *Map* **9H9** ▥ 36
rms and 22 suites ▣ 52 ▧ ◨
AE ⊙ ⊙ VISA *Tube Green Park.*
*Location: St James's, near Green Park
and St James's Palace.* In a gas-lit
courtyard, a small but rather grand
hotel opened in 1906 and occupying
what was once presumably
someone's Upstairs-Downstairs town
house. Dukes was pleased when an
enthusiastic guest described it as "the
smallest castle in England." Only in

London could a location be so pretty and tranquil yet so close to the throbbing heart of the city. Despite its being almost claustrophobically small, Dukes offers full hotel facilities, including 24hr service. It has recently undergone refurbishment, with improved suites and reception rooms.

⌂ ‡ 🗔 🖼 🖋 👥

Durrants Hotel

George St., W1 ☎ *935-8131*
☎ *894919. Map 9F9* 🔲 *to* 🎽 *100 rms* 🔲 *70* ⇥ *AE* 🖸 🖸 *VISA Tube Bond Street.*
Location: Near Oxford St. In a street which is, as its name suggests, Georgian, this attractive small hotel is perennially popular, although rooms are small and in need of attention. A portrait of a Durrant patriarch, dating back to 1782, hangs among the delightful collection of oils and prints. There are leather chairs and pretty desks in the writing room, antiques on sale to guests, an open fire in the bar, Devenish beer in the bottle, pheasant for dinner when it's in season, and brass bedsteads.

‡ 🗔 *those rooms with bath* 🖼 🖋
👥

Ebury Court ⬛

26 Ebury St., SW1 ☎ *730-8147. Map 17J8. 39 rms* 🔲 *12* ⇥ 🖸 *VISA Tube Victoria, Sloane Square.*
Location: Victoria/Pimlico. Cottagey, quaint and under the proud eye of the owners, Mr and Mrs Topham, who have been there since the 1930s and live on the premises. To be a guest is thus to stay in the Topham's home. Their full English breakfast includes haddock and kippers, there is home-baked bread and roast duckling for dinner on weekends. In order to have a drink, though, it is necessary to pay a nominal fee to join the Topham's club; this is no place for libertines, despite one or two four-poster beds. In the lobby a list is posted detailing the times at which the Guards pass on their way to Buckingham Palace; they are best seen from a balconied first-floor room.

‡ 🖼

Eleven Cadogan Gardens

11 Cadogan Gdns., SW3 ☎ *730-3426* ☎ *8813318. Map 16J7* 🎽 *58 rms* 🔲 *58. Tube Sloane Square.*
Location: Belgravia, near Sloane Square. So discreet that it has no sign even on the door, which is kept locked. No wonder it is favored by diplomats. Late Victorian exterior, with decor to match: a glorious

marble fireplace in one room; a drawing room with open fire. Full English breakfast in bed, and they'll send out for a bottle of champagne (the establishment has no liquor licence); they'll even deliver you to the airport in a Rolls.

⌂ 🖼 🖋 ⚓

Gore ✿

189 Queen's Gate, SW7 ☎ *584-6601* ☎ *296244. Map 15/4* 🎽 *54 rms* 🔲 *54* ⇥ *AE* 🖸 🖸 *VISA Tube South Kensington.*
Location: Kensington, near the Albert Hall and Hyde Park. With ivy outside, potted plants inside, and good furniture in the more expensive rooms (with beautifully tiled modern bathrooms), this warm and welcoming hotel has few of the usual hallmarks of a chain member, in this case, Best Western. Of the honeymoonish deluxe rooms, one has a four-poster, real log fire and leaded windows, and another, in Italian style, has a bed which reputedly belonged to Judy Garland, but the Gore also caters to many business visitors from Continental Europe. There is a small, intimate bar, and a coffee shop which is open throughout the day.

‡ 🗔 🖼 🖃 ▼

Goring

15 Beeston Pl., Grosvenor Gdns., SW1 ☎ *834-8211* ☎ *919166. Map 17J9* 🎽 *90 rms* 🔲 *90* 🔲 ⇥ *AE* 🖸 🖸 *VISA Tube Victoria.*
Location: Victoria, near Buckingham Palace. A book on Buckingham Palace written by the hotel's founder is provided for each guest along with the Bible, and royal carriages may occasionally be seen calling at the Goring to collect diplomat guests. The thorough-minded Mr Goring was the first hotelier in the world to fit all of his rooms with central heating and baths, and he would undoubtedly be pleased to know that the hotel is still in the family three generations later. There are, after all, few full-service hotels of this size still in private hands. Some of the original furniture, including brass bedsteads, is still in use, and the policy has clearly been to renovate rather than replace, although many of the rooms have now been given a proper facelift. The public rooms are elegant and inviting (though the color scheme in the newly revamped front hall has excited some controversy) with an excellent writing room, a small bar and a good restaurant that is worth sampling.

‡ 🗔 🖼 🖋 👥 ▼

Hotels

Great Eastern
Liverpool St., EC2 ☎ *283-4363*
⊚ *886812. Map* **13E17** ▥ *164 rms*
▭ *129* ⊟ ᴀᴇ ⊙ ⓒ ᴠɪsᴀ *Closed
Christmas. Tube Liverpool
Street.*
Location: *The City.* Away from the
West End (though only a few stops
on the tube), and in the heart of old
London. Handy, too, for those
wishing to travel on to the eastern
counties of England or to Continental
Europe. There is a genuinely
traditional quality about railway
hotels like this one. Spacious, high-
ceilinged bedrooms, though with
twin beds more available than
doubles, and simple fittings. Some
bedrooms have wash basins, but the
majority also have bathrooms,
usually with big, deep tubs, though
often without showers. High ceilings
in the public rooms, too, with ornate
moldings. A magnificent stained-
glass dome hangs over the carvery
(one of three restaurants in the
building).
‡ ▢ ◪ ▱ ☲ ☙ ♈

Great Western Royal
Praed St., W2 ☎ *723-8064*
⊚ *263972. Map* **7F5** ▯ *165 rms*
▭ *165* ⇌ ᴀᴇ ᴄʙ ⊙ ⓒ ᴠɪsᴀ *Tube
Paddington.*
Location: *Paddington.* When the
great engineer Brunel built this
hotel, he intended it to be the
starting point of journeys by way of
his adjoining, and architecturally
magnificent, station and Great
Western Railway, via Bristol and his
Great Western steamship, to New
York. It has slumbered somewhat
since then, though 1988 has seen a
great deal of sprucing up. Prices, for
London, are reasonable.
‡ ▢ ▱ ☙ ♈

Grosvenor House 🏨
Park Lane, W1 ☎ *499-6363*
⊚ *24871. Map* **8G7** ▥ *466 rms,
70 suites, 160 apartments* ▭ *696*
⊟ ▱ ⇌ ᴀᴇ ᴄʙ ⊙ ⓒ ᴠɪsᴀ *Tube
Marble Arch.*
Location: *Mayfair, overlooking Hyde
Park.* The flagship of the Trust
House Forte group is something of a
modern-day grand hotel in its scale
and in the extent of its service and
facilities, which include a pool,
solarium, gymnasium and Jacuzzi.
Built in 1928 as apartments, and a
social center during World War II when it
accommodated American officers,
the Grosvenor House is famous for
its huge banqueting room. There's a
pianist to accompany afternoon tea at
which, despite the grandeur of the
place, the atmosphere is relaxing and

children are welcome. A well-run
hotel.
‡ ⅋ ▢ ▱ ◁« ⇋ ☙ ☙ ♈ ♫ ♉

Halcyon
81 Holland Park, W11 ☎ *727-7288*
⊚ *226721 Map* **6H1** ▥ *44 rms*
▭ *44* ⊟ ⇌ ᴀᴇ ⊙ ⓒ ᴠɪsᴀ *Tube
Holland Park.*
Location: *Close to Kensington High St.*
Expensive and very *à la mode* the
Halcyon is ideally placed for the
visitor: away from the hurly-burly in
gracious and exclusive Holland Park,
but just a short taxi ride from the city
center. The interior is a kind of
modern rendition of the *belle epoque*,
luxurious and very soothing. There's
a classy, pastel-shaded restaurant, the
Kingfisher, opening onto a small
garden where drinks can be taken in
summer, as well as 24hr room
service.
‡ ⅋ ▢ ▱ ☙ ♈ ♉

Hazlitt's ♧
6 Frith St., W1 ☎ *434-1771. Map*
10F10 ▯ *22 rms and 1 suite*
▭ *23* ⊟ ⊙ ⓒ ᴠɪsᴀ *Tube
Tottenham Court Rd.*
Location: *Soho.* There are precious
few hotels of character at this price
range in central London, certainly no
others in Soho; a pity, for it makes an
amusing and convenient location. So
Hazlitt's, named after the essayist
William Hazlitt who resided and died
here in 1830, is a welcome
newcomer. Unpretentious and
refreshingly simple — even
puritanical — in appearance, it has
cream-painted walls, plain antique
furniture and wobbly, uneven floors
and staircases. Bedrooms are spotless
and comfortable: bathrooms are
great fun, with free-standing
Victorian baths and matching loos
and basins, antique prints on the
walls and stone busts balancing on
window sills. Ambience and a
pleasant professional young staff
make up for the lack of 'extras.'
▢ ▱

Hilton
22 Park Lane, W1 ☎ *493-8000*
⊚ *24973. Map* **9H8** ▥ *501 rms*
▭ *501* ⊟ ▱ ⇌ ᴀᴇ ᴄʙ ⊙ ⓒ ᴠɪsᴀ
Tube Hyde Park Corner.
Location: *Mayfair, overlooking Hyde
Park.* Great excitement when the
28-story new Hilton presented itself
in Park Lane in the early 1960s, and
some controversy about its modern
style and proportions; today, it is
part of the scenery, with its **Trader
Vic's** restaurant and bar almost an
institution. Improvements have
recently been carried out and there is

a food and drink service in the **Lobby Lounge**, as well as the **British Harvest** restaurant serving English specialties. The **Roof Restaurant**, with its marvelous views, remains, and the room service still offers Middle Eastern gastronomic specialties. The rooms have very large beds but are otherwise quite simple. One whole floor is devoted to nonsmokers. The public areas are very busy, with theater, secretarial and British Airways ticket desks.
⬚ □ 🖼 📠 ≪ 👗 ♈ ⦿

L'Hôtel

28 Basil St., SW3 ☎ *589-6286*
⊕ *919042 Map 16/7* ▌▌ *11 rms and 1 suite* ▭ *12* ⇥ 🅰🅴 🆅🅸🆂🅰 *Tube Knightsbridge.*
Location: Next to Harrods. A very upscale version of the big-city B & B, whose well-heeled clientele feel that it's a relief to get away from the relentless pace of a large, bustling full-service hotel once in a while. Rooms are fairly small, attractive without being glamorous; breakfast is taken in the smart basement **Métro** wine bar, which is also open to nonresidents for light French lunches and dinners. As befits an establishment owned by the same couple who own the **Capital** next door, staff are courteous and professional and they welcome families.
⌂ ⬚ □ 🖼

Howard

Temple Pl., WC2 ☎ *836-3555*
⊕ *268047. Map 11F13* ▌▌▌▌ *117 rms and 24 suites* ▭ *141* ⇥ 🅰🅴 🅲🅱 ⊕ 🅲🅾 🆅🅸🆂🅰 *Tube Temple.*
Location: Overlooking the Thames, on the edge of The City. Annoyingly for visiting businessmen with little time on their hands, the City was until recently deprived of hotels. Then came the Tower Thistle at St Katharine's Dock (☎ *481-2575* ▌▌▌▌), which is now joined farther upstream by the Howard. Exhorbitant prices are evident from the over-the-top decor in the public rooms, although the bedrooms are more understated and luxurious. Business facilities are legion and service is appropriately smooth. More hotels are scheduled for this area of London — all of them in futuristic Docklands.
⌂ ⬚ □ 🖼 🍴 �}🌱 👗 ♈

Hyatt Carlton Tower 🏨

2 Cadogan Pl., SW1 ☎ *235-5411*
⊕ *21944. Map 16/J7* ▌▌▌▌ *224 rms* ▭ *224* ▥ ▱ ⇥ 🅰🅴 🅲🅱 ⊕ 🅲🅾 🆅🅸🆂🅰 *Tube Knightsbridge, Sloane Square.*

Location: Between Knightsbridge and Chelsea, off Sloane St. Whether your requirement is for enormous breakfasts or a kosher dinner (and guests range from rock stars to foreign politicians), American-cut beef or contemporary French cuisine, the Carlton Tower can meet your wishes, and you can always make your penances in the new health club, the **Peak**. The hotel has always had an individuality, perhaps because the very building itself is distinctive: a handsome rectangular structure with a matching 15-floor tower that looks more 1930s than 1960s (which it is). Under the Hyatt banner it has undergone major cosmetic surgery and, with a well-equipped business center, can vie as one of the best business hotels in London. The location, in a quiet square, has a character of its own.
⌂ ⬚ □ 🖼 🌱 ≪ 🕭 👗 ♈

Imperial

Russell Sq., WC1 ☎ *837-3655, reservations 278-7871* ⊕ *263951. Map 10E11* ▌▌ *447 rms* ▭ *447* ▱ ⇥ 🅰🅴 ⊕ 🅲🅾 🆅🅸🆂🅰 *Tube Russell Square.*
Location: Bloomsbury, near the British Museum. This modern, purpose-built hotel is the flagship of a small group owned by one family. It stands on the site of a previous Imperial hotel which was famous for its Turkish baths. The present Imperial is much more functional, but provides well-equipped accommodations in a convenient location.
⬚ 🚿 □ 🖼 👗

Inn On The Park 🏨

Hamilton Pl., Park Lane, W1 ☎ *499-0888* ⊕ *22771. Map 9H8* ▌▌▌▌ *202 rms and 26 suites* ▭ *228* ▤▤ ▱ ⇥ 🅰🅴 🅲🅱 ⊕ 🅲🅾 🆅🅸🆂🅰 *Tube Hyde Park Corner.*
Location: Mayfair, overlooking Hyde Park. The only European hotel in the Four Seasons group, built in 1970, kept in superb condition, and favored by stars, though it is better known as the home of Howard Hughes during one of his most demanding years. Despite its being such a recent building, the Inn On The Park has architecturally a 1950s look, and some of its suites are in a 1930s style, though each is individually appointed, and the hotel is lavishly furnished with antiques. In the Queen Anne-style lounge, ten different teas are offered, with a pianist or harpist to provide additional soothing. Service in the hotel is outstanding, and there are two good restaurants, **Four Seasons**

and **Lanes**. Many people speak of this as London's best hotel.
✳ ♿ ☐ 🖾 ⛵ 🛳 ♥

Inter-Continental 🏨
1 Hamilton Pl., Hyde Park Corner, W1 ☎ *409-3131* ✆ *25853. Map 9H8* ▥▥▥ *500 rms* 🛏 *500* ▦ 🍽 AE CB ✆ 💳 VISA *Tube Hyde Park Corner.*
Location: Hyde Park Corner, overlooking Hyde Park. Very much the American style of luxury hotel, despite its now being owned by the large British group Grand Metropolitan: spacious rooms, often with separate sitting areas; individual heating and air-conditioning controls; dual-voltage; doorbell; telephone extension in the bathroom, free in-house movies, not to mention scales and a clothesline. A coffee house with sufficient privacy for breakfast meetings, and no wonder female executives seem to favor this hotel, with its Aquascutum and Cartier shops. Excellent cocktail barman, and excellent restaurant, **Le Soufflé**. Rolls-Royces available for rental.
✳ ♿ ☐ 🖾 ⛵ 🛳 ♥ ● ⤴

Kensington Close
Wrights Lane, W8 ☎ *937-8170* ✆ *23914. Map 14/3* ☐ *to* ▥▥▥ *524 rms* 🛏 *524* 🍽 ⤴ AE CB ✆ 💳 VISA *Tube Kensington High Street.*
Location: Kensington High St. With goldfish ponds in its award-winning garden (with tables in the summer, and illumination in the evening), a swimming pool, squash courts, sauna and even 'health' cocktails, this is the ideal medium-price hotel for a keep-fit freak. This Trust House Forte hotel in a converted apartment block is otherwise a rather sprawling and conventionally modern building.
✳ ☐ 🖾 ⛵ ≋ 🛳 ♥

Kensington Palace
De Vere Gdns., W8 ☎ *937-8121* ✆ *262422. Map 15/4* ▥▥▥ *298 rms* 🛏 *298* ⤴ AE CB ✆ 💳 *Tube Kensington High Street.*
Location: Opposite Kensington Gardens. Beautifully and lavishly refurbished a few years back as one of the London showpieces of the Scottish group Thistle Hotels. In true Scottish style, kippers and black pudding are proudly featured on the breakfast buffet menu, and they can be enjoyed in an elegant restaurant overlooking the park. Rooms are attractive and comfortable. The hotel is much used by airline staff and executives. Another excellent middle-market Thistle hotel is the

Royal Horseguards (*Whitehall Court, SE1* ☎ *839-3400*) with splendid views from its river-facing rooms from the 4th to 9th floors.
✳ ☐ 🖾 ◁€ 🛳 ♪

Kingsley ♣
☎ *242-5881* ✆ *211517. Map 10E11* ▥▥▥ *146 rms* 🛏 *146* ⤴ AE CB ✆ 💳 VISA *Tube Tottenham Court Road.*
Location: Bloomsbury, near British Museum. Warm and inviting hotel, ideal for families, offering accommodations at good-value prices in a very convenient location. The Kingsley is a full-scale hotel, with a bar and carvery restaurant, owned by the Mount Charlotte Group.
✳ ☐ 🖾 🛳 ♥

May Fair
Stratton St., W1 ☎ *629-7777* ✆ *262526. Map 9G9* ▥▥▥ *322 rms* 🛏 *322* ▦ ⤴ AE CB ✆ 💳 *Tube Green Park.*
Location: Mayfair, just off Piccadilly. The most entertaining hotel in London. With its own inbuilt theater and cinema, the May Fair continues to pursue the performing arts, though in a lower key than it did during the big band era, with its long-gone Candlelight Room. The rooms are well-decorated with huge beds and attractive bathrooms — you can even have a spa bath if that is what turns you on. An Intercontinental hotel.
✳ ☐ 🥂 🛳 ♥ ⤴ �

Meridien Piccadilly 🏨
Piccadilly, W1 ☎ *734-8000* ✆ *25795. Map 10G10* ▥▥▥ *254 rms and 30 suites* 🛏 *284* ▦ ⤴ AE CB ✆ 💳 VISA *Tube Piccadilly Circus.*
Location: Near Piccadilly Circus. Reopened in late 1985 after a lavish year-long refurbishment program, the Piccadilly has been transformed into a top-class luxury hotel and is now owned by the Air France company, Meridien. The Edwardian extravagance of the interior, protected by preservation orders, has been restored to its former glory with the Oak Room as its superb *pièce de la résistance* (see *Restaurants*), while the pillared roof terrace has been glassed in to create a stunning conservatory-style brasserie. Executives in particular will be lured by the extensive conference facilities, and the luxurious basement health club complex, which number a pool, a gym, squash courts and Turkish baths.
✳ ☐ 🖾 ≋ 🛳 ♥ ● ♪ 🍸

Montcalm

Great Cumberland Pl., W1 ☎ *402-4288* ● *28710. Map 8F7* ▮▮▮▮ *104 rms and 12 suites* ▭ *116* ▤ ⇥ AE CB ⊕ ⊕ VISA *Tube Marble Arch.*

Location: *Near Marble Arch and Oxford St.* Behind its dignified Georgian facade, a hotel which quietly evinces all the pampering luxury and style required by the international businessman or his wife. The antique gilt reception desk, lavish leather sofas and military chests set the tone, and there are spiral staircases within the suites.

◠ ‡ ❑ ⬚ Ⱡ

Park Lane

Piccadilly, W1 ☎ *499-6321* ● *21533. Map 9H8* ▮▮▮▮ *300 rms and 24 suites* ▭ *324* ▤ *partial* ◠ ⇥ AE ⊕ ⊕ VISA *Tube Green Park.*

Location: *Piccadilly, overlooking Green Park.* This lovely old establishment is still privately-owned, one of the largest in London. From its needlessly misleading name (Piccadilly is every bit as grand as Park Lane), the hotel is full of quirkiness and character. The French château is decorated with carved paneling from J.P. Morgan's home, and the ballroom is a magnificent consummation of the Art Deco themes which pervade the hotel. Rooms are spacious, with walk-in closets and often with mahogany, 1920s-style beds. The beauty salon offers aromatherapy.

‡ ❑ ⬚ ⊟ ⬥ Ⱡ ♪

Pembridge Court

34 Pembridge Gdns., W2 ☎ *229-9977* ● *298363. Map 6G2* ▯ *to* ▮▮▮ *26 rms and 12 suites* ▭ *24* ⇥ AE ⊕ ⊕ VISA *Tube Notting Hill Gate.*

Location: *Notting Hill, 1 mile (1.5km) w of center.* The Notting Hill locals who enjoy the French cooking and countrified ambience of **Caps** restaurant aren't always aware that this is part of a hotel. Caps in fact doubles as a breakfast room, apart from which there is only a small lounge and bar and the rooms, small but bright, impeccably kept, and comfortable. Recently upgraded rooms have en-suite bathrooms, while all others have showers. Many of the walls are adorned with a collection of Victorian fans and lacework. The hotel has very much a family feeling. Loyal clients include antique dealers who visit **Portobello Road** market (see *Shopping*).

◠ ‡ ❑ ⬚ ⬥ Ⱡ

Portobello

22 Stanley Gdns., W11 ☎ *727-2777* ● *268349* ▮▯ *to* ▮▮▮ *25 rms* ▭ *7* AE ⊕ ⊕ VISA *Tube Notting Hill Gate.*

Location: *Just N of Holland Park.* An idiosyncratic small hotel which people tend to love or hate. Rooms vary greatly in style, quality and size and are priced accordingly; ones termed 'cabins' are tiny. Only suites and 'special rooms' have bathrooms (all others have showers) and these are spacious and fun — a good choice for a romantic weekend. An added bonus for escapees is the 24hr food and drink service, though it can be erratic.

◠ ‡ ❑ ⬚ ⊟ Ⱡ

Ritz ▦

Piccadilly, W1 ☎ *493-8181* ● *267200. Map 9G9* ▮▮▮▮ *116 rms and 14 suites* ▭ *130* ⇥ AE CB ⊕ ⊕ VISA *Tube Green Park.*

Location: *Near St James's and Green Park.* The first hotel to bear the name of César Ritz was in Paris, and he brought with him the architectural style of the Rue de Rivoli when he opened this London establishment at the beginning of the 1900s. He even imported French craftsmen to work on the Louis XVI interior. In the early days of the Ritz, the Prince of Wales used to dance there; later it became a favored lunch place for Noël Coward, and postwar residents included millionaires such as Getty and Gulbenkian. With the disappearance of such grandiosity, the Ritz has faced the difficult task of adapting itself to a less richly textured world. Sadly, one of its two famous bars has long gone, but other features are happily immovable, like the staircase and rotunda; the restaurant (see *Restaurants*), with its magnificent view and *trompe-l'oeil* ceiling, and the spectacular **Palm Court**, with its ornate marble fountain. The decor and furnishings in the Palm Court have been restored, and afternoon tea is served there, while on Fri and Sat nights there is dancing to a 12-piece orchestra. The Ritz has been through patchy times recently but it has now re-established itself as one of the world's great hotels.

‡ ❑ ⬚ ⬰ ⬇ ⬥ Ⱡ ♪

Royal Lancaster

Lancaster Terrace, W2 ☎ *262-6737.* ● *24822. Map 7G5* ▮▮▮▮ *418 rms* ▭ *418* ▤ ◠ ⇥ AE ⊕ ⊕ VISA *Tube Lancaster Gate.*

Location: *Bayswater, opposite Kensington Gardens.* A comfortable

Hotels

and well-maintained modern hotel in the Rank group, in an excellent location, from which some rooms have lovely views of the park. The rooms are well-appointed, and the hotel has an informal café serving pasta dishes and grills, as well as its Anglo-French restaurant.

‡ ⚲ ⬜ ◪ ⬱ ☀ ☂ ☒

Sandringham ◼︎ ✿
3 Holford Rd., Hampstead, NW3 ☎435-1569. Map **21C4** ⬜ 14 rms ▭ 4. Tube Hampstead.
Location: Hampstead, N of center, near the heath. Every guest believes this bed-and-breakfast hotel is his or her own secret, but it turns out to be quite well known — unsurprisingly, in the light of its being owned by Mrs Dreyer, whose friendliness and helpfulness has enhanced the visit of many a stranger to London. Though she has retired now, her son Anthony and his wife continue the tradition, and are gradually redecorating many of the rooms. Dried flowers on the tables, well-filled china cupboards, a breakfast room overlooking the garden. Small, immaculate rooms, with baths and showers. A Victorian house in a villagey Hampstead street, with panoramic views of London. Perhaps because Hampstead has so many bookstores, the Sandringham is popular with academics.

⌂ ◪ ⬱ ◁≪

Savoy ⌂
Strand, WC2 ☎836-4343 ☎ 24234. Map **11G12** ▨ 153 rms and 49 suites ▭ 202 ▤ partial ⬱ ⚌ AE CB ⬩ VISA Tube Charing Cross.
Location: Strand, near Covent Garden and South Bank. The Earl of Savoy built a palace on this site in 1245, and the present hotel was opened in 1869 by Richard D'Oyly Carte, who first staged the operettas of Gilbert and Sullivan in the adjoining **Savoy Theatre**, which is still functioning. With its tucked-away entrance at the front, and gardens facing the Thames at the back, the Savoy is full of extravagant treats. An open fire greets guests, afternoon tea is served in a garden setting with a new gazebo, and recent renovation has uncovered yet more 1920s features. The emphasis is on thorough hotel-keeping and comfort, with Irish linen sheets on the beds, and mattresses made by the Savoy's own workshop. Most bathrooms have marble floors and satisfyingly deep tubs. There are two restaurants to choose from, the famous **Grill** and the **Savoy** restaurant. A new addition is the

Upstairs Bar, beautifully decorated, for anything from a cup of coffee to a meal.

‡ ⬜ ◪ ◪ ⬱ ◁≪ ☀ ☒ ⌂ ☒

Sheraton Park Tower ⌂
101 Knightsbridge, SW1 ☎235-8050 ☎ 317222. Map **16/7** ▨ 295 rms ▭ 295 ▤ ⬱ ⚌ AE ⬩ CB ⬩ VISA Tube Knightsbridge.
Location: Knightsbridge/Belgravia, near Hyde Park. European flagship of the group, and very much the metropolitan, luxury type of Sheraton, as opposed to some of the smaller ones in American provincial cities. The hotel towers above Knightsbridge in an outwardly ugly cylindrical shape. All the rooms have a view, and are spacious and luxurious, recently redecorated in pretty English chintzes with walnut paneling on the walls. Floors ten to 17 are devoted to 'executive rooms' providing accommodations for groups of visitors from blue-chip corporations, but as a matter of policy the hotel does not accept conventions. Superb bathrooms, beauty salon, barbershop and valeting service to keep guests well-groomed.

‡ ⚲ ⬜ ◪ ⬱ ◁≪ ☒

Stafford
St James's Pl., SW1 ☎493-0111 ☎ 28602. Map **9H9** ▨ 62 rms ▭ 62 ⚌ AE ⬩ Tube Green Park.
Location: St James's near Green Park. Elegant and discreet hotel in gentlemanly St James's, where almost every house is of historical interest. The Stafford's 300yr-old wine cellars once belonged to St James's Palace (and the hotel today has the distinction of employing not one but two master sommeliers). Much of the interior is in the style of Adam, though the brickwork facade is much later. The building once housed the Public Schools Club, and during World War II accommodated American officers and French resistance workers. It is a beautifully kept hotel, with four comfortable salons which are rented for business meetings.

⌂ ‡ ⬜ ◪ ◪ ⬱ ☀

Strand Palace ✿
369 Strand, WC2 ☎836-8080 ☎ 24208. Map **11G12** ▮▯ 771 rms ▭ 771 ⚌ AE CB ⬩ ⬩ CD VISA Tube Covent Garden.
Location: Strand, near Covent Garden. When it was built in the early part of this century, a 900-bedroom hotel was by definition a palace. Now, the

Strand has slimmed a little, been extensively modernized, and turned its attention to a different business: that of providing good value accommodations. It does so from a vantage point right opposite the **Savoy**, in a location handy for many theaters and for city sightseeing. The Strand Palace has most of the facilities to be expected in a large hotel, though there is no room service. There are tea and coffee-making facilities in each room and a 24hr coffee shop, Neapolitan chefs in the *pizzeria*, and an American-style cocktail bar. A Trust House Forte hotel.
‡ □ ⌨ 🖥 Y

Waldorf Hotel
Aldwych, WC2 ☎ *836-2400*
🕾 *24574. Map* **11F12** ▥▥ *311*
▭ *311* ⇌ AE ◉ ◍ VISA *Tube Aldwych.*
Location: N *side of the Aldwych.*
Exemplifying the Edwardian era with its crystal chandeliers, marble floors and vast pot plants, the Waldorf is a comfortable hotel, offering both old-world charm and excellent service and facilities. These include mini-bars in the bedrooms, a video channel for in-house movies, a hairdresser and valet service. There is a *thé dansant* on Fri and Sat.
‡ ⌖ □ ⌨ 🖥 ▭ ▭

Westbury
Conduit St., W1 ☎ *629-7755*
🕾 *24378. Map* **9G9** ▥▥ *229 rms and 14 suites* ▭ *243* ⇌ ▤▤ AE
CB ◉ ◍ VISA *Tube Bond Street.*
Location: Mayfair, near Bond St. and Oxford St. The first Westbury Hotel,

on Madison Avenue, New York, was named by a polo buff after the ground on Long Island. Like its New York counterpart, the London Westbury still has a bar called the **Polo**, and its martinis are of American dryness. When it opened in 1955, the London Westbury was the first hotel in Britain to be operated by an American chain, but since 1977 it has been owned by Trust House Forte. Its library-style lounge, with an open fire in winter, and its comfortable rooms nonetheless sustain the feeling of a 1950s American hotel.
‡ ⌖ □ ⌨ ▭ 🖥 Y

White House ✿
Albany St., NW1 ☎ *387-1200*
🕾 *24111. Map* **3D9** ▥▥ *589 rms*
▭ *589* ⇌ ⇌ AE ◉ ◍ VISA *Tube Great Portland Street.*
Location: Near Regent's Park. A handy location for sightseeing, shopping, and taking relaxing walks in the park, though this is not a hotel area. The White House is a well-appointed hotel, offering 24hr room service and all the other amenities of a luxury hotel at more modest rates. The fact that the preferences and whims of guests are kept on computer gives some indication of the rate of repeat reservations, but also suggests a high rate of occupancy by business visitors. Despite its name, the White House is a British hotel (the building is actually shaped like the Union Jack), and is owned by the Rank group. The block is large enough to shrug off the traffic that swarms around it.
‡ ⌖ □ ⌨ 🖥 Y

Eating in London

Recent years have seen something of a revival of English cooking, blighted two centuries ago by the disruption of the world's first industrial revolution. The invasion by foreign cuisines, with the French leading, was thorough, but now the ethnic diversity of London's restaurant world is being tempered by the resurgence of the native table. Just as *nouvelle cuisine* brought French cooking up to date, so English cooking is now being reworked by many chefs — often under the loose term of New English Cookery. There is a whole new breed of English chefs now operating who look as much to Britain as to France for their inspiration.

There are, of course, some excellent French restaurants of unimpeachable authenticity in London, and equally notable standard-bearers of many another national cuisine. Even local cooking illustrates London's propensity for absorbing outside influences. Those who can muster the appetite to begin the day with the great British breakfast might find that the kippers come from Scotland, the bacon from Ireland (or, more lately, Denmark), and the tea from India. This is a meal which draws upon the tradition of home cooking, like that other British specialty, high tea (see *Cafés and tearooms*); to sample them the visitor should go to one of the grand old hotels rather than a restaurant.

So much is the blind Folly of this Age, that they would rather be imposed on by a French Booby, than Give Encouragement to a good English Cook!

Mrs Glasse, *The Art of Cookery*, 1747

The English are traditionally eager carnivores, and feast day dishes are still usually some sort of roast meat. The South Downs of Kent and Sussex produce the finest English lamb and mutton. It's odd that Sussex also claims to have invented the steak-and-kidney pudding, when the most famous beef is produced far away in Hereford or Scotland. Presumably it was the time taken to transport the beef that led, in the days before refrigeration, to its being preserved by pickling — hence the Londoners' beloved boiled beef. There seems to be less doubt about the origins of sweet puddings and pies, filled with the apples, cherries and soft fruits of Kent and Essex.

Among geographical influences on London's own specialties, the Thames is paramount. Cockles, mussels and whelks are sold for immediate consumption by vendors in many open markets (see *Shopping*). Shellfish from the estuary and beyond are very much the capital's own love, and the well-heeled diners of Mayfair throng to oyster bars like **Bentley's**, Swallow St., W1, or **Green's**, 36 Duke St., SW1; City folk have **Sweetings**, Queen Victoria St., EC4. Fish specialties like whitebait and eel were originally pulled from the river itself. Street sellers still offer jellied eels, while the stewed version is the stock in trade of the pie-and-mash shop, one of London's own 'ethnic' eating places, usually to be found near a street market.

Whisper it not, but that other tradition, fried fish and chips, was brought to Britain by immigrants from Italy and Belgium respectively, and they seem to have met in the North of England. Still, Londoners do make good fish and chips; apart from fashionable places like **Geale's** or **Sea Shell**, the capital is well endowed with fish-and-chip shops of varied quality.

Choosing a restaurant

London has at least 2,000 fully accoutered restaurants. Like most things in the city, their keynote is diversity. They are widely dispersed, although the areas best served by good restaurants are Covent Garden, Soho, Chelsea and South Kensington.

As a great city not only of its old empire but also of Western Europe, London is richly cosmopolitan. The ubiquitous Italians of London have a remarkable number of fashionable restaurants in the middle to upper price brackets, many of which are notably similar in style: quarry-tiled floors, white-painted walls, foliage, discreet spotlights, a fairly basic menu and cheerful waiters. This trattoria style was popularized in the sixties; more recent fashions include the new style in *haute cuisine* which seems to have been established by the Roux brothers, and the upscale French restaurant with the ambience of a brasserie.

From farther afield are the various cuisines of which Chinese and Indian are the most obvious. As in many cities, 'ethnic' eating can be remarkably good, and an excellent value. Chinese and Indian restaurants in particular have also become known for producing good take-out foods, and late at night a Londoner might simply declare that he is going "for an Indian" or "for a Chinese." These two and other ethnicities are manifest in dozens of inexpensive restaurants, and a few grander ones: Gerrard St. (W1) for Chinese; the British Post Office Tower area (W1), Westbourne Grove (W2) or Hammersmith (W6) for Indian; and Charlotte St. (W1) for Greek.

London also boasts humbler eating places, many doing their trade mostly by day. The pub is certainly more likely to serve meals at lunchtime, and is usually cheap; the fare will range from French bread and cheese to, typically, steak-and-kidney pie or shepherd's pie. Wine bars also offer inexpensive eating, some of them content to serve quiche and pâté, others stretching to full meals. At a pace more agreeable than fast food, and in a restaurant ambience, chains like Pizza Express, Bistro Bistingo and Bistro Vino offer good value. The carvery types of dining room in some hotels are also a good value, providing a selection of roast meats, often for a set price.

When to eat

Restaurants in the West End and The City are busy at lunchtime, with a largely business clientele, but those dining for pleasure tend

---

Vintage chart

A guide to the major areas and the general qualities of recent vintages. See key below.

	1978	1979	1980	1981	1982	1983	1984	1985	1986	1987
Red Bordeaux										
Médoc/Graves	●*	●*	◑*	●*	●*	●*	●	○ *	●	○
Pomerol/St-Emilion	●*	●*	◑*	●*	●*	●*	●	●	●	◑
White Bordeaux										
Sauternes & sweet	◑*	◑*	●*	●*	◑*	●*	○*	●	●	◑
Graves & dry	●*	◑*	●*	●*	●*	●*	○*	●*	◑*	
Red Burgundy and neighbours										
Côte d'Or	●*	◑*	○*	○	●*	●*	●*	◑*	●	◑
Beaujolais	●*	◑*	○*	◑*	●*	◑*	●*	●*	◑*	●*
White Burgundy and neighbours										
Côte d'Or	●*	◑*	◑*	◑*	●*	◑*	●*	◑*	◑*	○
Chablis	●*	◑*	◑*	◑*	●*	●*	◑*	●*	●*	◑
Alsace	●*	●	◑*	●*	◑*	●*	◑*	●*	◑*	●
Rhône	●*	●*	◑*	●*	●*	○*	●*	◑*	●	◑

Best vintages of other wines
Italy. Chianti: 1971, 1975, 1977, 1978, 1980, 1982, 1985, 1986; Piemonte: 1971, 1975, 1978, 1979, 1980.
Germany. Mosel: 1975, 1976, 1979, 1983, 1985, 1986; Rhine: 1975, 1976, 1977, 1979, 1983, 1985, 1986.
Spain. Rioja: 1970, 1974, 1976, 1978, 1982, 1983, 1985.
California. Red: 1973, 1974, 1975, 1977, 1978, 1980, 1981, 1985, 1987; White: 1977, 1979, 1980, 1981, 1983, 1985, 1987.
Vintage port: 1960, 1963, 1966, 1967, 1970, 1975, 1977, 1980, 1983, 1985.

Key: ● above average to outstanding ◑ average
○ acceptable * for drinking now

to come out at night, usually 8 or 9pm. Restaurants close after lunchtime, re-open at about 6 to 7pm, and wind down after about 10 to 11pm. The more famous and well-established restaurants are nearly always fully reserved before they open; it is usually possible to find somewhere good to eat on the spur of the moment, but the careful diner will always reserve a table first.

Price

Set-price menus are relatively uncommon in London, although appearing more often of late. Many of the best restaurants have excellent value set lunch menus which enable the less affluent to take advantage of them. They include **La Tante Claire**, the **Oak Room**, and the **Bombay Brasserie**. On all menus look out for items which might bump up the quoted or apparent price: check whether VAT (Value Added Tax) and service are included, and whether salads and vegetables are going to be expensive. Pre- and after-dinner drinks can also prove costly — don't be afraid to ask. If service is not included, and you are happy with your treatment, give a tip of 10-15%.

Wine and food

Wine is one area where French dominance continues. Italian and German white wines are also almost universally available, and Spanish and Californian wines are to be found on several lists. There is a small, and growing, English wine industry, producing mainly white wine, rarely on offer in London.

Away from the mainstream of Anglo-French-Italian cooking, wine might not always be the best bet; beer goes well with Indian and much Oriental food, and jasmin tea can be ordered with a Chinese meal.

Aperitifs and after-dinner drinks

The English have long been leading consumers of fortified wines, and have played a leading part in the sherry and port trade. If there is a traditional aperitif in England, it is dry sherry, which whets the appetite perfectly; however, London restaurants will generally be able to cater to most tastes.

After dinner, the English gentleman traditionally 'takes' port. It is one of the longest-lived wines, and develops great complexity — do not dismiss it as a 'sweet' drink. Alternatives usually available are brandy, liqueurs, or perhaps malt whisky.

Restaurants classified by area

Battersea/Wandsworth
L'Arlequin ▮▮▮ Fr
Harvey's ▮▮▭ to ▮▮▮ Eng/Fr
Nancy Lam's Enak Enak ▮▭ Indo
Bayswater
Le Chef ▮▮▭ Fr
Kalamares ▮▭ Gr
Belgravia/Knightsbridge
Capital Hotel ▮▮▮ ⌂ Fr
Hyatt Carlton Tower ▮▮▮ ⌂ Fr
Ménage à Trois ▮▮▭ to ▮▮▮ Fr/Eng
Mr Chow ▮▮▭ to ▮▮▮ Ch
St Quentin ▮▮▮ Fr
Salloos ▮▮▮ Pak
San Lorenzo ▮▮▭ to ▮▮▮ It
Shezan ▮▮▮ Pak
Camden Town/Euston
Diwana Bel Poori ▭ ✿ ● Ind
Nontas ▮▭ Gr

Chelsea/South Kensington
Bangkok ▮▭ Th
Bibendum ▮▮▮ Eng/Fr
Brinkley's ▮▮▮ Eng/Fr
Daphne's ▮▮▮ Fr
Daquise ▭ to ▮▭ ● Pol
Drakes ▮▮▮ Eng
Eleven Park Walk ▮▮▭ It
English House ▮▮▮ Eng
La Famiglia ▮▮▭ It
Gavvers ▮▮▭ ✿ Fr
Lou Pescadou ▮▮▭ Fr fish
Ma Cuisine ▮▮▮ Fr
Meridiana ▮▮▭ to ▮▮▮ It
Nikita's ▮▮▭ to ▮▮▮ Rus
Paper Tigeer ▮▭ to ▮▭ Ch
Read's ▮▮▭ to ▮▮▮ Eng
San Frediano ▮▮▭ It
Le Suquet ▮▮▮ Fr fish

Tai-Pan ⬛⬜ to ⬛⬛ Ch
La Tante Claire ⬛⬛ to ⬛⬛ △
Walton's ⬛⬛ to ⬛⬛ Eng/Fr
City
Le Poulbot ⬛⬛ Fr
Sweetings ⬛⬜ Eng
Covent Garden/Strand
Calabash ⬛⬜ ●
Food for Thought ⬜ ♣ ● Eng
Inigo Jones ⬛⬛ △ Fr
Joe Allen ⬜ to ⬛⬜ Am
Luigi's ⬛⬜ It
Mon Plaisir ⬛⬜ Fr
Porter's ⬛⬜ Eng
Simpson's-in-the-Strand ⬛⬜ to ⬛⬛
  Eng
East End
Bloom's ⬛⬜ Je
Hammersmith/Fulham
Anarkali ⬛⬜ Ind
Hiders ⬛⬜ ♣ Eng/Fr
Hampstead
Keat's ⬛⬛ to ⬛⬛ Fr
Islington/Kings Cross
Ganpath ⬜ Ind
M'sieur Frog ⬛⬜ Fr
Kensington/Notting Hill
Ark ⬛⬜ ♣ Fr
Bombay Brasserie ⬛⬜ Ind
Geale's ⬜ ● Eng
Leith's ⬛⬛ Eng
192 ⬛⬜ Fr/Eng
Marylebone/West End
L'Etoile ⬛⬛ to ⬛⬛ Fr
Gaylord ⬛⬜ Ind
Ikkyu ⬜ to ⬛⬜ ♣ ● Jap
Little Akropolis ⬛⬜ Gr
Odins ⬛⬛ Fr
Rue St Jacques ⬛⬛ Fr
Sea Shell ⬜ ♣ ● Eng
Mayfair
Al Hamra ⬛⬜ ♣ Leb
Cecconi's ⬛⬛ It

Chicago Pizza Pie Factory ⬜ ●
  Am
Connaught Hotel ⬛⬛ △ Fr/Eng
Le Gavroche ⬛⬛ △ Fr
Hard Rock Cafe ⬛⬜ Am
St James/Piccadilly
Auberge de Provence ⬛⬛ Fr
Bentley's ⬛⬜ Eng fish
Cage Royal ⬛⬛ △ Fr
Le Caprice ⬛⬜ Eng/Fr
Langan's Brasserie ⬛⬜ to ⬛⬛ Fr
Oak Room, Meridien Hotel ⬛⬛ △
  Fr
Ritz ⬛⬛ to ⬛⬛ △ Eng/Fr
Smollensky's Balloon ⬜ to ⬛⬜ Am
Suntory ⬛⬛ Jap
Wilton's ⬛⬛ △ Eng
Soho
Alastair Little ⬛⬛ Eng/Fr
Bahn Thai ⬛⬜ Th
La Bastide ⬛⬛ Fr
La Capanina ⬜ to ⬛⬜ It
Chuen Cheng Ku ⬜ to ⬛⬜ It
Cranks ⬜ ♣ ● Eng
L'Escargot ⬛⬜ to ⬛⬛ Fr
Fung Shing ⬛⬜ to ⬛⬜ ♣ Ch
Gallery Rendezvous ⬛⬜ Ch
Gay Hussar ⬛⬜ to ⬛⬛ Hung
Au Jardin des Gourmets ⬛⬜ to ⬛⬛
  Fr
Kettners ⬜ to ⬛⬜ It/Am
Manzi's ⬛⬜ ♣ It fish
Melati ⬜ to ⬛⬜ ● Indo
Poons ⬜ to ⬛⬜ ♣ Ch
Red Fort ⬛⬜ Ind
Soho Brasserie ⬜ ⬛⬜ Fr
Victoria/Pimlico
Memories of China ⬛⬜ Ch
Simply Nico ⬛⬛ Fr
Tate Gallery Restaurant ⬛⬜ to ⬛⬛
  Eng
Westminster
Lockets ⬛⬛ Eng

Key to types of cuisine

Afr **African**	Gr **Greek**	Jap **Japanese**	Pol **Polish**
Am **American**	Hung **Hungarian**	Je **Jewish**	Rus **Russian**
Ch **Chinese**	Ind **Indian**	Leb **Lebanese**	Th **Thai**
Eng **English**	Indo **Indonesian**	Pak **Pakistani**	Turk **Turkish**
Fr **French**	It **Italian**		

Alastair Little
4a Frith St., W1 (Soho) ☎ 734-
5183. Map 10F10 ⬛⬜ *Closed
Sat, Sun, 3 weeks Aug,
Christmas. Tube Leicester
Square.*
Much-vaunted media hang-out with
an equally high profile chef/
proprietor, the eponymous Mr
Little. His dining room, with the
kitchen in view, is tiny, and pretty
stark: Venetian blinds, bare floor-
boards, curly tube lighting on the
ceiling, glossy cream walls, black
tables set with paper napkins, hard

black chairs. "Designer setting for
designer food," says one disparaging
critic. But whatever label you give
the food, it is good: reminiscent of
Californian cuisine but more
vigorous. Little is a talented,
instinctive cook, able to change his
menu twice daily according to what
he finds in the market. Meat and fish
are simply cooked — grilled, stir-
fried, steamed — and served with
vivid sauces and excellent vegetables
and salads. The evening clientele is
usually less uncompromisingly
trendy than at lunchtime.

151

Restaurants

Al Hamra ♣
31-33 Shepherd Market, W1 (Mayfair) ☎ *493-1954. Map 9H8* ▥ ▯ ▭ ▦ ⊕ ⊚ ▨ *Closed Christmas Day, Jan 1. Tube Green Park.*

Even the most jaded palettes will buck up at the sharp, fresh tastes of Lebanon's superb cuisine. London's best example is to be found at this smart, comfortable, mainly business oriented restaurant in Mayfair. Make a selection from the list of 65 hot and cold hors d'oeuvres (more properly called *meze*), possibly baulking at the grilled lambs' testicles, but including perfect renditions of well-known Lebanese dishes, such as *tabouleh*, *hommos* and stuffed vine leaves, as well as *montabel*, *loubeih* and mixed fresh vegetables with herbs and Lebanese bread, all quite delicious. Main courses are more perfunctory, but well flavored.

Anarkali
303-305 King St., W6 (Hammersmith) ☎ *748-1760/6911* ▥ ▯ ▭ ▦ ⊚ ▨ *Tube Ravenscourt Park.*

Anarkali was one of the first Indian restaurants in London to win widespread gastronomic attention, and it inspired the others. Its cooking is Punjabi, with a tendency to creaminess, exemplified by the excellent chicken *korma*. Start with outstanding *samosas*, and have *niramish* vegetable. A distinguished former chef gives his name to **Aziz** (*116 King St., W6* ☎ *748-1826*), handily positioned for the Lyric Theatre.

Ark ♣
122 Palace Gardens Terrace, W8 (Kensington) ☎ *229-4024. Map 6G3* ▥ ▯ ▭ ▰ ⊕ ⊚ ▨ *Closed Sun lunch, Easter and four days at Christmas. Tube Notting Hill Gate.*

This funky wooden hut looks most unpromising, but is regarded with great affection by a loyal clientele, many of whom remember its inception as a '60s bistro, with prices which are by local standards reasonable. Posters, photographs and paintings on the walls. Very hearty servings of basic, somewhat variable, bistro food from a short menu: good soups, smoked chicken pancakes, sole *bonne femme*, medallions of beef with tarragon, and very acceptable wines in a list of equally sensible brevity. There are two Arks; this wooden one is fractionally less expensive, but nonetheless gastronomically held in slightly

higher regard than its sister at 35 Kensington High St., W8 ☎ 937-4294.

L'Arlequin
123 Queenstown Rd., SW8 (Battersea) ☎ *622-0555. Off Map 17M8* ▥ ▯ ▭ ▰ ▦ ⊕ ⊚ ▨ *Closed Sat lunch, Sun, three weeks Aug. Tube Clapham Common.*

Nico Ladenis (see **Simply Nico**) has deserted Queenstown Rd. for a more refined address, but those other top-class restaurateurs Christian and Geneviève Delteil still choose to remain in the unlikely setting of this dark and dingy street. L'Arlequin is very impressive. The soberly pretty, rather formal dining room is beautifully run by Mme. Delteil, while her husband creates such light and inventive delicacies as asparagus mousse, breast of chicken with scallops and fresh noodles or beef with bone marrow and grapes, and wonderful sorbets. The wine list is very expensive, but the house wine is reliable.

Auberge de Provence
St James's Court Hotel, Buckingham Gate, SW1 (St James's) ☎ *834-6655. Map 17L10* ▥ ▯ ▭ ▰ ▦ ⊕ ⊚ ▨ *Tube St James's.*

In the new European Flagship of Taj Hotels, the St James's Court, is to be found a genuinely Provençal restaurant, masterminded by one of France's globe-trotting super-chefs Jean-André Charial from L'Oustau de Baumanière at Les Baux. He devised the menu of Provençal dishes, beautifully adapted to modern tastes, imported his wine list and his superb dining and kitchen staff, including the talented resident chef. He visits regularly, often bringing consignments of local produce with him. Under a rough-cast vaulted ceiling, savor a pungent *charlotte d'agneau et d'aubergines*, a perfect *daube de boeuf* or a succulent baby leg of lamb *en croûte*, plus superb accompanying vegetables (and a wide choice of vegetarian main dishes). The best wines of the region figure on the *carte*: Côteaux de Baux, Bandol, Vignelaure. Finish with a glass of Baume de Venise.

Bahn Thai
21a Frith St., W1 (Soho) ☎ *437-8504. Map 10F10* ▥ ▯ ▭ ▰ ▦ ⊚ ▨ *Closed Christmas and Easter. Tube Leicester Square.*

A few years ago it was smart Indian restaurants popping up on every corner; today Thai cuisine is in the ascendant. The number in London has more than quadrupled in the past five years. Bahn Thai is one of the best; but don't try it unless you like spicy food — in Thailand hot means hot. Among starters look for satay, boned stuffed chicken wings and squid in batter, among soups for hot and sour seafood with lemon grass. Drink Thai beer or a balancing white wine such as Gewürztraminer or Sauvignon. For devotees of dear departed Bianchi's, a visit here is somewhat unnerving, for it's the same premises, still creaking and faded, but now with Oriental touches. The pace is relaxed and leisurely, in true Thai tradition. Also excellent, with more of a party atmosphere, is the **Blue Elephant** (*4-5 Fulham Broadway, SW6* ☎*385-6595* 💵).

Bangkok

9 Bute St., SW7 (South Kensington) ☎*584-8529. Map 15J5* 💵 ⊡ *Closed Sun. Tube South Kensington.*
The Bangkok pioneered Thai food in London, and although its cooking is not as fine as some of the newer Thai establishments it's a good choice for a simple meal in bustling, unobtrusive surroundings. The restaurant can become very crowded, but devotees don't mind. You might start with excellent satay, followed by sweet and sour pork or stir-fried beef with ginger and mushroom sauce.

La Bastide

50 Greek St., W1 (Soho) ☎*734-3300. Map 10F10* 💵 ⊡ 🍴 🅰 🅰🅴 ⓪ 🅾 🆅🅸🆂🅰 *Closed Sat lunch, Sun. Tube Tottenham Court Rd.*
Nicholas Blacklock's restaurant is one of those places it feels good to be in: comfortable and elegant, a place to dress up for. With its pre- and post-theater menus it's popular with theater-goers and players alike, and full of buzz, especially later on. The cooking is classic French, brasserie style with a strong emphasis on regional dishes: there are set-price regional menus as well as a constantly changing *carte*; also, helpfully, a special light lunch menu. The wine list is regional too, featuring country wines from the s and sw Jura; for example the inexpensive and good Côtes de Gasgogne.

Bentley's

11 Swallow St., W1 (Piccadilly Circus) ☎*734-4756. Map 10G10* 💵 ⊡ 🅰🅴 🅲🅱 ⓪ 🅾 🆅🅸🆂🅰 *Closed Sun. Tube Piccadilly Circus.*

Oyster bars and fish restaurants of long-established reputation abound in London. Some have tended to live on their reputation, but Bentley's has remained, on the whole, reliable. Although the restaurant's ownership changed in 1981, oysters are still provided by the family's beds near Colchester.

For devotees of oysters, the very best in town are to be found at **Green's Champagne Bar** (see *Bars*).

Bibendum

Michelin House, 81 Fulham Rd., SW3 (South Kensington) ☎*581-5817. Map 16J6* 💵 ⊡ 🅰🅴 ⓪ 🅾 🆅🅸🆂🅰 *Closed Sat eve, Sun. Tube South Kensington.*
Lunch is a particular delight at this, London's most exciting new restaurant. Light streams through huge windows into the first floor dining room, brilliantly designed by Sir Terence Conran, and graced at either end by two splendidly jolly Michelin men in stained glass. Seating is spacious and supremely comfortable, and the food, by Simon Hopkinson, is just right: definite, appealing and carefully presented. The midday set menu, for example, may reveal perfect mushroom soup, gravlaks, calves' liver with mustard grain sauce and coffee granita. The ground floor of the famous Michelin building now houses the Conran shop and an oyster bar, open from 10am to 11pm.

Bloom's

90 Whitechapel High St., E1 (East End) ☎*247-6001/6835. Map 13F18* 💵 ⊡ 🅾 🆅🅸🆂🅰 *Closed Fri eve, Sat, Jewish hols. Christmas Day. Tube Whitechapel.*
While Manhattan's Jewish families were migrating from Lower East to Upper West Side, London's were making an almost identical journey. Even Bloom's restaurant opened a branch in Golders Green, NW11, but its soul remains in Whitechapel, where the nostalgia is thicker than the *borsche* and noisier than the *matzos*, and the waiters as crotchety as any on Lower East Side. Eat here on Sun after visiting **Petticoat Lane** and **Brick Lane** markets (see *Shopping*).

Bombay Brasserie

Courtfield Close, Courtfield Rd., SW7 (Kensington) ☎*370-4040. Map 15J4* 💵 *lunch* 🍴 🍴 🅰🅴 ⓪ 🅾 🆅🅸🆂🅰 *Tube Gloucester Road.*
For sheer scale and lavishness, with a huge conservatory leading off the

153

Restaurants

palatial 1920s main dining room, this European vanguard of India's thoroughbred Taj Hotels group must rank as one of London's most imposing restaurants. But the food impresses too; regional home cooking (Goa, Bombay, Punjab), changing daily, with such delights as halibut *ambotik*, crab *malabar*, mutton *achari* and superb *gulab jamun*. The staff is cosmopolitan; service can be somewhat erratic, occasionally badly so. The restaurant is open every day of the year, with last orders at midnight. Though Bombay Brasserie is generally expensive for an Indian restaurant, the set price buffet lunch is certainly an outstanding value.

Brinkley's
47 Hollywood Rd, SW10 (Chelsea South Kensington) ☎351-1683. *Map 15L4* ▥▥ ▅ ━ ⌂ ▤ ⒶⒺ ⓋⒾⓈⒶ *Closed lunch, Sun. Tube West Brompton.*
Hardly a secret, but not very well known for a restaurant of such qualities, original in both menu and ambience. Starters include duck and walnut terrine with onion marmalade; main courses range from grilled fillet of gravlaks with vermouth and dill sauce to sliced breast of duck with fresh figs and brandy; puddings (as the menu likes to call them) from crêpes to homemade sorbets. In summer you can eat in the delightful garden. Next door is the **Wine Gallery**, one of four similar and very popular wine bars under the same management as Brinkley's.

Café Royal
68 Regent St. W1 (Piccadilly Circus) ☎439-6320 *Map 10G10* ▥▥ ▅ ━ ⒶⒺ ⒸⒷ ⓄⒹ ⓋⒾⓈⒶ *Tube Piccadilly Circus.*
Oscar Wilde's name is the one most bandied about, but the Café Royal is remembered as the haunt of many wits, writers and artists in the late 1800s and early 1900s. The 1890s interior of the Grill Room is as dazzling as ever, but the Café Royal is long past the bloom of youth. Nor does its formal mood encourage bohemian impetuosity. The cuisine is classical French, with some excellent fish dishes, and prices are predictably haughty. The Café Royal's Le Relais restaurant has now been transformed into the **Nicols** restaurant, where a carvery-style buffet has been created mainly to attract groups of businessmen before they retire to the Café Royal's private function rooms.

Calabash ☻
38 King St., WC2 (Covent Garden) ☎836-1976. *Map 10G11* ▥ ⌂ ⒶⒺ ⓄⒹ *Closed Sat lunch, Sun, Christmas Day. Tube Covent Garden.*
The Africa Centre offers Black and Muslem studies, exhibitions and the Calabash restaurant, which has the feel of an Oxbridge refectory, despite African rugs on the walls and exotic taped music. The service tends to be languid, and the menu is very limited indeed, but still spans both former British and Francophone Africa. Specialists include African stews and fish dishes, and there are North African wines and Tusker beer.

La Capannina
24 Romilly St., W1 (Soho) ☎437-2473. *Map 10F10* ▥ ▅ to ▥▥ ⌂ ⒶⒺ ⓄⒹ ⓋⒾⓈⒶ *Closed Sat lunch, Sun. Tube Leicester Square, Piccadilly Circus.*
A good example of the type of unpretentious, inexpensive, friendly Italian restaurant in which Soho specializes. Well-prepared basic Italian dishes like *gnocchi*, *raviolini*, *crespolini*, sea-bass with fennel, beef braised in Barolo, rabbit in white wine.

Capital Hotel ⌂
22 Basil St., SW3 (Knightsbridge) ☎589-5171. *Map 16/7* ▥▥ ⌂ ▤ ⒶⒺ ⒸⒷ ⓄⒹ ⓋⒾⓈⒶ *Tube Knightsbridge.*
Having quickly established itself as one of the finest hotel restaurants in London, the Capital has lately suffered a downturn in its culinary fortunes with the loss of its Michelin star. (The chef who brought it to prominence has now opened his own restaurant in Walton St., SW3, **Turners** ☎584-6711.) The cuisine is French and decidedly *haute*, as are the prices. The dining room, decorated by Nina Campbell, has been given the full treatment, all pink and festooned and candlelit.

Le Caprice
Arlington House, Arlington St., SW1 (Piccadilly) ☎629-2239. *Map 9G9* ▥▥ ▅ ⒶⒺ ⓄⒹ ⓋⒾⓈⒶ *Closed Sat lunch. Tube Piccadilly Circus.*
Long famous as a restaurant, Le Caprice was given a new image a few years ago, and now, all chrome and glass and black-and-white Bailey photographs, it's an even more fashionable rendezvous for West End glitterati than **Langan's** across the road. The food is surprisingly good and just right for the ambience: steak tartare, onion tart, rack of lamb,

imaginative salads, white and dark chocolate mousse. And it's perhaps the best place in London for Sunday brunch. Reserve well ahead.

Cecconi's
5 Burlington Gdns., W1 (Mayfair) ☎434-1509. Map **9G9** ▥ ▢ ▤ ▧ ⊙ ⊚ ▨ *Closed Sat, Sun. Tube Piccadilly Circus.*
So Venetian, in the grand hotel mood, that surely the lone diner in the corner is Thomas Mann (or Dirk Bogarde)? Signor Cecconi was at the Cipriani, and he even brought with him the Bellinis, not to mention ten champagnes and three sparkling waters, as well as faithful clientele of extremely well-heeled Italians. The food, which is also Venetian, of course, is always dependable without being exceptional, which cannot be said for the prices.

Le Chef ▧
41 Connaught St., W2 (Bayswater) ☎262-5945. Map **8F6** ▥ ▢ ▤ ⊕ ⊙ ⊚ ▨ *Closed Sat lunch, Sun, Mon, 2 weeks Aug. Tube Marble Arch.*
Outdoor sidewalk tables are hard to find in London, though the idea has gained a little ground in recent years. When the weather is favorable, the handful of gingham-covered tables outside Le Chef brings a soupçon of Paris to the streets of London. In less clement weather, the cramped and rather rickety interior is a reminder of many a simple Paris *bistrot*. The menu also brings flavors from other regions of France, and a distinct quality of home cooking, both deriving from the diligence of the resident proprietors. Quality can be uneven, though the pungent fish soup with wine is always excellent.

Chicago Pizza Pie Factory
17 Hanover Sq., W1 (Mayfair) ☎629-2669. Map **9F9** ▢ ▢ *Tube Oxford Circus.*
Chicago adman Bob Payton left his London job to do his own thing and he does it with zest. His huge pizzas are of the deep-dish style, soft and seductive if a little bland. Doggie bags are cheerfully produced for leftovers. Music is taped from a Chicago radio station and there are video tapes of baseball and other All-American games.

Chuen Cheng Ku ♣
17 Wardour St., W1 (Soho) ☎437-1398. Map **10G10** ▢ to ▥ ▢ ▧ ▤ ⊙ ⊚ ▨ *Tube Leicester Square.*

Dim sum snacks, served in wobbly basketwork pagodas, are a popular lunch among the workers of Soho, not to mention the local Chinese community. The long-time favorite scene of such pleasures is the Chuen Cheng Ku, locally known as the CCK, which also has a respectable gastronomic reputation for other types of Cantonese dish. It is not necessary to reserve; the CCK has the advantage of apparently endless floors, each with countless rooms, so that the restaurant can expand magically to accommodate Soho's appetite.

Connaught Hotel ⌂
Carlos Pl., W1 (Mayfair) ☎499-7070. Map **9G8** ▥ ▢ *restaurant* ▬ *Grill Room* ▰ ⊙ *Grill Room closed Sat, Sun. Tube Bond Street.*
Amid the fluctuating fortunes of many other top hotel restaurants, the Connaught remains implacably serene — and supreme. There is a restrained *frisson* of excitement in the air at the prospect of a meal here, no mean feat by chef Michel Bourdin in an atmosphere as clubby and dignified (one critic called it somber) as this. His offerings are a near faultless marriage of French flourish and English tradition, all marked by top quality ingredients and superb cooking skills. Service is always superbly orchestrated.

Cranks ♣ ☙
8 Marshall St., W1 (Soho ☎437-9431. Map **10F9** ▢ ▢ *Closed Sun. Tube Oxford Circus.*
Vegetarian restaurant which has over the years become the best-known in London, helped no doubt by its ironic name, but also by its thoroughgoing approach to the joys of health food. Less of a true restaurant than a cafeteria-style lunch place, but its popularity brooks no argument as well as ensuring that it gets very crowded. Plain wooden tables, and a shop for health food, accessories and books. Branches in Covent Garden market and at 9-11 Tottenham St., W1.

Daphne's
112 Draycott Ave., SW3 (Chelsea/ South Kensington) ☎589-4257. Map **16K6** ▥ ▢ ▤ ▧ ⊙ ⊚ ▨ *Closed lunch Sat, Sun. Tube South Kensington.*
Long-favored French restaurant with a penchant for game dishes, classical cuisine, and careful but usually inspired innovation. Smart without being pretentious.

Restaurants

Daquise ●

20 Thurloe St., SW7 (South Kensington) ☎589-6117. Map 15F5 □ to □ □ □ VISA Tube South Kensington.

A home away from home for the Polish community, and a welcome refuge for hungry students. This is a littly corner of Eastern Europe in central London. Fifties decor, lots of nostalgia, huge helpings of Polish fodder such as borscht (barszcz), goulash, steamed buckwheat (kasza). The ground-floor room is more informal that the neat, wood-paneled basement dining room.

Diwana Bhel Poori ♣ ●

121 Drummond St., NW1 (Euston) ☎387-5556. Map 4C10 □ □ ■ AE ● ● VISA Tube Warren Street.

Deliciously spicy vegetarian Gujerati (western Indian) cooking at Indian rather than English prices. The set lunch thali is satisfying and filling; or try crispy samosas and dose — long pancakes with a savory filling. Drink lassi or fruit juice or bring your own wine. Surroundings are very basic and seating is hard and cramped, but that doesn't deter from the spotless hygiene and good food. There's more space and less bustle at the branch at 50 Westbourne Grove, W2 ☎221-0721.

Drakes

2a Pond Pl., SW3 (Chelsea/South Kensington) ☎584-4555/6669. Map 15K5 ■ □ ▤ AE ● ● VISA Tube South Kensington.

Game, English-style, but within a bright and innovative menu, at a very fashionable restaurant. Sauces and stuffings are likely to be made with fruit, marmalade or chestnuts, and there are some splendidly sweet English puddings; on Sundays spit roast beef is on offer. The same blend of tradition and invention is clear in the interior design, though modernity wins, and the atmosphere is more airy than intimate.

Eleven Park Walk

11 Park Walk, SW10 (Chelsea/South Kensington ☎352-3449. Map 15L4 ■ □ ▤ AE ● VISA Tube South Kensington.

Northern Italian: the menu, a goodly sprinkling of the diners, and the chic. Relaxed and friendly ambience. Apart from standard pasta dishes such as taglioni, and crespelle, there are simpler ones such as crudités with bagna cauda and bollito misto. A favorite lunch place for middle-aged pop stars.

English House

3 Milner St., SW3 (Chelsea) ☎584-3002. Map 16J6 ■■ □ ■ lunch AE ● ● VISA Tube Sloane Square.

Here is old-English cooking under the eye of historian, food writer and TV chef Michael Smith. The rooms are small and intimate and manners more refined than in Georgian times. Dishes include potted Arbroath smokies and historical ways with pork and venison.

L'Escargot

48 Greek St., W1 (Soho) ☎437-2679. Map 10F10 ■■ □ to ■■ □ ▤ AE ● ● VISA Closed Sun. Tube Tottenham Court Road.

Soho rejoiced when young wine importer Nick Lander gave a new lease of life to the venerable Escargot. He and his wine-writer wife Jancis Robinson created a global selection of wines, but the food is, as chef Martin Lam puts it, "modern English, obviously influenced by French." The downstairs brasserie-type menu is a lighter version of what's on offer to the media-folk in the upstairs dining rooms. Graphically-arresting snail-trails on the carpets, and the marbled eau-de-nil walls to the lofty skylights. It's life-force is maîtresse d' Elena, enticed from the much-loved, now defunct Bianchi's. L'Escargot, now under new management, has competition these days from, among others, the Groucho Club (44 Dean St. ☎439-4685), current hot-spot for Soho's media execs.

L'Etoile

30 Charlotte St., W1 (West End) ☎639-7189/1496. Map 10E10 ■■ to ■■ □ ▭ AE ● ● VISA Closed Sat, Sun, three weeks in Aug. Tube Goodge Street.

Old-fashioned bourgeois French restaurant which could be in Paris, a pervasive feeling which is intensified by the excellence of the wine list and in no way diminished by the establishment's cosmopolitan touches, or its long years of residence in a neighborhood better known for its Greek tavernas. Nor has the sumptuous intimacy of L'Etoile been dimmed by the proximity of noisy and inexpensive neighbors.

La Famiglia

7 Langton St., SW10 (Chelsea) ☎351-0761. Map 15M4 ■■ □ AE ● ● VISA Tube South Kensington.

Southern Italian outpost of restauranteurs Alvaro and Corrado, in the World's End neighborhood of Chelsea, a needlessly pessimistic name, as several restauranteurs have found in a congenial district in which to establish themselves; Alvaro's fishier **La Nassa** (*438 King's Rd.* ☎*351-4118*) is just around the corner. La Famiglia is longer-established, with good pasta and that slightly boisterous friendliness that usually characterizes its establishments. Celebrities can often be spotted among the diners; indeed London's 'Italians' are renowned less for their food than for their star-appeal.

Food for Thought ♣ ⛴
31 Neal St., WC2 (Covent Garden) ☎*836-0239. Map 10F11 ▢ ▭ ▤ Closed Sun. Tube Covent Garden.*
Youthful vegetarian restaurant so popular that Covent Garden lunchers line in the street for the privilege of eating in the cramped cellar. Good salads, soups and pastas as well as hot vegetarian dishes. Open until 8pm.

Fung Shing
15 Lisle St., WC2 (Soho) ☎*437-1539. Map 10G10 ▥ to ▥▥ ▤ ◉ ⊙ ⅥⅤ Tube Leicester Square.*
Chinatown presents a bewildering choice of restaurants to the newcomer, perhaps wandering through after the theater (no need to reserve, although you might have to wait for a table). Most are perfectly reasonable, but **Poons**, for lunch or a quick supper, **Chuen Cheng Ku** (for good *dim-sum* and an amusing venue), **New World** (*Gerrard Pl.* ☎*734-0677*), for the best *dim-sun*, and Fung Shing stand out. Fung Shing is small and rather cramped, with bland un-Oriental decor. Its Cantonese food, however, is the very best in Chinatown: one delicious meal for two consisted of state of the art *wun-tun* soup, crunchy quail baked with salt and chili, green vegetables with slivers of garlic, and slices of duck with lemon sauce.

Gallery Rendezvous
53 Beak St., W1 (Soho) ☎*734-0445. Map 9G9 ▥ ▭ ▤ ▤ ◉ ⅥⅤ Tube Piccadilly Circus.*
Diners don't necessarily always want an ethnically-authentic ambience when they eat the food of a particular culture, and the creators of the Rendezvous chain perhaps had that in mind when they created their calm, spacious restaurants in which to serve Perking-style food of genuine quality. The set menus are the best value.

Ganpath
372 Grays Inn Rd., WC1 (King's Cross) ☎*278-1938. Map 5C12 ▢ ▭ ▯ Tube King's Cross St Pancras.*
South Indian food is very different from that of the northern part of the subcontinent, which is more commonly found in Britain. Southern cooking is usually (though not always) hotter, and this particular restaurant also gives it a vegetarian emphasis, though fish and meat dishes are available on a menu which is authentic, interesting and varied. Gracious service, too, but don't go too late — the restaurant starts to close around 10.30pm. Try spiced green bananas, *avial* (vegetables in coconut and yogurt) and *masala dosa*.

Le Gavroche △
43 Upper Brook St., W1 (Mayfair) ☎*408-0881. Map 9F8 ▥▥▥▥ ▭ ▆ ▆ ▤ ▤ ◉ ⊙ ⅥⅤ Closed Sat, Sun. Tube Bond Street.*
For the money you could fly to Paris, but even there you wouldn't get the wonderful creations of Albert and Michel Roux. The brothers are from Charolles, in Burgundy, and theirs is widely regarded as one of the two or three best French restaurants in London. The menu is sufficiently varied to meet most requirements, and it does list a few popular classics among the heavenly sauces and soufflés, mousses and *mousselines*. Although Le Gavroche doesn't specialize in fish, its *mousseline* of lobster and *turbotin au porto* are notable delights. Burgundian the brothers may be, but their lengthy wine list pays equal homage to Bordeaux. Service is attentive, courteous and helpful, and the ambience formal but unstuffy. The set lunch is almost a bargain.

Gavvers ♣
61-63 Lower Sloane St., SW1 (Chelsea) ☎*730-5983. Map 16K7 ▥▥ ▆ ▤ ◉ ⊙ ⅥⅤ Closed lunch, Sun, one week Christmas. Tube Sloane Square.*
There are few restaurants where fixed-price means what it says, but this young relation of **Le Gavroche** is one of them. From the crisp vegetable canapés to the final cup of coffee not a single extra creeps onto the bill. Included in the price is a half bottle per person from a small but excellent selection of house wines. The Parisian chef, who has his vegetables brought by truck from France, changes his imaginative menu every Monday. Service is good

and the atmosphere lively, though the tables could be better spaced.

Gay Hussar
2 Greek St., W1 (Soho), ☎437-0973. Map **10F10** ▯▯ to ▯▯▯▯ ▭ lunch ▤▤ Closed Sun. Tube Tottenham Court Road.

The name predates any sexual connotation, and persuasions are more obviously political in this famous plotting place. It is an irony that a Hungarian emigré establishment should be so well patronized by leading socialist politicians, but they obviously enjoy such central European sustainers as cherry soup, pressed boar's head, goose, mallard, dumplings and lemon cheese pancakes. A considerable choice at modest prices on the lunch menu. The famous Mr Sassie orchestrates proceedings with panache, but sadly his retirement seems imminent.

Gaylord
79 Mortimer St., W1 (West End) ☎580-3615. Map **9E9** ▯▯ ▭ ▰ ▤▤ AE ⊕ ⊙ VISA Tube Oxford Circus.

The first Gaylord was in Delhi, but the London branch, which opened in 1966, has probably done most to spread the name of this family of restaurants, with their own delicate style of Indian *haute cuisine*. The Gaylords boast that they open for lunch and dinner '365 days a year.' The *pilaus*, lamp *pasanda* and *korma* dishes are an impressive introduction to Indian cooking for the timid or skeptical.

Geale's ☉
2 Farmer St., W8 (Notting Hill) ☎727-7969. Map **6G2** ▯ ▭ ⊙ Closed Sun, Mon, three weeks July. Tube Notting Hill Gate.

Fish and chips should be eaten out of a newspaper held hotly in the hand, in the course of a winter's evening stroll; every true Briton knows that in much the way that all Americans prefer their franks to be served at a ball-game. The notion of a fish-and-chip restaurant is to the purist heresy enough, and a fashionable one defies the logic of the world's greatest take-out food. Geale's became fashionable when it was patronized by people like then-soccer star George Best, in search of simple pleasures. Success hasn't spoiled the place, which remains very basic, with excellent fish, despite such nonsense as a wine-list (better tea would be more appropriate) and rather feeble desserts. No reservations.

Hard Rock Cafe
150 Old Park Lane, W1 (Mayfair) ☎629-0382. Map **9H8** ▯ ▭ Tube Hyde Park Corner.

The best hamburgers in London by common consent and, in fact, better than most in the United States. Steaks, sandwiches, chili in winter, American beer, and good ice cream plus a collection of pop memorabilia. Not a place for conversation, though; it might better be called the Loud Rock Cafe. No reservation, and, of course, the legendary line.

Harveys
2 Bellevue Rd., SW17 (Wandsworth) ☎672-0114 ▯▯ to ▯▯▯▯ ▭ ▰ AE ⊙ VISA Closed Sat lunch, Sun. Train Wandsworth Common.

An unlikely setting for some of the most creative cooking currently on offer in London, this recently face-lifted dining room in a gentrified backwater overlooking Wandsworth Common. But this is where Marco Pierre White, an explosive, driven young Yorkshireman has decided to unleash his considerable talents. His commitment to the culinary art and his fresh approach are evident in every beautifully presented dish, whether it be tagliatelle with oysters, shellfish soup or baby pigeon with truffles. Cheese and desserts stand up well. The food is good value, especially the set lunch; it's only a shame that there are no house wines, or inexpensive ones to keep the price down. The young French staff are courteous and professional, belying the tumult going on unseen in the kitchens.

Hiders ♣
755 Fulham Rd., SW6 (Fulham) ☎736-2331 ▯▯ ▭ ⊙ VISA Closed Sat lunch, Sun. Tube Parsons Green.

A great favorite with local Fulhamites, Sloanes and yuppies alike as well as people from farther afield. It's informal, intimate and sophisticated in a country house style — swags and drapes, mirrors, chandelier and a roaring (gas) log fire downstairs. The food is appreciated for its quality at less than West End prices. Dishes turn out to be a lot less fussy than they sound on the menu, to whit: medallions of veal and lobster tail served on a duo of sauces, one sherry and the other shellfish with cognac. There is an intelligent wine list spread across the price range, with fair-priced house red and white.

Hyatt Carlton Tower ⌂
Cadogan Pl., SW1 (Belgravia)
☎235-5411. *Map* 16*I7* ▢ ▭
▦ ᴀᴇ ⊙ ⊚ ᴠɪsᴀ *Tube Sloane
Square.*

Two excellent but quite different restaurants under one roof in this pleasant, relaxing hotel. The one offers roast beef, American cut, in impressive quantity and quality; the other contemporary French cuisine of the highest standards. The beef is to be found in the **Rib Room** which also has an oyster bar: the *haute cuisine* in the **Chelsea Room**, whence its *maître d'* and chef make frequent forays to all parts of France to keep sharp their gastronomic wits.

Ikkyu ➹ ✿
*Basement, 67 Tottenham Court
Rd., W1 (West End)* ☎636-9280.
Map 10*E10* ▢ *to* ▣ ▭ ▦ ᴀᴇ
⊙ ⊚ ᴠɪsᴀ *Closed Sat, Sun lunch.
Tube Goodge St.*

A world away from Suntory with its serious, expense account clientele, Ikkyu is one of the cheapest and most humble Japanese restaurants in town; its also the most fun, with some of the best food. The entrance, down steep steps beneath an electronics store, is easy to miss and positively tacky. The room itself is not much of an improvement, but it's a relaxed and amusing place to dig into big portions of *sushi*, *sashimi* or *yakitori*, or *robatayaki*, the country cooking of Japan, which might include stewed meat with potato, or rolled conger in seaweed. The set menus are incredibly cheap. Drink whiskey (sold by the bottle), saké or lager, or free green tea.

Inigo Jones
*14 Garrick St., WC2 (Covent
Garden)* ☎836-6456. *Map* 10*G11*
▥ ▭ ▦ ▦ ⇥ ᴀᴇ ⊙ ⊚ ᴠɪsᴀ
*Closed Sat lunch, Sun. Tube
Covent Garden.*

Mainly *nouvelle cuisine* dishes in a roaming menu which changes monthly; excellent wines too. Very expensive, though there is a set-price menu at lunchtime and for a pre-theater dinner. An interestingly-designed restaurant which has some attractive souvenirs from the building's days as a stained-glass factory.

Au Jardin des Gourmets
5 Greek St., W1 (Soho) ☎437-1816. *Map* 10*F10* ▥ *to* ▥ ▭ ▦
⇥ ᴀᴇ ⊙ ⊚ ᴠɪsᴀ *Closed Sat
lunch, Sun. Tube Tottenham
Court Road.*

Although it is especially noted for its fine wines — one of the best lists in London, acquired with great care and served with love — this elegant, discreet classical French restaurant has for years been a firm Soho favorite. Theater-goers can split their meal: starter and main course before curtain-up, dessert and coffee after.

Joe Allen
*13 Exeter St., WC2 (Covent
Garden)* ☎836-0651. *Map* 11*F11*
▢ *to* ▣ ▭ ▦ ⇥ *Tube Covent
Garden.*

Branch of the New York restaurant, and very similar in style and decor, though somehow less intimate and more bustling. Very popular with journalists and actors, more for its social ambience than its food. Sizeable menu on a chalkboard, with salads, burgers (called 'chopped steak'), etc., and American desserts. Cocktails at the bar. Open late, until 1am.

Kalamares
*76-78 Inverness Mews, W2
(Mega) and 66 Inverness Mews,
W2 (Micro) (Bayswater)* ☎727-9122. *Map* 6*G3* ▥ ▭ ᴀᴇ ⊙ ⊚
ᴠɪsᴀ *Closed lunch, Sun. Tube
Bayswater.*

An unprepossessing mews leads to these two ever-popular Greek tavernas. Micro, nearest is smaller, rather cramped, unlicensed and cheaper; Mega, farther down, is more spacious. The food at both is equally good, the atmosphere relaxed and very jolly. An incomprehensible menu is patiently decoded by helpful waitresses (although it's impossible to remember everything they tell you — how much simpler it would be to print translations). Starters tend to be more exciting than main courses: try deep-fried squid, *melitzanes skordalia* (fried eggplant with garlic dip) and the *loukanika* (spicy sausages). Wine is Greek too.

Keats
*3 Downshire Hill, NW3
(Hampstead)* ☎435-3544. *Map*
21*C4* ▥ *to* ▥ ▭ ⇥ ᴀᴇ ⊙ ⊚
ᴠɪsᴀ *Closed Sat lunch, Sun. Tube
Hampstead.*

In bookish Hampstead, even the restaurants look like libraries, but such an erudite and worldly district is most exacting in the matter of gastronomy. The classical French menu, which might include such delights as *châteaubriand aux trois sauces* and wild duck, features new dishes every month, and the wine list is outstanding.

Restaurants

Kettners
29 Romilly St., W1 (Soho) ☎437-6437/734-6112. Map **10F10** □ to □ ⬛ ▢ ☰ 🍷 ♪ ⓘ ● ● VISA Tube Leicester Square, Tottenham Court Road.

A famous London restaurant in days gone by, Kettners is now home to yet another Pizza Express (there are 18 branches in London, at two of which, **Pizza on the Park**, 11 Knightsbridge, SW1 ☎235-5550 and **Pizza Express**, 10 Dean St., W1 ☎437-9595, live jazz can be heard nightly). This is all to the good, since it means that those with only a few pounds to spend can enjoy their tasty pizzas and hamburgers in splendidly plush surroundings (avoid the modern, tiled dining room if you can). There is also a champagne bar and cocktail lounge with pianist, where you may be serenaded by Alfredo, the singing *maître d'*.

Langan's Brasserie
Stratton St., W1 (Piccadilly) ☎493-6437. Map **9G9** ▥▥ to ▥▥▥ □ ☰ 🍷 AE ⓘ ● VISA Closed Sat lunch, Sun. Tube Green Park.

Michael Caine, the archetypal knowing cockney, was one of the founding members of this headquarters of London's café society, where the famous are not only sketched on the menu but also seated at the tables. Londoners have always enjoyed the watering-holes, such as **Odins**, established by extrovert Irish restauranteur Peter Langan. Even though Peter Langan is now only rarely in evidence, having decamped to warmer climes, his buzzing and crowded brasserie has lost none of its pizazz, despite the presence of more tourists and soccer stars than moguls and movie stars. The food, under the control of roving chef Richard Shepherd, may have lost some of its edge of late, but it remains surprisingly superior (try the spinach soufflé, *croustade d'oeufs de caille*, profiteroles with chocolate sauce). Langan's may not be at its zenith, but this is still the most exciting dining room in London, a huge space, wonderfully lit, filled with white-covered tables, black-aproned waiters, beautiful modern paintings, and above all, people.

Leith's
92 Kensington Park Rd., W11 (Notting Hill) ☎229-4481. Map **6G2** ▥▥▥ ▬ ➤ ☰ AE ⓘ ● VISA Closed lunch, Aug hol weekend. Tube Notting Hill Gate.

A school of food and wine, a farm growing produce for the restaurant, and an impressive *ouevre* as a cookery writer, all underpin the work of Prue Leith and her partners in this Victorian building, with an interior by expatriate American architect Nathan Silver. The result is an ambience of discreet, glittering comfort, of respect for food by the kitchen and diners alike. Leith's is a temple of the very best English food and an especially inventive (though nonetheless usually simple) style, served from a very short menu. The restaurant is well known for its trolley of cold starters, on which a typical item might be smoked trout pâté parcels wrapped in smoked salmon. Stilton soup is a favorite, perhaps followed by charcoal-grilled lamb steak and thyme. Superb vegetables, an excellent, if expensive, wine list, and delicious desserts such as ginger syllabub.

Little Akropolis
10 Charlotte St., W1 (West End) ☎636-8198. Map **10E10** ▥ □ AE ⓘ ● VISA Closed Sun lunch, Sun, three weeks Aug. Tube Goodge Street.

Comfortable, old-established restaurant offering carefully-prepared Greek dishes at medium prices. Very good *avgolemono*, excellent *kleftiko*, and rose-petal pancakes.

Lockets
Marsham Ct., SW1 (Westminster) ☎834-9552. Map **18H11** ▥▥▥ □ ▬ ▬ AE ⓘ ● VISA Closed Sat lunch, Sun. Tube Westminster.

Members of Parliament like Lockets not only because it is convenient for the Palace of Westminster (it is even fitted with a Division Bell) but also because it provides traditional English food of mostly excellent quality. Just the place to take a counterpart from Brussels or a visiting congressman who might choose mousse of Arbroath smokies, spiced beef cooked in ale, or duck with black cherries.

Lou Pescadou
241 Old Brompton Rd., SW5 (South Kensington/Earl's Court) ☎370-1057. Map **14K3** ▥▥ □ AE ⓘ ● VISA Tube Earl's Court.

Most seafood restaurants in London are fiendishly expensive, so it's good to know of this humble younger sister of **Le Suquet**. The surroundings are suitably rustic, with plenty of nautical nic-nacs designed to induce you (in vain) into believing that you are not in Earl's

Court, but in a small French fishing port. The food does a much more evocative job than the decor, with a tureen of delicious reddy-brown *soupe de poisson*, a traditional oniony *pissaladière*, excellect pizzas, *moules marinière*, pasta with *palouredes* (clams), *calamar frit*, and so on. To drink, try one of the rosés, which makes a refreshing change from red or white wine. No reservations are accepted.

Luigi's

15 Tavistock St., WC2 (Covent Garden) ☎ *240-1795. Map 10G10* ▥▢ 🞐 ⬚ VISA *Closed Sun. Tube Covent Garden.*

Theater-goers who exit stage east, in the Strand/Covent Garden/Drury Lane area, flock to Luigi's, a bustling old favorite on several floors. Typical Italian menu, with good *pastas* and *zabaglione*.

Ma Cuisine

113 Walton St., SW3 (Chelsea/ South Kensington) ☎ *584-7585. Map 16J6* ▥▥ ⬚ 🞐 🞐 *Closed Sat, Sun. Tube South Kensington.*

Patron Guy Mouilleron is once again at the stove of this excellent and popular restaurant, and his cooking is some of the most assured in London. Daily special dishes are announced at the table, according to what was fresh in the market that morning, although their prices have to be guessed at and a knowledge of French is a bonus. Ma Cuisine is small and intimate, not to say crowded, and often it is necessary to reserve a week ahead. Prices, for food of this quality, are very reasonable, though the wine list bumps up the cost.

Manzi's ✿

1 Leicester St., WC2 (Soho) ☎ *734-0224. Map 10G10* ▥▥ ⬚ AE 🞐 🞐 VISA *Closed Sun lunch. Tube Leicester Square.*

This Italian fish restaurant has been a much-loved London institution for more years than anyone can remember, including including Mr Manzi. Its atmosphere is less overtly Italian than between-the-wars 'Continental.' Downstairs, Manzi's is all bustle and lunchtime and pre-theater dining. Upstairs, the Cabin Room is calmer, for pre-theater dinners, or romantic assignations. Good starters, excellent scallops, sole, crab, lobster, simply prepared, are characteristic. Custardy strawberry flan is an essential dessert. The whole thing is unpretentious and good fun.

Melati ⬤

21 Great Windmill St., W.1 (Soho) ☎ *437-2745. Map 10G10* ▢ *to* ▥▢ ⬚ ▤ AE 🞐 🞐 VISA *Tube Piccadilly Circus.*

Excellent Indonesian food, with some Malaysian/Singaporean dishes, in a little Soho spot just behind Berwick St. market. *Satay*, of course, with the distinctive flavor of lemon grass powder, but also a wide variety of soups, noodle dishes, seafood and vegetarian specialties. Very helpful staff.

Memories of China

67-69 Ebury St., SW1 (Victoria) ☎ *730-7734. Map 17J8* ▥▢ ⬚ ▥ ▤▤ AE 🞐 🞐 VISA *Closed Sun. Tube Victoria.*

The gastronomic memories are those of Ken Lo, the grand old man of Chinese cookery. He also has a cookery school, and a shop around the corner from the restaurant selling Chinese spices and kitchen utensils. The restaurant features regional dishes, especially from the north, as well as some more innovative creations. The overall style of cooking inclines to the light and crispy or crunchy, and the airy, cool interior seems to match it. On the menu you will find Shantung hand-shredded chicken in garlic sauce, Shanghai long-cooked braised knuckle of pork, barbecue of lamb in lettuce puffs and iron-plate sizzled chicken.

Ménage à Trois

15 Beauchamp Place, SW3 (Knightsbridge) ☎ *589-4252/584-9350. Map 10I6* ▥▢ *to* ▥▥▥ ⬚ AE 🞐 🞐 VISA *Closed Sun. Tube Knightsbridge.*

Just the spot for lunch after a hard morning's shopping at Harrods. The 'all starters and puddings' menu is perhaps better suited to daytime rather than evening eating and to delicate female rather than voracious male appetites. Certainly it's popular amongst Sloane Ranging women for an intimate *tête à tête* where, between scintillating pieces of gossip, they can sample light, intricate and utterly delectable dishes, prettily presented *à la mode*. Two dishes apiece, perhaps the trio of creamed eggs followed by baby fillets of lamb, beef and veal in a curry cream sauce, or terrine of lobster, salmon and broccoli followed by stuffed boned quail in pastry, will just keep the wolf from the door; any more and the price becomes altogether exorbitant for such very tasty but insubstantial fare.

Restaurants

Meridiana

169 Fulham Rd., SW3 (South Kensington) ☎589-8815/25. *Map 15K5* ▥ *to* ▥ ▭ ▱ AE ⊕ ⊚ VISA *Tube South Kensington.*

Meridiana's popularity dates back to the Swinging Sixties, but these days it's rather a serious Italian restaurant with a plethora of oversize peppermills being wielded by the waiters. There is a new owner and a new conservatory which covers the roof terrace overlooking Fulham Rd. Excellent pasta and risottos.

Mon Plaisir

21 Monmouth St., WC2 (Covent Garden) ☎836-7243. *Map 10F11* ▥ ▭ ▱ *lunch. Closed Sat lunch, Sun, Aug. Tube Covent Garden.*

The cheese board at Mon Plaisir is so good that one day a diner will order it for all four courses. The notion has been discussed, but no one has yet dared risk the wrath of the staff, who can at times be very Parisian. The distinctly patchy cuisine is more tuned to country cooking such as *coq au vin* and *escargots Bourguignons*, and the atmosphere is bistro-like. Mon Plaisir is on the edge of the Covent Garden area in something of a no-man's land, but by no means inconvenient, and it has for years been everyone's favorite secret. Small, intimate, and pleasantly busy.

Mr Chow

151 Knightsbridge, SW1 (Knightsbridge) ☎589-8656/7347. *Map 16I6* ▥ ▭ ▱ AE CB ⊕ ⊚ VISA *Tube Knightsbridge.*

In the late 1960s, when fashion decreed that to be trendy a restaurant must have exuberant Italian waiters and an Apicella-style interior, Chow had a good idea. Why not do that, with Italian waiters, but serve the food of his native China, particularly Peking? It turned out that, while people certainly wanted to follow fashion, they didn't necessarily want to eat *mozarella* every night; the rest is history. Mr Chow became the most fashionable restaurant in town. It may have been superseded these days, but it's still there.

M'sieur Frog

31a Essex Road., N1 (Islington) ☎226-3495. *Map 21C5* ▥ ▭ ▱ VISA *Closed Sat lunch, Sun, one week in Aug, one week at Christmas. Tube Angel.*

The neighborhoods of northeast London are not the best-served gastronomically, but fashionable Islington does its bit. M'sieur Frog is a well-respected bistro serving robust, often northern, French cooking, in a warm, friendly atmosphere. Typical dishes might include *noisettes de lotte au poivre rose* and *magret d'oie aux prunes.*

Nancy Lam's Enak Enak

56 Lavender Hill, SW11 (Battersea) ☎924-3148 ▥ ▭ ⊚ VISA *Closed lunch, Sun. Train Clapham Junction.*

Enak Enak, so Nancy says, means yum yum, and so it is. Hers is a homespun venture, but it succeeds because she is an excellent cook as well as being both sincere and an authentic 'character.' Give her half a chance and she will show you her family snapshots, but she's often too busy cooking in a minute area at the back of the ground-floor dining room. Her tasty Indonesian cooking is full of individual touches. Don't miss the satay or the treasure hunt chicken. Drink Tiger beer.

Nikita's

65 Ifield Rd., SW10 (Chelsea/South Kensington) ☎352-6326. *Map 14L3* ▥ *to* ▥ ▭ AE ⊕ ⊚ *Closed lunch, Sun. Tube West Brompton.*

Pepper vodka? Tarragon vodka? At least ten versions of the Slav spirit, and often more, are served at this predictably lively Russian restaurant. The atmosphere is that of a bistro with subdued lighting; the prices are definitely those of a restaurant; but no one leaves without having been infused with at least one sort of spirit. Nor does anyone leave hungry, after dill-flavored chicken *consommé* with dumplings, veal with caviar, and pancakes with chilled cream. If you want a bit of peace and quiet, ask for one of the booths when you reserve.

Nontas

16 Camden High St., NW1 (Camden Town) ☎387-4579 ▭ *to* ▥ ▭ AE ⊕ ⊚ *Closed Sun. Tube Camden Town.*

The Greek Cypriot ethnic neighborhoods of London are Camden and Kentish Towns, and points NW, and throughout this area are inexpensive local restaurants of greatly varying quality. In Camden Town, Nontas is an excellent local Greek restaurant, full of life, with very flavorsome cooking and good lamb and fish dishes, varied *mezze* and delicious Hymettus honey and yogurt to finish what should be a most pleasant meal.

Oak Room ⌂
*Piccadilly Meridien Hotel,
Piccadilly, W1 (Piccadilly)* ☎734-
8000. *Map* **10G10** ⬜ ◼ ▰
🅰🅴 🅲🅱 ⊙ ⓒⓓ 🆅🅸🆂🅰 *Tube Piccadilly
Circus.*
Yet another luxury restaurant
(**L'Auberge de Provence** and **Ninety
Park Lane** are others) which is
guided from afar by a luminary
French chef, in this case Michel
Lorain from A La Côte St-Jacques at
Joigny. Together with chef David
Chambers he has won a Michelin star
for this sumptuous hotel dining room
(see *Hotels*), second only in
Edwardian splendor to the **Ritz**.
The food is creative and complex,
spectacularly garnished. With the
removal of Anton Mossiman from
the Dorchester to his own restaurant,
Mossiman's (*11b West Halkin St.,
SW1* ☎235-9625), and indeed the
closure of the Dorchester for
refurbishment, the Oak Room makes
the best place for a money-no-object
celebration.

Odins
*27 Devonshire St., W1
(Marylebone)* ☎935-7296. *Map*
9E10 ⬜ ▤ 🅰🅴 ⊙ ⓒⓓ 🆅🅸🆂🅰 *Closed
Sat lunch, Sun. Tube Regent's
Park.*
Peter **Langan's** other place, less
excitable than the restaurant that
bears his name, and more private and
romantic. Restful and engrossing in
its collection of paintings;
gastronomically it reaches very high
standards at times. Don't miss the
wonderful chocolate dessert to finish
your meal.

192 ♨
*192 Kensington Park Rd., W11
(Notting Hill)* ☎299-0482. *Map*
6G1 🅸⬜⬜ ▰ 🅰🅴 ⓒⓓ *Closed
Sun evening. Tube Ladbroke
Grove.*
Though it's probably meant to be
stunning, the all-glass front of this
restaurant-cum-wine bar is somehow
rather uninviting, as is the self-
consciously stylish post-modern/'50s
interior, with its mainly blank eau-
de-nil walls and tightly packed
seating. What does impress is the
wine and the food, which for their
price are very good value: the check,
which includes no hidden extra
charges, is usually a very pleasant
surprise. Warm salads, red mullet,
goat's cheese all feature on the
modern menu. The restaurant is
often crowded — 192 is the local
canteen for Notting Hill's designer
crowd. Ask for a table upstairs for
preference.

Paper Tiger
*10-12 Exhibition Rd., SW7 (South
Kensington)* ☎584-3737. *Map*
15J5 🅸⬜ *to* �⬜ ⬜ ▤ ▤▤ 🅰🅴 ⊙
ⓒⓓ 🆅🅸🆂🅰 *Tube South Kensington.*
Szechuan food has not really caught
on in London, despite the overall
great popularity of Chinese cooking.
So, for its Szechuan dishes alone,
such as bang-bang chicken and
crispy duck, Paper Tiger was a
welcome addition to the scene. It also
has some Peking dishes, and is much
more comfortable, airy and relaxing
than a cellar restaurant, even one so
meandering, has any right to be.

Poons ♨
4 Leicester St., WC2 (Soho)
☎437-1528. *Map* **10G10** ⬜ *to* 🅸⬜
⬜ ◼ *Closed Sun. Tube
Leicester Square.*
One of Chinatown's best
establishments: good, tasty dishes;
smart, clean cafeteria-style
surroundings; efficient service.
Poons' specialty is wind-dried food
— salty but addictive sausages, pork
and duck — as well as excellent
Singapore-style noodles, steamed
scallops, eel with pork and garlic, or
sweet and sour *wun-tun*. Reservations
recommended.

Porter's
*17 Henrietta St., WC2 (Covent
Garden)* ☎836-6466. *Map* **10G11**
🅸⬜ ⬜ ◼ *lunch* ⓒⓓ 🆅🅸🆂🅰 *Tube
Covent Garden.*
The raised pie is one of the principal
themes of traditional English
cooking, and it has the natural
advantage that it is easy to handle
and to prepare ahead. Thus it makes
an ideal dish for quick lunches in a
busy restaurant, as Porter's has
discovered. The same is true of soups
and potted meats, which go to make
up an emphatically traditional but
quickly-served menu at a restaurant
which arrived with the revival of
Covent Garden.

Le Poulbot
45 Cheapside, EC2 (City) ☎236-
4379/248-4026. *Map* **12F15** ⬛⬜ ◼
🅰🅴 🅲🅱 ⊙ ⓒⓓ 🆅🅸🆂🅰 *Closed
evenings, Sat, Sun. Tube St
Paul's.*
Haute cuisine's only outpost in The
City, and inevitably a popular place
in which to plot or consummate a big
business deal. Very discreet, and
excellent, as might be expected from
one of the Roux brothers'
establishments (see **La Gavroche**).
Lunch only, with a short menu
which changes daily. Superb cheese
board.

Restaurants

Reads
152 Old Brompton Rd., SW5 (South Kensington) ☎373-2445. Map **15K4** ▮▮▯ to ▮▮▮▮ ▮▮ lunch ━ ▮Æ▯ ⑩ ⓒ◎ VISA *Closed Sun evening, two weeks Christmas. Tube South Kensington.*

This is a charming restaurant, pretty and filled with flowers. The atmosphere is convivial and unstuffy, generated by the informal but dedicated approach of the proprietors. "We hate restaurants which are nothing but shrines to good food," says co-owner Keith Read, who has built up an interesting and well-explained wine list (he particularly recommends his Pomerols) and orchestrates the efficient table service. The food, described as "English . . . with imagination," is accomplished and beautifully presented with some good ideas, such as *millefeuille* of fresh frogs' legs or deliciously stuffed rare filet steak. Try to find room for a dessert, or at least a homemade *petit four*. The roast beef Sunday lunch is one of the best in town.

Red Fort
77 Dean St., W1 (Soho) ☎437-2115/2525 Map **10F10** ▮▮▯ ⌑ ▮▮ ⓨ ▮Æ▯ ⑩ ⓒ◎ VISA *Tube Leicester Square.*

Indian restaurants have gone upscale. At least in London, flock wallpaper and piped music are definitely out, to be replaced instead by Osborne and Little wallpaper and cocktail bars, or alternatively an evocation of the last days of the Raj. This, **Bombay Brasserie** and **Lal Quila** (*117 Tottenham Court Rd., W1* ☎387-4570 ▮▮▯), are vanguards of the new-wave 'Indian' and have all proved successful. In neutral, soothing surroundings, on two floors, the Red Fort dispenses above-average if not outstanding North Indian cooking, which can be uneven. Good starters, prawn dishes, quails marinated in yogurt, Goan-style fish and vegetable dishes. To drink, stick to lager if you can; the wine list is unadventurous and pricey.

Ritz △
Piccadilly, W1 (Piccadilly) ☎493-8181. Map **9G9** ▮▮▮▮ to ▮▮▮▮ ⌑ ▮Æ▯ ⓒⒷ ⑩ ⓒ◎ VISA *Tube Green Park.*

London's prettiest dining room continues to produce food that almost, but not quite, lives up to the ravishing pink and marbled Empire surroundings. Keith Stanley, from the Savoy Grill, is the third successive English chef to try luck here, and reviews have so far been mixed. Best to stick to the plainer dishes such as whole Dover sole or collops of monkfish and oysters in a chive butter sauce. Desserts are disappointing. Service is almost back to its former balletic efficiency. Prices are high, but a meal here is still worth every penny for the sheer thrill of being in this definitively legendary room.

Rue St Jacques
5 Charlotte St., W1 (West End) ☎637-0222. Map **10E10** ▮▮▮▮ ⌑ ▮Æ▯ ⑩ ⓒ◎ VISA *Closed Sat, Sun. Tube Goodge Street.*

With its sophisticated, glossy decor, its almost faultless culinary offerings and its lavish prices, this restaurant has already established itself on the international circuit, although it opened only in 1984. Chef Gunther Schlender (who was at the now defunct Carrier's for many years) rekindles the jaded palettes of businessmen with elastic expense accounts and society ladies alike with such delights as guinea fowl in a caramel glaze with mangoes, or sweetbreads with sorrel and mushroom sauce. Altogether a safe bet for the very rich, but perhaps lacking in individuality. A classic restaurant very much in the modern style.

St Quentin
243 Brompton Rd., SW3 (Knightsbridge) ☎589-8005. Map **16/6** ▮▮▮▮ ⌑ ━ ▤▤ ▮Æ▯ ⑩ ⓒ◎ VISA *Tube Knightsbridge, South Kensington.*

Open a helpful seven days a week, St Quentin has the atmosphere of a bustling, upscale Parisian bistro: all mahogany, mirrors, and starched white table cloths. The food is typical too, and of fairly high standard, although there are mistakes (such as dishes arriving tepid rather than hot). Choose upstairs for the people, downstairs for the calm.

Salloos
62-64 Kinnerton St., SW1 (Belgravia) ☎235-4444. Map **16/7** ▮▮▮▮ ⌑ ▤▤ ▮Æ▯ ⑩ ⓒ◎ VISA *Closed Sun. Tube Knightsbridge.*

A rare Pakistani restaurant. The ethnicity is a matter of some pride to patron 'Salloo' Salahuddin, who also has a restaurant in Lahore. What it really indicates is the food of the NW corner of the subcontinent, with an emphasis on kebabs and other roasted meats. Although there are ethnic touches, the restaurant is basically modern in design, and smart but subdued. Specialties include lamb in wheatgerm, chicken in cheese and tandoori quails.

San Frediano
62 Fulham Rd., SW3 (South Kensington) ☎*584-8375. Map 15K5* ▮▯ ⌧ ▭ ▤ ▣ ⦿ ▨ *Closed Sun. Tube South Kensington.*
The friendly and caring service in this extrovert and somewhat Tuscan restaurant doesn't seem to have faded since it first became popular well over a dozen years ago. The food is good, too; arguably the best among this style of Italian trattoria, at prices which represent very fair value. Mouthwatering cold table, and good, inexpensive Italian wines.

San Lorenzo
22 Beauchamp Pl., SW3 (Knightsbridge) ☎*584-1074. Map 16I6* ▮▯ *to* ▮▮ ▭ ▱ *see below. Closed Sun. Tube Knightsbridge.*
Still the most fashionable Italian restaurant in London with, many would argue, the best food. Much loved for its conservatorial interior, and roof which opens in summer. Favored dishes include *crudités* and *bagna cauda* and delicious veal San Lorenzo.

Sea Shell ♣ ⬥
51-53 Lisson Grove, NW1 (Marylebone) ☎*723-8703. Map 8E6* ▯ ▭ ✳ *Closed Sun, Mon. Tube Marylebone.*
Once it was a humble fish-and-chip shop, then people started coming in Rolls-Royces, and now it is a restaurant. The Sea Shell offers a notably wide variety of excellent quality fried fish in generous helpings — not only the traditional cod and haddock but also skate, plaice, sole, and others — followed by better apple pie than might be expected. It has recently changed hands: hopefully the food and the proud, friendly service will remain intact.

Shezan
16-22 Cheval Pl., SW7 (Knightsbridge) ☎*589-7918/0314. Map 16I6* ▮▮ ▭ ▤ ▤ ⦿ ▨ *Closed Sun. Tube Knightsbridge.*
One of the best of the 'gourmet' restaurants from the Indian sub-continent, though the delicacy of its spicing and individual approach to one or two dishes can disappoint the diner who prefers something more

ethnic. The intention is to provide Pakistani *haute cuisine*, and the clientele in this coolly smart, almost austere, restaurant seems to include many successful businessmen from the subcontinent. Pleasing choices from the menu include *murg tikka Lahori, kofta Kashmiri* and *pulao Lizazi*.

Simply Nico
48a Rochester Row, SW1 ☎*630-8061 (Victoria) Map 17J10* ▮▮ ▰ ⌧ ▤ ⦿ ▨ *Closed Sat, Sun. Tube St James's Park.*
Nico Ladenis is undoubtedly one of Britain's best chefs. He is also totally committed, highly temperamental, and peripatetic — three moves in two years have landed him at present in the hinterland of Victoria. If ever a restaurant deserved to be named for its proprietor, it is this one, for Nico's presence, sometimes belligerent, is always palpable, and his idiosyncratic, intensely flavored cooking is as strong in character as its creator. The wine list, too, is uncompromising — the best bottles, regardless of cost.

Simpson's-in-the-Strand
100 Strand, WC2 (Strand) ☎*836-9112. Map 11G12* ▮▮ *to* ▮▮ ▭ ▤ ⦿ ▣ ▨ *Closed Sun. Tube Covent Garden.*
The most famous home of roast beef, saddle of lamb, Aylesbury duck, and other traditional English favorites. The roast meats are brought on a trolley and carved at the table. Good English apple pie, or finish the meal with a savory such as angels on horseback (oysters in bacon on toast). Very male atmosphere, very British.

Smollensky's Ballon
1 Dover St., W1 (Piccadilly) ☎*491-1199. Map 9G9* ▮▮ *to* ▮▮ ▭ ▽ ♪ ✳ ▤ ⦿ ▣ ▨ *Tube Green Park.*
Open all day, this is a lively, busy restaurant-plus, very much in the American mold, successful because what it does, it does well. Getting down to basics, the steaks are properly charcoal-grilled, and they are big. On top of that, the service is notably friendly and prompt, there's an abundance of unfunny jokes on the walls, live music, entertainers for the children at weekends (reserve well in advance), a crowded cocktail bar, heart-shaped steaks on St Valentine's Day, and more in the same style. The formula works, and owner Mike Gottlieb is opening a new branch in the Strand.

Restaurants

Soho Brasserie
*23-25 Old Compton St., W1
(Soho)* ☎439-3758. Map **10F10**
□ to Ⅲ □ ▤ ¥ ⓐ ⓞ ⓞ ⓥⓘⓢⓐ
Tube Leicester Square.
The moment the blue and cream
doors of this brewery-owned
establishment were opened a few
years ago, it became the newest place
in the area to see and be seen,
whether taking a croissant or a
cocktail in the front bar (with small
tables and chairs, not stools) or a
more substantial meal in the
restaurant behind. If you are looking
for a light but tasty lunch this is a
good choice: the bar menu includes
excellent fish soup (be warned: you'll
be treated like a leper after you've
eaten the pungent accompanying
rouille), good cheese and charcuterie.
The restaurant menu has its
moments too: the turbot and brill
dishes are to be recommended.

Suntory
*72 St James's St., SW1 (St
James's)* ☎409-0201. Map **9H9**
Ⅲ Ⅲ ▤ ⓐ ⓞ ⓞ ⓥⓘⓢⓐ *Closed
Sun. Tube Green Park.*
In surroundings of simple elegance,
with cool Japanese screens, Suntory
dispenses Shabu-Shabu dishes in one
room, and Teppan cooking in
another. The restaurant is owned by
the Japanese vineyard, distilling and
brewing company Suntory, and is
something of a showpiece of the
country's cuisine, in preparation,
presentation and service. On the
menu, all dishes are described in
detail in English, and service is
helpful. Prices are geared to Japanese
expense accounts.

Le Suquet
*104 Draycott Ave., SW3 (Chelsea/
South Kensington)* ☎581-1785.
Map **16J6** Ⅲ □ 🚗 ⓐ ⓞ ⓞ ⓥⓘⓢⓐ
*Closed Christmas. Tube South
Kensington.*
This is the best of Pierre Martin's
growing chain of Gallic fish
restaurants (see also **Lou Pescadou**).
The atmosphere is very French, as is
the service, but it is the quality of the
fish, and the cuisine, that have made
them so successful. Treat yourself to
the huge *plateau de fruits de mer*, or
perhaps *filet de loup bordelaise* or
raie au beurre noir. It is essential to
reserve for both lunch and dinner.

Sweetings
39 Queen Victoria St., EC4 (City)
☎248-3062. Map **12F15** Ⅱ □
*Closed evening, Sat, Sun. Tube
Mansion House.*
Unchanged for 150yr, Sweetings

remains an old friend to countless
pin-striped City workers who jostle
for a seat at the bar or in the small
back dining room with its communal
tables (no reservations). They are
there for fish, prepared in a no-
nonsense British way, without fuss or
frills: oysters, shellfish salads,
delicious crab and salmon
sandwiches, and so on. For dessert
there are such favorites as jam roly-
poly, bread-and-butter pudding and
spotted dick.

Tai-Pan
*8 Egerton Garden Mews, SW3
(Chelsea/South Kensington)*
☎589-8287/584-2499. Map **16J6**
Ⅲ to Ⅲ □ ▤ ⓐ ⓞ ⓞ ⓥⓘⓢⓐ .
Tube South Kensington.
Hunan cooking was introduced to
London by the Tai-Pan at the
beginning of the 1980s, and the
restaurant takes great pride in its
authentic dishes in this style. A
genuinely exotic menu includes
frogs' legs Hunan, tigers' whiskers
and squirrel fish. There are also
Szechuan and Peking dishes, in a
short menu which always features
daily specials. A busy restaurant,
with an expensive clientele, in an airy
basement.

La Tante Claire ⌂
*68 Royal Hospital Rd., SW3
(Chelsea)* ☎352-6045. Map **16L6**
Ⅲ to Ⅲ □ ▀ ▅ ⓐ ⓞ ⓞ ⓥⓘⓢⓐ
*Closed Sat, Sun, two weeks
Easter, two weeks Christmas,
three weeks Aug. Tube Sloane
Square.*
It was the Roux brothers' **Le
Gavroche** that gave birth to Pierre
Koffman's La Tante Clair, and any
argument as to which is the finest
restaurant in London is inclined to
polarize between these two. Both are
noted, as *haute cuisine* surely should
be, for their exquisite and complex
sauces. Tante Claire has recently
expanded and been redecorated and
is now more spacious and
comfortable, but still delightfully
unpretentious. It can be reserved
weeks in advance, especially in the
evenings. The set lunch remains
excellent value, and gives lesser
mortals the chance to savor London's
haute cuisine.

Tate Gallery Restaurant
Millbank, SW1 (Pimlico) ☎834-
6754. Map **18K11** Ⅲ to Ⅲ □ ▀
*Closed evening, Sun. Tube
Pimlico.*
Not a museum snack bar but a
full-scale restaurant whose
reputation rests on its inexpensive

and excellent wine list, and the beauty of its Rex Whistler mural. The olde-English cooking — Joan Cromwell salad, Hindle Wakes — is badly faltering, as is the service.

Walton's
117 Walton St., SW3 (Chelsea/ South Kensington) ☎*584-5297. Map 16J6* ▮▮▮ *to* ▮▮▮▮ ▭ ▬ ▬ ▦ *AE* *CB* *⊕* *⊙* *VISA* *Closed Sun evenings. Tube South Kensington.*
Renowned for its plushness and privacy. Its menu is basically French, but with British touches: Stilton soup; *noisettes* of Welsh lamb

with lobster meat and *béarnaise* sauce; moneybags of curried mussels.

Wilton's ⌂
55 Jermyn St., SW1 (St James's) ☎*629-9955. Map 10H10* ▮▮▮▮ ▭ *AE* *⊙* *⊙* *VISA* *Closed Sat lunch, Sun, three weeks July-Aug. Tube Green Park.*
Clubby and rather male, with an atmosphere redolent of the '30s and '40s, this old-established restaurant has recently moved location, but little has changed. The English menu is traditional, relying on prime fresh ingredients simply prepared.

Cafés and tearooms

Britain's colonial adventures made her controller of the world's tea trade; united with a rich tradition of cakes, biscuits and breads, this resulted in an institution nobody has copied — afternoon tea. The traditional meal is a substantial affair, with cakes, toasted teacakes or crumpets, perhaps even fish or cold meat. Popular today is the 'cream tea': scones, jam and whipped cream. It is more than mere refreshment — it is a graceful, sometimes even formal, social occasion.

Most of the better hotels offer a traditional afternoon tea between about 3.30-5.30pm. Taking tea there is a uniquely metropolitan experience. A choice of India or China tea, or Earl Grey, camomile or even tilleul (linden or lime-blossom) if you care to ask is offered at the **Ritz Hotel**, W1 (it is essential to reserve); on Sun afternoons at the Ritz there is a *thé dansant* — also at the **Waldorf**, WC2, on Fri and Sun. Those who enjoy the full gastronomic delights favor **Brown's Hotel**, W1, and the **Hyde Park Hotel**, W1, but those more concerned with the drink itself incline to the Ritz and to the **Savoy** group (which includes **Claridges** and the **Connaught**, both W1, and the **Berkeley**, SW1), which has its own blend. At La Chinoiserie in the **Hyatt Carlton Tower**, SW1, and on Sat and Sun in the **Savoy**, there is a harpist; piano accompaniment is on hand at most grand hotels.

One of the most stylish locations in which to take afternoon tea is **Fortnum & Mason**, Piccadilly, in the Fountain restaurant, which serves excellent sandwiches, salads and cakes. Among the department stores which offer afternoon tea, **Harrods** also provides a pianist, and has a fairly expensive set price for which you can eat as much as you like. Opposite Harrods, on Brompton Rd., SW3, is a branch of **Richoux**, at which rather high prices are matched by an expensive ambience.

The opening of a tea shop may not seem a headline-maker, but the 1981 revival of the **Lyons Corner House**, Strand, WC2, along established institution, made waves in the London media, and attracted afternoon lines for weeks afterward. Upstairs, Lyons is happy to serve at any time of day an order comprising nothing more than a cup of tea ('cuppa'), perhaps with a Chelsea bun, although egg and bacon or a snack are available. Downstairs, lunches are served, and orders for just tea are taken only between 3-5.30pm. Whether in the abrasive 1980s the company can sustain the idea of a relaxed atmosphere, with very low prices, and adequate, if slightly fast-foodish, quality on busy sites, only time will tell.

The upstairs-downstairs arrangement is followed in a slightly different manner at the **Ceylon Tea Centre**, 22 Regent St., W1. Upstairs for waitress service, down for cafeteria, but at either level it is possible to order a solo 'cuppa', and there is an excellent choice of different teas. Lunches are also available. The **India Tea Centre**, 343 Oxford St., W1, even serves curries. Since the classic English teas are blends of Ceylon and India, these establishments offer as authentic a selection as can be sampled on the spot. Unfortunately, The City, where the tea trade has its roots, now has only countless anonymous snack bars.

London has long been sufficiently cosmopolitan to have a number of good patisseries. For gossipy ambience, try **Valerie**, 44 Old Compton St., Soho, W1; for privacy and good pastries, visit nearby **Maison Bertaux**, 28 Greek St., W1; for excellent pastries, **Maison Bouquillon**, 45 Moscow Rd., W2.

Pubs

In most countries, it is difficult for even the experienced traveler to visit a strange town and immediately spot a place where it will be possible to relax and, with luck, meet a few friendly natives. Apart from the welcome, each painted sign outside a pub heralds a singularity of identity which is its quintessential charm.

The public house contrives to be unmistakable whatever its origins, and pubs can vary considerably. Being one of England's older cities, London has pubs which grew out of every period of the country's history, and their names reveal their backgrounds. A pub which stands on the site of a colonial Roman taverna may be called The Vines or The Grapes; a hostel for workers on some medieval construction project might be The Builders, The Castle or The Bridge; a monastery hospice for pilgrims, The Angel or The Salutation. Though the term 'public house' was not used in official language until the mid-1880s, that's what they all are, whether they were built as coaching inns, Georgian coffeehouses or gin palaces for the new city-dwellers of the Victorian period.

The first purpose of the pub is to provide for conversation in an informal setting, and most London pubs do concentrate on just that, though, as in Shakespeare's time, there are hostelries which present live entertainment. There are plenty of pubs, too, which serve meals, but a greater number employ the impenetrable pork pie as a defense against would-be diners, thus freeing themselves to concentrate on the serving of drink, which is the second purpose of the pub.

What to drink in the London pub? The fact that England's national spirit is London Dry Gin is easily overlooked, perhaps because the average publican's skills in the matter of mixed drinks don't stretch much further than the addition of tonic.

The true stock-in-trade of the pub is beer. Because London is so close to the hop gardens of Kent, it has long had a tradition of especially 'hoppy' beers. Two London breweries, Whitbread and Watneys, are national giants, while the truly local breweries are small firms, Fuller's (London Pride) and Young's. The latter in particular have championed the unique British tradition of having their beer conditioned at the pub, in the cask, whence it is drawn by a hand pump or 'beer engine' at a natural cellar temperature. An ale should never be cold, but served like a red wine, which surprises many tourists.

Another puzzler for foreigners is the lack of waiter service, though you may find it in some 'lounge' bars. The public bar is where you will find the darts board, and the purist who likes to stand up while he enjoys his pint, and to drink it from a straight, handle-less glass.

Drinking laws
Britain's old, inconvenient drinking laws are better known. They were devised during World War I to curb drunkenness and were finally relaxed in 1988. Pubs may now stay open from 11am-11pm Mon-Sat and Sun noon-3pm, 7-10.30pm; within these limits the exact opening hours are at the discretion of the landlord. Opening hours tend to be longer in and around obvious tourist attractions. In the financial and commercial heart of The City, pubs may close early and remain shuttered on weekends. Ten minutes before closing, the barman sings out "last orders." Closing time is announced as "time gentlemen please," and customers are given up to 20 minutes to drink up.

Central London

Anglesea
Selwood Terrace, SW7. (Kensington) Map 15K5
On Chelsea borders. Drink outside in summer. Inside, a pewter beer engine dispenses such country specialties as Brakspeare's and Ruddle's. Fairly basic pub snacks. Nearby on the corner of Old Church St. and Fulham Rd., publican-turned-novelist Sean Tracey entertains literati and artists in the delightfully scruffy **Queen's Elm**.

Black Friar
174 Queen Victoria St., EC4. (Blackfriars) Map 12F14
The astonishing interior, in marble, alabaster, bronze and copper, with friezes depicting bacchanalia among the friars who gave the neighborhood its name, dates from 1905-24 and is an outstanding manifestation of the later period of the Arts and Crafts Movement. This busy pub, with seats outside, is handy for the Mermaid Theatre (see *Nightlife*) and for *Fleet Street* and *The City*. Don't miss the tiny nook at the back of the main bar. A good range of real ale is served. Closed Sat evenings and all day Sun.

Bunch of Grapes
207 Brompton Rd., SW3. (Knightsbridge) Map 16I6
This pub, w of Harrods, on the way to the *Victoria and Albert Museum*, has a beautiful Victorian interior, with grapes carved in wood, leaded-glass partitions and 'snob screens' to prevent bar staff from eavesdropping on your conversation. Pleasantly dark, with intimate little bar at the back. Country beers from Everard's and Wells. Substantial hot snacks available.

Cheshire Cheese
Wine Office Court, EC4. (Fleet St.) Map 11F13
The pub is on the N side of *Fleet St.*, and scribes from the street of saints and sinners still favor Dr Johnson's old pub for its low-ceilinged friendliness and Marston's beer, despite its inevitably being a tourist haunt. No food in the pub, but the adjoining restaurant offers its famous steak, kidney and game pudding in winter, and a similar pie in summer. Reservations are advisable.

French House
49 Dean St., W1. (Soho) Map 10F10
The definitively picaresque Soho hangout, in which even the bar staff fits the image. Visitors either adore 'The French' or wholly fail to be engaged by its perverse charm, but true Soho-lovers have been loyal for decades. Bare except for fading photographs of French boxers and stage stars, and the pewter water-cooler (for your pastis). Indifferent beer and unexciting wine: try the champagne. 'The French,' like such neighboring pubs as **The Swiss Tavern** in Old Compton St., the

Pubs

Coach and Horses in Romilly St., and **The Sun and 13 Cantons**, Gt. Pulteney St., is a reminder of Soho's ethnic past.

George
77 Borough High St., SE1.
(Lambeth) Map 12H15
This type of inn, with galleries from which patrons could watch shows presented by strolling players in the courtyard, inspired the layout of the first theaters, including Shakespeare's Globe. The George is the last galleried inn in London, and only a part of it still stands. It is most attractive and comfortable, with four small bars, one serving bar food, as well as two restaurants. Wethered's Bitter is dispensed from a 150yr-old beer engine.

Grenadier
18 Wilton Row, SW1. (Belgravia)
Map 17H8
At Hyde Park Corner, down a tiny unpromising mews called Old Barrack Yard. Said to have been the Duke of Wellington's local. You can drink outside this pretty pub, and eat full meals inside at reasonable restaurant prices. Ruddle's County beer.

Guinea
30 Bruton Place, W1. (Mayfair)
Map 9G9
In the heart of London, a tiny, basic pub that would pass for a village local if it weren't full of advertising account executives and book editors. Hard to find, down a mews, but worth the effort. The adjoining restaurant serves excellent beef and good claret, but is very expensive indeed. The Guinea is a Mayfair outpost for Young's brewery in much the way that a nearby mews pub, the **Star Tavern**, Belgrave Mews West, SW1, just off Belgrave Sq., is a showpiece in Belgravia for Fuller's brewery.

King's Head and Eight Bells
50 Cheyne Walk, SW3 (Chelsea).
Map 16L6
In lovely Cheyne Walk overlooking the river, a pub which is more than 400yrs old. 18thC decor, prints of old Chelsea on the walls. There's a permanent buffet and Wethered's and Flowers on tap.

Lamb and Flag
Rose St., WC2. (Covent Garden)
Map 10F11
The poet Dryden dubbed this pub 'The Bucket of Blood' after being mugged in the adjoining alley. It's as dark and poky as ever, but you will meet none more intimidating than the graphic design crowd, spreading themselves almost into Garrick St.

Magpie and Stump
18 Old Bailey, EC4. (City) Map 12F14
The lawyers regularly to be seen drinking here can no longer watch the fruits of their labors; the pub was once a vantage point from which to view public executions, and the neighborhood's Newgate Prison has long gone. But the *Old Bailey* (the Central Criminal Court) is still very much in business. The pub, rebuilt in 1931 but still rich in atmosphere, serves Charrington's IPA.

The Olde Watling
29 Watling St., EC4. (City) Map 12F15
In the shadow of *St Paul's Cathedral*, a Wren-built pub restored in the course of this century. Oak-beamed and very busy, serving City types with draft Bass, and traditional English pies.

Red Lion
2 Duke of York St., SW1.
(Piccadilly) Map 10G10
Behind Simpson's store and gentlemanly Jermyn St. Said to be the best example of a small Victorian gin palace. Burton's beer; hot snacks.

Salisbury
Cecil Court, St Martin's Lane, WC2 (Trafalgar Sq.) Map 10G11
Art Nouveau bronze nymphs and equally decorative predominantly male clientele inhabit this spectacular theaterland pub. Draft Guinness. Cold buffet.

Sun
63 Lamb's Conduit St., WC1. (Bloomsbury) Map 10D12
Specialty beer pub offering never less than a dozen out-of-town brews, usually ranging from Bateman's Good Honest Ales (Lincolnshire) to Timothy Taylor's Ram-Tam (Yorkshire). Landlord Roger Berman will proudly show you his cellars (reserve in advance) when he is not too busy slaking the thirsts of medics from Great Ormond St. Hospital, or feeding them tasty hot snacks.

Farther along this charming little street is the **Lamb**, said to have been Dickens' local (see *Dickens' House*), which has an attractive Victorian interior. Young's beer is served here.

Barnes

Sun
Church Rd., SW13
The village pond lies opposite, alive
with ducks and fringed with weeping
willows and oak trees. There are
seats by the pond, but you could just
as well sit outside the pub with a pint
of Taylor Walker's beer. Inside, it is
low-ceilinged and cozy. Remarkably
rural for a place which is a double-
decker bus ride (no.9) from
Piccadilly. Barnes has lots of
interesting pubs. Just down the High
Street are the **Bull's Head** for jazz,
and the **White Hart** for its riverside
veranda. Both of these sell Young's
beer.

Epping Forest

Traveller's Friend
*496 High Rd., Woodford
Green*
Epping Forest is a rural part of the
London area rarely visited by
tourists, yet full of interest. This
pub, within reach of Woodford
Station on the tube (Central line), is a
good starting point for a visit to the
area. It also offers Victorian snob
screens and a rare opportunity to
sample Ridley's beer.

Greenwich

Cutty Sark
Ballast Quay, SE10
Named after the famous tea clipper,
which is permanently berthed
nearby, this pub is Georgian in style,
and dates from the early 1800s. It
serves draft Bass. Another nautical
public house, which is located
nearby, at 60 Greenwich Church St.,
is the **Gipsy Moth**, serving Taylor
Walker beer. Greenwich also has a
fine Victorian pub in the **Rose and
Crown**, 1 Croom's Hill, serving
Courage's beer on traditional hand
pumps.

Hammersmith

Dove
19 Upper Mall, W6
Riverside pub, with terrace, just
upstream from the splendid
Hammersmith Bridge. Part of the
pub was built by George III's son,
Prince Augustus Frederick. Rich in
historical and literary associations.
Fuller's beer. Closer to the bridge is
the **Blue Anchor**, 13 Lower Mall,
W6, with a fine pewter bar and
enormous beer engine serving
Courage's beer.

Hampstead

Bull and Bush
North End Way, NW3
Popularized in song by a star of the
19thC music hall, Florrie Forde. The
'Bull' recalls the days when it was the
site of a farm, and the 'Bush' was a
clump of trees planted when it was
the home of Hogarth, the cartoonist
and moralist. Among the notables
who have drunk here, in the
intervening years, Dickens perhaps
forges the link between the
earthiness of the music hall and the
artiness of Hampstead. The pub is
not far from Hampstead Heath, has
its own garden, and serves Taylor
Walker beer. There are two other
historically interesting pubs nearby:
Jack Straw's Castle, also in North
End Way, and the **Spaniards Inn**,
Spaniards Rd.

Flask
Flask Walk, NW3
Among the well-known Hampstead
pubs, this is the best-liked locally. It
is a genuine neighborhood pub, with
interesting tiling inside and out, a
lively regular clientele, and Young's
beer. It is in a pretty alleyway, near a
couple of bookstores, just around the
corner from Hampstead tube station.
There is another **Flask** across the
Heath at 77 Highgate West Hill, N6,
full of historical interest, and serving
Taylor Walker beer. Both take their
name from the flasks once used to
carry water from wells in
Hampstead.

Richmond

Orange Tree
45 Kew Rd., Richmond
Theater pub opposite Richmond
station (*for details of shows* ☎ *940-
3633*). Victorian, large and rambling,
yet somehow intimate. Young's beer
and good range of bar meals.
Richmond has several good pubs;
also especially recommended is the
Old Ship, 3 King St. (which faces the
main George St.), for its Young's
beer and its cheering, open fires in
winter.

Southwark

Goose and Firkin
47 Borough Rd., SE1
The beer is brewed in the cellar;
bitters with names like Goose,
Borough, Dogbolter and
Earthstopper bring in an
enthusiastic, young clientele.
Drinkers can see the brewery

through a window at the same proprietor's **Fox and Firkin**, at 316 Lewisham High St., SW13, farther s. On the other side of town, a third pub in this growing mini-chain is the **Frog and Firkin**, 41 Tavistock Crescent, W11, not far from Portobello Rd. A firkin is a nine-gallon cask.

Mayflower
Rotherhithe St., SE16
Close to the jetty whence the Mayflower set sail, this well-restored pub, with a veranda over the river, serves Charrington's IPA. Next door is the Wren church of St Mary's. In the same dockland area is one of Pepys' favorite pubs, the **Angel**, at

101 Bermondsey Wall East, SE16, serving Courage's beer.

Wapping

Prospect of Whitby
57 Wapping Wall, E1
Recently completely refurbished and still desperately touristy pub in old dockland, although the history and location are genuinely interesting. The nearby **Tower of Ramsgate**, 62 Wapping High St., E1, is a more honest-to-badness pub, where hanging once took place. This East End riverside area always had a marrow-chilling mood which has been heightened by economic depression.

Nightlife and the arts

After dark, the most evident activity in the West End of London (The City dies after the evening rush hour) is theater-going. It is far less formal and self-conscious than in some European cities, but even Broadway can hardly match the elegant bustle of Shaftesbury Avenue as the black cabs deposit and reclaim theater-goers. Although the best seats for a big show are expensive, the London theater does offer its patrons a wide range of prices, so only the most determinedly philistine visitor fails to catch at least one production. (Those with a busy schedule might also note that many theaters present a matinee on Sat and one midweek day.)

For the Londoner, and for the visitor who thinks of it, a drink in a pub is a likely part of an evening at the theater, either as a rendezvous beforehand or for a nightcap afterward; that may depend upon whether you eat before or after the show. Since most of the West End theaters are near either Soho or Covent Garden, these two neighborhoods are the most convenient, and consequently the most lively, after dark. Don't be put off by the seediness of Soho; it has lots of reasonably priced Chinese (Gerrard, Lisle and Wardour Sts.) and Italian (Frith St.) restaurants, and is a safe place to walk, provided you avoid the darkest alleys. For a simple stroll, Covent Garden might seem more relaxing. Elegant Mayfair has a villagey enclave called Shepherd Market, with pleasant pubs, restaurants and ladies of the night (or, often, of the broad daylight), whose presence is not excessively assertive. Elsewhere, Mayfair is, in general, an area of expensive restaurants, private clubs and casinos. The main nocturnal area out of the center of town is outrageous Chelsea; along King's Rd. and Fulham Rd. parade the latest trends, strolling (skating, or whatever) in and out of pubs, wine bars and lively restaurants.

The closing hours of pubs and restaurants, and the paucity of late-night transportation, have won London a reputation that it only partly deserves from being insufficiently nocturnal. Like an aging, dignified actress, London cherishes its beauty sleep, but isn't above the occasional exploit in the small hours. The essential precaution is to lay plans carefully. Be aware that nightclubs may require membership to be arranged in advance; and after midnight, call for a cab from the restaurant or nightclub, rather than expecting to pick one up on the street.

Ballet and opera

Royal Opera House ▥
Bow St., WC2 ☎*240-1991 (info), 240-1066 (reservations). Map 11G11.*

Covent Garden was always a nocturnal enclave, and its more recent crop of wine and bars and restaurants has helped retain at least a hint of that. 'Covent Garden' is art critics' shorthand for the Royal Opera House, one of the most historically interesting theaters in London, with its Classical facade on Bow St. and its box office in Floral St. It is now one of the world's most important venues for opera and ballet, and the greatest artists appear regularly.

Originally named the Theatre Royal, its establishment derived from the first permissions granted by King Charles II for the opening of playhouses after the Restoration. The theater of Kean and Kemble was twice burned down before the present building was completed in 1858. The Royal Opera and Royal Ballet both perform at Covent Garden in seasons of alternating productions. Postal reservations open about six weeks before the beginning of a season, and tickets are quickly snapped up, but 65 seats up in 'the gods' (very high in this theater) are held until the day of the performance. Each person is permitted only one ticket, and there can be long lines, sometimes overnight.

Sadler's Wells Theatre
Rosebery Ave., EC1 ☎*278-8916 (info and reservation). Map 5C13.*

It is a strange name for a theater, and Islington is perhaps an unlikely location. The site was originally a garden in which there was a health-giving well, and its owner, whose name was Sadler, opened a 'musick house' there in 1683. The theater is the base for the Sadler's Wells Royal Ballet company, and has guest seasons including Gilbert and Sullivan productions. It was the original home of the company which became the Royal Ballet, and of the English National Opera.

London Coliseum
St Martin's Lane, WC2 ☎*836-7666 (info), 836-3161 (booking). Map 10G11.*

The theater which houses one of London's largest auditoriums is barely visible from the street, but its illuminated globe stands out in the night skyline. For a long time a music hall, it now houses the English National Opera, whose prestigious large-scale productions are usually sung in English.

Bars

The traditional cocktail bar is most easily found in hotels. The **Savoy's** inspired the famous *Savoy Cocktail Book*, and is believed to have been the first cocktail bar in Europe. The drinks are good, but the ambience is lacking. The **Park Lane Hotel**, the **Inn on the Park** and the **Hyde Park Hotel**, all W1, have good cocktail bars, as do many other hotels.

The younger generation of cocktail bar, featuring confections like the Margarita, Tequila Sunrise or Pina Colada, often doubles as a short-order restaurant, and may be obliged by law to ensure that at least a pastrami sandwich is consumed by each drinker. A

173

typical example is **Rumours** at 33 Wellington St., WC2 ☎836-0038. The well-known **Groucho Club**, 44 Dean St., W1 ☎439-4685, and **Zanzibar**, 30 Great Queen St., WC2 ☎405-8199, are private clubs, and visitors must be introduced by a member.

A change of mood is offered by the wine bar. The traditional kind, which grew out of wine merchants' shops, is typified by **El Vino**, 47 Fleet St, EC4, haunt of journalists and lawyers. It is a male-chauvinist establishment at which, although waitress service is extended to both sexes, ladies may not obtain their drinks at the bar.

There was a second growth of wine bars during the 1970s, and these are much more numerous. The most extrovert example, jostling with magazine folk and models, is **Brahms and Liszt** (cockney rhyming slang for the risqué 'pissed,' meaning drunk) at 19 Russell St., Covent Garden, WC2. For excellent wines and good food, visit the **Cork and Bottle**, 44-46 Cranbourn St., WC2; and, for Knightsbridge or Sloane St. shoppers, the **Ebury Wine Bar**, 139 Ebury St., SW1, is pleasant and well-run. It is not necessary to eat in wine bars, but most provide a range of cold and some hot food.

Brasseries and champagne bars have sprung up all over the West End in recent years, and make excellent places to meet for a drink and a bite to eat before the theater. Downstairs at **L'Escargot**, 48 Greek St., W1, is comfortable and well placed for West End theaters, as is the **Soho Brasserie**, 23 Old Compton St., W1. **Green's**, 36 Duke St., SW1, serves some of the best oysters in London in an attractive wood-paneled bar, and **Kettners**, 29 Romilly St., W1, also has a pleasant champagne bar.

Casinos

London does have casinos, but their numbers have in recent years declined drastically before the regulatory activity of the Gaming Board. Several famous names have vanished, or had their licenses suspended, and the future of others is uncertain. It is the more urbane type of casino, usually found in the Mayfair or Knightsbridge districts, which has fallen foul of the Board, but one or two brasher places still brightly proclaim their presence in Soho. Those casinos which have remained in business are not permitted to advertise, which includes mentions in guidebooks, but they are usually known to hotel concierges. In order to visit a casino, you must either join, which takes 48hr, or be the guest of a member.

Cinemas (movie theaters)

London has an enormous selection of cinemas, but a lesser choice of movies. Two chains, **Cannon** and **Odeon**, dominate, and concentrate on box-office hits. Art-house movies are more likely to be shown by independents, so check the *Evening Standard*, *Time Out* or *City Limits* for the following: the **Curzon Mayfair**, Curzon St., W1 ☎499-3737; the **Curzon Phoenix**, Phoenix St. (off Charing Cross Rd.), WC1 ☎240-9661; and the **Curzon West End**, Shaftesbury Ave., W1 ☎439-4805; the **Gate**, 87 Notting Hill Gate, W11 ☎221-0220; the **Renoir**, Brunswick Centre, Brunswick Sq., WC1 ☎727-4043; the **Camden Plaza**, 211 Camden High St., NW1 ☎485-2443; the **Chelsea Cinema**, 206 King's Rd., SW3 ☎351-3742; **Screen on the Hill**, 203 Haverstock Hill, NW3 ☎435-3366; **Screen on the Green**, 83 Upper St., N1 ☎226-3520; **Screen on Baker St.**, 96 Baker St., NW1 ☎935-2772; and the **Minema**, 45 Knightsbridge, SW1 ☎235-4225.

In Notting Hill, there's the offbeat **Electric Screen**, 191 Portobello Rd., W11 ☎229-3694. The **Institute of Contemporary Arts**, more commonly known as the ICA ☎930-3647, in The Mall, SW1, has a cinema; and the true celluloid freak heads for the **National Film Theatre** ☎928-3232, in the *South Bank Arts Centre*. It has two cinemas presenting a wide range of movies, with retrospectives on the work of individual directors and performers.

Concerts
Classical music
The two most important concert venues are the Royal Albert Hall and the Festival Hall (in the *South Bank Arts Centre*) — each belongs to a different era of optimism and grand gestures.

Royal Festival Hall, Queen Elizabeth Hall, Purcell Room �fi
South Bank, SE1 ☎928-3191 (info and reservation). Map 11G12.
The **Festival Hall**, built for the Festival of Britain in 1951, is part of the *South Bank Arts Centre*, with the **Queen Elizabeth Hall** and the **Purcell Room**. Said by Toscanini to have the finest acoustics in the world, the Festival Hall itself, with 3,000 seats, presents concerts by the leading British and international symphony orchestras. The Queen Elizabeth Hall has 1,100 seats, stages chamber music, string quartets and other small ensembles. The 372-seat Purcell Room presents solo performances and other small events. You can see and hear perfectly from all seats, so the cheaper ones are often a good buy. All three halls offer not only classical music but also pop and jazz. Early evening conversations with celebrities of the music world are held in the Chelfield Room of the Queen Elizabeth Hall.

Royal Albert Hall �fi
Kensington Gore, SW7 ☎589-3203/9465 (info, 589-8212 (booking)). Map 15I4.
The Albert Hall, named after the Prince Consort, is a spectacular manifestation of Victorian architecture, facing Kensington Gardens and the Albert Memorial. It is self-financing, operating independently under Royal Charter. Its best-known annual event is its 'Proms' ('promenade concerts'), founded in 1912 to bring the classics to a wider audience by recapturing the spirit of informal performances in London pleasure gardens. The center of the circular hall is cleared of seats for the Proms season, which runs from mid-July to early Sept, and a cheap ticket allows you to stand and wander at your leisure while you enjoy the music. Tickets are available at the door on the evening of the performance, except in the case of the Last Night of the Proms, a social event characterized by youthful nostalgia, which is reserved long in advance.

Although a wide range of classical music is performed at the Albert Hall, its keynote is eclecticism. The Hall plays host to pop singers, wrestlers, and the annual Miss World contest.

The new **Barbican Centre** (see *Theatres* p178) is now the home of the London Symphony Orchestra, which gives concerts regularly throughout the year.

There are several smaller halls. **Wigmore Hall**, Wigmore St., W1 ☎935-2141, is a famous small concert hall almost within earshot of Oxford St., where international musicians perform chamber music, particularly song and piano recitals and string quartets. One night a week debuts are performed. **Holland Park Court Theatre**, Holland Park, W8 ☎937-2542 ext.52, presents light opera and orchestral music in summer in the only remaining wing of the 17thC **Holland House**. **Kenwood Lakeside** ☎734-1877, is a venue for large-scale orchestral performances on Hampstead Heath on summer weekends. By the lake near Kenwood House is an orchestra shell which has accommodated the Royal Philharmonic and the London Symphony, among others. It is possible to reserve a deck chair, or to sit on the grass. There are also performances of chamber music in the **Orangery** of **Kenwood House**.

There are also a number of more offbeat venues, such as the cushion concerts held at the **Royal Academy**, during its Summer Exhibition of paintings; open only to those aged between 14 and 30, beyond which dignity does not permit people to sit on the floor (for times of concerts ☎379-6722). There are lunchtime recitals at some of London's most attractive and interesting churches, including **St-Martin-in-the-Fields** (on Mon and Tues at 1.05pm), and the famous boys' choir of **St Paul's** can be heard during Sun services at the Cathedral.

Folk music

The English Folk Dance and Song Society, at **Cecil Sharp House**, 2 Regent's Park Rd., NW1 ☎485-2206, has performances on Sat at 7.30pm; and there is traditional English Morris Dancing at **Westminster Abbey**, in front of the main gate of Broad Sanctuary, at 8pm on Wed in summer. British, Irish and American folk music is performed in a variety of clubs and pubs, with dates listed in *Time Out* and *City Limits*.

Jazz

Big-name jazz is always available in London, despite the fact that there are only a few jazz clubs. Almost every well-known name in international jazz has played at **Ronnie Scott's Club**, 47 Frith St., W1 ☎439-0747. It looks and feels like a club, and stays open until 3am, but anybody can enjoy the jazz; meals and drinks are served. Jazz is also performed on Mon at the **100 Club**, 100 Oxford St., W1 ☎636-0933.

On every evening of the week except Mon, leading British musicians, and occasional guests from other countries, perform at the **Pizza Express**, 10 Dean St., Soho, W1 ☎439-8722. Its companion, **Pizza on the Park**, 11 Knightsbridge, SW1 ☎235-5550, has jazz every evening except Sun. Both restaurants belong to the same jazz-crazed owner, who is also active in the Soho community conservation movement. Jazz cognoscenti have an affection for a pub called the **Bull's Head** ☎876-5241, despite its being in an unlikely villagey setting on the river at Barnes, SW13. It offers fine jazz nightly, and especially on Sun lunchtimes, noon-2pm, and serves Young's splendid beer.

Rock

London has an ever-lively and ever-changing rock scene. Clubs, concerts and pub dates are listed in *Time Out* and in rock newspapers such as *Melody Maker*. All the major rock venues are 30-45min from the West End. They are the **Odeon, Hammersmith**, Queen Caroline St., W6 ☎748-4081; the **Earls Court Exhibition Centre**, SW5 ☎385-1200; and the **Wembley Arena**, Empire Way, Wembley, Middlesex ☎902-1234. **Upstairs at Ronnie's**, 47 Frith St., Soho, W1 ☎439-0747, is above the famous jazz club. Also in Soho is the long-established **Marquee** club, 90 Wardour St., W1 ☎437-6603. In Covent Garden, the **Rock Garden**, a club and hamburger bar, is at 6-7 The Piazza,WC2 ☎240-3961. The **Camden Palace** is a converted movie theater at No. 1a Camden Rd., NW1 ☎387-428. Rock in pubs is a changing scene, but the **Half Moon**, 93 Lower Richmond Rd, SW15 ☎788-2387, and the **King's Head Fulham**, 4 Fulham High St., SW6 ☎736-1413, are particular favorites with fans

Nightclubs

If nightingales still sing in Berkeley Square, their songs are directed at the habitués of **Annabel's**, at no.44 ☎629-3558. "The world's best nightclub," says London's most garrulous gossip columinst, Nigel Dempster. It is hermetically discreet and expensive, and an introduction from a member is almost essential. This also applies to **Café de Paris**, 3 Coventry St., W1 ☎437-2036 (open Wed only), with its 1940s gilt and red plush decor, a glamorous haunt of the rich and famous. These and other similar clubs are not impossible to get into, but you must arrange something in advance.

Inside will be music and dancing, according to the current fashion, bars, and, in the more exclusive clubs, good meals will be served. Similar proscriptions apply to to the haunts of royals and pop stars, such as **Raffles**, 287 King's Rd., Chelsea, SW3 ☎352-1091; **Tokyo Joe's**, Clarges St., Mayfair, W1 ☎409-1832; **Stocks**, 107 King's Rd., SW3 ☎351-3461; and **Tramp**, 40 Jermyn St., SW1 ☎734-3174. It is in the nature of such diversions to be affected by fashion — discos have been known to open and close with alarming swiftness, or to announce a violent shift from one trend to another. Such shifts are best monitored through the several gossip columns of the *Evening Standard*, and the glossy magazine *Harper's & Queen*.

The (Roof) Gardens, 99 Kensington High St., W8 ☎937-8923 (open Thurs and Sat only), on top of the old Derry and Toms department store, has long been a stylish vantage point. Disco queen Regine failed with a nightspot here, then youthful music magnate Richard Branson took over and still runs the club.

Among nightspots open to anybody is **Dingwalls**, Camden Lock, NW1 ☎267-49967, an unpretentious and youthful spot for live music (reggae, rock, R&B, jazz), open until 2am. No reservations, so get there before 10pm. The **Empire Ballroom** in Leicester Sq., WC2 ☎437-1446, is an old-style dance hall; big-band alternates with American disco music and roller discos on Sun afternoons; open until 2am, and 3am at weekends. Another famous old dance hall out of town, now revamped and catering to all tastes, is the **Hammersmith Palais**, 242 Shepherds Bush Rd., W6 ☎748-2812. More exclusive is **Legends**, 29 Old Burlington St., Mayfair, W1 ☎437-9933, inspired by New York's Studio 54, with disco, French cuisine, and prices that are not prohibitive. Nonmembers are admitted at the discretion of the doorman, as at **Stringfellows**, 16-19 Upper St Martin's Lane, WC2 ☎240-5534. Glass dance-floor, suede walls and lots of chrome set the tone for what is intended to be an elegantly casual clientele. Proprietor Peter Stringfellow has also transformed the old Talk of the Town into the popular **Hippodrome**, Cranbourn St., WC2 ☎437-4311, particularly lively on Fri and Sat; dress up. **'Heaven,'** Underneath the Arches, Villiers St, WC2 ☎839-3852, is the best gay nightclub, with mixed nights on Tues and Thurs. **Villa dei Cesari**, 135 Grosvenor Rd., SW3 ☎828-7453, offers dinner and dancing, in an opulent Roman-style restaurant, overlooking the river near the Chelsea Embrankment; an expensive treat. Also recommended for dinner and dancing: **La Bussola**, 42 St Martin's Lane, WC2 ☎240-1148.

Theaters

Despite financial pressures, London remains one of the major world centers of theater, and the British still produce many of the greatest actors. The theater scene can be split into three broad categories: companies subsidized by the state, in impressive buildings, producing serious drama to the highest standards; commercial theaters, mainly built at the turn of the century in a style of cozy splendor, mounting lighter plays and musicals; and fringe or club theaters, which might do anything anywhere, but should not be missed by serious theater-goers. The major subsidized theaters usually have several plays in repertory at one time; most other theaters have a single play running as long as it is successful.

A booth on the w side of Leicester Sq., WC2, has half-price seats to same-day shows with spare tickets in West End theaters. There is a small service charge, a maximum of four seats per person, and there can be a long line, but it is a good deal. Many theater bars welcome advance reservations for interval drinks, a system which saves the crush, frustration and thirst. Most theaters close on Sun. Cheaper seats in some of the older theaters may allow only a partial view.

The National Theatre 🏛

*Upper Ground, South Bank, SE1 ☎633-0880 (info), 928-2252 (reservation). Map **11**G13.*
The National Theatre company, originally under the direction of Laurence Olivier, began its life at the Old Vic in the Waterloo Rd. Sir Peter Hall took over in 1973 ready for the opening of the new, purpose-built theater, a modern architectural landmark, in the *South Bank Arts Centre*. He was succeeded by Richard Eyre in 1988. 'The National' actually comprises three theaters within one building. The largest, the **Olivier**, has an amphitheater setting; the **Lyttelton** has a proscenium stage; and the **Cottesloe** is a studio theater. The three present a wide range of classical and modern British and international works. Before performances there is live music in the foyers, picture galleries are open, and there are early-evening lectures, poetry readings and short plays, from 6pm. Although many performances are heavily reserved, the National always retains some seats for sale on the day, and has reduced-price standby tickets. There are also backstage tours.

Barbican Theatre (Royal Shakespeare Company)

*Barbican Centre, EC2. Map **11**E15 ☎628-8891.*
The finest productions of the world's greatest dramatist, many would say. In any case, the RSC enjoys worldwide repute. This is its London base, which complements its Stratford home (see *Excursions*), where many of the theater's productions originate. Besides Shakespeare, the company also performs a wide variety of standard and new plays. With *Nicholas Nickleby* and *The Greeks*, the company pioneered productions in which one major work spanned two or three performances. It also runs a studio theater, **The Pit**, in the Barbican (reservations through same box office).

The Royal Court Theatre

*Sloane Sq., SW1 ☎730-1745. Map **16**J7.*
Despite its name, this theater has a distinguished record of

anti-establishment drama. George Bernard Shaw's plays were presented here in the 1920s and 1930s; and John Osborne, the original 'angry young man,' and Arnold Wesker made their names here in the 1950s and 1960s. John Arden, Edward Bond and David Storey are more recent examples. There is also a smaller **Theatre Upstairs** ☎730-2554.

The oldest theater in London is the **Theatre Royal**, Drury Lane, WC2 ☎240-9066, which specializes in musicals and hit shows. The most elegant is the **Theatre Royal, Haymarket**, SW1 ☎930-9832, presenting a range of 'legitimate' theater. Both date back to the Restoration. The most famous is probably the **London Palladium**, Argyll St., W1 ☎437-7373, which has a policy of family entertainment, and plays host to most of the top international stars. **Regent's Park Open Air Theatre**, NW1 ☎486-2431, presents Shakespearean works throughout the summer.

A few of the more permanent fringe theaters are listed below; publications such as *Time Out* will give details of the smaller, more transient ones. An exquisite 1895 auditorium has been lovingly retained inside a modern concrete shell at the **Lyric, Hammersmith**, King St., W6 ☎741-2311, offering serious classical and modern drama. Neighbors are **Riverside Studios** ☎748-3354, and **The Bush** ☎743-3388, a pub theater. Another pub theater is the **King's Head**, 115 Upper St., N1 ☎226-1916. Other well-regarded venues away from the center include the **Hampstead Theatre Club**, Avenue Rd., Swiss Cottage, NW3 ☎722-9301, and the **Greenwich Theatre**, Crooms Hill, SE10 ☎858-7755.

Other theaters include:

Aldelphi (commercial)   Strand, WC2 ☎836-7611
Albery (commercial)   St Martin's Lane, WC2 ☎836-3878
Aldwych (commercial)   The Aldwych, WC2 ☎836-6404
Ambassadors (commercial)   West St., WC2 ☎836-6111
Apollo (commercial)   Shaftesbury Ave., W1 ☎437-2663
Apollo Victoria (commercial)   Wilton Rd., SW1 ☎828-8665
Arts Theatre Club (commerial)   6/7 Gt Newport St., WC2 ☎836-3334
Astoria (commercial)   157 Charing Cross Rd., WC2 ☎437-1801/8772
Cambridge (commercial)   Earlham St., WC2 ☎379-5299
Cockpit (fringe)   Gateforth St., NW8 ☎402-5081
Comedy (commercial)   Panton St., SW1 ☎930-2578
Criterion (commercial)   Piccadilly Circus, W1 ☎930-3216
Donmar Warehouse (fringe)   41 Earlham St., WC2 ☎379-6565
Duchess (commercial)   Catherine St., WC2 ☎836-8243
Duke of York's (commercial)   St Martin's Lane, WC2 ☎836-5122
Fortune (commercial)   Russell St., WC2 ☎836-2238
Garrick (commercial)   Charing Cross Rd., WC2 ☎379-6107
Globe (commercial)   Shaftesbury Ave., W1 ☎437-3667
Her Majesty's (commercial)   Haymarket, SW1 ☎839-2244
ICA (club)   The Mall, SW1 ☎930-3647
Jeanetta Cochrane (subsidized)   Southampton Row, WC1 ☎242-7040
Lyric (commercial)   Shaftesbury Ave., W1 ☎437-3686
Mayfair (commercial)   Stratton St., W1 ☎629-3036
Mermaid (subsidized)   Puddle Dock, EC4 ☎236-5568
New London Theatre (commercial)   Drury Lane, WC2 ☎405-0072
Old Vic (commercial)   Waterloo Rd., SE1 ☎928-7616

Palace (commercial)   Shaftesbury Ave., W1 ☎434-0909
Phoenix (commercial)   Charing Cross Rd., WC2 ☎836-2294
Piccadilly (commercial)   Denman St., W1 ☎437-4506
Players Theatre Company (club)   Villiers St., WC2 (lodged in Duchess theatre until Autumn 1989) ☎839-1134
Prince Edward (commercial)   Old Compton St., W1 ☎734-8951
Prince of Wales (commercial)   Coventry St., W1 ☎839-5989
Queen's (commercial)   Shaftesbury Ave., W1 ☎734-116
St George's (commercial/ fringe)   49 Tufnell Park Rd., N7 ☎607-1128
St Martin's (commercial)   West St., WC2 ☎836-144¾
Savoy (commercial)   Savoy Court, Strand, WC2 ☎836-8888
Shaftesbury (commercial)   Shaftesbury Ave., WC2 ☎379-5399
Strand (commercial)   Aldwych, WC2 ☎836-2660
Theatre Royal, Stratford East (fringe)   Gerry Raffles Sq., E15 ☎534-0310
Vaundeville (commercial)   Strand, Wc2 ☎836-9987
Victoria Palace (commercial)   Victoria St., SW1 ☎834-1317
Whitehall (commercial)   14 Whitehall, SW1 ☎930-7765
Wyndhams (commercial)   Charing Cross Rd., WC2 ☎836-3082
Young Vic (fringe)   The Cut, SE1 ☎928-6363

Shopping

It is nothing as mundane as shopping that you do in London. It is promenading in the trendy King's Rd. on a Saturday afternoon after having strolled along the Portobello Rd. in the morning. It is listening to the spiel in Petticoat Lane's street market on a Sunday morning. It is exploring the world's most famous department store, **Harrods**, in Knightsbridge, and comparing its food with the exotica at **Fortnum & Mason** in Piccadilly. It is window-dreaming of jade and jewels in Bond St. Depending upon your inclinations, it is the sensation of silk in **Liberty**, or of snuff in Jermyn St. It is relaxing in Covent Garden and wondering whether you need a French horn (**Paxman**, 116 Long Acre) or a quill pen (**Philip Poole**, 182 Drury Lane).

These neighborhoods form a jigsaw stretching five or six miles across the center of London from Chelsea in the w to Petticoat Lane in the E. Each of them is worth half a day of anyone's time, and every one leads to another. None of them is London's principal shopping street, though several of them are linked by it. The main shopping thoroughfare, and the most democratic, is Oxford St., which itself runs from w to E (assuming that you see the most traditional end first). It is a giant version of the main shopping street of every town or city in Britain.

Prices

In London, prices are not generally negotiable, although bargaining is acceptable in some street markets. In most shops, all major credit cards are accepted.

Exemption from Value Added Tax on goods bought for export is offered by some shops. VAT is not a negligible percentage, and can be added a substantial amount to the price of any item costing a few pounds or more, so do ask. You will need to be able to show your passport, and the shop will ask you to fill in a form.

Hours

Shops do not stay open as late as in some other countries. Most shops open Mon-Sat from 9am-5.30pm, with 'late-night' shopping once a week. The Chelsea and Knightsbridge area stays open until 7pm on Wed, and Oxford Street until 8pm on Thurs. Some consolation is that few shops close for lunch. Some shops in Bond St. and a few others in the West End close on Sat. Central London shops do not as yet open on Sun, although new laws may change that in future.

Although central London has few 'local' or 'corner' shops, inner-city neighborhoods have plenty, and they often open until mid-evening, or even midnight, and on Sun.

Antiques

At the top end of the price range, and for the best that money can buy, visit the specialty shops in Bond St., W1, and the adjoining streets and arcades. Examples range from the **Antique Porcelain Company**, at 149 New Bond St., to **The Leger Galleries**, for old masters, at 13 Old Bond St., or **Sac Frères**, for amber, at 45 Old Bond St. The serious buyer will also want to head out to Kensington Church St., W8, which has several high-quality shops. At the s end of this hilly street, **Simon Castle**, upstairs at no.38, deals in wooden objects, particularly inlaid boxes and models; **Michael German**, on the ground floor, specializes in walking sticks and firearms; farther up is **The Lacquer Chest**, at no.75; at the Notting Hill end, **Philip and Bernard Dombey** sell antique clocks at no.174. Nearby is Westbourne Grove, W2, for cheaper antiques, and for fascinating shops like **Dodo**, at no.185, which deals in interesting old advertising materials. The New King's Rd. beyond World's End has also become peppered with quality antique shops, and, farther on, the Wandsworth Bridge Rd. with shops dealing in pine.

In recent years, several permanent, indoor antique markets have been established. In the Bond St. area, **Gray's Mews Antique Market** is at 58 Davies St. and 1-7 Davies Mews, W1; there are about 300 stalls, in a pleasant, well-appointed former factory building, with a lot of Art Nouveau and Deco, and several excellent stalls for tin toys. Across Oxford St., Gee's Court or Duke St. leads to the long-established market in **Barrett St.**, W1, with silver, jewelry, antiques and bric-a-brac.

Among the indoor markets, the insiders prefer **Alfies**, rather isolated from shopping areas in Marylebone, at 13-25 Church St., NW8, selling old lace, antique photographic equipment, genuine antique street signs, etc., with the added interest of the bustle, gossip and dealing. The other neighborhood for indoor markets is Chelsea/Kensington. The **Chelsea Antique Market**, at 245-53 King's Rd., SW3, is a maze of stalls, run by seasoned dealers in all types of antiques. **Antiquarius**, 135-41 King's Road at the corner of Flood St., has always been very conscious of trends.

(See also *Street markets* p187.)

Auction houses

Auctions are a part of London's metropolitan life. If you would like to look, don't be intimidated by newspaper stories of six-figure bids; most items go for much less, and, if you keep your hand firmly on your lap, you can enjoy the auction without parting with any money. It is not necessary to reserve a seat, and there are always viewing days beforehand. The most renowned salesrooms are the following.

Bonhams Montpelier St., SW7 ☎584-9161. Especially good for furniture and paintings. You may pick up a bargain.
Christie's 8 King St., SW1 ☎839-9060. One of the two great names. Fine art, and specialty auctions, including wine sales.

Christie's other salesroom at 85 Old Brompton Rd., South
Kensington, SW7, is worth visiting for less expensive items of
general interest.
Phillips 7 Blenheim St., W1 ☎629-6602. Prices usually in the
medium range. Objets d'art, and various collectibles.
Sotheby's 34/5 New Bond St., W1 ☎493-8080. The other great
name, and the biggest. Fine art, porcelain, jewelry, clothing,
books, Victoriana and decorative arts.

Books
The street for the bibliophile is Charing Cross Rd., WC2, with
numerous stores, including **Foyles** (one of the world's biggest) at
no.119, and the excellent **Waterstone's** next door. In fascinating
alleys like Cecil Court, hours pass quickly in the secondhand book
stores. Regular shops of particular interest are **Zwemmer** at no.80,
for art, architecture and cinema; and **Collet's** no.129-31, for
political and philosophical works of the Left. Away from Charing
Cross Rd., the most comprehensive selection is to be found at
Dillon's, 82 Gower St., WC1. **Hatchards**, in Piccadilly, is a
pleasant, well-stocked general bookstores. **The Children's Book
Centre**, in **Young World**, 229 Kensington High St., W8, has a
huge stock for children up to age 13.

China
The English invented bone china, and the famous names display
themselves proudly in Regent St., W1, especially Wedgwood and
Spode at **Gered**, no.158. There is an even more opulent display at
Thomas Goode, 19 South Audley St., W1, with its Minton
elephants within range of the hunting rifles across the road at the
gunsmith's **James Purdey & Sons**.

China, glassware, and all sorts of elegant household goods can be
found at the **General Trading Company**, 144 Sloane St., SW1,
near Sloane Sq., and at department stores like **Liberty, John
Lewis, Selfridges** and **Harrods** (see pp184-5). For its selection,
Chinacraft, in Regent St., W1, New Bond St., W1, and branches,
is noteworthy.

Clothes
Clothes for children
Britain's maritime tradition is upheld even for children by Rowes
in the **White House**, 51 New Bond St., W1, which began by
making clothes for the children of naval families. This traditional
line shares the store with such children's classics as button-bar
shoes and velvet-collared tweed coats. Visit **Liberty** (see
Department stores p184), **Zero Four**, in South Molton St., W1,
Baby B's, 779-81 Fulham Rd., SW6, and **Anthea More-Ede**, 16
Victoria Grove, W8.
Clothes for men
Savile Row is the place for suits, Jermyn St. for accouterments —
definitive addresses for the English gentleman.

In Savile Row, W1, the appositely named **H. Huntsman and
Sons**, at no.11, is famous for riding clothes and has been a tailor to
royalty for more than hundred years; very expensive, and no credit
cards. Other renowned names in Savile Row include **Gieves &
Hawkes**, at no.1, **Anderson & Sheppard** at no.30, and **Tommy
Nutter**, fraternized by Elton John and Mick Jagger, at no.19. For
classic and casual suits, try **Blades of Savile Row**, at 8 Burlington
Gardens, W1. Also nearby is **Austin Reed**, 103 Regent St., W1,
and **Aquascutum**, 100 Regent St., W1. At 35 Dover St., **Crolla**
sells wonderfully *outré* clothes for men (and women) in beautiful

rococo brocade prints. And **Paul Smith** in Covent Garden, at 43 Floral St., is another trendy menswear store that has made a name for itself.

In Jermyn St., SW1, a man can no longer sweat out a hangover in the Turkish baths, but he can still have a shave and haircut, buy himself a clean shirt, and prepare to face the world. It is still a male street, in the debonair sense of the word. Buy mustache wax or a badger-hair shaving brush at **Ivan's**, no.20, or an antique meerschaum at **Astleys**, no.109. Top-quality shirts are available from **Harvie and Hudson**, at nos. 77 and 96, or the extrovert **Turnbull and Asser**, at no.71. For a bowler hat (a 'derby' to Americans), for townwear, where better to go than the originators of the style, **James Lock**, nearby at 6 St James's St., SW1. For a tweed cap, visit **Bates**, at 21a Jermyn St., where the shop's late cat (it died in 1921) watches you from a glass case. Of the department stores watches you from a glass case. Of the department stores **Simpson's**, 203 Piccadilly, W1, is noted both for menswear and women's clothes.

Clothes for women

Young British designers are very much in the international limelight these days, and London's importance as a fashion center has never been greater.

The Bond St. area has the premises of international designers such as **Giorgio Armani**, 123 New Bond St., **Chanel**, 26 Old Bond St., and **Valentino**, 160 New Bond St., and of internationally-known British designers like **Zandra Rhodes**, weaving fantasies from chiffon at 14a Grafton St., W1; and the 'Royal Wedding' **Emanuels**, at 26a Brook St., W1.

For more accessible creations, nearby South Molton St., W1, is browsily full of interesting clothes and best known for high fashion and sporty items at the several **Browns** shops. Similar lines and accessories abound in shops like **Nicole Farhi** and **Mulberry** in St Christophers Pl., W1, just across Oxford St.

Head w via Knightsbridge, Sloane St. and Brompton Rd., dropping in at department stores like **Harvey Nichols**, Knightsbridge, SW1, and **Harrods' Way In** boutique (see *Department Stores* p184) for a wide range of British designer clothes and blouses (9 Harriet St., SW1, and branches) and Joseph Ettedgui's Sloane St. empire, **Joseph Bis**, **Joseph Tricot** and **Esprit** for trendy monochrome clothes, finally reaching Beauchamp Pl., SW3. This pretty little street is crammed with fashion, from smart **Caroline Charles** at no.11, by way of up-to-the-minute **Jasper Conran** at no.37 and ethereal **Monsoon** at no.53 to **The Beauchamp Pl. Shop** at no.55, selling British and foreign designer clothes. No one would consider visiting these establishments unless provocatively clad in lingerie by **Janet Reger** at no.2.

Head toward South Kensington, where top British designer Katharine Hammett has her flagship store at no.264 Brompton Rd.; continue to the King's Rd., Chelsea, SW3, best known these days for the bizarre, and often ephemeral, but never failing to offer a wide variety of visual stimuli. Punk was popularized at no.153, at a shop originally called 'Acme Attractions,' then renamed **Boy**. Some of the most flamboyant attractions are grouped around a shop which is named after its location, **World's End** (but remembered by early punks as 'Seditionaries'), at no.430; look out for the high-speed clock which whirls around backward.

A number of shops where you can rent glamorous evening dresses and ballgowns have opened throughout London. They include **One Night Stand**, 44 Pimlico Rd., SW1 ☎730-8708 (appt. advisable), **Hetherington**, 289 King's Rd., SW3, and, for maternity dresses, the basement of **Mum's the Word**, 283 New King's Rd.

The best furs can be bought at **Calman Links**, 241 Brompton Rd., SW3 — you can visit the workshops upstairs. Alternatively, rent one for an evening from **Moss Bros.**, Bedford St., WC2. For hats, the center of the **Frederick Fox** millinery business is a tiny salon at 87 New Bond St., W1.

(See also *Department stores* below. All have women's fashion departments.)

Knitwear

The hugely successful Italian chain, **Benetton**, have branches all over London, including 23 Brompton Rd., SW3. British specialties, such as chunky knits and tweeds, can be bought from **Ireland House Shop**, 150 New Bond St., W1. **The Scotch House**, 2 Brompton Rd., SW3, 84 Regent St., W1, and branches, is the shop for Fair Isle, Shetland, Pringle, Ballantyne and tartans. More imaginative sweaters are to be found at **Scottish Merchant**, 16 New Row, Covent Garden; it sells handmade designers' sweaters in beautiful patterns and colors. Visit **Peal & Co.** for cashmere and luxury, in majestic Burlington Arcade, W1, one shop for women and men. More economical are the branches of **Westaway and Westaway**, 65 and 92 Great Russell St., WC1, famous for bargains, and **Marks and Spencer** (see *Department stores* below).

Outerwear

For both men and women, tweed jackets, high-quality trench coats and double-breasted raincoats are the specialties at **Aquascutum**, 100 Regent St., W1. Plaid-lined raincoats and fine cashmere coats are the hallmarks of **Burberrys**, 18-22 Haymarket, SW1. For walking stick or umbrella go to **James Smith & Sons**, 53 New Oxford St., WC1.

Crafts

Contemporary Applied Arts, 43 Earlham St., Covent Garden, WC2, sells original ceramics and jewelry. Also in Covent Garden, on Sat, is Britain's largest display of crafts, at the Jubilee Market. If you feel you need to know a little more before you go shopping for this particular type of merchandise, visit the **Crafts Council**, 8 Waterloo Pl., SW1, off Pall Mall — not a shop but an exhibition center. However there is a good **Craft Council Shop** in the V & A. Other specialty craft shops are the **Craftsman Potter's Shop**, Marshall St., W1, on the site of William Blake's house in Soho, noteworthy for stoneware, and the **Contemporary Textiles Gallery** at 10 Golden Sq., W1. **The Design Centre**, 28 Haymarket, SW1, is an essential port of call for those interested in contemporary British products.

Department stores

Household names abound, especially along Oxford St., where **Selfridges** introduced the American concept of the department store in 1909. Closer to Oxford Circus, a much more British response can be seen in the sober but reliable **John Lewis**. Four stores are tourist attractions in themselves.

Fortnum & Mason   181 Piccadilly, W1, is an aristocratic and exotic grocery store with tail-coated assistants, founded by a footman to Queen Anne, and famous for preserves, biscuits, and the like. Have afternoon tea in the Fountain restaurant. The upstairs floors are devoted to fashion and other items.

Harrods   Knightsbridge, SW1 (actually in Brompton Rd.), is the biggest and best-known department store. Imperial flourishes like the zoo have been trimmed, but the food hall still feels and looks like Britain's greatest provisions merchant. Harrods will get you anything, even if it has to be ordered. In fashion and homemaking, a very wide range of tastes is met.

Liberty Regents St., W1, gave its name to a design style embracing fabrics, silver, glassware and furniture during the Art Nouveau period. 'Liberty prints' and 'Liberty silks' are still renowned. This heritage is evident, as are the store's origins as an important or Oriental goods, although today's range of merchandise is much wider. Worth a visit just for its 1924 mock-Elizabethan building.

Marks and Spencer 458 and 173 Oxford St., W1, and branches. It is for knitwear and other items of well-made, mainly British clothing that visitors go to M & S; local office workers shop there for superb convenience food. Whatever you buy, it will be a good value. It is not a department store in the traditional sense, but what a metamorphosis from the utilitarian 'Marks & Sparks' of the past!

Fine art

The commercial galleries are predominantly in two short and elegant streets, Cork and Albemarle, in Mayfair, W1, and in nearby parts of Bond St. Of special note is **Thomas Agnew & Son**, 43 Old Bond St., selling paintings from all periods. For contemporary art, go to **Browse and Darby**, 19 Cork St., **Christies**, 8 King St., and **Marlborough Fine Art**, 6 Albemarle St., which often deals in the really big names. The occasional gallery has opened in Covent Garden, WC2.

Food and drink

Don't visit London without 'laying down' an English Christmas pudding from one of the great department stores (see above). Their food halls offer an experience which is uniquely metropolitan, even if the biscuits come from Bath or Carlisle, the shortbread and whisky from Scotland, and they all have well-presented gift packs of teas and other specialties. Their hampers, which can be sent abroad, are costly but fabulous.

Gourmet foods also dazzle the eye at **Hobbs**, 29 South Audley St., W1. All these shops and food halls incorporate excellent wine merchants; a specialty vintner of note is the long established **Berry Bros. & Rudd**, 3 St James's St., SW1, whose shop contains a superb pair of antique scales. For the finest selection of Scotch Whiskies (single malts, not the commercial blends) go to the **Soho Wine Market**, 3 Greek St., W1.

Other specialty food shops include the following.

For chocolates **Bendicks**, which holds the royal warrant, at 55 Wigmore St., W1, 107 Long Acre, WC2 and branches; **Charbonnel et Walker**, 28 Old Bond St., W1; and **Prestat**, 40 South Molton St., W1.

For the best English cheese and ham **Paxton & Whitfield**, 93 Jermyn St., SW1.

For health foods, including a superb range of breads **Cranks**, 8 Marshall St., W1, or the extraordinary selection of shops in Neal's Yd., Earlham St., Covent Garden, WC2.

Household goods

Conran, 81 Fulham Rd., SW3, and **Habitat**, 206 King's Rd., SW3, and branches, are the names that have dominated British household design in the past couple of decades, and the new Conran Shop, which has moved across the road into the old

Michelin garage, is more stylish and impressive than ever. A stunning collection of Bauhaus-inspired furniture, Oriental-style flooring, colorful ethnic fabrics and rugs is displayed upstairs, while a vast array of ornaments, accessories, gifts, books and toys are to be found in the basement. There is also an attractive, affordable oyster bar on the ground floor, perfect for an elegant lunch. Habitat is also merged with **Heal's** at 196 Tottenham Court Rd., W1, both are now part of the Conran empire. For more traditional furniture, try **Maples**, at no.141.

Jewelry

London's diamond center is Hatton Garden, EC1. The emphasis is on the trade, but some shops, like **R. Holt**, at no.98, welcome the public. The royal jewelers are **Garrard**, at 112 Regent St., W1. Anything from a jewel box to a gold plated toothbrush can be had at **Asprey**, 165 New Bond St., W1; in the same street is **Cartier**, at no.175. For very fashionable jewelry, visit **Butler and Wilson**, at 189 Fulham Rd., SW3, and 20 South Molton St., W1.

Music

The biggest record shop is **HMV**, 363 Oxford St., W1, with a vast stock covering all categories. Specialty shops include: **Virgin Records**, 14-16 Oxford St., W1, for British rock and new wave; **Rough Trade**, some way out of the center, geographically as well as musically, at 130 Talbot Rd., W11; **Collets**, 129-31 Charing Cross Rd., WC2, for Eastern European folk music; and jazz buffs will also want to see the famous **Dobells**, at 21 Tower St., W1, off Shaftesbury Ave. (☎240-1354). **The Gramophone Exchange**, 3 Betterton St., WC2 (☎836-0976) specializes in second-hand records. Classical music is available from **Farringdon Records**, 52 High Holborn, WC1 (☎242-1877), and **Tower Records**, Swan & Edgar Building, Piccadilly Circus, W1 (☎439-2500).

Perfumers

All the international brands are best bought in department stores. For English flower perfumes, visit the established **Floris**, 89 Jermyn St., SW1, or the fashionably traditional **Penhaligon's**, 41 Wellington St., WC2.

Pharmacies

Harley Street's supplier, **John Bell and Croyden**, nearby at 50 Wigmore St., W1, can meet any pharmaceutical need, and the shop carries cosmetics. Homeopathic specialist **A. Nelson**, at 73 Duke St., W1, by appointment to the Queen, has wonderfully Victorian premises. For more conventional needs, **Boots** and **Underwoods** have branches all over London.

Photographic supplies

To buy a camera, try **City Camera Exchange**, 124 High Holborn, WC1, and branches, or **Dixons**, 88 Oxford St., W1, and branches. For films, use the **Boots** or **Underwood** chains, which also develop films fast. **Fotofast**, Green Park Station, Piccadilly, W1, and branches, sells film, and has a six-hour processing service. **Foto Inn** proposes a one-hour service at 35 South Molton St., W1.

For emergency repairs: **Advance Technical**, 9 St Anne's Ct., W1, and **Sendean**, 105 Oxford St., W1.

Shoes

Fashion shoe shops abound in Bond and South Molton Streets, W1. Men who want the best and can wait for it order custom-made boots fit for royalty from **John Lobb** at 9 St James's St., SW1; Lobb keeps on the premises a wooden last of every customer. Sturdy, traditional footwear can be bought nearby at **Maxwell's**, 11 Savile Row, W1, and slightly less expensively at **Tricker's**, 67 Jermyn St., SW1.

The most expensive and stylish shoes in London are hand-made and sold by **Manolo Blahnik** at 48-51 Old Church St., SW3. Excellent quality Italian leather shoes are available from **Ferragamo**, 24 Old Bond St., W1, **Bruno Magli**, 49 New Bond St., and branches, and **Rayne**, 15-16 Old Bond St., and branches, where the Queen buys shoes. Well-made shoes at more affordable prices are sold by **Bertie**, 48 South Molton St., W1, **Hobbs**, 47 South Molton St., and **Pied à Terre**, 19 South Molton St.; all three have other branches in London.

Street markets
The famous ones are still fun, but see some of the others, too. London has 50 or 60 street markets and it is here that the town best demonstrates its wit, wisdom and elusive code. If you demonstrate your own, you might knock prices down. You will not find credit accepted, only English checks, so take cash.

Portobello Road Sat antique market, especially well known for its silver. Easy to find — and to explore, since it is basically one street — but it stretches for more than 1 mile. Start by taking the underground to Notting Hill Gate, and walk via Pembridge Rd., W11, following the crowd. Antiques and junk come first, then freaky shops, and finally food, at the N end of the street.

Petticoat Lane Middlesex St., E1. Junk market in the East End on Sun, and only one part of a maze of street trade where the patois embraces cockney rhyming slang, Yiddish and Bengali. Serious bargain-hunters start at the improbable hour of 4am with the Cheshire St. (E2) and Brick Lane (E1) areas, where the action subsides well before 9am. The more touristic Petticoat Lane itself

---

Clothing sizes
When shops give clothing sizes in inches or centimeters, use the following conversion scale to determine the correct size

12 in	16	20	24	28	32	36	40	44	48
30 cm	40	50	60	70	80	90	100	110	120

When standardized codes are used, although these may be found to vary considerably, the following provides a useful guide.

Women's clothing sizes
UK/US sizes	8/6	10/8	12/10	14/12	16/14	18/16
Bust in/cm	31/80	32/81	34/86	36/91	38/97	40/102
Hips in/cm	33/85	34/86	36/91	38/97	40/102	42/107

Men's clothing sizes
European code (suits)	44	46	48	50	52	54	56
Chest in/cm	34/86	36/91	38/97	40/102	42/107	44/112	46/117
Collar in/cm	13½/34	14/36	14½/37	15/38	15½/39	16/41	16½/42
Waist in/cm	28/71	30/76	32/81	34/86	36/91	38/97	40/102
Inside leg in/cm	28/71	29/74	30/76	31/79	32/81	33/84	34/86

Men's and women's shoe sizes
UK/US sizes	3/4½	4/5½	5/6½	6/7½	7/8½	8/9½	9/10½	10/11½	11/12½
European	36	37	38	39	40	41	42	43	44

(real name, Middlesex Street) is in full swing by then, and impossibly crowded by 11am. Take lunch at Bloom's (see *Restaurants*); you'll have to line up, but after that early start, the chicken soup will be manna. The nearest underground stations are Liverpool Street and Aldgate East.

Camden Passage Camden Passage, N1. Wed morning and all day Sat for the good-quality antiques; Tues for coins; Thurs and Fri for books. A permanent shop here, **Chiu**, at 10 Charlton Pl., N1, helped pioneer interest in Art Deco, something of a theme in the market, especially in the Athenai Arcade. Everyone goes to the Camden Head pub or Natalie's coffee shop. Alternatively, lunch at M'sieur Frog (see *Restaurants*). Go by tube to Angel and walk up Islington High St.

Bermondsey (New Caledonian) Long Lane and Tower Bridge Rd., SE1, on Fri. The insiders' antique market, where the cognoscenti hunt by flashlight at 5am, grab their purchases by 8.30am at the latest, then retire for breakfast at the Rose Dining Rooms. As if that weren't a sufficiently daunting venture, the market is also hard to find — through such challenges, Bermondsey has remained a market for the seriously interested. Go by underground to London Bridge, and walk down Bermondsey St.

Camden Lock Camden High St./Chalk Farm Rd., NW1. Sun market with an entertaining mix of junk and attractions, including books, musical instruments, clothing and snacks. It stretches for a mile from Chalk Farm underground. The main market is by Regent's Canal.

Toys

The biggest toy shop in the world is **Hamleys**, 188 Regent St., W1. Parents who believe play should be educative favor **Galt Toys**, within Liberty (see *Department Stores* p184). Victorian reproductions are available at **Pollock's Toy Museum**, 21 Scala St., W1, and Covent Garden Market, WC2.

Biographies

A list of the famous whose names are linked with London would be endless. The following personal selection pays particular attention to those mentioned in this book.

Adam, Robert (1728-92)
The great Scottish Neo-Classical architect and designer brought new refinement to the town and country houses of London.

Albert, Prince (1819-61)
Queen Victoria's consort endeared himself to Londoners, despite his German origin. He left his stamp on the capital in the massive *Kensington* museum and learned society complex.

Bacon, Sir Francis (1561-1626)
The great philosopher and statesman of the Elizabethan and Jacobean period was a member of *Gray's Inn*.

Boadicea (died AD 61)
Now considered a national heroine, the warlike queen led her Iceni tribe against the Romans, razing London to the ground before her defeat. Her statue graces Westminster Bridge.

Browning, Robert (1812-89)
Apart from 15yr spent in Italy with his wife Elizabeth Barrett of

Wimpole St. fame, the Victorian poet spent most of his life in London, largely by the *Grand Union Canal* at Little Venice.

Carlyle, Thomas (*1795-1881*)

Author of *The French Revolution* and in many ways the essential Victorian intellectual, Carlyle lived for 47yr in *Chelsea* in preference to his native Scotland. *Carlyle's House* is as he left it.

Charles I (*1600-49*)

The most ambitious of Britain's royal patrons ended his reign on the scaffold after defeat in the Civil War with Parliament. He was led to his execution from his own *Banqueting House*.

Charles II (*1630-85*)

Perhaps the most flamboyant of kings, Charles II enjoys enduring fame thanks to his indiscreet relationships with the likes of Nell Gwynne. More significantly, he was a great patron of the London theater, developed the royal parks and presided over the rebuilding of *The City*.

Chaucer, Geoffrey (*c. 1340-1400*)

The greatest of the medieval English poets was for many years a senior customs official of the port of London. The pilgrims of *The Canterbury Tales* set off from a Southwark inn.

Churchill, Sir Winston (*1874-1965*)

The steadfastness of the wartime national leader helped Londoners endure the horrors of the German bombing of their city — the Blitz. This he successfully organized from his secret *Cabinet War Rooms* bunker in *Whitehall*.

Constable, John (*1776-1837*)

The great painter of the English countryside lived for many years in *Hampstead*. Several of his finest works, on view at the *Victoria & Albert Museum*, show views of the Heath. He is buried in Hampstead parish churchyard.

Coram, Thomas (*c. 1668-1751*)

This bluff sea captain became one of the 18thC's leading philanthropists in his retirement, setting up the Foundling Hospital. The *Coram Foundation* displays works by the artists whom Coram enlisted into his fund-raising efforts.

Cubitt, Thomas (*1788-1855*)

To this energetic man can be credited some of the finest housing in London. Establishing the first modern building firm and inventing the concept of 'speculative builder,' he constructed much of *Bloomsbury* and *Belgravia*.

Dickens, Charles (*1812-70*)

In novels such as *Oliver Twist* and *The Old Curiosity Shop*, Dickens drew attention to the appalling social deprivations of Victorian London.

Edward the Confessor (*c. 1002-66*)

This pious king began the Normanization of England that culminated in the Conquest. He also reinforced the importance of London by establishing his palace at *Westminster*.

Flamsteed, John (*1646-1719*)

The first Astronomer Royal, working largely at the Royal Observatory at *Greenwich Observatory*, recorded no fewer than 3,000 stars.

Garrick, David (*1717-79*)

The English stage's greatest actor/manager, Garrick established the naturalistic style which modern acting takes for granted. Most of his performances were in *Covent Garden*.

Gibbons, Grinling (*1648-1721*)

Wren's master-carver decorated many of the great architect's outstanding buildings with incomparably naturalistic flowers, leaves, fruits, musical instruments — all sculpted in wood or stone

with Baroque exuberance. The greatest profusion is to be seen at
St Paul's Cathedral or *Hampton Court*.

Gibbs, James *(1682-1754)*
Continuing where Wren had left off, this Scottish architect
introduced some of the more theatrical elements of the Italian
Baroque to London church building. Excellent examples can be
seen at *St Mary-le-Strand* and *St Martin-in-the-Fields*.

Gresham, Sir Thomas *(1519-79)*
Founder of the *Royal Exchange*, Gresham was one of the great
merchants and financiers of the Elizabethan age, when London
began to establish its dominance in international commerce.

Henry VIII *(1491-1547)*
The heavy hand of this powerful monarch was repeatedly felt in
London — not least in the dissolution of the monasteries. Among
more positive achievements, he moved the chief royal palace to
Whitehall (giving Westminster to Parliament) and built up *St.
James's Palace* and *Hampton Court*.

Hogarth, William *(1697-1764)*
With the sharpest of all eyes for social foible or moral weakness,
Hogarth in his paintings and engravings has given us an
unforgettable picture of the seamier sides of life in 18thC London.
Hogarth's House at *Chiswick* is now a museum.

Johnson, Dr. Samuel *(1709-84)*
The giant of 18thC letters patronized the pubs of *Fleet Street*, the
coffeehouses of *Covent Garden* and wrote his famous dictionary
at *Dr. Johnson's House* nearby.

Jones, Inigo *(1573-1652)*
With this architect, the ideas of the Italian Renaissance came to
England with bold vision can be seen in the Queen's House at *Greenwich*,
the *Covent Garden*.

Keats, John *(1795-1821)*
The perfect romantic poet, and a consumptive to boot, wrote
much of his best work at *Hampstead* (see *Keats' House*).

Marx, Karl *(1818-83)*
Writing in German in the *British Museum*, the political
economist whose theories have split the world down the middle
lived for most of his life as an exile in *Soho* and N London.
Pilgrims flock to where he is buried in the Cemetery at *Highgate*.

Nash, John *(1752-1835)*
Marble Arch, Regent's Park and Carlton House Terrace in *The
Mall* are the visible legacies of this Regency architect. Just as
significant is the fine town planning scheme of which Regent St.
forms the main axis.

Pepys, Samuel *(1633-1703)*
Recording the Great Plague and Fire of London, Pepys' diary is an
outstanding social document, presenting an irresistible account of
daily life in the 17thC city.

Prince Regent *(1762-1830)*
In many ways a ludicrous figure, the Regent (later George IV) led
the nation in fashion and sport, and backed the ambitious town
planning schemes of **John Nash**.

Seifert, Richard *(born 1910)*
This uncompromising architect's works are a dominant and
controversial feature of the modern London skyline. **Centrepoint**
at St Giles Circus is the best known: to the conservationists, it
symbolizes uncontrolled speculative development.

Shakespeare, William *(1564-1616)*
The London stage saw the first productions of almost all the bard's
plays — usually in the theaters of *Southwark*, where he worked,

although sometimes in the halls of the *Inns of Court*.

Sloane, Sir Hans (*1660-1753*)
The *British Museum*, *Natural History Museum* and *Museum of Mankind* all ultimately owe their existence to this successful physician's vast collections, bequeathed to the nation.

Tyler, Wat (*died 1381*)
After his capture of the *Tower of London*, the leader of the great Peasant's Revolt of 1381 was personally killed by the Lord Mayor of London while attempting to parley with Richard II at Smithfield.

Wellington, Duke of (*1769-1852*)
The leading British general of the Napoleonic Wars, Wellington ultimately defeated Napoleon at the Battle of Waterloo. He went on to become an authoritarian prime minister, during which time he lived at *Apsley House*, now the Wellington Museum.

Whittington, Dick (*1358-1423*)
A rich merchant and the greatest medieval Lord Mayor of London, Whittington has passed into legend. In the quintessential rags-to-riches story, he paused in flight from the city on Highgate Hill (accompanied by his famous cat), when the bells of *St Mary-le-Bow* called him back to greatness.

William the Conqueror (*c. 1027-87*)
Having defeated the English and declared himself their first Norman king, William consolidated by building the massive *Tower of London*.

Wolsey, Cardinal (*c. 1473-1530*)
Promoted by Henry VIII but falling from favor when he failed to secure the king's divorce, this powerful churchman's palaces at *Whitehall* and *Hampton Court* were confiscated and became the favorite royal residences.

Wren, Sir Christopher (*1632-1723*)
The dazzling career of the greatest British architect includes a staggering number of major buildings, most of which are in London — a feat made possible by the ravages of the Great Fire of 1666. Numerous city churches, *St Paul's Cathedral*, major parts of *Hampton Court* and *St James's Palace* testify to his genius.

Sports and activities

For information on all sports: **Sportsline** ☎222-8000

Athletics (track and field)
Major athletic events are held at the **Crystal Palace National Sports Centre**, SE19 ☎778-0131. Information from **The Amateur Athletic Association**, Francis House, Francis St., SW1 ☎828-9326.

Bicycling
This can be an affective way of exploring the city and one of the quickest ways of getting around. Bikes can be rented from **On Your Bike**, 52-54 Tooley St., SE1 ☎407-1309, or **Porchester Cycles**, 8 Porchester Pl., W2 ☎723-9236. For more serious cycling, contact the **British Cycling Federation**, 16 Upper Woburn Pl., WC1 ☎387-9320, or **London Cycling Campaign**, Tress House, 3 Stamford St., SE1 ☎928-7220, which publishes a booklet of routes.

Sports and activities

Cricket
The most baffling of sports to the newcomer, but an integral part of the English summer; from Apr-Sept club matches are played all over London, in parks and on greens, mainly on Sat and Sun afternoons. First-class professional matches, also on weekdays, at **Lord's** (the Middlesex club), NW8 ☎289-1615, and **The Oval** (the Surrey club), SE11 ☎735-4911. Both stage a test match every year: Lords in June, The Oval in Aug or Sept.

Fishing
Fishing in the Thames is forbidden unless you have a license from the Thames Water Authority, obtainable through the **London Anglers Association**, Forest Rd. Hall, Hervey Park Rd., E17 ☎520-7477, which you have to join. It is also possible to fish in Osterley and Hyde Park; licenses from **The Royal Parks Department**, The Storeyard, Hyde Park, W2 ☎262-5484.

Football (soccer)
Football (soccer) matches are generally played on Sat afternoons from Aug through to Apr, with some matches on midweek evenings. The FA Cup Final, the biggest single match, is played in May at **Wembley Stadium**, Middlesex ☎902-1234, also the scene of England's international matches, usually played on Wed evenings. The principal clubs are:

Arsenal   Highbury Stadium, Avenall Rd., N5 ☎359-0131
Charlton   Selhurst Park, Whitehorse Lane, SE25 ☎771-6321
Chelsea   Stamford Bridge, Fulham Rd., SW6 ☎385-5545
Crystal Palace   Selhurst Park, Whitehorse Lane, SE25 ☎653-4462
Fulham   Craven Cottage, Stevenage Rd., SW6 ☎736-6561
Orient   Brisbane Rd., E10 ☎539-2223
Queen's Park Rangers   South Africa Rd., W12 ☎743-0262
Tottenham Hotspur (Spurs)   White Hart Lane, High Rd., N17 ☎808-1020
West Ham United   Green St., Upton Park, E13 ☎472-2740
Wimbledon   49 Durnsford Rd., SW19 ☎946-6311

Gardens
Apart from the parks and gardens that are open to the public, the **National Gardens Scheme**, 57 Lower Belgrave St., SW1 ☎730-0359, runs a program whereby private gardens both in London and the country are open to the public for perhaps one day a year. The **Royal Horticultural Society** holds periodic shows in summer at its home in Vincent Sq., SW1, and stages the massive **Chelsea Flower Show** in May (see *Calendar of events* in *Planning*).

Golf
Most courses are private and will only allow you to play if you have an introduction from a member or from your own club. Public courses, however, will allow you to play on payment of a green fee, and some will rent out clubs. The only major professional course near London is **Wentworth**, in Surrey. The most central are at:
Richmond Park   Roehampton Gate, SW15 ☎876-3205
Royal Epping Forest Gold Club   Forest Approach Chingford, E4
Wimbledon Common   Camp Rd., SW19 ☎946-0294 (Mon-Fri). Players must wear a pillar-box red top, and there are no clubs for rental here.

Greyhound racing
Traditionally a pastime favored by the London working man

without his woman, 'the dogs' are now gaining prestige and at most tracks the races can be watched from a restaurant. Ring for times. London's tracks are:

Catford   Ademore Rd., SE26 ☎692-2261
Hackney   Waterden Rd., E15 ☎986-3511
Walthamstow   Chingford Rd., E4 ☎531-4255
Wembley Stadium   Middlesex ☎902-8833
Wimbledon   Plough Lane, SW17 ☎946-5361(09327)

Health clubs
Westside, 201-207 Kensington High St., W8 ☎937-5386, offers gymnasiums, aerobic classes, saunas and treatments. **The Sanctuary**, 11 Floral St., WC2 ☎240-9635, is for women only.

Popular with office workers in Covent Garden at lunchtime are the dance/keep-fit sessions at **The Fitness Centre**, 11 Floral St., WC2 ☎836-6544, and **Pineapple**, 7 Langley St., WC2 ☎836-4004.

Horseback racing
There are many large racecourses within easy reach of London: to the w, **Ascot** and **Newbury**; to the sw, **Sandown, Epsom** and **Kempton**. No races on Sun. There are long overlaps between the summer (flat) and the winter (jumping) seasons. All races will be well covered in the daily newspapers, and it is possible to bet from betting shops that are not on the course.

Ice-skating
The major public rinks, which will rent out skates are:
Queens Ice Skating Club   Queensway, W2 ☎229-0172
Richmond Ice Rink   Clevedon Rd., Twickenham ☎892-3646
Streatham Ice Rink   386 Streatham High Rd., SW16 ☎769-7861

Riding
Stables are conveniently located near major parks:
Ross Nyes Riding Establishment   8 Bathurst Mews, W2 ☎262-3791, for Hyde Park.
Roehampton Gate   Priory Lane, SW15 ☎876-7089, for Richmond Park.

Several major show-jumping events are held at Wembley, Middlesex ☎902-1234 (for leading examples see *Calendar of events* in *Planning*).

Roller-skating
The best places to skate are on the Embankment between County Hall and The National Theatre, and also in Battersea Park. There is an indoor roller-skating area where you can rent skates at **Finsbury Leisure Centre**, Norman St., EC1 ☎253-4490. Check opening hours before you go.

Rowing
Rowboats and sailing dinghies may be rented on the Serpentine, in Battersea Park and Regents Park, as well as on some stretches of the Thames. For rowing events see *Calendar of events* in *Planning*. For details contact the **Amateur Rowing Association**, 6 Lower Mall, W6 ☎748-3632.

Rugby
Rugby Union, a 15-a-side sport, restricts its players to amateur status in the same way that track and field does. Matches are played on Sat afternoons from Sept-Apr, with international and

major games taking place at the sport's headquarters at **Whitton Rd.**, Twickenham ☎892-8161. The principal clubs are:

Blackheath   Charlton Rd., SE13 ☎858-1578
Harlequins   Craneford Way, Twickenham ☎892-0822
London Irish   The Ave., Sunbury-on-Thames ☎83034
London Scottish   Kew Foot Rd., Richmond ☎940-0397
London Welsh   Kew Rd., Richmond ☎940-2520
Rosslyn Park   Upper Richmond Rd., SW15 ☎876-1879
Saracens   Green Rd., N14 ☎449-3770
Wasps   Repton Ave., Wembley ☎902-4220

Squash
Addresses from **Squash Rackets Association**, Francis St., SW1 ☎828-3064.

Swimming
Major indoor pools with all facilities include:
Chelsea Sports Centre   Chelsea Manor St., SW3 ☎352-6985
Fulham Pools   Normand Park, Lillie Rd., SW6 ☎381-4494
Marshall St. Baths   14-15 Marshall St., W1 ☎439-4678
Oasis Pool   32 Endell St., WC2 ☎836-9555
White City Pool   Bloemfontein Rd., W12 ☎743-3401
    For outdoor swimming during the summer, major pools are:
Hampstead Ponds   NW3 ☎435-2366
Parliament Hill Lido   NW5 ☎485-3873
The Serpentine   Hyde Park, W2 ☎262-3751

Tennis
Information from **The Lawn Tennis Association**, Queen's Club, Baron's Ct., W14 ☎385-2366. For major annual tennis tournaments see *Calendar of events* in *Planning*.

London for children

Information
To find out what's on in London for children buy the inexpensive *Children's London* published by the London Tourist Board. For specific questions ring **Kidsline** ☎222-8070 between 4-6pm (9am-4pm during school vacations).
    Many of London's museums have special features of particular interest to children and often produce questionnaires to make a child's visit more directly interesting.

Ways of seeing London
An ideal introduction to London, from a child's point of view, is to go on a Round London Sightseeing Tour in a double-decker bus. River trips to *Hampton Court* and *Greenwich* are also popular. (See *Useful addresses* in *Basic information* for departure points of buses and boats.)

Eating in London
Most restaurants tolerate children — Italian ones are often the most friendly — and some less expensive restaurants will supply children's portions. Hamburger and other fast-food restaurants are plentiful. **Wimpy**, **Macdonalds** and **Spaghetti House** restaurants all cater to children; also **Eats and Treats** at Hamleys, 188 Regent

St., W1 ☎734-3161; **Lyons Corner House**, The Strand, WC2 ☎930-9381; **Smollensky's Balloon**, 1 Dover St., W1 ☎491-1199.

Fares
On London Regional Transport, children under 5 travel free and children between 5-16 travel for a reduced fare, although children aged 14 and 15 need a photocard (available from any post office).

Christmas
Seeing the Christmas lights and decorations in London, particularly in Regent St. and Trafalgar Sq., makes a good early evening's entertainment. Children can also see Santa Claus at Hamleys, Harrods and Selfridges as well as other large department stores during the season. The windows at Selfridges are another special attraction.

Parks
Hyde Park and Kensington Gardens (separated only by a road) are the most central and well-known of London's parks. As well as wide open spaces allowing large-scale games to be played, there are many special attractions. Boats and paddle craft can be rented on the Serpentine, part of which is cordoned off and used as a swimming area in the summer. Kensington Gardens also has unique Sun entertainments — men sail their model boats on the Round Pond, and there are kites to admire. Nearby is the playground donated by J.M. Barrie with its statue of *Peter Pan.* Another statue to look out for is the beautifully carved *Elfin Oak*, near Bayswater Rd., supposedly restored by the fairies (with a little help from Spike Milligan). Puppet shows are staged here on Aug afternoons.

Regent's Park also has rowboats to rent, but the main attraction is the *Zoo*.

Hampstead Heath, though not particularly central, also offers wide open spaces as well as a deer park, a pond for model boats, an outdoor swimming pool and a playground.

Coram's Field in Holborn is a park donated to children in London by Sir Thomas Coram — adults are only allowed in if accompanied by a child.

In addition to these parks are the many supervised adventure playgrounds, which have imaginative materials and equipment created by the children themselves. Information from **London Adventure Playground Association**, 28 Underwood Rd., E1 ☎377-0314. Younger children can go to the council-run **One O'Clock Clubs** where they can play with the equipment provided. Under-5s must be accompanied by an adult. Information from local borough councils.

Theaters and cinemas (movie theaters)
Some London theaters have special performances for children. *The Little Angel Marionette Theatre* 14 Dagmar Passage, Cross St., N1 ☎226-1787, shows regular puppet plays, on weekend afternoons and on weekdays during school vacations; performances for small children take place on Sat mornings. *Polka Children's Theatre* 240 The Broadway, SW19 ☎543-4888, stages regular plays for children, and has exhibitions of puppets and toys. *The Unicorn Theatre* 6 Great Newport St., WC2 ☎836-3334, also stages plays suitable for children aged between 4-12 on weekend afternoons.

During the school vacations in particular, major cinemas show a wide selection of children's movies. Both the **National Film Theatre** and the **Institute for Contemporary Arts** cinemas (see *Nightlife*) have children's movie clubs on weekend afternoons.

Funfairs and circuses

Touring circuses and fairs often come to London for bank holiday weekends (see *Public holidays* in *Basic information*) and usually take place in the larger parks. Information can be obtained from the **London Tourist Board** ☎730-3488. Fireworks and other celebrations on Nov 5 often include funfairs. See *Calendar of events* in *Planning*.

Brass-rubbing

This can be a fascinating way of passing a wet afternoon. The **London Brass Rubbing Centre**, St Martin-in-the-Fields, Trafalgar Sq., WC2 ☎427-6023, has a large collection, and **Westminster Abbey**, SW1, and **All-Hallows-by-the-Tower**, Byward St., EC3 ☎481-2928 (*open mid-May-Oct*), also have facilities. There is also brass rubbing at the *Trocadero*. In the churches, admission is free but you must pay for your materials.

Baby-sitters

Babysitters Unlimited	271-273 King St., W6	☎741-5566
Childminders	67a Marylebone High St., W1	☎935-2049

Farms

There are a surprising number of farms in the Inner London area. The most interesting are:

Freightliners	Paradise Park, Sheringham Rd., N7	☎609-0467
Kentish Town City Farm	1 Crossfield Close, NW5	☎482-2861
Mudchute Community Farm	Pier St., E14	☎515-5901
Spitalfields Farm	Buxton St., E1	☎247-8762
Stepping Stones Farm	Stepney Way, E1	☎790-8204
Vauxhall City Farm	24 St Oswald's Pl., SE11	☎582-4204

Toy shops See *Shopping*

Excursions

In Britain, all roads lead to London, and they can also be taken in the opposite direction, as can the commuter railway routes to such historically interesting cities as Canterbury, Salisbury and Winchester. London's hinterland covers the half-dozen 'home counties' of the SE and beyond to cities like Cambridge, Oxford and even Bath. These cities, and to an even greater extent Stratford, repay a weekend visit, with a little exploration on the way. All of them are popular with visitors, and at the height of the summer are over-subscribed to the point of suffocation.

Stately homes around London

London's own countryside, where the nobility once lived in stately homes, begins in the suburbs, then fans out into Epping Forest, the Thames Valley, the Downs, and the Chilterns. Much of this countryside can be reached by tube, and there are several 'country' homes open to the public within the capital, especially in West

London (see houses at *Chiswick*, *Ham*, *Orleans* and *Syon*, and *Osterley Park*). Beyond, there are about 50 houses and castles within 100 miles. Most of these close on Mon, but are open on bank holidays, then close the following day.

Audley End House   40 miles (64km) from London, 15 miles (24km) s of Cambridge ☎(0799) 22842. Drive through the pretty Roding Valley on the M11, or take the train from Liverpool Street to Audley End, then walk or take a bus. Open April-Oct Tues-Sun, closed Mon and Good Friday. One of the best examples of a Jacobean mansion, with extensive later work by Vanbrugh and Robert Adam. Much fine 18thC furniture, and a collection of stuffed birds. Large grounds, with a miniature railway.

Beaulieu (pronounced Bewlee)   80 miles (128km) from London, 14 miles (22km) s of Southampton ☎(0590) 612345. By car, A3, A31 or M3, A33. Train from Waterloo to Southampton, then bus. World famous for its **Motor Museum**, with 200 veteran cars, early Rolls, land-speed record breakers, and a monorail. The house, home of auto enthusiast Lord Montagu, was built as the gatehouse of the 13thC Beaulieu Abbey, the ruins of which can be visited. Museum and ruins can be visited all year, as can the stately home. Nearby is the **New Forest**, and there is a **Maritime Museum** at Buckler's Hard, a village with shipbuilding associations dating from Nelson's time.

Broadlands   80 miles (128km) from London, 6 miles (10km) NW of Southampton ☎(0794) 516878. By car, as above. Train to Southampton, changing for Romsey. Open Apr-Sept Tues-Sat. The Prince and Princess of Wales spent part of their honeymoon at Broadlands, thus bringing public attention to the home of the late Lord Mountbatten, and in an earlier time of Lord Palmerston. Broadlands is now the home of Lord and Lady Romsey. There is a **Mountbatten exhibition** in the house, which is a Palladian mansion with landscaping by Capability Brown.

Chartwell   25 miles (40km) from London, 5 miles (8km) SW of Sevenoaks ☎(0732) 866368. By car, A21, A233, B2026. Bus from Victoria Coach Station. Train to Sevenoaks from Charing Cross, then bus to Westerham, then a 25min walk. Open Mar and Nov Wed, Sat, Sun, Apr-Oct Tues-Thurs afternoons, Sat, Sun. Winston Churchill's country home for 40yr. Victorian, chosen for its tranquility and views. Churchill's study and library can be visited. An unfinished canvas still stands in his studio in the beautiful gardens. Five miles (8km) away is **Hever Castle**, trysting place of Anne Boleyn and Henry VIII and 20thC home of William Waldorf Astor (with Holbeins and a Titian), and **Penshurst Place**, birthplace of Sir Philip Sidney (with a toy museum, costume display, Italian gardens and nature trail), is also nearby.

Hatfield House   21 miles (33km) N from London ☎(07072) 62823. By car, A1000. Train from King's Cross or Moorgate to Hatfield. Open Tues-Sun (grounds daily) Apr-Oct. Royal mementos dating back to Elizabeth I, paintings, tapestries and armor, and special exhibitions on crafts and collectibles. Within the grounds is a part of the palace in which Elizabeth I lived as a girl. Her Secretary of State, Robert Cecil, built Hatfield House, and his descendant, the Marquess of Salisbury, still lives there. Six miles (10km) N is **Knebworth House**, begun in 1492 and completed in the 1800s, known for its books and manuscripts, paintings and furniture, narrow-gauge railroad and occasional rock concerts.

Leeds Castle   36 miles (57km) from London, 5 miles (8km) SE of Maidstone. By car, A20 and M20. By train and bus, inclusive ticket available from Victoria Station ☎(0622) 65400. Open

Apr-Oct daily, Nov-Mar Sat, Sun. Fairytale medieval castle on two islands in a lake. Built about 1120, restored in the 1800s. Henry VIII converted it into a royal palace; Elizabeth I was a prisoner here. A garden with many species of flowers is named after another resident, Lord Culpeper, who was Governor of Virginia in the 1600s and founder of the herbalist shop.

Luton Hoo 30 miles (48km) from London, 2 miles (3km) from Luton ☎(0582) 22955. By car, A1(M1). Train from St Pancras Station, then local bus. Fabergé jewels and mementos of Tsarist Court, Renaissance jewels, bronzes, porcelain, in a house built by Robert Adam. Gardens by Capability Brown. Open Apr-Sept Sun, Mon, Wed, Thurs, Sat.

Polesden Lacey 20 miles (32km) from London, 2 miles (3km) from Dorking ☎(0372) 52048. By car, A24. Train from Waterloo to Box Hill or Bookham, then a taxi, or bus plus walk. The playwright Sheridan lived, gardened and farmed here, but his house was demolished in the early 1800s and replaced by a Regency villa. After having several private owners, the property was bequeathed to the National Trust. The lovely house, with a much-admired rose garden, contains a substantial collection of porcelain, and paintings by Sir Joshua Reynolds and Sir Henry Raeburn. The gardens are open all year, daily, but the house in the afternoon only, Apr-Oct Wed-Sun.

Waddesdon Manor 38 miles (60km) from London, 5 miles (8km) w of Aylesbury ☎(0296) 651211. By car, A41. Train from Marylebone to Aylesbury, then a taxi or bus, plus a strenuous walk. Open Apr-Oct Wed-Sun afternoons. Château-like house built by Baron Ferdinand de Rothschild. Family mementoes, French royal furniture, carpets, paintings. Extensive grounds with deer.

Wilton House 80 miles (128km) from London, 2½ miles (4km) w of Salisbury ☎(072-274) 3115. By car, A30. Train-and-bus excursions by British Rail Awayday from Waterloo Station. Open Apr-Oct Tues-Sat, Sun afternoons. Whimsical Inigo Jones house, with Chippendale and Kent furniture and Van Dyck paintings. Wilton House's more offbeat attractions include some 7,000 brightly-painted model soldiers and a lock of Queen Elizabeth I's hair.

Bath

116 miles (186km) from London. Population: 85,000.
Getting there: By train, 70min from Paddington, trains hourly; by car, 2hr, M4 to Junction 18, then A46 ☎ *code (0225)* **i** *Abbey Churchyard* ☎462831.

One-day excursion: An effortless day out by comfortable high-speed train, with good views of gentle countryside, especially between the Vale of the White Horse and the Lambourn Downs, and where the edges of the Cotswolds form a valley with the Marlborough Downs. Fast by car, too, though the temptation is to make it a weekend, with detours into the hills and stops at ancient sites like **Stonehenge** or **Avebury**, or walks by the Kennet and Avon Canal.

The warm springs which gave Bath its name are said to have been discovered by King Lear's father, but their celebrity can more accurately be dated from the devotions of the Romans. The renewed enthusiasm for taking the waters in Georgian times spawned a second layer of history, and an architectural elegance which remains remarkable. Bath is easy to explore on foot and, being set amid hills like Rome itself, it best rewards those with willing legs. The center of the city is very crowded in summer.

A first glimpse of that hillside majesty, embellished with Georgian crescents, is well taken from the train as it slows out of Brunel's tunnel at Box and rumbles toward Bath Spa Station. Out of the station, the immediate impression is uninteresting, but a walk straight ahead down Manvers St. leads to the Georgian Bath in **North** and **South Parades**. A left turn along North Parade leads to **Sally Lunn's Tea House**, after which a traditional English bun is named. The premises are said to be the oldest house in Bath, and the establishment is reputed to have been a haunt of Beau Nash, the dandy and arbiter of social graces who helped make Bath fashionable in Georgian times. Cut through York St. to the **Abbey Churchyard**, the heart of the city. The **abbey** itself was begun in the 15thC, but some of its most striking features are Victorian.

Across the churchyard are the **Roman Baths** and **Pump Room**, completed in 1799 (*open 9am-5.30pm*). A guided tour of the baths affords the opportunity to see the fruits of constant excavations there, ranging from coins to a sacrificial altar. About 10yr ago it was discovered that Bath's water had been contaminated by an ameba. Bore holes now reach down below the level of contamination to an uncontaminated source. The water can be sampled from a fountain in the elegant and restful Pump Room. Since the water tastes, in the words of Dickens' Sam Weller, like a "warm flat iron," it is perhaps as well that the Pump Room serves morning coffee and afternoon tea, sometimes to the accompaniment of string music.

The most spectacular Georgian homes were built on the hillsides to provide their owners with panoramic views. Walk along Bath St. (colonnaded to protect itinerant bathers), turning right at the end, then left into Sawclose, past the city's lively theater and a restaurant area, up Gay St. to The Circus, then along Brock St, to the **Royal Crescent**, built 1765-75, where the house at no.1 is open as a museum in summer (*open Tues-Sat 11am-5pm, Sun 2-5pm*). Return via The Circus to the **Assembly Rooms**, home of an outstanding **Museum of Costume** (*open Mon-Sat 9.30am-6pm, Sun 10am-6pm*).

Return downhill by Lansdown Rd. which becomes in turn Broad St. and High St., with the Guildhall and the covered market, noted for another of the city's culinary delights, the Bath Chap — this turns out to be a pig's jowl!

Such indulgences may subsequently call for a diet of Dr Oliver's remorselessly plain biscuits, for which the city is also known (the more luxurious chocolate-coated version seems at odds with his ascetic intentions), or simply a Bath bun. Determined walkers can do a little more shopping under cover of Pulteney Bridge, an Italianate delight designed by Robert Adam. This leads into another fine Georgian street named Argyle St., and thence to nowhere in particular except perhaps, at the end of Forrester Rd., a place where boats can be rented on the River Avon. At weekends, pleasure trips can also be taken on the Kennet and Avon Canal, from Sidney Wharf, near Bathwick Hill, or from the Top Lock, at the far end of North Parade Rd.

A unique attraction a couple of miles out of the city, at Claverton Down, is the **American Museum in Britain** (*open Tues-Sun 2-5pm*). This has Indian and folk art, interiors of early American homes, including Shaker and Pennsylvania Dutch settings, relics of the West, and gardens which replicate George Washington's at Mount Vernon. Audiovisuals, a collection of old maps and other exhibits will be featured in a new gallery, scheduled to open in 1989. The museum bakes its own selection of cakes and gingerbread, making for a delicious afternoon tea.

In town, Bath is especially well endowed with museums, catering to a wide variety of interests. These include: the **Geology Museum**, 18 Queen Sq.; the **Herschel Museum** (astronomy and music), 19 New King St.; the **National Centre of Photography** in the Octagon, Milsom St. (the building itself merits a visit, and the street has elegant shops); the **Postal History Museum**, 8 Broad St.

Maritime enthusiasts might wish to see **SS Great Britain**, in the nearby city of Bristol. In the opposite direction, a drive into the Mendip Hills leads to the small city of **Wells**, with one of Britain's most beautiful cathedrals.

The **Priory** (see below) and the **Royal Crescent Hotel** ☎319090 are especially comfortable and full of personal touches. The friendly **Pratt's**, South Parade ☎60441 and the more sophisticated **Francis**, Queen Sq. ☎24257 are both centrally placed. There are many bed-and-breakfast places along Pulteney Rd., and Wells Rd. Recommended is **Eagle House**, Church St., Bathford ☎859946 a Georgian mansion 3 miles (2km) outside Bath.

The Tourist Information Centre also has an accommodations register.

One of the most famous restaurants in England, the **Hole in the Wall**, is in Bath, at 16 George St. ☎25242 where fresh ingredients are inventively incorporated into a French-style menu. Rich but subtle sauces feature in the opulent restaurant at the **Priory Hotel**, Weston Rd. ☎331922 A new French restaurant has opened; it is called **Clos du Roy**, 7 Edgar Buildings, George St. ☎64356 and is run by flamboyant chef Philippe Roy. Less expensive is **Popjoys**, named after Beau Nash's mistress and in his house, serving English food at Sawclose ☎60494 Other well-regarded places are **Woods**, 9-13 Alfred St. ☎314812 **Clarets** wine bar, 6-7 Kingsmead Sq. and **Flowers**, 27 Monmouth St. Or try **Evelyn Owens**, Bartlett St., or **Sweeney Todds**, 15 Milsom St., for a pizza.

Brighton

53 miles (85km) from London. Population: 162,000. Getting there: By train, 51min from Victoria, trains twice hourly: by car, A23 then M23 ☎ code (0273) i Marlborough House, 54 Old Steine ☎23755; also at King's Rd., on the seafront, in summer.

One-day excursion: The speed and frequency of the trains and the labyrinthine quality of the roads out of South London deter most day-trippers from taking a car, but weekenders might wish to do so to explore the Downs and the Sussex countryside around Brighton.

This seaside resort is beloved by many Londoners for its wry mix of Regency elegance and Graham Greenean seediness. A day out in Brighton is an English experience. The craze for sea-bathing in the late 1700s, and the Prince Regent's subsequent attentions, gave Brighton a social status which it has never entirely surrendered and to which its residents still cling.

The Regency terraces, squares and crescents provide the elegance, crowned by the extravagant fantasies of the Royal Pavilion, the exploration of which is an essential feature of a first-time visit to Britain. Such an Aladdin's cave of Orientalia is an appropriate centerpiece to a town noted for its antique stores, the most celebrated of which, along with some interesting fish restaurants, are in a neighborhood called The Lanes. Not far away, an antique electric railroad, the first in Britain, runs from one of the town's two Victorian piers along the pebbly beach to the swimming pool and marina. The journey can be continued by open-topped bus, or on foot, to the village of Rottingdean.

From the railway station, Queen's Rd. and Trafalgar St. are the boundaries of an antiques-and-boutiques area called **North Laine**, which is less pretty but also less expensive than The Lanes. Within this area, there is a Sat-morning flea market.

A half-mile walk down Queen's Rd. leads to Church St. on the left and **Brighton Museum and Art Gallery** (*open Tues-Sat 10am-5.45pm, Sun 2-5pm*) housing a major Art Deco collection as well as English watercolors and Old Masters. Just beyond is the **Royal Pavilion** (*open Jan-May, Oct-Dec 10am-5pm, June-Sept 10am-6pm*). The royal flourish was bestowed upon Brighton by the Prince Regent, later to be George IV, who is said to have gone there to get away from his father. While there in 1785 he secretly and illegally married a Catholic, Mrs Fitzherbert, a twice-widowed commoner. The Pavilion was his summer palace, though he left it soon after its completion. The bizarre mock-Indian architecture, most of it by Nash, derives from the fashionability of Oriental themes during a period of great trade with the East. There was room for discordance within this preoccupation; the interior was decorated in 'the Chinese taste.' The Pavilion affords visitors a good hour's browse through eccentric splendor, with huge dragons, exotic birds and chandeliers, in a whole series of room settings.

From the Pavilion one wanders into **The Lanes**, where the fashionable and fascinating shops often close on Sun, and stay open late on Wed and Thurs. From there it is a few minutes' walk down to the seafront. To the right, about half a mile along the beach, is the West Pier, built in 1866, and a century later the memorable setting for the film *Oh, What a Lovely War*. The pier now stands forlorn, unsafe, closed to visitors, and with an uncertain future. In that direction are some fine Georgian buildings, notably in **Regency Square**, as Brighton blends into its sister town of **Hove**.

In a more central position on the seafront is the **Palace Pier**, built in 1891, a rich symbol of British seaside frolics. Nearby in King's Rd. Arches, Lower Promenade is a **Penny Arcade Museum** containing Edwardian machines, including working expositions, of 'What The Butler Saw.'

Just to the left of the pier is the **Aquarium** (*open Apr-Sept 10am-6pm, Oct-Mar 10am-5pm*) dating from 1872, with a Dolphinarium. From this point, **Volk's Electric Railway** (see above) begins its journey. The railroad, named after its founder, was opened in 1883, but at its terminus now is the largest yachting marine in Europe. Visitors can walk along the breakwaters, and there are pleasure trips and deep-sea angling. Beyond the marina, the resort which once popularized sea bathing machines now has an area of beach set aside for those who prefer nudity. This bracing facility is a whistle away from one of England's most famous girls' schools, **Roedean**, on the way to **Rottingdean**. There is a toy museum, a local history collection and Rudyard Kipling memorabilia at **The Grange**, Rottingdean, where the great writer lived toward the end of his life (*open Mon-Sat 10am-5pm, Sun 2-5pm; closed Tues and Fri 1-2pm, and Wed*).

✎ Brighton has an enormous selection of hotels, and the Tourist Information Centre has a reservation service. Two famous Victorian seafront hotels are the **Metropole** ☎ 775432 **⦙⦙▢** — rather unfairly notorious for furtive weekend couples — and the **Grand**, bombed with tragic consequences by the IRA at the 1984 Conservative Party Conference and now renovated and reopened ☎ 21188 **⦙⦙⦙▢** Both are in King's Rd., as is the **Old Ship Hotel** ☎ 29001 **⦙▢** which has a fine ballroom.

🍴 In The Lanes, **English's Oyster Bar**, 29 East St. ☎ 27980 **⦙⦙▢** is something of an institution. Despite its name, it is a full-scale restaurant and it is advisable to reserve in advance. In King's Rd. at no.64 is **Wheeler's** ☎28372 *III* a branch of the famous London chain of fish restaurants, known for its sole. In Market St., at no.23, is the **Ceres Health Foods Restaurant** *▢* which is a self-service establishment. At the edge of The Lanes, a tea shop called **The Mock Turtle**, at 4 Pool Valley, sells homemade cakes and lunchtime snacks. Elsewhere in Brighton, **Le Grandgousier**, 15 Western St. ☎772005 *III* ▬ is a bistro offering a good value.

Outside Brighton

Walkers enjoy the South Downs, a range of chalk hills that runs just inland from Brighton and stretches for 80 miles (128km). A bus from the seafront to the crest of **Devil's Dyke** offers superb views and a half-hour walk to the **church at Poynings**. The Tourist Information Centre has detailed information on walks.

In the Sussex countryside, several towns and villages are worth a visit, including **Lewes** (with a castle, interesting pubs and good walks), **Sheffield Park** (for its Capability Brown gardens, and a full-scale steam railroad), and **Arundel** (another castle, a sometimes grotesque museum of curiosities, housing an arts festival held in late Aug).

Cambridge

54 miles (86km) from London. Population: 105,000. Getting there. By train, about 75min from Liverpool Street (direct) or King's Cross (faster route), two or three trains hourly; by car, M11, 90min ☎ code (0223) i Wheeler St. ☎322640.
One-day excursion: Being linked to London by motorway, Cambridge is easily reached by car. The town is encircled with parking lots, and cars should not be taken into the center.

The first scholars came from Oxford to Cambridge in 1209, and the first college, **Peterhouse**, was founded in 1284. Modern times have seen F.R. Leavis, a lion among literary critics, the splitting of the atom by Rutherford and the work of Crick and Watson in establishing the double helix structure of DNA. For all its architectural similarities to Oxford, this 'younger' of Britain's two great university cities is distinguished by the larger scale of its colleges, its lower skyline (unlike Oxford, it is not an industrial town), its paler stone, and its geographical setting on the edge of flat and water-laced Fen country. Cambridge makes good use of its river, the Cam or Granta, along which half a dozen of its colleges are set. Most of the colleges can be visited except between mid-May and mid-June, and there are several tours daily Apr-Dec, starting from the Tourist Information Centre on the hour (times vary through the year). It is advisable to reserve an hour before the tour starts.

Close to the bus station is **Emmanuel College**, where John Harvard was a pupil in the 1600s. Emmanuel's chapel is one of several fine Wren buildings in Cambridge. Across St Andrew's St., in Downing St., are the **Museums of Geology and Archaeology**. Downing St. bends into Pembroke St., and **Pembroke College**, which also has a Wren chapel. Parallel with Pembroke St. is Botolph Lane, beyond which lies **Corpus Christi**, with its fine 14thC collegiate building in Old Court.

Turn left from Pembroke St. into Trumpington St. for the **Fitzwilliam Museum** (*open Tues-Sat 10am-5pm, Sun 2.15-5pm*), which has an outstanding collection, including paintings by Gainsborough, Turner, Rembrandt, Renoir and Degas, drawings by Hogarth, Dürer, Michelangelo and Leonardo, and Blake's illuminated books, as well as Roman, Greek, Egyptian and Eastern antiquities and English pottery and porcelain. Return along

Trumpington St., turning left for two more colleges, **St Catherine's** and **Queens'** (1448), the latter with its Tudor courtyard, Cloister Court and Mathematical Bridge.

Nearby, at Mill Lane (and farther along, at Magdalene Bridge), row boats and punts can be rented on the river. Along this stretch of the water are five more colleges, **King's**, **Clare**, **Trinity**, **St John's** and **Magdalene**. The grassy bank facing the first two of these colleges is known as The Backs.

King's College chapel is an outstanding example of Perpendicular architecture, built between 1446-1515, with glass by Flemish craftsmen. Amongs its treasures is *The Adoration of the Magi*, by Rubens. Nearby on King's Parade is the **Senate House**, a Georgian building in which the University's 'Parliament' sits.

Clare College was founded in 1326, but the present building, like a perfectly-proportioned tiny palace, was built in the 1600s. It has lovely gardens opposite the elegant Clare Bridge. Trinity, with its Great Court, fountain and many-windowed Wren library, is the largest and richest of the colleges. Its alumni have included Bacon, Byron, Macaulay, Tennyson and Thackeray. In the library are manuscripts by Tennyson, Thackeray and Milton. Two famous bookstores, **Heffers** and **Bowes & Bowes**, are in Trinity St., and nearby is **Belinda's**, for excellent teas and cakes.

St John's (1511), with its wedding-cake silhouette and Tudor gateway, is architecturally an acquired taste, but its 'Bridge of Sighs' is a splendid gesture. Properly known as New Bridge, it was built in 1831. St John's chapel was also built in the 1800s, by Sir George Gilbert Scott. At the end of this stretch of river, Magdalene College (1524), favored by the aristocracy, has Samuel Pepys' library, in the original bookcases.

Across the road from Magdalene St., in Castle St., the **Folk Museum** (*open Mon-Sat 10.30am-5pm, Sun 2.30-4.30pm*), in a converted inn, has an engrossing collection of domestic and agricultural objects from Cambridgeshire. In the opposite direction, in Bridge Street, is one of only five round churches in England, the **Church of the Holy Sepulchre**, modeled on its namesake in Jerusalem.

From Bridge St., turn left for **Jesus College**, which was once a convent. The windows in the chapel were designed by Burne-Jones and made in the William Morris workshop. Behind the college are Jesus Green and Midsummer Common, separated by Maid's Causeway and Short St. from another stretch of open grass and rather offhandedly known as Christ's Pieces.

Next to the railway station is another stretch of open grassland called Parker's Piece, with a restaurant called **Hobbs' Pavilion** which is popular with students. The restaurant is a converted cricket pavilion, and is named after that batsman Jack Hobbs. Nearby, in Lensfield Rd., is the **Scott Polar Research Institute**, named after the explorer, with relics of expeditions. In the same part of the town, off Trumpington Rd., are the University's **Botanic Gardens**. These uncrowded and beautifully scented gardens were laid out in 1846, primarily for the purpose of research.

✆ Student riots brought some unwelcome publicity to the **Garden House Hotel**, Mill Lane ☎63421 ◨ at the beginning of the 1970s, but guests with a nostalgic or vicarious interest can stay safely enough in what was already one of the city's best-known hotels, with a better-than-average restaurant, pretty gardens and river views.

Also on the river is the smaller, comfortable **Arundel House**, in a Victorian terrace at 53 Chesterton Rd. ☎67701 ☐ An excellent guesthouse is **May View** 12 Park Parade ☎66018.

Excursions

≋ There has been a gastronomic renaissance in Cambridge in recent years. Among the newcomers are **Midsummer House**, Midsummer Common ☎69299 ///▢ which serves imaginative English food in a converted common-keeper's cottage, and **Browns**, 23 Trumpington St. ☎461655 /▢ an American-style restaurant with polished wood floors, ceiling fans and bentwood chairs, where the fare includes pasta, salads, char-grilled steaks and hamburgers. In an unremarkable row house in Chesterton Rd., **Twenty Two** ☎351880 ///▢ produces the best food in Cambridge. Mouthwatering modern British dishes are served in an attractive, informal pink dining room. **Hobbs' Pavillion**, Park Terr. ☎67480 ▢ serves crêpes, salads and its own ice cream; and **Shao Tao**, 72 Regent St. ☎353942 /▢ is one of the city's numerous good Chinese restaurants. Local pubs serving good food are the **Free Press**, 7 Prospect Row, the **Fort St George** on Midsummer Common, and the crankily English **Tickell Arms** at Whittlesford, a mere 15 mins' drive away.

Oxford

56 miles (90km) from London, Population: 115,000. Getting there: By train, 60min from Paddington, trains hourly; by car, 90min, A40 then M40 ☎ *code (0865) i St Aldate's* ☎726871.

One-day excursion: Oxford is a finely-crafted jewel of a city, which has to be protected against incursion. There are several pedestrian streets, a ring of parking lots, and a 'Park and Ride' bus service.

It has been a university town since the 1200s, and has provided its country with enough prime ministers to make a cricket team; with writers ranging from Wilde to Tolkien, and with adventurers from Raleigh to Rhodes. Oxford's colleges and quadrangles dominate the center of the city, rich in their architectural diversity, though with a preponderance of Gothic among their turrets, towers and dreaming spires. Some of the colleges are walled, though most of them can be visited in the afternoons (and all day during vacations, usually for a month around Christmas and Easter, and July-Sept). As a seat of learning, Oxford also has institutions such as the Bodleian Library and Ashmolean Museum and famous bookstores. There is punting on the river with unstrenuous walks by the waterside. Beyond, the countryside reaches out to both the Chiltern and the Cotswold Hills.

An impressive start to a day in Oxford might be at the **Ashmolean Museum** (*open Tues-Sat 10am-4pm, Sun 2-4pm*), one of Britain's finest museums, with riches ranging from Michelangelo and Raphael drawings, past silverware and musical instruments, to John Tradescant's natural-history collection. The Victorian Ashmolean building is at the corner of Beaumont St. and St Giles, from which Magdalen St. runs into Broad St., the address of the famous **Blackwell's** bookstores (this and Foyle's in London are the two most extensive bookstores in Britain); browsers are welcome. Also housed in Broad St. is a small and friendly pub called the **White Horse**.

On this stretch of walk are the rival colleges of **Trinity**, with charming 17thC buildings and a rose garden, and **Balliol**, founded in the 13thC and especially influential in the development of the university, with a beautiful garden quadrangle. Opposite Balliol on Broad St. is **Exeter College**, the place of conception of the pre-Raphaelite Brotherhood.

To the right off Broad St. is the **Sheldonian Theatre**, the first building designed by Wren, in 1662. The theater, modeled on those of ancient Rome and named after its benefactor Archbishop Sheldon, is used for university functions and concerts. Behind it is the **Bodleian Library** (*open Mon-Fri 9am-5pm, Sat 9am-12.30pm*), named after Sir Thomas Bodley, who donated his own collection in

1598. This is said to be the oldest library in the world, and contains three million books. The part known as the Divinity School, with a beautiful late Gothic low-vaulted ceiling, has folios and first editions of works by Shakespeare, Milton, Swift and Pope, among others. Also within the Bodleian is the **Radcliffe Camera**, a striking domed rotunda designed by James Gibbs in 1739. To the left across Catte St. is **All Souls College**, with its celebrated twin towers by Hawksmoor. Behind All Souls is **New College**, founded in 1379, which has a magnificent chapel and parts of the medieval city wall in its gardens. There are a number of tea shops in nearby Holywell St., which serve delicious cream teas.

Holywell St. leads into Longwall, from which the Magdalen deer park can be seen. Where Longwall reaches High St. a turn to the right along Merton St. leads to **Merton College**, with the oldest quadrangle in Oxford, dating from the 1300s. A turn to the left, through Christ Church Meadows, leads to **Magdalen College**, the most beautiful of the colleges with its Perpendicular bell tower from which the choir sings at 6am on May Day morning. At Magdalen and Folly Bridges it is possible to rent a punt. From Rose Lane, a footpath runs around Christ Church Meadow, following the River Thames. Alongside Rose Lane are the **Botanic Gardens**, which date back to 1621.

Blenheim Palace is 8 miles (13km) from Oxford. The Churchill's ancestral home and nearby burial place would have a magnetic appeal even without the grand Baroque design of Vanbrugh and the landscaping of Capability Brown, but the combination of the historic with the esthetic is irresistible.

The enormous Blenheim Palace and Park (*open Mar-Oct 10.30am-6pm*) are at the small town of **Woodstock**, which has resonances quite different from those of its American descendant, and there are buses every half hour from Cornmarket. Apart from its assembly of Churchill artifacts, the palace has a large collection of tapestries, paintings, sculpture and furniture. Perhaps the most magnificent room is the Long Library, which contains more than 10,000 volumes as well as 17thC Oriental porcelain, and has carvings by Grinling Gibbons.

The palace was built by a grateful Queen Anne for John Churchill, First Duke of Marlborough, to mark his victory over the French at the Battle of Blenheim in 1704. Winston Churchill, grandson of the Seventh Duke, was born there on Nov 30, 1874. He is buried in the churchyard at Bladon, which is on the edge of the park.

✍ For a city which attracts many visitors, Oxford does not flaunt its hotel, but the Tourist Information Centre ☎726873/4 does have a special telephone accommodations register. Among the better-known hotels are the **Randolph**, Beaumont St. ☎24781 ▥ with its Edwardian plush, and the **Ladbroke Linton Lodge**, Linton Rd. ☎53461 ▥ with pleasant gardens. There are lots of bed-and-breakfast places around Abingdon Rd., St John's St. and Walton St. 7 miles (10km) E of Oxford is **Le Manoir aux Quat' Saisons** at Great Milton ☎(08446) 8881 ▥ Raymond Blanc's much-praised and visited hotel and restaurant.

🍽 There are several first-class restaurants in Oxford, all of them offering French cuisine: **Le Petit Blanc**, 61A Banbury Rd. ☎53540 ▥ ❧ occupying Raymond Blanc's former premises; **Elizabeth**, 84 St Aldate's ☎242230 ▥ and **La Sorbonne**, 130a High St. ☎241320 ▥ ⬛ For less expensive eating, cold buffet and Sun lunch, **Cherwell Boathouse** ☎52746 ▥ on the river off Bardwell Rd. makes for a pleasant experience, as does **Brown's**, Woodstock Rd. ☎511995 ▢ and **15 North Parade**, ☎513773 ▥ a friendly bistro, which serves delicious food geared to the health-conscious.

Stratford-upon-Avon
96 miles (154km) from London. Population: 22,000. Getting there: By train, about 2hr 30min from Paddington, changing at Leamington Spa, 6 trains a day; by train and bus, 2hr from Euston, changing at Coventry, 7 trains a day; by car, 2hr 30min-3hr, A40, M40 to Oxford, then A34 ☎ code (0789) **i** *1 High St. ☎293127, recorded info ☎67522.*

One-day excursion or longer: An awkward journey, but still a seemingly inescapable trip for visitors from overseas. Stratford is not really within London's hinterland, belonging less to the South than to the Midlands, and is most comfortably visited as part of a trip taking in **Warwick** or **Kenilworth castles**, **Coventry Cathedral**, or the northern part of the **Cotswold Hills**.

In the 16thC, as now, playwrights found their audiences and their milieu in London, and Shakespeare was a metropolitan writer. However, he was born in Stratford, retired and died there, and was buried there. Soon after his death in 1616, people started going to Stratford to see his birthplace, and today they can also watch his plays performed by the Royal Shakespeare Company during its long season. There is much worth seeing in the town, despite exploitation which would surely draw a satirical sting from the subject of its purported devotions. There is little left of the Forest of Arden, setting for several of the plays, except for the odd clump, but its trees remain in the timbering of some fine Elizabethan and Tudor buildings. When its streets are not sighing under the weight of visitors, Stratford is a quiet and peaceful town, especially in the evenings.

From the railway station, Alcester Rd., Greenhill St. and Windsor St. lead to the half-timbered **Shakespeare's House** in Henley St. (*open Apr-Sept Mon-Sat 9am-6pm, Sun 10am-6pm, Oct Mon-Sat 9am-5pm, Sun 10am-5pm, Nov-Mar Mon-Sat 9am-4.30pm, Sun 1.30-4.30pm*) where the playwright was born, probably on April 23, 1564. The interior has been carefully restored — notice the engraved signatures of pilgrims such as Carlyle, Tennyson and Sir Walter Scott in the room where the birth is said to have taken place.

A short walk along Henley St., High St. (past the family home of John Harvard, founder of the university) and Chapel St. is **New Place**, to which Shakespeare retired, and where he died at the age of 52. The house no longer stands, but the garden, laid out in the characteristic Elizabethan 'knot' patterns, can still be enjoyed. Farther along, when the same thoroughfare has become Church St., is the **Shakespeare Birthplace Trust**, which offers a combined ticket for the several properties historically linked to the bard. Another of these properties, just around the corner in Old Town, is **Hall's Croft** (*hours as Shakespeare's House, but closed Sun Nov-Mar*). This building is named after John Hall, who married Shakespeare's daughter; its principal interest, however, is the fact that Hall was a doctor, and the equipment within provides insight into the medical techniques of the 17thC.

Old Town meets Trinity St. at the churchyard where Shakespeare was buried. The gravestone is inscribed with an imprecation, attributed to Shakespeare, to leave him in peace. On the chancel wall is a monument, and at the font is a reproduction of the register recording his baptism and burial.

Back along the Southern Lane and Waterside, by the Avon, is the **Royal Shakespeare Theatre**. There were performances in Stratford even in the days of strolling players, but the first serious attempts to honor Shakespeare began in the late 1700s. The original Shakespeare theater was built in 1879, and burned down in 1926. The present red-brick building was opened in 1932, and The Royal Shakespeare Company, one of the world's finest theater companies, presents at least 12 Shakespearean productions in a season stretching from Apr-Jan.

The RSC also has a studio theater in the town, known as **The Other Place** and a new Jocobean-style theater, **The Swan**, which opened in 1986 and is where lesser-known Shakespeare and his contemporaries' plays are staged. Recorded reservation information for all theaters can be obtained around the clock ☎(0789) 69191, for the box office ☎295623. The Royal Shakespeare Theatre has an interesting and informative picture gallery containing paintings of great actors in Shakespearian costume, in surviving section of the original building. It also has extensive gardens. In the part near the church are rare trees and a court for Nine Men's Morris, an ancient game mentioned in *A Midsummer Night's Dream*; the part near the Shakespeare monument — **Bancroft Gardens** — makes a pleasant picnic spot.

Two further scenes from the *Seven Ages of Shakespeare* are to be seen just outside the town. **Anne Hathaway's thatched cottage**, which was her home before her marriage to Shakespeare, is 2 miles (3km) away at **Shottery** (hours as Shakespeare's Birthplace). The contents include Shakespeare's 'second best bed', a four-poster which he willed to his wife. The cottage can be reached by a very pleasant walk along a signposted footpath from Evesham Pl.; there is also a bus service from the bottom of Bridge St. A longer and sometimes muddy walk along a canal towpath N from Bridgefoot, or a short train journey, leads the 4 miles (6km) to **Wilmcote**, home of Shakespeare's mother, Mary Arden (hours as Hall's Croft). This was a typical Warwickshire farmstead, and was in use as such until 50yr ago. It still has an informality which makes it a revealing museum of English rural life.

🛏 The thespian hotel, also ejoyed for its food and drink, is **The Arden**, at Waterside ☎294499 🏠 which has a country-house atmosphere. There are several other hotels in Stratford with this kind of ambience, though the rooms have usually been modernized. For the full modern treatment there is the **Moat House** at Bridgefoot ☎414411 🏠 **Caterham House**, 58-9 Rother St. ☎67309 🛏 is a good bed and breakfast. Others tend to gather on the roads into Stratford from Oxford, Evesham and Alcester. The Tourist Information Centre has an accommodations register.

🍴 The **Royal Shakespeare Theatre** ☎69191 has two restaurants and offers a package-deal ticket for a play and dinner ♣ 🏠 Or reserve in the morning for a pre-theater dinner at **Shepherd's**, Stratford House Hotel, Sheep St. ☎68233 🏠 After the theater, Sheep St. has several late restaurants, Italian and Greek, among which the Greek-biased **Debut** is a lively highlight ☎293546 🏠 In the same street, there are good pub lunches at the **Rose and Crown**, while actors favor the '**Dirty Duck**' (**Black Swan**), at Waterside, near the theater.

Windsor

21 miles (34km) from Central London. Population: 30,000.
*Getting there: By train, 53min from Paddington, changing at Slough for Windsor and Eton Central, trains hourly, or 47min direct from Waterloo to Windsor Riverside, trains twice hourly; by car, 1hr, M4 then A308 ☎ code (0753) from London **i** Central Station (Apr-Dec) ☎852010.*

One-day excursion: Windsor and Eton are compact and busy, and surrounded by walking country. A car is not essential.

With its royal castle and Great Park, on a pretty stretch of the River Thames, and with Eton, famous for its boys' school, just across the footbridge, a visit to Windsor is, understandably, an almost mandatory day trip for the visitor to London, or worth even a hasty half-day. Hotels are not listed as Windsor is too close to London to warrant an overnight stay.

Even in William the Conqueror's time it was within a day's march of London, which is why he chose it for the site of one of the nine castles with which he decided to encircle the city. Since the Royal Family still spend time at **Windsor Castle** it is both a national monument and a private home, and it is the largest and oldest inhabited castle in the world. The precincts are open to visitors, and there is admission to the State Apartments when the Queen is not in official residence. There are walks in **Windsor Great Park**, which stretches for 6 miles (10km) in the direction of **Ascot racecourse**. A similar distance up the willow-fringed river is Boulter's Lock, still much as it was when Jerome K. Jerome described it in *Three Men in a Boat* in 1889, and the town of **Maidenhead**.

A couple of miles farther upriver is **Cliveden House**, built by Barry in 1851, once owned by the Astors, and on occasion the breeding ground of political scandal. The house is now a hotel, but a small part is open to members of the National Trust on Thurs and Sun afternoons in summer. The magnificent gardens with beautiful views can be visited from Mar-Oct daily 11am-6pm. Cliveden is close to the village of **Cookham**, where the painter Stanley Spencer lived. One of his paintings hangs in the church, and others are in King's Hall.

Across the river from Windsor, **Eton High St.** is dotted with craft and antique stores.

Unless you intend to take a long walk in the Great Park or along the river, the places of interest in Windsor and Eton are all within a radius of about a mile. It is possible to take a perhaps brisk look at each in the course of one day, and there are reasons to see Windsor in the morning and Eton in the afternoon. From Riverside Station, a walk along Datchet Rd. and Thames St. leads to the castle. Central Station is closer; there is a parking lot opposite, housed in the ugly King Edward Court shopping center, and a walk up Peascod St. and Castle Hill leads to the castle.

The **Changing of the Castle Guard** can be seen at 11am Mon-Sat from mid-Mar to mid-Aug and every 48hrs excluding Sun from mid-Aug to mid-Mar. The new guard leaves from the Royal Mews at 10.55am and marches to the castle. The old guard returns at 11.30am. On the High St. the **Guildhall**, completed by Wren after the death of the original architect, has an exhibition including royal portraits.

Up Church Lane, in Church St., Nell Gwynne's house is now a coffee shop called **The Drury House**. At the top of Church St., King Henry VIII Gate is the main entrance to the castle. Straight ahead within the castle is the finest example of Perpendicular architecture in England, **St George's Chapel** (*open summer Mon-Sat 10.45am-4pm, Sun 2-4pm, winter Mon-Sat 10.45am-3.45pm, Sun 2-3.45pm, closed Jan*), where several monarchs are buried in the choir. The architectural style, with external buttresses providing much of the support, permits a spacious interior, with the light from stained-glass windows filling the magnificent nave. There are elaborate carvings in the nave and stalls. On the opposite side of the castle precincts are the **State Apartments** (*open May-Sept Mon-Sat 10.30am-4.30pm, Sun 1.30-4.30pm, Oct-Mar Mon-Sat 10.30am-2.30pm, closed Sun, usually for a month at Christmas and Easter, and for Ascot race week in June*), decorated with paintings from the royal collection, including

works by Van Dyck and Rubens, and with carvings by Grinling
Gibbons. There are also drawings by Leonardo da Vinci and
Holbein in the hall near the main entrance to the State
Apartments. Within the same complex are a **coach museum** and
an extraordinary delight, **Queen Mary's Dolls' House**, also near
the entrance. This has running water, working elevators and a
library with commissioned writings by Kipling and miniature
paintings. The house, designed by Sir Edwin Lutyens, is on a scale
of 12:1. From the castle, Long Walk runs for 3 miles (5km)
through Home Park to a statue of *George III*. Beyond stretches
Windsor Great Park, with Smith's Lawn, where Prince Charles
plays polo. Nearby, the **Savill Garden** (*open Mon-Fri 10am-6pm,
Sat, Sun 10am-7pm*) contains a large collection of rhododendrons,
roses, herbaceous borders and alpine plants, set in 35 wooded
acres.

An exploration of the Great Park and Savill Garden may well
demand an afternoon, but the alternative is to return to the town,
and from Thames St. cross the footbridge (a pretty Victorian
structure in cast iron) to **Eton**, which may prove a less crowded
place in which to have lunch. The town of the boating song and
playing fields on which Britain's battles were allegedly won
instantly proclaims itself; from the bridge, the Eton College
boathouses can be seen on the left. In the High St. near a splendid
Victorian pillar box, and with punishment stocks outside, is a
timbered building dating from 1420, where cock-fighting used to
take place. Known as **The Cockpit**, it is now, incongruously, an
international restaurant. Among the antique shops in the High St.
is **F. Owen**, at no.113, notable for militaria; covering one wall of
the shop are photographs of customers who were Eton boys. **Eton
College** (*open Apr-Sept 2-4.30pm, holidays 10.30am-5pm; parties of
10 or more must reserve in advance* ☎863593), cradle of great British
poets and prime ministers, was founded in 1440 by Henry VI, and
some of the oldest parts of the school can be seen in a quadrangle
called The Cloisters. The 15thC chapel in the Pependicular style
contains wall paintings from the time of its foundation.

⇌ Gastronomes will cut short their sightseeing to spend time and money at
the **Waterside Inn**, Bray, near Maidenhead ☎(0628) 20691 ▥▥ which is the
country establishment of the Roux brothers, owners of Le Gavroche in
London (see *Restaurants*). Windsor itself cannot match such gourmet
delights as the exquisite lightness of touch in the Waterside's cuisine, though
La Taverna at 2 River St., off Thames St., ☎863020 ▥▥ is worth visiting
for pasta and veal dishes. For the determined sightseer, the schedule might
favor a really excellent snack at the **Eton Wine Bar**, or a hot pub lunch at the
Christopher, both in the High St., Eton.

Index

Individual hotels, restaurants and shops have not been indexed, because they appear in alphabetical order within their appropriate sections. The sections themselves, however, have been indexed. Similarly, streets are listed in the gazetteer and not the index, with a few notable exceptions, such as Fleet Street and Pall Mall, being indexed as well.

Page numbers in **bold** type indicate the main entry. Numbers in *italic* refer to the illustrations and plans.

Index

Index

Index

Index

Index

Index

Gazetteer of street names

Numbers after the street names refer to pages on which the street is mentioned in the book. Map references refer to the maps that follow this gazetteer.

It has not been possible to label every street drawn on the maps, although of course all major streets and most smaller ones have been named. However, some streets that it has not been possible to label have also been given map references in this gazetteer because this serves as an approximate location that will nearly always be sufficient for you to find your way.

Gazetteer

Gazetteer

224

LONDON

1

LEGEND

City Maps

0   100   200   300   400   500 YDS.

-      Major Place of Interest
-      Other Important Building
-      Built-up Area
-      Park
- † †   Cemetery
- ✝ †   Named church, church
- ☾   Mosque
- ✡   Synagogue
- ✠   Hospital
- ℹ   Information Office
- ⊠   Post Office
- ✋   Police Station
- ⬤   Parking Lot
- ⊖   Underground Station
- →   One Way Street
-      Footpath, arcade
- **10**   Adjoining Page No.

Area Maps

- ■   Place of Interest
-      Built-up Area
-      Wood or Park
- ═○═   Superhighway (with access point)
- ꞊꞊꞊   Superhighway under construction
- ═══   Main Road – Four Lane Highway
- ▬▬▬   Other Main Road
- ▬▬▬   Secondary Road
- ▬▬▬   Railroad
- ✈   Airport
- ✦   Airfield

LONDON BUS CHART

	Aldwych	Angel	Baker St.	Bank	Chelsea/King's Rd.	Earls Ct.	Elephant and Castle	Euston	Hammersmith	Hampstead	Highgate	High St. Kensington	Holborn	Hyde Pk. Corner	Kew	King's Cross	Knightsbridge/Harrods	Liverpool St.
Aldwych																		
Angel	4/171																	
Baker St.	13	30																
Bank	6/9	43	6/13															
Chelsea/King's Rd.	11	22/38	22/30	11/22														
Earls Ct.	30/9	74/38	22	74/12	31													
Elephant and Castle	1/68	17	L	133	12/4	A												
Euston	68/77A	30/73	18/6	68/6	68/11	30	68											
Hammersmith	11	73	27	9/8	11	9/3	9/12	73										
Hampstead	168	24/30	18/30	24/30	24/8	24/22	M	24/73	24/73									
Highgate	134/176	43	134/30	43	134/8	134/22	134/30	134/176	134/73	210								
High St. Kensington	9	73	27	9/8	31	31	9/12	73	9/73	73/24	73/134							
Holborn	68/77A	19/73	8/74	6/25	22	68/22	68/7	7/73	9/24	8/134	19	8/19						
Hyde Pk. Corner	9	19/73	30/74	9/25	22	9/30	14/7	9/73	73/24	73/134	9/73	19	25					
Kew	27/9	27/73	27	27/31	27/31	31	B	27	27/24	27/134	27	C	27/73	9/77A				
King's Cross	77A	30/73	18/30	M	73/22	30	45/63	14	73	30/134	73	77A	14/73	73/27	77A			
Knightsbridge/Harrods	9	73	27	9/8	19/22	30/74	9/12	73	9/73	73/134	9/73	22	14/30	9/27	30	30		
Liverpool St.	6	43†	6/159	6/8	11	E	45/188	6	11	6/135	6/134	8	8/14	D	77A	8/22	14	6
Ludgate Circus	6/9	4	6/159	6/8	11	E	45/63	6	11	6/135	6/134	9	8	14	D	45	9	6
Marble Arch	6/15	30	30/24	6/8	18/22	74	12	30/73	73	73/134	73	72	8	30/73	73/30	8	30/74	6
Monument	15	43	15/159	21/43	15/22	E	10/35	15	15	15/73	F	43	15/501	E	15/77A	15	15/74	35
Notting Hill Gate	28/9	12/73	27	12/8	31	31	12	12/73	27	27/134	31	12/25	28/72	52	27	73/12	52	12/73
Olympia	9	73	27	9	73/6	73/22	73	73	73/24	73/134	73	9/25	8/72	27	73	9/73	9/137	73
Oxford Circus	6/15	73	13/6	8	73/22	73/12	74	12	73	73/134	73	73/8	8/25	73	73	73/73	137/8	8
Oxford St./Selfridges	6/15	30/73	13/6	8/22	73/22	74	12	73	73	73/134	73	73/8	8	30/73	73	73/73	73	8
Paddington	15	27/9	27	15	27/31	27/31	15/12	27/73	27	27/134	27	27/7	8/36A	27/36	27	27/73	27/36	9
Piccadilly Circus	6/9	19	13/159	6/15	22	9/30	12/53	14A	9	14/24	134	9	22B	9/14	14A	14	14A	14/22
Richmond	27/9	27/73	27	27/31	27/31	31	B	27	27/24	27/134	27	C	27/73	27	27/73	27/9	G	
St. Paul's	4/6	4	6/13	11	11	11	11/66	24	11	24/134	11	9	8/68	9	C	27	27/9	8
Sloane Sq.	11	19	19/74	11	11/30	19/22	19/30	11	137/24	137/134	19/137	19	E	19	137/19	11		
South Kensington	14/9	30	30	14/8	49	30	14/176	30	49/14	14/134	49	14	30	14/49	49/30	30	14	
Tate Gallery/Millbank	77A	88/73	2B	77A	28/22	30	10	77A	28/30	88/9	1	9	77A	36	J	77A	28/36	4
Tottenham Ct. Rd.	176	73	27/27	8/25	19/22	30	176	73	73	24	134	173	8/25	14/73	73	73	14/19	8
Trafalgar Sq.	6/9	24/73	13/159	6/11	11	9/30	12/53	77A	9	24	9/134	9	77A	9/27	77A	9	9/27	6
Victoria	11	38	2B/74	11	11/25	29/10	10	73	11	24/52	52	38	28/73	52	24/27	52	52	11
Warren St.	24/8	30/73	27	29/25	73/22	30	14	176	27/24	24/134	27	73	8/73	14/27	27	30/73	30	24
Waterloo	1/68	4	L	76/501	1/11	K	1/68	68	1	176/9	178/9	8/68	5/68	K		5		14
Westminster	77/77A	71/4	159	11	11	E	12/53	77/77A	11	24	29/13	9	77/77A	E	77A	29/9		

To find the route numbers of buses linking any two locations on this chart, follow the rows of squares horizontally and vertically to the square where the two rows meet. If a square is coloured you must change buses as indicated in the key.

Change at Aldwych
Change at High St. Kensington
Change at Hyde Pk. Corner
Change at Oxford Circus
Change at Tottenham Ct. Rd.
Change at Trafalgar Square
Change at Warren St.

* Buses run Mon-Fri only.
† From Liverpool St. walk along Eldon St.
  to Moorgate for direct bus service (43).

The following journeys are difficult by bus, involving two changes and the alternative tube connections are suggested:
A Bakerloo line to Embankment then change to District line
B District line to Embankment then change to Bakerloo line
C District line to Earls Ct. then change to Piccadilly line
D Circle line to Sth. Kensington then change to District line
E District line direct
F Escalator link to Bank then change to Northern line
G District line to Sth. Kensington then change to Circle line
H Circle or District lines direct
I Victoria line from Pimlico to Warren St. then change to Northern line
J Victoria line from Pimlico to Victoria then change to District line
K Bakerloo or Northern line to Embankment then change to District line
L Bakerloo line direct
M Northern line direct

	Ludgate Circus	Marble Arch	Monument	Notting Hill Gate	Olympia	Oxford Circus	Oxford St./ Selfridges	Paddington	Piccadilly Circus	Richmond	St. Paul's	Sloane Sq.	South Kensington	Tate Gallery/Millbank	Tottenham Ct. Rd.	Trafalgar Sq.	Victoria	Warren St.	Waterloo	Westminster
15																				
15 6																				
12 6 88	12 15																			
6 73	9 15	27 28																		
15 6 7	15	12 88	73																	
15 6 7	15	12 88	73	6 7																
15 7 15	15	27	27	7 15	7 15															
7 9 73	E	27	27	27 73	27 73	27 9														
6 15	15	6 12	9	6 15	6 15	6 15	27 9													
11	137	137 15 9	137 52	137	137	137 36	19 22	11												
4 9	30	H	49	14 73	30	14 36	14	49 27	14 19											
8 15	88	10	88 36 9	88	88	36	88	J	2B 19 14	28 14										
6 6 73	88	8 176 15	73	8 25	8 73	7	14 22	24 27	22	14	88									
11	28 73	11 15	52	2B 6	25	28 9	36	38	11 9 14	11	88 24 25									
4 73	30	27	27	73 135	30 73	27	73 3	27	137 73	30	24 29 88	24 29								
76	1 6 501 513	1 12 9	1 15	176	1 6	1 15	24 15	K	4	1 11	25 14	176 1 68	176	1 76	70 76	1 24				
11	12 88	77 15	88	24 15	12 88	12 15	24 88	12 15	E	11	11	77A 88	24 29	24 29	24 29	24 29	70			